REINVENTING
YOUR LIFE

JEFFREY E. YOUNG, PH.D., AND
JANET S. KLOSKO, PH.D.

REINVENTING
YOUR LIFE

HOW TO BREAK FREE FROM
NEGATIVE LIFE PATTERNS

A DUTTON BOOK

DUTTON
Published by the Penguin Group
Penguin Books USA Inc., 375 Hudson Street, New York, New York, 10014, U.S.A.
Penguin Books Ltd., 27 Wrights Lane, London W8 5TZ, England
Penguin Books Australia Ltd., Ringwood, Victoria, Australia
Penguin Books Canada Ltd, 10 Alcorn Avenue, Toronto, Ontario, Canada M4V 3B2
Penguin Books (N.Z.) Ltd, 182–190 Wairau Road, Auckland 10, New Zealand

Penguin Books Ltd, Registered Offices:
Harmondsworth, Middlesex, England

First published by Dutton, an imprint of New American Library,
a division of Penguin Books USA Inc.
Distributed in Canada by McClelland & Stewart Inc.

First Printing, May, 1993
3 5 7 9 10 8 6 4

■ REGISTERED TRADEMARK—MARCA REGISTRADA

LIBRARY OF CONGRESS CATALOGING IN PUBLICATION DATA
Young, Jeffrey E.
    Reinventing your life : how to break free from negative life patterns / Jeffrey Young
and Janet Klosko.
        p.   cm.
    ISBN 0-525-93584-3
    1. Self-defeating behavior.   2. Self-management (Psychology).   I. Klosko, Janet.
II. Title.
    RC455.4.S43Y68   1993
    158'.1—dc20   92-34584
                                                                              CIP

Printed in the United States of America
Set in Century Old Style and Newtext

Designed by Steven N. Stathakis

*For Manny, Ethel, and Hannes, who have loved
and supported me unconditionally.*
—JEFFREY YOUNG

*For my mother, father, Michael, and Molly, who
all gave me the space to write this book.*
—JANET KLOSKO

ACKNOWLEDGMENTS

Reinventing Your Life has special meaning. This book represents the culmination of years of personal and professional growth for each of us. For this reason, we have many people to thank, past and present, who have in some important way contributed to our development.

We are indebted to Dan and Tara Goleman, without whose guidance, faith, advice, gentle prodding, and of course, friendship, we would never have undertaken such an overwhelming project; to Arthur Weinberger, for his suggestions and encouragement during many years of developing the schema-focused model; to William Zangwill, who, in his invaluable role as devil's advocate and critic, has inspired us to sharpen and refine our ideas; to David Bricker, who, through his involvement in new approaches to psychotherapy, continually offers us fresh perspectives to consider; to Cathy Flanagan, for her help in running the Center, her intelligent comments, and her warmth; to Bill Sanderson, who has played an important role as Director of Training at the Cognitive Therapy Center of New York and as co-director at the Cognitive Therapy Center of Long Island; to Marty Sloane, Richard Sackett, Jayne Rygh, and all our other friends and colleagues in New York who have contributed to the development of this approach; and to our editors Deb Brody and Alexia Dorszynksi, who helped give the book its form and tone, and to our agent Pam Bernstein, who helped make the book possible.

—JY and JK

I would like to extend my personal thanks to several other people who have played important roles in my development. To Janet Klosko, for making this collaboration so stimulating and fruitful. I could not have "reinvented" anyone better to work with; to Will Swift, who, like my father, has always had supreme confidence in me, even when I was not so sure—thank you for helping me get my ideas on tape, and for providing crucial feedback over the past eight years; to Aaron (Tim) Beck, who, through his clinical wisdom, penetrating intelligence, and empirical approach to personal and professional problems, has served as my mentor. To Peter Kuriloff and Arthur Dole, my graduate school advisors, for their friendship, for having confidence in me, and for being open enough to give me the freedom to pursue cognitive therapy before it was widely accepted; to Candice, for putting up with me and for her devotion in shouldering much of the responsibility I cannot handle; to Richard and Diane Wattenmaker, Bob Spitzer, Janet Williams, Gene D'Aquili, and many others who have contributed in ways they probably do not realize.

I have been fortunate throughout my life to have a family that I can always rely on for praise, reassurance, and acceptance, regardless of what I have gone through personally. For accepting all my quirks, I would like to thank my parents, grandparents, brother Stephen, sister Debra, and the other members of my extended family. I have learned through working with patients less fortunate than I not to take such support for granted.

—JY

I would like to thank all the other people who helped me become the psychologist that I am. I would like to start by thanking Jeff Young, for being such an exemplary model, and for giving me the best form of therapy I have ever known. I would like to thank my mentor, David Barlow, for teaching me the meaning of the word "professional," and for encouraging me to fulfill my talents. I would like to thank my supervisor in New York City, Will Swift; Ann De Lancey, Mike Burkhardt, and my fellow interns and other advisors from Brown University; and from SUNY at Albany— Jerry Cerny, Rick Heimberg, John Wapner, Glen Conrad, Robin Tassinari, Jim Mancuso, Robert Boice, Bill Simmons, Alan Cohen, my warm supportive classmates, and others. Finally, I would like to thank the other members of my family and close friends, for everything they have given me.

—JK

Contents

Foreword by Aaron Beck, M.D.   xi

Preface   xiii

1 Lifetraps   1

2 Which Lifetraps Do You Have?   14

3 Understanding Lifetraps   23

4 Surrender, Escape, and Counterattack   35

5 How Lifetraps Change   42

6 "Please Don't Leave Me!": The Abandonment Lifetrap   58

7 "I Can't Trust You": The Mistrust and Abuse Lifetrap   83

8 "I'll Never Get the Love I Need": The Emotional Deprivation Lifetrap   109

9 "I Don't Fit In": The Social Exclusion Lifetrap   129

10 "I Can't Make It on My Own": The Dependence Lifetrap   155

11 "Catastrophe Is About to Strike": The Vulnerability Lifetrap   184

12 "I'M WORTHLESS": THE DEFECTIVENESS LIFETRAP   207

13 "I FEEL LIKE SUCH A FAILURE": THE FAILURE LIFETRAP   239

14 "I ALWAYS DO IT YOUR WAY!": THE SUBJUGATION LIFETRAP   258

15 "IT'S NEVER QUITE GOOD ENOUGH": THE UNRELENTING STANDARDS LIFETRAP   294

16 "I CAN HAVE WHATEVER I WANT": THE ENTITLEMENT LIFETRAP   314

17 A PHILOSOPHY OF CHANGE   341

REFERENCES   353

INDEX   355

FOREWORD

BY AARON BECK, M.D.

I am delighted that Jeffrey Young and Janet Klosko have tackled the difficult issue of personality problems, drawing upon the techniques and principles of cognitive therapy. The authors have done pioneering work in developing and making available to the public a powerful set of tools for making significant life changes in relationships and at work.

Personality disorders are self-destructive, lifelong patterns that bring patients tremendous unhappiness. People with personality disorders have long-term problems with living, in addition to specific symptoms like depression and anxiety. They are often unhappy in their intimate relationships or chronically underachieve in their careers. Their overall quality of life is usually lower than they desire.

Cognitive therapy has been expanding to meet the challenge of treating these difficult, chronic patterns. In treating personality problems, we address not only sets of symptoms—depression, anxiety, panic attacks, addictions, eating disorders, sexual problems, and insomnia—but also underlying *schemas,* or controlling beliefs. (The authors refer to schemas as *lifetraps.*) Most patients come to therapy with certain core schemas that are reflected in many symptom areas. Addressing these core schemas in treatment can have beneficial effects that reverberate throughout many areas of the patient's life.

Cognitive therapists have found that certain signs point to the likelihood of a schema-level issue. The first is that the patient discusses a problem and says, "I have always been this way, I have always had this problem." The problem feels "natural" to the patient. Secondly, the patient seems unable to carry out homework assignments that the therapist and patient have agreed upon during sessions. There is a sense of being "stuck." The patient both wants to change and resists changing. Thirdly, the patient seems unaware of his or her effects on other people. There may be lack of insight about self-defeating behaviors.

Schemas are hard to change. They are supported by cognitive, behavioral, and emotional elements and therapy must address *all* of these elements. Change in only one or two realms will not work.

Reinventing Your Life addresses eleven of these chronic, self-defeating personality patterns, known in the book as *lifetraps*. This book takes very complicated material and makes it simple and understandable. Readers will easily grasp the idea of lifetraps, and quickly be able to identify their own. A wealth of case material, drawn from actual clinical experience, will help readers relate to the lifetraps in a personal way. Furthermore, the techniques the authors present are powerful in producing change. Their approach is integrative: it draws on cognitive, behavioral, psychoanalytic, and experiential therapies, while maintaining the practical, problem-solving focus of cognitive therapy.

Reinventing Your Life presents practical techniques for overcoming our most painful, lifelong problems. The book reflects the tremendous sensitivity, compassion, and clinical insight of its authors.

PREFACE

Why another self-help book?

We believe that *Reinventing Your Life* fills an important gap in the books currently available for self-improvement. There are many excellent self-help books, just as there are many fine therapy approaches. However, most of these are limited. Some books only deal with one specific problem, like codependency, depression, lack of assertiveness, or making poor partner choices. Some deal with many problems, but only use one means of change, like inner-child work, couples exercises, or cognitive-behavioral methods. Other books are inspirational or do a great job of describing a universal problem like loss, but the solutions they offer are so vague that we don't know how to go about changing once we have the inspiration.

In *Reinventing Your Life,* Janet Klosko and I share with you a new therapy for changing major life patterns. Lifetrap therapy addresses *eleven* of the most destructive problems we encounter every day in our practices. To help you change these lifetraps, we combine techniques from several different therapies. As a result, we think this book will provide you with a far more thorough and comprehensive approach to a variety of lifelong problems than most books you have read so far.

Since this book is about personal growth and change, I'd like to describe the path I followed leading to the development of lifetraps therapy.

In many respects my development as a therapist mirrors the journey of self-discovery we outline for you in this book.

It began in 1975 when I was a graduate student at the University of Pennsylvania. I remember my first experience doing therapy as an intern at a community mental-health center in Philadelphia. I was learning Rogerian therapy, a nondirective approach. I remember feeling stymied much of the time. Patients would come to me with serious life problems, expressing powerful emotions, and I was taught to listen, to paraphrase, and to clarify so patients could arrive at their *own* solutions. The problem, of course, was that often they didn't. Or, if they did come to their own resolution, it took so long that I became terribly frustrated by the time therapy was over. Rogerian therapy did not fit my temperament, my *natural inclinations.* Perhaps I am too impatient, but I like to see change and progress relatively quickly. I become easily frustrated in circumstances where there is a serious problem and I have to sit by helplessly watching, unable to correct it.

Within a short time, I began reading about behavior therapy, an approach that stresses rapid, concrete behavior change. I felt an enormous relief. I could be active and offer advice to patients instead of being so passive. Behavior therapy offered a well laid out framework that explained why patients had specific problems and exactly which techniques to use. It was almost like a cookbook or technical manual. In comparison with the vague approach I had originally learned, the behavioral model was very appealing. It was geared toward fast, short-term change.

After a couple of years, I became disillusioned with behavior therapy as well. In focusing so narrowly on what people *do,* I began to feel that behavior therapy had gone too far in ignoring our *thoughts* and *feelings.* I was missing the richness of patients' internal worlds. At this point I read Dr. Aaron Beck's book, *Cognitive Therapy and the Emotional Disorders,* and became excited again. Beck was combining the practicality and directness of behavior therapy with the richness of patients' thoughts and beliefs.

After graduate school in 1979 I began studying cognitive therapy with Dr. Beck. I loved demonstrating to patients how their thoughts were distorted and showing them rational alternatives. I also liked pinpointing problem behaviors and rehearsing new ways of handling everyday situations. Patients began to change in dramatic ways: their depression lifted, anxiety symptoms went away. I also found that the techniques of cognitive therapy were extremely valuable to me in my personal life. I began spreading the word about cognitive therapy to other professionals through lectures and workshops in the United States and Europe.

After a few years, I started my own private practice in Philadelphia. I continued to have dramatic results with many patients, especially those with specific symptoms like depression and anxiety. Unfortunately, as time went on, I built up a backlog of patients who were not responding at all or who showed only slight improvement. I decided to sit down and figure out what these patients had in common. I also asked colleagues of mine who were cognitive therapists to describe their resistant patients. I wanted to see whether their therapy failures were similar to my own.

What I found in trying to distinguish difficult patients from the ones who responded quickly was a revelation to me. The most difficult patients tended to have *less* severe symptoms; in general, they were less depressed and anxious. Many of their problems concerned intimacy: these patients had patterns of unsatisfactory relationships. Furthermore, most of these resistant patients had experienced their problems for most of their lives. They were not coming to therapy because of a single life crisis, like divorce or the death of a parent. These patients all had *self-destructive* life patterns.

Next I decided to make a list of the most common themes or patterns in these difficult patients. This became my first list of schemas, or lifetraps. It only had a few of the eleven patterns described in *Reinventing Your Life,* such as deep feelings of defectiveness, a sense of profound isolation and loneliness, a tendency to sacrifice their needs for those of other people, and an unhealthy dependence or reliance on others. These lifetraps proved invaluable to me in working with patients who previously had been unresponsive to treatment. I found that by developing a list of lifetraps, I could break down patients' problems into manageable parts. I could also develop different strategies for solving each problem or pattern.

In retrospect, my search for broad themes and patterns was also very consistent with my own personality. I've always longed to see various aspects of my life as part of an organized whole, with some sense of order and predictability. I've always felt that I could gain control over my own life by extracting these general themes or patterns. I remember as a college student trying to classify my roommates into various categories of friendship, depending on how much I felt they could be relied upon.

Another thread in my own development as a therapist has been my increasing desire to integrate and blend, rather than eliminate or criticize. Many therapists feel they must choose one approach to therapy and follow it with devotion. That is why we have strict Gestalt therapists, family therapists, Freudian therapists, and behavior therapists. I have come to believe that integrating the best components of several therapies is far more effective than any one alone. There is much of value in psychoanalytic, experiential, cognitive, pharmacological, and behavioral approaches, but each has significant limitations when used alone.

On the other hand, I am also opposed to combining many different techniques haphazardly without a unifying framework. I believe that the eleven lifetraps provide that unifying framework, and that techniques drawn from several approaches can be combined, like an arsenal of weapons, to fight these lifetraps. Furthermore, as described in the chapters that follow, these lifetraps can provide you with a sense of continuity over the course of your life; the past and present can be seen as part of a consistent whole. Each lifetrap has an understandable origin in childhood that intuitively feels right to us. We can understand, for example, why we are drawn to critical partners, and why we feel so badly about ourselves when we make a mistake, once we grasp how demanding and punitive our own parents were.

I hope that *Reinventing Your Life* fills the need for a book that deals comprehensively with a broad range of deeply felt, lifelong problems we all face. I also hope that it provides you with a useful framework for understanding how these patterns developed, along with powerful solutions for each lifetrap, drawn from many different psychological approaches that can really work for you.

JEFFREY YOUNG
September 1992

1

LIFETRAPS

- Are you repeatedly drawn into relationships with people who are cold to you? Do you feel that even the people closest to you do not care or understand enough about you?
- Do you feel that you are at your core somehow defective, that no one who truly knows you could possibly love and accept you?
- Do you put the needs of others above your own, so your needs never get met—and so you do not even know what your real needs are?
- Do you fear that something bad will happen to you, so that even a mild sore throat sets off a dread of more dire disease?
- Do you find that, regardless of how much public acclaim or social approval you receive, you still feel unhappy, unfulfilled, or undeserving?

We call patterns like these *lifetraps*. In this book, we will describe the eleven most common lifetraps and will show you how to *recognize* them, how to understand their *origins,* and how to *change* them.

A lifetrap is a pattern that starts in childhood and reverberates throughout life. It began with something that was *done* to us by our families or by other children. We were abandoned, criticized, overprotected, abused, excluded, or deprived—we were damaged in some way. Eventually the lifetrap becomes part of us. Long after we leave the home we grew up in, we continue to create situations in which we are mistreated,

1

ignored, put down, or controlled and in which we fail to reach our most desired goals.

Lifetraps determine how we think, feel, act, and relate to others. They trigger strong feelings such as anger, sadness, and anxiety. Even when we *appear* to have everything—social status, an ideal marriage, the respect of people close to us, career success—we are often unable to savor life or believe in our accomplishments.

JED: A THIRTY-NINE-YEAR-OLD STOCKBROKER WHO IS EX-TREMELY SUCCESSFUL. HE CONQUERS WOMEN, BUT NEVER REALLY CONNECTS WITH THEM. JED IS CAUGHT IN THE *EMO-TIONAL DEPRIVATION* LIFETRAP.

When we were first developing the lifetraps approach, we began treating an intriguing patient named Jed. Jed perfectly illustrates the self-defeating nature of lifetraps.

Jed goes from one woman to another, insisting that none of the women he meets can satisfy him. Each one eventually disappoints him. The closest Jed comes to intimate relationships is infatuation with women who sexually excite him. The problem is that these relationships never last.

Jed does not *connect* with women. He *conquers* them. The point at which he loses interest is exactly the point at which he has "won." The woman has started to fall in love with him.

JED: *It really turns me off when a woman is clingy. When she starts hanging all over me, especially in public, I just want to run.*

Jed struggles with loneliness. He feels empty and bored. There is an empty hole inside—and he restlessly searches for the woman who will fill him up. Jed believes he will never find this woman. He feels that he has always been alone and always will be alone.

As a child, Jed felt this same aching loneliness. He never knew his father, and his mother was cold and unemotional. Neither one of them met his *emotional* needs. He grew up emotionally deprived, and continues to recreate this state of detachment as an adult.

For years Jed inadvertently repeated this pattern with therapists, drifting from one to another. Each therapist initially gave him hope, yet ultimately disappointed him. He never really connected with his therapists;

he always found some fatal flaw that in his mind justified terminating therapy. Each therapy experience confirmed that his life had not changed, and he felt even more alone.

Many of Jed's therapists were warm and empathic. This was not the problem. The problem was that Jed always found some excuse to avoid the intimacy with which he was so unfamiliar and uncomfortable. Emotional support from a therapist was essential, but not enough. His therapists did not *confront* his self-destructive patterns often or forcefully enough. For Jed to escape his Emotional Deprivation lifetrap, he had to stop finding fault with the women he met and begin to take responsibility for fighting his own discomfort about getting close to people and accepting their nurturance.

When Jed finally came to us for treatment, we challenged him over and over again, trying to chip away at his lifetrap each time it reasserted itself. It was important to show him that we were genuinely sympathetic with how uncomfortable it felt for him to get close to anyone, in light of his extremely icy parents. Nevertheless, whenever he insisted that Wendy was not beautiful enough, Isabel was not brilliant enough, or Melissa was just not right for him, we pushed him to see that he was falling into his lifetrap again, finding fault with others to avoid feeling warmth. After a year of this *empathic confrontation,* balancing emotional support and confrontation, we were finally able to see significant change. He is now engaged to Nicole, a warm and loving woman:

JED: *My previous therapists were really understanding, and I got a lot of insight into my grim childhood, but none of them really pushed me to change. It was just too easy to fall back into my old familiar patterns. This approach was different.*

I finally took some responsibility for making a relationship work. I didn't want my relationship with Nicole to be another failure, and I felt like this was it for me. Although I could see that Nicole wasn't perfect, I finally decided that either I would have to connect with someone or resign myself to being alone forever.

The lifetrap approach involves *continually confronting* ourselves. We will teach you how to track your lifetraps as they play themselves out in your life, and how to counter them repeatedly until these patterns loosen their grip on you.

HEATHER: A FORTY-TWO-YEAR-OLD WOMAN WITH TREMEN-
DOUS POTENTIAL, TRAPPED IN HER OWN HOME BECAUSE HER
FEARS ARE SO CRIPPLING. ALTHOUGH SHE TAKES THE TRAN-
QUILIZER ATIVAN TO TREAT HER ANXIETY, SHE IS STILL STUCK
IN THE *VULNERABILITY* LIFETRAP.

In a sense, Heather has no life; she is too afraid to do anything. Life is
fraught with danger. She prefers to stay home where it is "safe."

HEATHER: *I know there's lots of great stuff to do in the city. I like the
theater, I like nice restaurants, I like seeing friends. But it's just too
much for me. I don't have fun. I'm too worried all the time that
something horrible is going to happen.*

Heather worries about car crashes, collapsing bridges, getting mugged,
catching a disease such as AIDS, and spending too much money. It certainly is not surprising that a trip to the city is no fun for her.

Heather's husband Walt is very angry with her. He wants to go out
and do things. Walt says—and rightly so—that it is not fair for him to be
deprived. More and more, he goes ahead and does things without her.

Heather's parents were exceptionally overprotective of her. Her parents were Jewish Holocaust survivors who spent much of their childhoods
in concentration camps. They treated her like a china doll, as she put it.
They continually warned her about possible (but unlikely) threats to her
welfare: she might catch pneumonia, be trapped in the subway, drown, or
be caught in a fire. It is no wonder that she spends most of her time in a
painful state of anxiety, trying to make sure that her world is safe. Meanwhile, almost everything that is pleasurable is draining out of her life.

Before coming to us, Heather tried several anti-anxiety medications
over a three-year period. (Medication is the most common treatment for
anxiety.) Most recently, she went to a psychiatrist who prescribed Ativan.
She took the pills every day, and the medication did provide some relief.
She *felt* better, less anxious. Life became more pleasant. Knowing she had
the medication made her feel more able to cope with things. Even so, she
continued to avoid leaving the house. Her husband complained that the
medication just made her happier to sit around at home.

Another serious problem was that Heather felt dependent on the Ativan:

HEATHER: *I feel like I'm going to have to stay on this for the rest of my
life. The idea of giving it up terrifies me. I don't want to go back to being
scared of everything all the time.*

Even when Heather coped well with stressful situations, she attributed all her success to the medication. She was not building a sense of mastery—the sense that she could handle things on her own. (This is why, particularly with anxiety treatments, patients tend to relapse when the medication is withdrawn.)

Heather made relatively rapid progress in lifetrap therapy. Within a year, her life was significantly better. She gradually started entering more anxiety-provoking situations. She could travel, see friends, go to movies, and she eventually decided to take on a part-time job that required commuting.

As part of her treatment, we helped Heather become better at estimating the odds of bad things happening. We continually demonstrated how she exaggerated the risk of catastrophe in harmless situations; and we showed her that she overestimated her own vulnerability and weakness outside her home. She learned to take *reasonable* precautions. She stopped asking her husband and friends for reassurance. Her marriage improved. And she got more pleasure from her life.

THE IRONY OF REPETITION

Jed and Heather illustrate two of the eleven lifetraps: Emotional Deprivation and Vulnerability. As we discuss other patients, you will read about the other lifetraps: Subjugation, Mistrust and Abuse, Abandonment, Defectiveness, Entitlement, Dependence, Failure, Unrelenting Standards, and Social Exclusion. You will probably recognize elements of yourself in several of these.

That we keep repeating the pain of our childhood is one of the core insights of psychoanalytic psychotherapy. Freud called this the *repetition compulsion*. The child of an alcoholic grows up to marry an alcoholic. The abused child grows up to marry an abuser, or becomes an abuser himself. The sexually molested child grows up to be a prostitute. The overly controlled child allows others to control her.

This is a baffling phenomenon. Why do we do this? Why do we reenact our pain, prolonging our suffering? Why don't we build better lives and escape the pattern? Almost everyone repeats negative patterns from childhood in self-defeating ways. This is the strange truth with which therapists contend. Somehow we manage to create, in adult life, conditions remarkably similar to those that were so destructive in childhood. A lifetrap is all the ways in which we recreate these patterns.

The technical term for a lifetrap is a *schema*. The concept of a schema comes from cognitive psychology. Schemas are deeply entrenched beliefs about ourselves and the world, learned early in life. These schemas are central to our sense of *self*. To give up our belief in a schema would be to surrender the security of knowing who we are and what the world is like; therefore we cling to it, even when it hurts us. These early beliefs provide us with a sense of predictability and certainty; they are comfortable and familiar. In an odd sense, they make us feel at home. This is why cognitive psychologists believe schemas, or lifetraps, are so difficult to change.

Let us now look at how lifetraps affect the *chemistry* we feel in romantic relationships.

PATRICK: A THIRTY-FIVE-YEAR-OLD BUILDING CONTRACTOR. THE MORE HIS WIFE, FRANCINE, HAS AFFAIRS WITH OTHER MEN, THE MORE HE DESIRES HER. PATRICK IS CAUGHT IN THE ABANDONMENT LIFETRAP.

Patrick is acutely unhappy. His wife keeps having affairs with other men. Whenever she has an affair, he becomes desperate.

PATRICK: *It's like I'll do anything to get her back. I can't stand it. I know if I lose her I'll fall apart. I can't understand why I put up with this; it's as if I love her more when I know she's not there for me. I start thinking, "If only I could be better, she wouldn't need to do this. If only I were better, she would stay with me." I can't stand the* uncertainty.

Francine keeps promising to be faithful, and each time Patrick believes her. And each time his hopes are dashed.

PATRICK: *I can't believe she's doing this to me again. I can't believe she'd put me through it. After last time I was sure she would stop. I mean, she saw what she did to me. I was almost suicidal. I can't believe she would do it* again.

Patrick's marriage is a roller coaster. He rides, out of control, from wild hope to despair, rising and crashing again and again.

PATRICK: *The hardest part for me is the waiting. Knowing what she is doing and waiting for her to come home. There have been times when I have waited* days. *Just sat there and waited for her to come home.*

While Patrick waits, he alternates between sobbing and rage. When Francine finally comes home, there is a scene. A few times he has hit her, afterward always begging her forgiveness. He wants to get off the roller coaster. He says he wants some stability and peace. Yet this is the irony of the Abandonment lifetrap: the more unpredictable Francine is, the more he is drawn to her at a deep emotional level. He feels more *chemistry* when she threatens to leave.

Patrick's childhood was fraught with loss and unpredictability. His father abandoned the family when Patrick was only two years old. He and his two sisters were raised by their mother, an alcoholic who neglected them when she was drunk. These feelings are familiar to him, and he has managed to recreate them by marrying Francine and tolerating her infidelity.

Patrick was in psychoanalysis (Freudian therapy) for three years. He saw his analyst three times a week for fifty minutes each time—at considerable expense.

PATRICK: *I would go in and lie down on the couch and talk about whatever came into my mind. It was very lonely for me. My analyst said very little in the whole three years. Even if I was crying or yelling at him he usually wouldn't say anything. I felt like he wasn't really there.*

He talked a lot about his childhood, and about what it felt like to lie there on the couch.

He became frustrated with analysis. He found his progress very slow. He *understood* his problems better, but he still had them. (This is a common complaint about psychoanalysis: Insight is not enough.) He wanted a therapy that was quicker and more directive. He wanted more guidance.

The lifetrap approach offered Patrick the guidance he needed. Instead of being distant and neutral with Patrick, we *collaborated* with him. We helped him see exactly what his pattern was and how he could break it. We taught him how to become more selective in his relationships with women. We warned him of the danger in romantic relationships of being drawn to destructive partners who generate a lot of sexual chemistry. He was confronted with the painful reality that he, like many of us, had fallen in love with a partner who reinforced his lifetrap.

After a year and a half of lifetrap therapy, Patrick decided to end his marriage to Francine. In that time he had given her every chance. He had tried to correct his behaviors that were destructive to the relationship—and that were inadvertently driving her away. He had stopped trying to control her. He had given her more freedom. He had asserted himself when she treated him badly. But through it all Francine had not changed. In fact, things had grown worse.

When we first asked if he had considered leaving Francine, Patrick insisted that he was too afraid he would fall apart. But when he finally left her and ended his marriage, he did not fall apart. Instead, he became calmer and more self-confident. He saw that he could have a life apart from Francine. We think he was right to leave the self-destructive relationship.

Patrick slowly started seeing other women. At first, he dated women who were just like his wife—unstable and unable to support him. It was as though he were running through the whole cycle again in fast motion. We gradually helped him to make healthier choices, even though the chemistry he felt was not quite as high. He has been living for six months with Sylvia, a very stable and reliable woman who seems devoted to him. While she is less glamorous than Francine, for the first time in his life Patrick is learning to be content in a consistent, nurturing environment.

The lifetrap approach shows you exactly what types of relationships are healthy for you to pursue, and what types to avoid, given your particular lifetraps. Often, this is not easy. Like Patrick, you may have to make choices that are painful in the short run and even go against your gut feelings in order to escape a rut that you have been mired in throughout your life.

CARLTON: THIRTY YEARS OLD, WORKS FOR HIS FATHER IN A FAMILY TEXTILE BUSINESS. HE IS NOT VERY GOOD AT MANAGING OTHER PEOPLE AND WOULD MUCH RATHER BE DOING SOMETHING ELSE. CARLTON IS CAUGHT IN THE *SUBJUGATION* LIFETRAP.

Carlton is a people-pleaser. He puts everyone's needs before his own. He is the one who always says, "I don't care, you decide," when other people ask him what he wants.

Carlton tries to please his wife by saying "yes" to everything she says and wants. He tries to please his children by never saying "no." He tries to please his father by going into the family business, even though it means doing a job he does not like.

Ironically, despite the fact that he tries so hard to please, other people often feel irritated with Carlton. He is so self-sacrificing. His wife is angry that he has no backbone. Although the children take advantage of his permissiveness, at some level they are angry that he fails to set limits. His father is constantly annoyed with Carlton's weakness and lack of aggressiveness at work, particularly in dealing with employees.

Although Carlton does not know it, he is angry, too. Deep inside he is angry about having denied his own needs for so long. This is a pattern he learned early in life. His father is considered a tyrant; he thrives by domineering and controlling others. Everything has to be his way. As a child, if Carlton disagreed or argued, his father spanked and belittled him. His mother adopted a completely passive role. She was depressed much of the time, and Carlton often found himself in the role of caretaker, trying to make her feel better. There was no place he could go to get *his* needs met.

Before coming to us, Carlton was in an experiential treatment called Gestalt therapy for two years. His therapist encouraged him to stay in the present and get in touch with his feelings. For example, the therapist had him try imagery exercises in which he would picture his father and practice talking back to him. This approach was helpful. He started to feel how angry he was.

The problem was that the therapy lacked direction. It did not have a consistent focus. Carlton drifted from session to session, exploring whatever feelings were most prominent at the moment. Naturally, his anger at his loved ones kept surfacing, but he did not *act* on his feelings and he did not understand why. The therapist did not draw all the components of his problem together for him and then teach him specific change techniques to overcome his subjugation.

Lifetrap therapy provided Carlton with a simple, straightforward *conceptual framework* that allowed him to see that subjugation was a primary theme running through his life, and he learned ways to change it. He made rapid progress. We often find that the Subjugation lifetrap takes the least amount of time to break.

Carlton developed a stronger sense of *self*. He became more aware of his own desires and feelings, which he had learned to suppress. He started developing opinions and preferences. He also became more assertive with his father, employees, and his wife and children. Particularly, he worked on expressing anger; he learned to state his needs in a calm and controlled manner. Although his wife and children put up some minor resistance at the beginning, once they recognized they were losing power, they soon settled down. In truth, they liked him better. They wanted him to be strong.

He had a more difficult battle with his father. Although his father tried to squelch Carlton's rebellion and reassert his dominant position, Carlton discovered that he had more leverage with his father than he realized. When he threatened to leave the business if his father would not let him assume a more equal role, his father backed down. Carlton is now beginning to take over many of his father's responsibilities as his father prepares for retirement. He has also discovered that his father has a newfound respect for him.

This case illustrates the importance of going beyond getting in touch with our feelings. Many so-called experiential therapies, such as inner-child work, provide a valuable role in helping us *feel* the links between what we experience in our daily lives today and what we felt as children. But these approaches rarely go far enough. Participants often feel much better after therapy sessions or workshops, but they usually drift back to their old patterns quickly. The lifetrap approach provides structured behavioral homework assignments and continual confrontation to help you maintain progress.

THE COGNITIVE THERAPY REVOLUTION

Lifetrap therapy is an outgrowth of an approach called cognitive therapy, developed by Dr. Aaron Beck in the 1960s. We have incorporated many aspects of this treatment into the lifetrap approach.

The basic premise of cognitive therapy is that the way we *think* about events in our lives (cognition) determines how we *feel* about them (emotions). People with emotional problems tend to distort reality. For example, Heather was taught by her mother to view everyday tasks such as riding a subway as dangerous. Lifetraps lead us to view certain kinds of situations in an inaccurate manner. They push our cognitive buttons.

Cognitive therapists believe that if we can teach patients to become more accurate about the way they interpret situations, we can help them feel better. If we can show Heather that she can travel on her own without much danger, then she will be less frightened and can begin living again.

Dr. Beck suggests that we examine our thoughts logically. When we are upset, are we exaggerating, personalizing, catastrophizing, etc.? Do our thoughts really make sense? Are there other ways to look at the situation? Further, Beck says we should *test* our negative thoughts by performing little experiments. For example, we asked Heather to walk around the block alone during the winter to see that nothing harmful would happen to her, even though she was convinced she would get sick or be mugged.

Cognitive therapy has gained wide respect. A large, growing body of research supports its effectiveness with such disorders as anxiety and depression. It is an active approach that teaches patients to control their own moods by controlling their thoughts.

Cognitive therapists usually combine cognitive methods with behavioral techniques, which are designed to teach patients practical skills they may never have learned such as relaxation, assertiveness, anxiety management, problem solving, time management, and social skills.

However, we have found over the years that cognitive and behavioral methods, while invaluable, are not sufficient to change lifelong patterns. Thus we developed the Lifetrap approach, which combines cognitive and behavioral techniques with psychoanalytic and experiential techniques. Madeline, the final patient we will discuss in this chapter, demonstrates both the value and limitation of using only cognitive behavioral methods.

MADELINE: A TWENTY-NINE-YEAR-OLD ACTRESS AND SINGER. SHE WAS SEXUALLY ABUSED BY HER STEPFATHER, AND CONTINUES TO SUFFER THE EFFECTS. MADELINE IS STILL PLAYING OUT THE *MISTRUST AND ABUSE* LIFETRAP.

Madeline has never had a long-term relationship with a man. Instead, she has gone from one extreme to the other: either she has avoided men altogether or she has been promiscuous.

Until she went to college, Madeline avoided boys. She never dated or had a boyfriend.

MADELINE: *I never let a guy near me. I remember the first time a boy kissed me. I ran away. When I sensed that a boy liked me, I acted really cold until he went away.*

In her first two years of college, Madeline started drinking and doing drugs. During this period, she had sex with more than thirty men. "None of them meant anything to me," she says.

MADELINE: *I went wild in college. I slept around. There was one fraternity where every guy in there had slept with me. I was miserable. I felt cheap and dirty. I felt used. I just couldn't say no. I would go out with a guy and end up sleeping with him even though I had promised myself I wouldn't. I figured it was the only reason guys would go out with me. I really don't know why I did it. That whole time was just like running out of control.*

The experience of sexual abuse by her stepfather damaged her sexuality and capacity for intimacy with men. For her, sex and abuse are inextricably mixed.

Now, Madeline is back to avoiding men. She has not dated in many years and is worried that she will never be able to marry and have children.

The first treatment Madeline tried was conventional cognitive therapy. Her therapist focused on the present—on Madeline's current avoidance of men. It was rare, for example, for Madeline to discuss her childhood in therapy. Instead, she and her therapist designed homework for her to do between sessions, such as striking up conversations with men or going to parties. The therapist helped her fight her distorted thoughts, such as "Men are only out for sex," by asking her for examples of men she knew who were caring and wanted intimacy.

Therapy went on for several months. Madeline began to date again, but she was drawn to abusive men. Although she recognized that many men were considerate, her experience with boyfriends did not bear this out. Madeline realized she needed something more to change her deeply ingrained pattern.

MADELINE: *I felt like my therapist was asking me to change without understanding why I was the way I was. I mean, I know I have to change in the ways that she said. I have to start trusting men and stop avoiding closeness. But there are* reasons *why I avoid men. I need to understand what they are.*

Madeline became angry at any man who seemed to approach her romantically. She could see that the anger was the result of distorted thoughts, but she still felt it. Madeline needed to direct her anger toward its true object— her stepfather. She needed to express her anger and have it validated.

During the first year and a half of lifetrap therapy, we helped Madeline to uncover her memories of abuse through imagery. We pushed her to ventilate her anger at her stepfather and to confront him with her accusations. We encouraged her to join a support group for survivors of incest. We also showed her how she maintained her pattern of abuse by selecting abusive boyfriends.

Madeline slowly resumed dating. Although she was still attracted to abusive men, she stayed away from them at our insistence, focusing instead on men who treated her respectfully, even though the chemistry was less intense. She worked on *demanding* respect, rather than leaving it to the man to give it to her. She learned to say "no."

About a year later she fell in love with Ben, a gentle, sensitive man. Even with him, however, she experienced serious sexual inhibition. Ben was willing to work with her to overcome her sexual difficulties. She is now considering marriage.

In Chapter 16, we will provide many suggestions for changing the Mistrust and Abuse lifetrap. However, we want to emphasize that many lifetraps, Mistrust and Abuse in particular, take a long time to change and should be approached with the help of a therapist or support group.

Madeline's treatment illustrates how lifetrap therapy retains the practical focus of cognitive and behavioral therapies: it builds skills and makes changes. But we are interested in more than short-term behavior modification. We also want to address lifelong issues, especially difficulties in relationships, self-esteem, and career problems. We want to address behavior, but we also want to address the ways that people *feel* and *relate*.

The next chapter begins with a questionnaire to help you discover which lifetraps apply to you.

2

WHICH LIFETRAPS
DO YOU HAVE?

In this chapter, we will help you identify which lifetraps seem most pertinent to *your* life.

Rate each of the next twenty-two statements in terms of how true each is of you on this six-point scale.

SCORING KEY

1 Completely untrue of me
2 Mostly untrue of me
3 Slightly more true than untrue of me
4 Moderately true of me
5 Mostly true of me
6 Describes me perfectly

First, rate how true the statement was of you as a *child*. If your answer would be different for various times in your childhood, choose the rating that best fits the way you felt in general up until the age of twelve. Then, rate how true each item is of you now, as an *adult*. If your answer would be different for various periods of your adult life, choose the rating that best applies to you in the past six months.

THE LIFETRAP QUESTIONNAIRE

AS A CHILD	NOW	DESCRIPTION
		1. I find myself clinging to people I'm close to because I'm afraid they'll leave me.
		2. I worry a lot that the people I love will find someone else they prefer and leave me.
		3. I am usually on the lookout for people's ulterior motives; I don't trust people easily.
		4. I feel I cannot let my guard down around other people or they will hurt me.
		5. I worry more than the average person about danger —that I will get sick or that some harm will come to me.
		6. I worry that I (or my family) will lose money and become destitute or dependent on others.
		7. I do not feel I can cope well by myself, so I feel I need other people to help me get by.
		8. My parents and I tend to be overinvolved in each other's lives and problems.
		9. I have not had someone to nurture me, share him/herself with me, or care deeply about what happens to me.
		10. People have not been there to meet my emotional needs for understanding, empathy, guidance, advice, and support.
		11. I feel like I do not belong. I am different. I do not really fit in.
		12. I'm dull and boring; I don't know what to say socially.
		13. No one I desire who knew the real me—with all my defects exposed—could love me.
		14. I am ashamed of myself; I am unworthy of the love, attention, and respect of others.
		15. I am not as intelligent or capable as most people when it comes to work (or school).
		16. I often feel inadequate because I do not measure up to others in terms of talent, intelligence, and success.

		17. I feel that I have no choice but to give in to other people's wishes; otherwise they will retaliate or reject me in some way.
		18. People see me as doing too much for others and not enough for myself.
		19. I try to do my best; I can't settle for good enough. I like to be number one at what I do.
		20. I have so much to accomplish that there is almost no time to relax and really enjoy myself.
		21. I feel that I shouldn't have to follow the normal rules and conventions other people do.
		22. I can't seem to discipline myself to complete routine, boring tasks or to control my emotions.
		YOUR TOTAL SOCIAL EXCLUSION SCORE (Add your scores together for questions 1-10)

USING THE SCORE SHEET

Now you are ready to transfer your scores from the questionnaire to the score sheet. The sample questionnaire and sample score sheet below show you how to do this:

SAMPLE QUESTIONNAIRE ITEMS		
AS A CHILD	NOW	DESCRIPTION
		1. I find myself clinging to people I'm close to because I'm afraid they'll leave me.
		2. I worry a lot that the people I love will find someone else they prefer and leave me.

SAMPLE OF MATCHING SCORE SHEET						
√	LIFETRAP	CHILD	NOW	CHILD	NOW	HIGHEST SCORE
√	Abandonment	1. 3	1. 2	2. 5	2. 4	5

Questions 1 and 2 are both part of the Abandonment lifetrap. Let's start with Question 1. Take your score for this item as a *child* and transfer it to the box just to the right of the word ABANDONMENT on the score sheet, next to the number 1 (under the *Child* column). Now take your score for this item *now* (as an adult) and transfer it to the next box 1 (under the *Now* column).

Next, look at your score for question 2 as a *child*. Transfer it to box 2, under the Child column. Then take your score for question 2 *now* and transfer it to the next box 2, under the Now column.

Look at all four of your scores for the Abandonment lifetrap. Which one is highest? Transfer your highest score (1, 2, 3, 4, 5, or 6) into the last box on the Abandonment row. If your highest score is 4, 5, or 6, put a check mark in the first column. This √ means that Abandonment is probably one of your schemas. If your highest score is 1, 2, or 3, leave the box blank. This means Abandonment is probably *not* one of your schemas.

Now go ahead and fill in the rest of the score sheet in the same way.

LIFETRAPS SCORE SHEET						
√	LIFETRAP	CHILD	NOW	CHILD	NOW	HIGHEST SCORE
	Abandonment	1.	1.	2.	2.	
✓	Mistrust and abuse	3.	3.	4.	4.	
✓	Vulnerability	5.	5.	6.	6.	
	Dependence	7.	7.	8.	8.	
	Emotional deprivation	9.	9.	10.	10.	
	Social exclusion	11.	11.	12.	12.	
	Defectiveness	13.	13.	14.	14.	
	Failure	15.	15.	16.	16.	
	Subjugation	17.	17.	18.	18.	
	Unrelenting standards	19.	19.	20.	20.	
	Entitlement	21.	21.	22.	22.	

INTERPRETING YOUR SCORES

We will now describe each of the eleven lifetraps briefly, just enough to acquaint you with each one. Refer to your score sheet: each lifetrap with a √ next to it is likely to apply to you. Naturally, the higher your scores for each lifetrap, the more powerful it probably is for you, and the more impact it probably has had on your life. You will want to read more about each of the relevant lifetraps later, after you have finished the introductory chapters.

If you are unsure about whether a lifetrap applies to you or someone close to you, do not worry about trying to be sure now. When you get to the chapter devoted to each lifetrap, we will give you a much more detailed test you can take to be sure that it fits.

THE ELEVEN LIFETRAPS, BRIEFLY

Two lifetraps relate to a lack of safety or security in your childhood family. These are *Abandonment* and *Mistrust*.

• ABANDONMENT •

The *Abandonment* lifetrap is the feeling that the people you love will leave you, and you will end up emotionally isolated forever. Whether you feel people close to you will die, leave home forever, or abandon you because they prefer someone else, somehow you feel that you will be left alone. Because of this belief, you may cling to people close to you too much. Ironically, you end up pushing them away. You may get very upset or angry about even normal separations.

• MISTRUST AND ABUSE •

The *Mistrust and Abuse* lifetrap is the expectation that people will hurt or abuse you in some way—that they will cheat, lie to, manipulate, humiliate, physically harm, or otherwise take advantage of you. If you have this lifetrap, you hide behind a wall of mistrust to protect yourself. You never let people get too close. You are suspicious of other people's intentions, and tend to assume the worst. You expect that the people you love will betray you. Either you avoid relationships altogether, form superficial relationships in which you do not really open up to others, or you form relationships with people who treat you badly and then feel angry and vengeful toward them.

Two lifetraps relate to your ability to function independently in the world. These lifetraps are *Dependence* and *Vulnerability*.

• DEPENDENCE •

If you are caught in the *Dependence* lifetrap, you feel unable to handle everyday life in a competent manner without considerable help from others. You depend on others to act as a crutch and need constant support. As a child you were made to feel incompetent when you tried to assert your independence. As an adult, you seek out strong figures upon whom to become dependent and allow them to rule your life. At work, you shrink from acting on your own. Needless to say, this holds you back.

 VULNERABILITY •

With *Vulnerability,* you live in fear that disaster is about to strike— whether natural, criminal, medical, or financial. You do not feel *safe* in the world. If you have this lifetrap, as a child you were made to feel that the world is a dangerous place. You were probably overprotected by your parents, who worried too much about your safety. Your fears are *excessive* and *unrealistic,* yet you let them control your life, and pour your energy into making sure that you are safe. Your fears may revolve around illness: having an anxiety attack, getting AIDS, or going crazy. They may be focused around financial vulnerability: going broke and ending up on the streets. Your vulnerability may revolve around other phobic situations, such as a fear of flying, being mugged, or earthquakes.

Two lifetraps relate to the strength of your emotional connections to others: *Emotional Deprivation* and *Social Exclusion.*

• EMOTIONAL DEPRIVATION •

Emotional Deprivation is the belief that your need for love will never be met adequately by other people. You feel that no one truly cares for you or understands how you feel. You find yourself attracted to cold and ungiving people, or you are cold and ungiving yourself, leading you to form relationships that inevitably prove unsatisfying. You feel *cheated,* and you alternate between being angry about it and feeling hurt and alone. Ironically, your anger just drives people further away, ensuring your continued deprivation.

When patients with emotional deprivation come to see us for therapy sessions, there is a loneliness about them that stays with us even after they have left the office. It is a quality of emptiness, of emotional disconnection. These are people who do not know what love is.

• SOCIAL EXCLUSION •

Social Exclusion involves your connection to friends and groups. It has to do with feeling isolated from the rest of the world, with feeling *different*. If you have this lifetrap, as a child you felt excluded by peers. You did not belong to a group of friends. Perhaps you had some unusual characteristic that made you feel different in some way. As an adult, you maintain your lifetrap mainly through avoidance. You avoid socializing in groups and making friends.

You may have felt excluded because there was something about you that other children rejected. Hence you felt socially *undesirable*. As an adult you may feel that you are ugly, sexually undesirable, low in status, poor in conversational skills, boring, or otherwise deficient. You reenact your childhood rejection—you feel and act inferior in social situations.

It is not always apparent that someone has a Social Exclusion lifetrap. Many people with this lifetrap are quite comfortable in intimate settings and are quite socially skilled. Their lifetrap may not *show* in one-to-one relationships. It sometimes surprises us to realize how anxious and aloof they may feel at parties, in classes, at meetings, or at work. They have a restless quality, a quality of looking for a place to belong.

The two lifetraps that relate to your self-esteem are *Defectiveness* and *Failure*.

• DEFECTIVENESS •

With *Defectiveness,* you feel *inwardly* flawed and defective. You believe that you would be fundamentally unlovable to anyone who got close enough to really know you. Your defectiveness would be exposed. As a child, you did not feel respected for who you were in your family. Instead, you were criticized for your "flaws." You blamed yourself—you felt unworthy of love. As an adult, you are afraid of love. You find it difficult to believe that people close to you value you, so you expect rejection.

FAILURE •

Failure is the belief that you are inadequate in areas of achievement, such as school, work, and sports. You believe you have failed relative to your peers. As a child, you were made to feel inferior in terms of achievement. You may have had a learning disability, or you may never have learned enough discipline to master important skills, such as reading. Other children were always better than you. You were called "stupid," "untalented," or "lazy." As an adult, you maintain your lifetrap by exaggerating the degree of your failure and by acting in ways that ensure your continued failure.

Two lifetraps deal with Self-Expression—your ability to express what you want and get your true needs met: *Subjugation* and *Unrelenting Standards*.

• SUBJUGATION •

With *Subjugation,* you sacrifice your own needs and desires for the sake of pleasing others or meeting their needs. You allow others to control you. You do this either out of *guilt*—that you hurt other people by putting yourself first—or *fear* that you will be punished or abandoned if you disobey. As a child, someone close to you, probably a parent, subjugated you. As an adult, you repeatedly enter relationships with dominant, controlling people and subjugate yourself to them or you enter relationships with needy people who are too damaged to give back to you in return.

• UNRELENTING STANDARDS •

If you are in the *Unrelenting Standards* lifetrap, you strive relentlessly to meet extremely high expectations of yourself. You place excessive emphasis on status, money, achievement, beauty, order, or recognition at the expense of happiness, pleasure, health, a sense of accomplishment, and satisfying relationships. You probably apply your rigid standards to other people as well and are very judgmental. When you were a child, you were expected to be the best, and you were taught that anything else was failure. You learned that nothing you did was quite good enough.

• ENTITLEMENT •

The final lifetrap, *Entitlement,* is associated with the ability to accept realistic limits in life. People who have this lifetrap feel *special.* They insist that they be able to do, say, or have whatever they want immediately. They disregard what others consider reasonable, what is actually feasible, the time or patience usually required, and the cost to others. They have difficulty with self-discipline.

Many of the people with this lifetrap were spoiled as children. They were not required to show self-control or to accept the restrictions placed on other children. As adults, they still get very angry when they do not get what they want.

Now you have an idea of which lifetraps apply to you. The next chapter will tell you about where lifetraps come from—how we develop them as children.

UNDERSTANDING LIFETRAPS

Lifetraps have three central features that allow us to recognize them.

RECOGNIZING LIFETRAPS

1. They are lifelong *patterns* or *themes*.
2. They are *self-destructive*.
3. They *struggle for survival*.

As we said in the first chapter, a lifetrap is a pattern or theme that starts in childhood and repeats throughout life. The theme might be Abandonment or Mistrust or Emotional Deprivation or any of the others we described. The end result is that, as an adult, *we manage to recreate the conditions of our childhood that were most harmful to us.*

A lifetrap is self-destructive. This self-defeating quality is what makes lifetraps so poignant for us as therapists to watch. We see someone like Patrick get abandoned *again,* or someone like Madeline get abused. Patients are drawn to situations that trigger their lifetraps, like moths to flame. A lifetrap damages our sense of self, our health, our relationships with others, our work, our happiness, our moods—it touches every aspect of our lives.

A lifetrap struggles hard for survival. We feel a strong push to maintain it. This is part of the human drive for consistency. The lifetrap is what we know. Although it is painful, it is comfortable and familiar. It is therefore very difficult to change. Furthermore, our lifetraps were usually developed when we were children as appropriate *adaptations* to the family we lived in. These patterns were realistic when we were children; the problem is that we continue to repeat them when they no longer serve a useful purpose.

HOW LIFETRAPS DEVELOP

A number of factors contribute to the development of lifetraps. The first is temperament. Temperament is inborn. It is our emotional makeup, the way we are *wired* to respond to events.

Like other inborn traits, temperament varies. It also covers a range of emotions. Here are some examples of traits we believe may be largely inherited.

POSSIBLE DIMENSIONS OF TEMPERAMENT

Shy	↔	Outgoing
Passive	↔	Aggressive
Emotionally Flat	↔	Emotionally Intense
Anxious	↔	Fearless
Sensitive	↔	Invulnerable

You might think of your temperament as the combination of your locations on all of these dimensions, and others we do not yet know of or understand.

Of course, behavior is influenced by environment as well. A safe and nurturing environment may make even a shy child relatively outgoing; and, if things get bad enough, even a relatively invulnerable child can be beaten down.

Heredity and environment shape and influence us. This is true (although to a lesser degree) even of traits that seem purely physical, such as height. We are born with a potential for a certain height, and whether we reach that potential depends in part on our environment—whether we are well fed, have a healthy environment, etc.

The most important early influence in our environment is our family. To a large extent, the dynamics of our family were the dynamics of our early world. When we reenact a lifetrap, what we are reenacting is almost always a drama from our childhood family. For example, Patrick reenacts what happened to him, his abandonment by his mother, and Madeline reenacts being abused.

In most cases the influence of family is strongest at birth and progressively declines as the child grows up. Other influences become important—peers, school, etc.—but the family remains the primal situation. Lifetraps develop when early childhood environments are destructive. Here are some examples:

EXAMPLES OF DESTRUCTIVE EARLY ENVIRONMENTS

1. One of your parents was abusive, and the other was passive and helpless.
2. Your parents were emotionally distant and had high expectations for achievement.
3. Your parents fought all the time. You were caught in the middle.
4. One parent was sick or depressed and the other was absent. You became the caretaker.
5. You became enmeshed with a parent. You were expected to act as a substitute spouse.
6. A parent was phobic and overprotected you. This parent was afraid to be alone and clung to you.
7. Your parents criticized you. Nothing was ever good enough.
8. Your parents overindulged you. They did not set limits.
9. You were rejected by peers, or felt different.

Heredity and environment interact. The destructive influences of our childhood interacted with our specific temperament in the formation of our lifetraps. Our temperament may partially determine how we were treated by our parents. For example, often only one child in a family is singled out for abuse. And our temperament partially determines how we responded to that treatment. Given the same environment, two children can react very differently. Both might be abused, but one becomes passive and the other fights back.

WHAT A CHILD NEEDS TO THRIVE

Our childhood does not have to be perfect for us to be reasonably well-adjusted adults. It just has to be, as D. W. Winnicott said, "good enough." A child has certain core needs for basic safety, connection to others, autonomy, self-esteem, self-expression, and realistic limits. If these are met, then the child will usually thrive psychologically. It is when there are serious shortfalls in meeting the child's needs that problems develop. These shortfalls are what we mean by lifetraps.

WHAT WE NEED TO THRIVE

1. Basic Safety
2. Connection to Others
3. Autonomy

4. Self-Esteem
5. Self-Expression
6. Realistic Limits

• BASIC SAFETY (LIFETRAPS: *ABANDONMENT* AND *MISTRUST AND ABUSE*) •

Some lifetraps are more core than others. Basic Safety lifetraps are the most core. They begin early. Even an infant can have them. To an infant, feeling safe is absolutely central. It is a matter of life and death.

Basic Safety lifetraps involve a child's treatment by *his or her own family*. The threat of abandonment or abuse comes from those who are most intimate—from those who are supposed to love us, take care of us, and protect us.

People who were abused or abandoned as children are the most damaged. There is nowhere they feel safe. They feel that at any moment something terrible might happen—someone they love might hurt them or leave them. They feel vulnerable and fragile. It takes very little to disrupt their equilibrium. Their moods are intense and erratic, and they are impulsive and self-destructive.

A child needs a secure, stable family environment. In a safe home, parents are predictably available. They are physically and emotionally there for the child. No one is being mistreated. Fighting is within normal bounds. No one dies or leaves the child alone for long periods.

Patrick, the man whose wife kept having affairs, did not have a stable home as a child. His mother was an alcoholic.

PATRICK: *Some nights she didn't even come home. She just wouldn't show up. And we'd all know where she was, though no one would talk about it. And when she was home, it didn't matter. She was either drunk, hung over, or getting drunk.*

If you had a parent who was a severe alcoholic, then your need for safety was almost certainly not fully met.

We might say that Patrick, as an adult, is *addicted* to instability. Unstable situations draw him like a magnet. Particularly, he feels a lot of attraction to unstable women. He feels a lot of *chemistry*. These are the women with whom he falls in love.

A child who feels safe can relax and trust. A core feeling of safety underlies everything. Without that feeling, little else is possible. We cannot proceed to other developmental tasks. So much energy is taken up with worrying about safety issues that there is little left.

Unsafe childhood situations are the most dangerous to repeat. You end up rushing headlong from one self-destructive relationship to another. Or you avoid relationships altogether, like Madeline did in her post-college years.

• CONNECTION TO OTHERS (LIFETRAPS: *EMOTIONAL DEPRIVATION* AND *SOCIAL EXCLUSION*) •

To develop a sense of connection, we need love, attention, empathy, respect, affection, understanding, and guidance. We need these things from both our family and our peers.

There are two forms of connection to others. The first involves *intimacy*. Usually intimate relationships are those with family, lovers, and very good friends. They are our closest emotional ties. In our most intimate relationships, we feel the kind of connection that one feels with a mother or father. The second form involves our *social* connections. This is a sense of *belonging*, of fitting into the larger social world. Social relationships are those with circles of friends and with groups in the community.

Connection problems can be subtle. You can look like you fit in perfectly well. You might have a family, loved ones, or be part of the community. Yet, deep down you feel disconnected. You feel alone, and long for a kind of relationship that you do not have. Only someone astute would notice that you are not really connecting with the people around you. You keep people at a little bit of a distance. You do not let anyone come too close. Or your problems may be more extreme. You may be a loner—a person who has always been alone.

Jed, the man described in the first chapter who is dissatisfied with one woman after another, has serious intimacy problems. He *recoils* from intimacy. He keeps even his closest relationships superficial. When he first started therapy, he could not name a single person to whom he felt close.

Jed grew up in an emotional vacuum. He barely knew his father, and his mother was cold and distant. There was no communication of feelings and no physical affection. We say there are three types of childhood deprivation: nurturance, empathy, and guidance. Jed was deprived of all three.

If you have connection problems, then loneliness is an issue for you. You may feel that no one really knows you deeply and cares about you (the Emotional Deprivation lifetrap). Or you may feel isolated from the world, that you do not fit in anywhere (the Social Exclusion lifetrap). It is a feeling of emptiness—a hunger for connection.

- AUTONOMY: INDEPENDENT FUNCTIONING (LIFETRAPS: *DEPENDENCE* AND *VULNERABILITY*) •

Autonomy is the ability to separate from our parents and function independently in the world, comparable to other people our own age. It is the ability to leave the house, have a life, an identity, and goals and directions of our own that are not solely dependent on the support or direction of our parents. It is the ability to act as an individual—to have a *self*.

If you grew up in a family that fostered autonomy, then your parents taught you self-sufficiency skills, encouraged you to accept responsibility, and taught you to exercise good judgment. They encouraged you to venture into the outside world and interact with peers. Rather than overprotecting you, they taught you that the world is safe and how to keep yourself safe in it. They encouraged you to develop a separate identity.

However, you may have had a more unhealthy childhood environment, one that fostered dependence and fusion. Your parents may not have taught you self-reliance skills. Instead, they may have done everything for you, and undermined your attempts to do things on your own. They may have taught you that the world is dangerous, and constantly warned you about danger and possible illness. They may have kept you from pursuing your natural inclinations. They may have taught you that you cannot rely on your own judgment or decisions to get by in the world.

Heather, the woman in Chapter 1 with numerous phobias, was overprotected as a child. Her parents constantly warned her about danger because they were constantly worried about danger themselves. They taught her to feel *vulnerable* in the world.

Heather's parents were not ill-intentioned. Rather, they were fearful themselves and were trying to protect her. This is often the case. Parents who overprotect their children can be quite loving. Heather has the Vulnerability lifetrap. Her ability to be autonomous in the world is impaired because she is too afraid to go out into the world and do things.

Feeling *safe* enough to venture into the world is one aspect of autonomy. Feeling *competent* to cope with everyday tasks and having a separate sense of *self* are other aspects. These last two have more to do with the Dependence lifetrap.

With Dependence, you fail to develop a sense of competence about your ability to function in the world. Perhaps your parents were overprotective: they made your decisions for you, and handled your responsibilities. They may even have subtly undermined you, criticizing you whenever you struck out on your own. As a consequence, as an adult you feel unable to cope effectively on your own without the guidance, advice, and financial support of people who you feel are stronger and wiser than you. Even if you leave your parents—and *many* never leave their parents—you just get into a relationship with another parental figure. You find a partner or boss who can serve as a parent substitute.

Dependent people often have an *undeveloped* or *enmeshed* sense of self. Their identities merge with the identities of their parents or spouses. The stereotype is the wife who becomes completely absorbed in her husband's life and loses the sense of her own identity. She does everything her husband wants her to do. She does not have friends of her own, interests of her own, or opinions of her own. When she talks, she talks about her husband's life.

Feeling safe enough to venture into the world, feeling competent, developing a strong sense of self—these are the components of autonomy.

• SELF-ESTEEM (LIFETRAPS: *DEFECTIVENESS* AND *FAILURE*) •

Self-esteem is the feeling that we are worthwhile in our personal, social, and work lives. It comes from feeling loved and respected as a child in our family, by friends, and at school.

Ideally we would all have had childhoods that support our self-esteem. We would have felt loved and appreciated by our family, accepted by peers, and successful at school. We would have received praise and encouragement without excessive criticism or rejection.

But this may not have been what happened to you. Perhaps you had a parent or sibling who constantly criticized you, so that nothing you did was acceptable. You felt *unlovable*. Perhaps you were rejected by peers. They made you feel undesirable. Or maybe you felt like a failure in school or sports.

As an adult, you may feel insecure about certain aspects of your life. You lack self-confidence in the areas where you feel vulnerable—intimate relationships, social situations, or work. Within your vulnerable areas, you feel inferior to other people. You are hypersensitive to criticism and rejection. Challenges make you very anxious. You either avoid challenges or handle them poorly.

The two lifetraps in the Self-Esteem realm are Defectiveness and Failure. They correspond to feelings of unworthiness in the personal and work realms. The Failure lifetrap involves a feeling of inadequacy in the realm of achievement and work. It is the sense that you are less successful, talented, or intelligent than your peers.

The Defectiveness lifetrap involves the sense that you are inherently flawed—that the more deeply someone knows you, the less lovable you are. The Defectiveness lifetrap often accompanies other lifetraps. Of the five patients we listed in the first chapter, three—Madeline, Jed, and Carlton—had the Defectiveness lifetrap in addition to their primary lifetraps.

Madeline is the patient who was sexually abused by her stepfather. It is very common for Mistrust and Abuse and Defectiveness to go hand in hand. Children almost always blame themselves for abuse, feeling that they must be very bad, or unworthy of love, to deserve the abuse.

Jed, the man who becomes involved with one woman after another, has profound feelings of defectiveness. He covers up these feelings by adopting a superior, aloof attitude. And Carlton, the people-pleaser, feels defective as well. Part of the reason Carlton denies his own needs is that he feels he is not worth more.

Injuries to our self-esteem cause us to feel *shame*. Shame is the predominant emotion in this realm. If you have the Defectiveness or Failure lifetrap, then you live a life filled with shame about who you are.

• SELF-EXPRESSION (LIFETRAPS: *SUBJUGATION* AND *UNRELENTING STANDARDS*) •

Self-expression is the freedom to express ourselves—our needs, feelings (including anger), and natural inclinations. It implies the belief that our needs count as much as other people's needs. We are free to act spontaneously without inordinate inhibition. We feel free to pursue activities and interests that make *us* happy, not just those around us. We are allowed time to have fun and play, not just encouraged to work and compete nonstop.

In an early environment that encourages self-expression, we are encouraged to discover our own natural interests and preferences. Our needs and desires are taken into account in making decisions. We are permitted to express emotions, such as sadness and anger, as long as they do not seriously harm other people. We are regularly allowed to be playful, uninhibited, and enthusiastic. We are encouraged to balance play and work. Standards are reasonable.

If you grow up in a family that discourages self-expression, you are punished or made to feel guilty when you express your needs, preferences, or feelings. Your parents' needs and feelings take precedence over yours. You are made to feel powerless. You are shamed when you act in a playful or uninhibited manner. Work and achievement are overemphasized at the expense of fun and pleasure. Your parents are not satisfied unless you perform perfectly.

Carlton, the people-pleaser, grew up in an environment that damaged his self-expression. His father was critical and controlling, and his mother was frequently depressed and ill.

CARLTON: *My father was never happy with who I was. He was always trying to change me, to tell me what I should be. My mother was in bed a lot. She was always sick and in bed. I tried to take care of her as best I could.*

Carlton's identity did not matter much. His parents used him for their own ends. He learned to push his own needs back lest he make a parent angry or depressed. His childhood was grim and selfless. "I feel like I never was a child," he says.

There are three signs that your self-expression is restricted. The first is that you are extremely *accommodating* to other people. You are always pleasing everybody else, always taking care of everybody. You are self-effacing, almost like a martyr. You do not seem concerned with your own needs. You cannot stand to see those around you in pain and will repeatedly sacrifice your own desires to help them. You may do so much for people that it makes them feel guilty to be with you. Inside, you may feel weak and passive, or resentful when all your giving is not appreciated. You are too much at the mercy of other people's needs.

A second sign that you have problems in this realm is that you are overly *inhibited and controlled*. You may be a workaholic—your whole life revolves around your work. Your work may be a career or it may be other things. You may work to look perfectly beautiful at all times, or to keep everything perfectly neat and clean, or to always do things in the perfectly proper, correct way.

You may be emotionally *flat*. There is no spontaneity in your life. You suppress your natural reactions to events. Whether it is because you feel you have to do what other people want (the Subjugation lifetrap) or because you have to live up to some impossibly high standard (the Unrelenting Standards lifetrap), you have the sense that you are not really enjoying your life. Your life is somber and joyless. You somehow rob yourself of fun, relaxation, and pleasure.

A third indication of problems in Self-Expression is having a great deal of *unexpressed anger*. Chronic resentment may simmer underneath, occasionally erupting unexpectedly, almost out of your control. And you may feel depressed. You are trapped in an unrewarding routine. Your life seems empty. You are doing everything you should, yet there is no pleasure in it.

• REALISTIC LIMITS (LIFETRAP: *ENTITLEMENT*) •

Realistic Limits problems are, in many respects, the opposite of Self-Expression problems. When you are not permitted Self-Expression, you are overly controlled. You suppress your own needs and attend to the needs of others. With Limits problems, you attend so much to your own needs that you *disregard other people*. You may do so to such an extent that others see you as selfish, demanding, controlling, self-centered, and narcissistic. And you may have problems with self-control. You are so impulsive or emotional that you have difficulty meeting your long-term goals. You always go for immediate gratification. You cannot tolerate routine or boring tasks. You learn that you are special, entitled to do everything your own way.

To have realistic limits means *to accept realistic internal and external limits on our own behavior*. This includes the capacity to understand and take the needs of others into account in our actions—to balance fairly our own needs with those of others. It is also the capacity to exercise enough self-control and self-discipline to reach our goals and to avoid punishment from society.

When we are raised in a childhood environment that sets realistic limits, our parents set up consequences for our behavior that reward realistic self-control and self-discipline. We are not *excessively* indulged or permitted excessive freedom. We are taught to be responsible. We have to do schoolwork and carry through on chores. Our parents help us learn to take the perspective of others and to be sensitive to other people's needs. We are taught not to hurt people unnecessarily. We learn to respect other people's rights and freedom.

But perhaps your childhood did not foster realistic limits. Your parents may have been overly indulgent and permissive. They gave you whatever you wanted. They rewarded you for manipulative behavior—whenever you threw a temper tantrum you got your way. They did not adequately supervise you. They permitted you to express anger without restriction. You never learned the notion of *reciprocity*. You were not encouraged to understand the feelings of others, nor to take the feelings of others into account. You were not taught self-discipline and self-control. All of these errors can lead to an Entitlement lifetrap.

In an alternative scenario, perhaps your parents were emotionally cold and depriving. You were constantly criticized and devalued. You developed a sense of Entitlement later in life to make up for, or escape, the deprivation and devaluation.

Entitlement can be damaging to your life. Eventually people get fed up with you. They either leave you or retaliate. Your partner breaks up with you, your friends stop spending time with you, you are fired from your job. If your Limits problems include difficulty with self-discipline and self-control, even your health can be affected. You might smoke too much, become addicted to drugs, get too little exercise, overeat. You might even commit criminal acts, such as losing your temper and assaulting someone or getting arrested for drunken driving. Self-discipline problems may also cause you to fail to reach your goals in life. You may have too much trouble disciplining yourself to do the necessary work.

People with Limits problems tend to be very *blaming*. Instead of recognizing themselves as the source of their problems, they blame others. Therefore it is unlikely that someone with Limits problems would be reading this book. They believe that *other* people have problems, not them. However, it *is* likely that many people reading this book are *involved* with someone who has Limits problems. None of the five patients in Chapter 1 had Limits problems. However, many were in self-destructive relationships with people who had Limits issues.

SUMMARY

To summarize, here is a chart of all the lifetraps in their appropriate categories:

THE ELEVEN LIFETRAPS

I. Basic Safety
   1. Abandonment
   2. Mistrust & Abuse

II. Connection to Others
   3. Emotional Deprivation
   4. Social Exclusion

III. Autonomy
   5. Dependence
   6. Vulnerability

IV. Self-Esteem
   7. Defectiveness
   8. Failure

V. Self-Expression
   9. Subjugation
   10. Unrelenting Standards

VI. Realistic Limits
   11. Entitlement

In the next chapter, we explain how lifetraps work, and how different people cope with their lifetraps.

4

SURRENDER, ESCAPE, AND COUNTERATTACK

Lifetraps *actively* organize our experience. They operate in overt and subtle ways to influence how we think, feel, and act.

Different people cope with lifetraps in different ways. This explains why children raised in the same environment can appear to be so different. For example, two children with abusive parents may respond to abuse very differently. One becomes a passive, frightened victim and remains that way throughout life. The other child becomes openly rebellious and defiant and may even leave home early to survive as a teenager on the streets.

This is partly because we have different temperaments at birth—we tend to be more frightened, active, outgoing, or shy. Our temperaments push us in certain directions. And it is partly because we may choose different parents to copy or model ourselves after. Since an abuser often marries a victim, their children have both serving as models. The child can copy the abusive parent *or* the victimized parent.

THREE LIFETRAP COPING STYLES: SURRENDER, ESCAPE, AND COUNTERATTACK*

Let us look at three different individuals: Alex, Brandon, and Max. Each one has the Defectiveness lifetrap. Deep down, all three feel flawed, unlovable, and ashamed. Yet they *cope* with their feelings of defectiveness in entirely different ways. We call these three styles *Surrender, Escape, and Counterattack.*

ALEX: HE SURRENDERS TO HIS SENSE OF DEFECTIVENESS.

Alex is a nineteen-year-old college student. When you meet him, he does not look you in the eye. He keeps his head down. When he speaks, you can barely hear him. He blushes and stammers, puts himself down in front of other people, and is constantly apologizing. He always takes the blame for things that go wrong, even if they are not really his fault.

Alex always feels "one down"—inferior to others, and he constantly compares himself to others unfavorably. He feels that other people are somehow better. Social events are invariably painful for this reason. In his first year of college, he went to parties but was too anxious to talk to anyone. "I couldn't think of anything to say," he explains. So far, in his second year, he has not attended a single college party.

Alex has begun dating a woman who lives in his dorm. She criticizes him all the time. His best friend is very critical of him as well. His expectation that people are going to be critical is often borne out.

THERAPIST: *Why do you criticize yourself so much?*
ALEX: *I guess I want to do it first, before other people do it for me.*

Alex has a lot of feelings of shame. He blushes and walks around with his head down because he feels ashamed of himself. He *interprets* events in his life as continual proof of his defectiveness, unlovability, and worthlessness.

ALEX: *I feel like such a social reject. We're halfway through the semester and I still don't know anyone in any of my classes. Other people sit around and talk, but I just sit there like a bump on a log. No one talks to me.*

---

*In schema therapy, these correspond to the coping styles of maintenance, avoidance, and compensation.

THERAPIST: *Do you ever talk to anyone?*
ALEX: *Nah. Who would want to talk to me?*

Alex *thinks, feels,* and *acts* as though he were defective. The lifetrap permeates his experience of life. This is how it is with Surrender as a coping style. The lifetrap is very much with us. Alex is well aware of his feelings of defectiveness.

When we Surrender, we *distort* our view of situations to confirm our lifetrap. We react with strong feelings whenever our lifetrap is activated. We select partners and enter situations that reinforce our lifetrap. *We keep the lifetrap going.*

Alex consistently distorts or misperceives situations so that they reinforce his lifetrap. His view of situations is inaccurate: he feels people are attacking and humiliating him even when they are not. He has a strong bias to interpret events as proving he is defective, exaggerating the negative and minimizing the positive. He is illogical. When we surrender, we continually misinterpret and misconstrue people and events in ways that maintain our lifetraps.

We grow up accustomed to certain roles and certain ways of being perceived. If we grow up in a family in which we are abused, neglected, yelled at, constantly criticized, or dominated, then that is the environment that feels most comfortable to us. Unhealthy as it may be, most people seek and create environments that feel familiar and similar to the ones where they grew up. The whole essence of surrendering is somehow managing to arrange your life so that you continue to repeat the patterns of your childhood.

Alex grew up in a family that criticized and demeaned him, a typical origin for the Defectiveness lifetrap. As an adult, he behaves in ways that ensure he will end up being criticized and demeaned. He chooses partners and friends who are very critical of him. He acts ashamed and apologetic. He criticizes himself in front of others. When people are nice to him, he distances or somehow undermines the relationship. Alex tries to maintain the *status quo*. When the environment becomes too supportive, he alters the situation so he can go back to that comfortable state of shame and dejection. If he feels superior or equal for a moment, he somehow manages to return to a lesser position.

Surrender includes all the self-destructive patterns we keep repeating over and over. It is all the ways we replicate our childhood lives. We are still that child, going through that same old pain. Surrender *extends* our childhood situation into our adult life. For this reason it often leads us to feel hopeless about changing. All we know is the lifetrap, which we never escape. It is a self-perpetuating loop.

BRANDON: HE *ESCAPES HIS FEELINGS OF DEFECTIVENESS.*

Brandon is forty years old and has never had a close relationship. He spends most of his spare time yakking with his buddies at the neighborhood bar. Brandon is most comfortable with casual, friendly relationships where nothing very personal is discussed.

Brandon is married to a woman who is out of touch with her feelings. She is very concerned with keeping up appearances. She is more interested in being married than in being married to Brandon particularly. She has close female friends, but does not expect closeness from Brandon. She wants a man just so she can fulfill the conventional role of wife. Their relationship is based on traditional roles, not on real intimacy. They rarely confide in each other.

Brandon has been an alcoholic his entire adult life. Although his family and friends have suggested Alcoholics Anonymous, he ignores them. He insists that he is not an alcoholic—he says he only drinks for recreation, and that he has control over his drinking. Besides drinking in his neighborhood bar, he tends to drink in social settings when he is around people he feels are better than he is.

Brandon became depressed, which is what originally brought him to therapy. But in contrast to Alex, he was not in touch with his lifetrap. He spent much of his life making sure that he was *not* in touch. When he first started therapy, he was only dimly aware of his feelings of defectiveness. When we asked him how he felt about himself, he denied having feelings of low self-esteem or shame. (Later in treatment these feelings came out very strongly.)

We had to battle his Escape on every front. When we asked him to write down his negative thoughts for homework, he did not do it. He claimed, "Why think about things? They only make me feel worse." When we asked him to close his eyes and picture himself as a child, he said, "I can't see anything. My mind is blank." Or he saw an image of a photograph of himself as a child, devoid of emotion. When we asked him how he felt about his abusive father, he insisted that he felt no anger. "My father was a good man," he said.

Brandon tries to escape his feelings of defectiveness. With Escape, we avoid *thinking* about our lifetrap. We push it out of our minds. We also escape *feeling* our lifetrap. When feelings are generated, we dampen them down. We take drugs, or overeat, or compulsively clean, or become a workaholic. And we avoid entering situations that might activate our lifetrap. In fact, our thoughts, feelings, and behaviors work as if the lifetrap never existed.

Many people escape whole areas of life where they feel vulnerable or sensitive. If you have the Defectiveness lifetrap, like Brandon you may avoid intimate relationships altogether, never letting anybody get too close. If you have the Failure lifetrap, you may avoid work, school tasks, promotions, or taking on new projects. If you have the Social Exclusion lifetrap, you may avoid groups, parties, meetings, conventions. If you have the Dependence lifetrap, you may avoid all situations that require you to be independent. You may be phobic about going into public places alone.

It is natural that Escape becomes one of the ways we cope with lifetraps. When a lifetrap is triggered, we are flooded with negative feelings—sadness, shame, anxiety, and anger. We are moved to escape from that pain. We do not want to face what we really feel because it is too upsetting to feel it.

The disadvantage of Escape is that we never overcome the lifetrap. Since we never confront the truth, we are stuck. We cannot change things that we do not admit are problems. Instead, we continue the same self-defeating behaviors, the same destructive relationships. In trying to coast through life without feeling pain, we rob ourselves of the chance to change the things that are causing us pain.

When we escape, we strike a bargain with ourselves. We will not feel pain in the short run, but in the long run we will suffer the consequences of having avoided the issue year after year. As long as he escapes, Brandon will never get what he wants most—to love and be loved by another human being who really knows him. Love is what Brandon was denied in childhood.

With Escape we give up our emotional life. We do not *feel.* We walk around numb—unable to experience real pleasure and pain. Because we avoid confronting problems, we often end up hurting those around us. We are also prone to the terrible consequences of addictions like alcohol and drugs.

MAX: HE *COUNTERATTACKS* TO COPE WITH HIS FEELINGS OF DEFECTIVENESS.

Max is a thirty-two-year-old stockbroker. On the surface he is self-confident and assured. In fact, he is a snob. He has an air of superiority. He is very critical of others while rarely acknowledging any faults in himself.

Max came to therapy because his wife was threatening to leave him. He insisted their problems were all her fault.

THERAPIST: *So your wife is pretty angry with you?*
MAX: *If you ask me, she's the one who's causing all the problems. She blows things out of proportion, and she demands too much from me.* She's the one who needs to be in therapy.

In fact, Max chose a very passive, self-sacrificing wife who worshiped him. Through the years, he had become so verbally abusive and selfish that she had finally insisted that either they start therapy or she would leave.

Max creates situations where he is one up. He chooses friends and employees who will flatter him, rather than challenge and confront him. He enjoys feeling superior. He devotes most of his energy to gaining prestige and status. He manipulates and uses people in any way necessary to achieve these ends.

He tried to stay one up in therapy as well. He questioned our credentials, approach, competence, level of success, and age. And he kept reminding us how successful he was. When we told him we thought he was treating his wife badly, he became infuriated. He insisted we did not understand his feelings. He insisted that we should be willing to give him appointments whenever he wanted them because he is an important person. When we refused, he again became angry. He felt he was not getting the special treatment he deserved.

Max is not in touch with his lifetrap yet it is very much with him. In feeling superior, Max experiences the *opposite* of what he felt as a child. He is trying to be as different as possible from the worthless child that his parents made him feel he was. We might say he spends his whole life trying to keep that child at bay and to fight off the attacks of those he expects to criticize and abuse him.

When we Counterattack, we try to make up for the lifetrap by convincing ourselves and others that the *opposite* is true. We feel, act, and think as if we are *special, superior, perfect, infallible*. We cling to this persona desperately.

Counterattack develops because it offers an alternative to being devalued, criticized, and humiliated. It is a way out of that terrible vulnerability. Our counterattacks help us cope. But when these counterattacks become too extreme, they often backfire and end up hurting us.

Counterattackers can *appear* healthy. In fact, some of the people we admire most in society are counterattackers—some movie stars, rock stars, and political leaders. But although they fit in well with society and are successful in the eyes of other people, they are usually not at peace with themselves. They frequently feel defective underneath.

They deal with these feelings of inadequacy by putting themselves in situations where they will get the applause of an audience. Winning this applause is actually an attempt to compensate for a deep sense that they are worthless. They can counterattack by masking their flaws with success before they are discovered and put down.

Our counterattacks isolate us. We become so invested in appearing to be perfect that we stop caring who gets hurt in the process. We continue to counterattack, no matter how much it costs other people. There are bound to be some negative effects. Eventually people leave us or retaliate in some way.

Our counterattacks also get in the way of real intimacy. We lose the ability to trust, become vulnerable, and connect at a deeper level. We have met some patients who would rather lose everything—including their marriage, a relationship with someone they love—than risk becoming vulnerable.

Eventually, no matter how perfect we try to be, we are going to fail at something. Counterattackers never really learn to cope with defeat. They do not take responsibility for their failures or acknowledge their limitations. However, when there is a *major* setback, the counterattack collapses. When this happens, they often fall apart and become very depressed.

Underneath, counterattackers are usually very *fragile*. Their superiority is easily deflated. Eventually there is a crack in the armor, and the whole world feels as if it is collapsing. At these times, the lifetrap reasserts itself with enormous strength, and the original feelings of defectiveness, deprivation, exclusion, or abuse return.

All three men—Alex, Brandon, and Max—have Defectiveness as a core lifetrap. Deep down, all three feel worthless, unlovable, and defective. Yet they *cope* with their feelings of defectiveness in completely different ways.

Alex, Brandon, and Max are relatively pure types. Each one uses one primary coping style. In fact such pure types are rare. Most of us use a combination of Surrender, Escape, and Counterattack. We must learn to change these coping styles in order to overcome our lifetraps and become healthy again.

The next chapter shows you how to confront your lifetraps effectively without surrender, without escape, and without counterattack.

5

HOW LIFETRAPS CHANGE

Lifetraps are long-term patterns. They are deeply ingrained, and like addictions or bad habits, they are hard to change. Change requires willingness to experience pain. You have to face the lifetrap head-on and *understand* it. Change also requires discipline. You have to systematically observe and change behaviors every day. Change cannot be hit-or-miss. It requires constant practice.

GENERAL STEPS IN LIFETRAP CHANGE

We will walk you through the steps of change using Danielle as an example. Danielle has the Abandonment lifetrap. She is thirty-one years old. She is in a relationship with a man, Robert, who will not make a commitment to her. They have been together for eleven years, and, although she has asked him many times, he will not marry her.

Every once in a while, Robert breaks up with her. When that happens, Danielle is devastated. She started therapy during one such breakup.

DANIELLE: *I just want to stop feeling this way. I can't take it anymore. All I can think about is Robert. I'm obsessed with him. I've got to get him back.*

This obsessiveness is characteristic of the Abandonment lifetrap. During breakups, Danielle occasionally dates other men, but she never becomes interested in anyone other than Robert. The stable, steady types bore her.

These are the steps Danielle followed in order to change her pattern, and that we recommend for our patients:

• 1. Label and Identify Your Lifetraps. •

The first step is to recognize what your lifetraps are. This can be accomplished by taking the Lifetrap Questionnaire in Chapter 2. Once you can identify a lifetrap and see how it affects your life, you will be in a better position to change it. By having a *name* for your lifetrap, like Defectiveness or Dependence, and reading about it in the second half of this book, you will understand yourself better. You will gain clarity about your life. This *insight* is the first step.

Danielle recognized her Abandonment lifetrap in a number of different ways. When she started therapy, we gave her the Lifetrap Questionnaire. She scored high on items in the Abandonment section.

DANIELLE: *I guess on some level I've always been aware that I have an issue about people abandoning me. I've always been afraid of it, I've always been worried it's bound to happen.*

Patients often have this sensation when they identify a lifetrap. It is a sense of becoming clear about something they have vaguely known all along.

Danielle could easily see how the theme of abandonment played itself out in her current life. She was in a long-term relationship in which abandonment was the main theme. She also learned about her lifetrap through imagery of the past. When we asked her to close her eyes and let images come of her childhood, the predominant theme was abandonment.

DANIELLE: *I see myself. I'm standing by the living room couch. I'm trying to get my mother to pay attention to me, but she's drunk. I can't get her to pay attention to me.*

Danielle's mother was an alcoholic as far back as she could remember. When Danielle was seven, her father left the family to marry another woman. He gradually drifted further away from the family as he had children with his new wife. He left Danielle and her sister with a mother who clearly could not take care of them adequately.

Danielle was abandoned by both parents. Her mother abandoned her through alcoholism, and her father abandoned her literally—by leaving the family. Their abandonment of her was the central truth of her childhood.

Eventually Danielle came to see the theme of abandonment weaving through her life from the past to the present. The idea of the lifetrap *organized her experience for her in a way she could clearly understand.*

Your lifetrap is your enemy. We want you to know your enemy.

- 2. UNDERSTAND THE CHILDHOOD ORIGINS OF YOUR LIFETRAP. *FEEL* THE WOUNDED CHILD INSIDE YOU. •

The second step is to *feel* your lifetrap. We have found that it is very difficult to change deep pain without first reliving it. We all have some mechanisms for blocking this pain. Unfortunately, by blocking the pain, we cannot get fully in touch with our lifetraps.

To feel your lifetrap, you will need to remember your childhood. We will ask you to close your eyes and let the images come. Do not force the images—just let one rise to the top of your mind. Get into each one as deeply as you can. Try to picture these early memories as vividly as possible. If you do this a few times, you will begin to remember what you felt as a child. You will feel the *pain* or emotions connected with your lifetrap.

This kind of imagery is painful. If you feel completely overwhelmed or frightened by the experience, that is a sign you need therapy. Your childhood was so painful that you should not remember it alone. You need a guide, an ally. A therapist can be this for you.

Once you have reconnected with your childhood self, we will ask you to open a dialogue with this child. This inner child is frozen. We want to bring it back to life, where growth and change are possible. We want this child to heal.

We will ask you to talk to your inner child. You can do this by actually talking aloud, or you can do it through writing. You can write a letter to this child in your dominant hand (the hand you usually write with), and have the child write a response in your non-dominant hand. We have found that your child-self can come out in the handwriting of your non-dominant hand.

The idea of talking to your inner child may sound strange at first.

You will understand more about it as the book proceeds. Here is an example of Danielle talking to her inner child. It is during the same scene we described above, when she is trying to get her drunk mother to pay attention to her.

THERAPIST: *I want you to talk to your inner child. Help her.*
DANIELLE: *Well . . . (pause) I come into the image and take little Danielle onto my lap. I say, "I'm so sorry this is happening to you. Your parents aren't able to be there for you the way you need. But I will be here for you. I will help you get through this and make sure you come out all right."*

Giving comfort to your inner child, offering guidance and advice, and empathizing with how the child feels are some of the things we will ask you to do. Even though these exercises may seem silly or uncomfortable to you at first, we have found that most people benefit enormously from them.

- 3. The Third Step is to Build a Case Against Your Lifetrap.
  Disprove its Validity at a Rational Level. •

Your life has utterly convinced you of the truth of your lifetrap. Danielle believes with her whole being that anyone she loves will abandon her. She accepts her lifetrap *emotionally* and *intellectually.*

This change step involves attacking your lifetrap on an intellectual level. In order to do this, you must prove that it is not true, or at least that it can be changed. You must cast doubt on the validity of your lifetrap. As long as you believe that your lifetrap is valid, you will not be able to change it.

To disprove your lifetrap, you will first list *all the evidence pro and con* regarding the lifetrap throughout your life. For example, if you feel *Socially Undesirable,* first you will list all the evidence that supports your lifetrap—that you are undesirable. Then you will make a separate list of all the evidence against your lifetrap—that you are socially desirable.

In most cases, the evidence will show that your lifetrap is false. You are not, in fact, defective, incompetent, a failure, doomed to be abused, etc. But sometimes the lifetrap *is* true. For example, you may have been so rejected and shunned all your life that you have failed to develop social skills, and thus really are socially undesirable in certain ways. Or you may have avoided so many school and career challenges that you have failed in your chosen field.

Look at your list of pros. Is any evidence supporting the lifetrap *inherently* true of you, or were you brainwashed into thinking this way by your family or peers during childhood? For example, were you *born* incompetent, or was your incompetence so drummed into you by a critical parent that you came to believe it was true (Dependence)? Were you *really* special as a child, or did your parents spoil and pamper you, and teach you to feel entitled to more than everyone else (Entitlement)? And ask yourself, is any evidence supporting the lifetrap *still* true of you? Or was it only true in your childhood?

If, after all this analysis, you still feel the lifetrap is true, then ask yourself, "How could I change this aspect of myself?" Explore what you could do to remedy the situation.

Here is a sample from Danielle's list of evidence supporting her Abandonment lifetrap:

EVIDENCE THAT EVERYONE I LOVE WILL ABANDON ME		
EVIDENCE	IS THIS INHERENTLY TRUE OR WAS I BRAINWASHED?	HOW COULD I CHANGE?
1. Unless I cling to Robert, he will leave me.	This isn't true. The truth is, when I cling to Robert, it turns him off. He gets mad at me and wants to get away from me. I think this way because I couldn't make my father stay with me as a child, no matter how I tried.	I could stop clinging to Robert and give him some space. I could learn to relax while I'm alone and not dwell on the possibility of abandonment.

Here is part of Danielle's list of evidence that her lifetrap is false:

EVIDENCE THAT NOT EVERYONE ABANDONS ME

1. My sister and I have been close all my life.
2. I've had several boyfriends who wanted to be with me, but I've been so obsessed with Robert that I never gave any of them a chance.
3. My therapist is there for me.
4. I have an aunt who has always taken an interest in me and tried to help.
5. I have friends who have been around for years and years.
6. Robert and I *have* stuck together for eleven years, even if it's been up and down.

After making your list, summarize the case against your lifetrap on a flashcard. This is a sample flashcard Danielle wrote:

ABANDONMENT FLASHCARD

Even though I *feel* that everyone I get close to will abandon me, it isn't true. I feel this way because when I was a child both my parents abandoned me.

Even though I have experienced a lot of abandonment in my life, in a lot of ways this is because I've been most attracted to men and friends who have trouble making commitments.

But the people in my life don't have to be like that. I can eliminate the people who really are like that from my life. And I can choose to associate with people who are able to be there for me and make a commitment.

A lot of times when I feel abandoned by someone, I should ask myself if I'm just being oversensitive. Even though I feel like the person's abandoning me, it may just be my Abandonment lifetrap being triggered. Something is reminding me of what happened when I was a child. People have a right to some space. I have to allow people some space.

Read this flashcard every day. Carry it with you. Keep a copy near your bed or some other place where you will see it every day.

- 4. WRITE LETTERS TO THE PARENT, SIBLING, OR PEER WHO HELPED CAUSE YOUR LIFETRAP. •

It is important to ventilate your anger and sadness about what happened to you. One thing that keeps your inner child frozen is all your strangled feelings. We want you to give your inner child a voice—to allow your inner child to express his or her pain.

We will ask you to write letters to all the people who hurt you. We realize you will probably have to overcome a lot of guilt to do this, particularly in regard to your parents. It is not easy to attack our parents. They may not have been malicious. They may have had good intentions. But we want you to put aside such considerations for a time, and just tell the truth.

Express your feelings in the letter. Tell them what they did that was hurtful, and how it made you *feel*. Tell them they were wrong to behave as they did. Tell them how you wished it could have been instead.

You will probably decide not to send the letter. It is the *writing* and *expressing* of your feelings that is most important. It is often *not* possible to change the feelings or behavior of your parents, anyway. You should know this from the start. The purpose of the letter is not to change your parents. It is to make you a whole person again.

Here is the letter Danielle wrote to her mother:

Dear Mom,

You have been an alcoholic for all my life. I need to tell you what it's done to me.

I feel like I never got to be a child. Instead, I had to worry all the time about stuff other kids never even dream of. I couldn't be sure that we would have food on the table. I had to do everything myself. While other kids were out playing and having fun, I was cooking dinner and cleaning the house.

You don't know how much humiliation I went through because of you. I remember learning to iron when I was six so the other kids wouldn't laugh at my wrinkled clothes. And I could never bring anybody to the house.

And you were never around like the other mothers. You never came to watch me at school. I couldn't talk to you about my problems. Instead you lay on the couch, drinking yourself senseless.

I would try so hard to get you to get up and be my mother. But you never did.

I feel so sad about what I missed. There were a few times that you were there for me, and those were special. Like the time I was upset about my high school boyfriend, and you got up and talked to me. I wish we could have had more of those times.

But instead I had to grow up with a big hole where there should have been a mother. And I'm still living with that big hole inside me. It wasn't right for you to do this to me. What you did was wrong.

A letter like this can set the record straight. It can tell your story aloud, perhaps for the first time.

• 5. Examine Your Lifetrap Pattern in Careful Detail. •

We want you to make explicit how your lifetrap plays itself out in your current life. The chapters on individual lifetraps will help you identify the self-defeating habits that reinforce your lifetrap.

We will ask you to write down the ways you surrender to your lifetrap, and how you can change them. On page 50 is a sample from one of Danielle's tables.

• 6. The Next Step is *Pattern-breaking*. •

After you have taken the Lifetrap Questionnaire in Chapter 2 and have identified your lifetraps, we want you to choose *one* lifetrap to work on first. Choose the one that has the most impact on your life now. If that seems too difficult, choose one that seems more manageable. We always want you to take manageable steps.

Danielle had more than one lifetrap. In addition to Abandonment, she had Defectiveness. She thought it was her fault that she could not make her father stay and did not have a better mother. As we mentioned earlier, it is very common for children to blame themselves when they are abused or neglected.

But Abandonment was Danielle's core lifetrap. It was the one she chose to work on first. She felt she needed a stable base from which to challenge her other lifetraps. We agreed.

Using the charts you filled out in Step 5, select two or three ways you

WAYS I REINFORCE MY ABANDONMENT LIFETRAP DAY-TO-DAY	HOW I CAN CHANGE
1. I cling to Robert and try to control him.	I could give Robert more free time without asking him a million questions about where he's going and what he's going to do. I could let him tell me when he's unhappy or angry about something in our relationship, instead of falling apart or arguing with him. I could stop asking him every five minutes if he loves me and wants to stay with me. I can stop getting so angry when he wants some space. I can stop feeling so threatened when something good happens in *his* life.
2. I get really angry when one of my friends doesn't return a call right away.	I can give my friends more space without getting so threatened when they're busy with their own lives.
3. I get obsessed with Robert's life and forget about my own.	I can turn my attention from his life to my own, and do the things that are important to me. I can see my friends, and paint, read, write letters. I can go do something fun. I can treat myself to something.

reinforce your lifetrap. Try to carry out the ways you can change. Select steps you feel able to do. We want you to have successful experiences.

Danielle started by trying to change her behavior toward her friends. She tried to stop alternating between clinging and anger with them. If they failed to return a call or invitation, she waited for a period and called again instead of calling them right away and getting angry, or getting excessively upset. She also worked on enhancing her relationships with her more committed friends and downplaying her relationships with her less committed ones. She decided to drop some friends who were particularly unsteady (and usually alcoholic) from her life. This was a loss, but at least it was *she* who was doing the deciding.

Use the techniques we describe in subsequent chapters to help you change your particular lifetrap. Work your way down your list of reinforcing behaviors. Once you have a reasonable degree of mastery with a lifetrap, move to the next one.

• 7. Keep Trying. •

Do not give up or get discouraged easily. Lifetraps *can* change, but it takes a long time and a lot of work. Persevere. *Confront yourself over and over again.*

Danielle has been in therapy with us for more than a year. Occasionally, events in her life still trigger her Abandonment lifetrap, but it happens less frequently, her feelings are less intense, and the whole thing is over more quickly. In addition, the triggering event has to be much more serious, such as the breakup of a relationship. Her life has changed.

The most dramatic changes have been in her relationship with Robert. She has learned to allow Robert a more normal amount of separation. He had been feeling smothered by her, and spent a lot of time trying to get away from her. Some of his lack of commitment was an attempt to resist her clinging. In addition, when she is angry, she tells him, but in a calm rather than a rageful way. She tries to listen when he tells her about his anger or his life. She tries to let him make his own decisions.

A few months ago, Danielle told Robert that either he had to marry her or she was going to end the relationship. He chose to marry her. Of course, things do not always work out this way. Sometimes relationships end. But we believe it is better to end a truly hopeless relationship than to stay caught in the Abandonment lifetrap.

• 8. Forgiving Your Parents. •

Forgiving your parents is not required. Particularly if there was severe abuse or neglect, you may never be able to forgive them. This is totally your choice. But we have found that, in most cases, forgiving one's parents is something that happens naturally, as the healing process progresses.

Patients gradually come to see their parents less and less as giant, negative figures in their mind, and more and more as just people with problems and concerns of their own. They see that their parents were caught within their own lifetraps, and were in fact more like children than giants. They become able to forgive them.

Again, this does not always happen. It may or may not happen to you. Depending upon what happened in your childhood, you may decide never to forgive them. In fact, you may even decide the opposite—to cut off all contact. At the end of your path there may or may not lie forgiveness, but you have to do what is right for you. We will support you either way.

OBSTACLES TO CHANGE

After working with many patients, we have made a list of the most common obstacles to change. We have also listed some possible solutions.

• OBSTACLE #1: YOU ARE COUNTERATTACKING INSTEAD OF ACKNOWLEDGING AND TAKING RESPONSIBILITY FOR THE LIFETRAP. •

If you are having trouble changing, you may still be blaming others for your problems or your lack of progress. You may still be having trouble admitting your mistakes or taking responsibility for changing. Or you may still be overcompensating by working harder, impressing people more, making more money, pleasing people more, and so on. (For more about Counterattacking, see Chapter 4.)

Jed, the man who moved from woman to woman, had to struggle hard to stop Counterattacking. His criticalness of women, his demand that they meet his impossibly high standards for beauty and status, and his need for constant excitement were ways he made himself feel better about his loneliness. He had to get beyond his Counterattacks to connect at a human level with a woman without criticizing her or trying to impress her. He had to get close enough to see beyond the lifetrap.

Here are some solutions to this obstacle:

Solution 1: Do an experiment. Make a list of all the choices you have regretted in your life. What if they *were* your fault? How would you feel? What if the criticisms others have of you *have* some validity? What would that mean about you?

Try to feel the pain of your flaws. Try to acknowledge the pain of your childhood—what you wanted but did not get.

Solution 2: Gradually start working less or making a little less money. Try to refrain from deliberately impressing others. Feel what it is like to be the same as everyone else rather than special or superior. Unless you can allow these feelings in, you will not make yourself vulnerable enough to change.

• Obstacle #2: You Escape from Experiencing Your Lifetrap. •

Escape is a common problem. Many patients have trouble giving up their escape routes. You may find that you have a similar difficulty. You do not allow yourself to think about your problems, your past, your family, or your life patterns. You keep cutting off feelings or dulling them by drinking or taking drugs.

We understand why you want to Escape. To stop avoiding means to lay yourself open to intense anxiety and pain. All five of the patients in Chapter 1 had to struggle with this issue. Patrick had to stop avoiding the problems in his life by obsessing about Francine. Madeline had to stop escaping the pain that sexual intimacy evoked for her. Heather had to stop avoiding activities that she considered dangerous. Jed had to stop escaping from emotional closeness. And Carlton had to stop running away from his own needs and preferences.

It takes motivation to overcome Escape as a coping style. You have to see the rest of your life before you—either stuck in the lifetrap or finally free of it.

Solution 1: You must allow yourself to think through your problems and feel your childhood pain before you can change.

Force yourself to try some of the childhood memory exercises we describe in your lifetrap chapter. Write down some criticisms of your parents or some of your flaws and vulnerabilities.

Keep doing this every day.

Solution 2: Make a list of the advantages and disadvantages of avoiding your feelings. Reread the list every day to remind yourself of why you are doing this.

Solution 3: Stop escaping through drinking, overeating, using drugs, overworking, etc., for a few days. Keep a diary in which you write down what you feel. Try some of the imagery exercises in your lifetrap chapter during these days. Go to a twelve-step program.

- OBSTACLE #3: YOU HAVE NOT DISPROVED THE LIFETRAP TO YOURSELF.
  YOU STILL ACCEPT IT ON A RATIONAL LEVEL. •

Another obstacle is continuing to believe the lifetrap is true. If you accept your lifetrap on a rational level, you are not going to try to change it. You have to cast enough doubt on the validity of your lifetrap for you to do some of the experiments to change.

For example, for a long time Heather felt extremely anxious in the situations she was entering. This was because she still *believed* the situations were dangerous and that catastrophe could strike at any moment. She maintained a hypervigilant state, ever alert for possible harm.

Heather still believed her lifetrap. She believed that she was excessively vulnerable to harm. She had to change her beliefs. She did this in a number of different ways: she educated herself about realistic appraisals of danger, worked continually to lower the odds she assigned to danger, and took reasonable precautions. She learned to relax her body in these situations. Her beliefs gradually yielded.

A lifetrap does not give way all at once. Rather, you must continually chip away at it, bit by bit, gradually weakening its pull.

Solution 1: Return to the exercises in your lifetrap chapter on disproving your lifetrap. Go through them again. Make a commitment to fighting your beliefs.

You may find it helpful to ask someone you trust to help you with the exercises. This person can provide a more objective point of view.

Solution 2: Look very carefully through your life for any evidence that challenges your lifetrap. Look for any possible avenues of change. Were there extenuating circumstances that invalidate the lifetrap? Were you abused? Did you avoid trying harder because you were afraid of rejection and failure? Did you choose friends, lovers, bosses, etc., who confirmed your lifetrap? Try to play devil's advocate in arguing against your lifetrap.

Solution 3: Write your flashcard and read it several times a day.

- OBSTACLE #4: YOU STARTED WITH A LIFETRAP OR TASK THAT WAS
  TOO DIFFICULT. •

Perhaps you have several lifetraps, and you started with the one that is most upsetting for you. If this lifetrap is too overwhelming, you may not be able to make progress.

Or, perhaps you have chosen an appropriate lifetrap, but your plan is too ambitious. You may have started with a change strategy that is too difficult. Carlton, the people-pleaser, is an example of this. When Carlton first started doing assertiveness exercises, he began by attempting to be assertive with his father. This was a mistake: it was too hard. Carlton would become very fearful and unable to express himself. Trying to confront his father right off the bat was setting himself up for failure.

Carlton eventually mastered assertiveness with his father. But he had to sharpen his skills and his confidence on less threatening people first. He started with strangers, such as salespeople and waitresses, gradually moved up to acquaintances and coworkers, and *then* began focusing on more intimate relationships.

This is one of the most important rules: *Always attempt manageable tasks.*

Solution 1: Break your plan into smaller steps.

Solution 2: Start with the easier steps. Slowly build a sense of mastery. Work your way up to the difficult steps.

• Obstacle #5: You Realize Your Lifetrap Is Wrong on a Rational Level, but Emotionally You Still Feel It Is Valid. •

This happens a lot. Most patients tell us that for many months they still *feel* deep down that the lifetrap is true, regardless of what logic and evidence tell them.

Patrick—the man whose wife kept having affairs—would say this. Even when he was in a healthy relationship with a stable woman who could be there for him, he would still *feel* like she was going to abandon him. If she seemed momentarily preoccupied or withdrawn, he became alarmed and began desperately trying to get her back. He would not allow the woman any space.

Patrick finally had to experiment by letting go. He had to learn to give her some space. He was not going to lose her. He had to learn that it was safe to let her go.

Solution 1: Remind yourself that *insight* comes quickly, but *change* comes slowly. Your healthy side will become stronger and stronger, and your lifetrap side will become weaker. Be patient. Your feelings *will* change.

Solution 2: You can speed up the process somewhat by doing more experiential exercises. Write dialogues between your healthy side and your lifetrap. Get angry at your lifetrap. Cry about the way you were treated as a child. Let yourself feel the injustice.

Solution 3: You can also speed up the process by working harder to change the behaviors that reinforce your lifetrap. As you change old patterns, you will see new evidence that contradicts your lifetrap. This new evidence will have a powerful effect on the way that you feel.

Solution 4: Finally, ask friends for help and support. Your friends can help you see that your lifetrap is invalid.

- OBSTACLE #6: YOU HAVE NOT BEEN SYSTEMATIC AND DISCIPLINED ABOUT CHANGING. •

You may approach change in a hit-or-miss fashion. Perhaps you only work on it once in a while. You miss steps. You skip from lifetrap to lifetrap. You resist doing all the writing that is required.

In this we are advocates of the cliché, "Slow and steady wins the race." Your lifetrap is like a rock which you must chip away with a hammer. If you only hammer it sporadically, sometimes on one part and sometimes on another, with half-hearted taps, the rock is going to be there for a long time. It is much more efficient and effective to hammer away systematically with hard, decisive taps.

Solution 1: Go back through the chapter on the lifetrap and make sure you have completed all the exercises. Did you do imagery? Did you list the evidence pro and con? Did you write a flashcard? Write a letter to your parents? Make a plan for behavior change? Do all the exercises in writing, not just in your head?

Solution 2: Set aside a few minutes every day to review your progress. Reread your flashcards. Was your lifetrap activated today? Did you do anything to surrender to your pattern? Push yourself to think, feel, or act differently *each day.*

- OBSTACLE #7: YOUR PLAN IS MISSING AN IMPORTANT ELEMENT. •

Perhaps you do not fully understand all the thoughts, feelings, and behaviors that reinforce your lifetrap. You are missing a change step that is necessary to making progress.

Carlton illustrates this. Despite becoming more assertive with his wife and children, he remained quite angry and unhappy. He would calmly tell them when he was angry, he would say "no" to unreasonable requests, he would ask them to change their behavior when it disturbed him. But he still *felt* subjugated and angry.

We realized what the problem was. It was really quite simple. He was not communicating what *he* wanted—his opinions and preferences. He was not telling other people what he wanted from them, and then was angry he was not getting it. Communicating his needs was an important element for Carlton.

Solution 1: Ask someone you trust to review your lifetrap and plan with you. Perhaps this person will notice something in your life pattern that you have missed.

Solution 2: Review the list of behaviors that are typical of your lifetrap more carefully. (See the chapter devoted to your lifetrap to find this list.) Did you overlook part of the pattern that really *does* apply to you?

• Obstacle #8: Your Problem Is Too Entrenched or Deep-rooted to Correct on Your Own. •

Before they come to us, many patients try very hard to change on their own. It is when they have little success at self-help that they start therapy.

This may happen to you. Even if you follow all the steps outlined in this book, you may still be unable to change. Despite all your efforts, the lifetrap still rules your life.

It may be that you cannot change alone. If this happens, seek out therapy. A close relationship with someone you trust may well be what you need. A therapist can reparent you, or confront you, or be more objective in pointing out problems.

Solution: Seek professional help from a therapist or group.

Now that you have an idea of our general plan of action, let us turn to the chapters on individual lifetraps. In this way, the change process can begin.

6

"Please Don't Leave Me!"
The Abandonment Lifetrap

ABBY: TWENTY-EIGHT YEARS OLD. SHE LIVES IN FEAR THAT
SHE IS GOING TO LOSE HER HUSBAND.

The very first thing Abby told me about herself was that her father had
died when she was a child.

ABBY: *I was seven years old when it happened. He had a heart attack at*
work.

It really hurts me to admit this, but I have only vague memories
of him left. And pictures, of course. He was big and warm. He hugged
me a lot.

After he was gone, I used to stand by the window and wait for him
to come home. (Starts to cry.) I guess I just couldn't accept that it had
happened.

I'll never forget the feeling I had waiting for him by the window.
THERAPIST: *Is that feeling with you anywhere in your life now?*
ABBY: *Yes, it's a feeling that's with me now. It's the way I feel when my*
husband goes away.

Abby and Kurt, her husband, are having problems about Kurt's frequent
business trips. Each time he leaves on a trip, Abby becomes very upset.

ABBY: *There is always a scene. I start to cry, and he tries to reassure me, but it doesn't work. While he's away, half the time I'm terrified and half the time I'm crying. I feel so* alone.

When he gets back I'm so angry at him for what he put me through. That's the irony of the whole thing. When he finally gets home, I'm so mad that I don't even want to see him.

Kurt has begun to dread coming home. Abby also calls him on the telephone too often when he is away. She once had him paged away from an important business meeting just because she wanted to hear his voice.

PATRICK: THIRTY-FIVE YEARS OLD. HE IS MARRIED TO A WOMAN WHO HAS AFFAIRS WITH OTHER MEN.

Patrick did not face such dramatic losses in his life. His story was more one of constant loss, day by day. Until Patrick was eight years old, his mother was an alcoholic.

PATRICK: *At her worst, she went on binges. She'd be gone for two or three days. I was never sure if she was coming back.*

Even at her best, when she was drinking at home, she wasn't there for me. Whether she was gone or home, if she was drinking, I was alone.

Patrick is married to Francine, a woman who has had a series of affairs with other men. She keeps promising that she will stop and be faithful to Patrick, but she does not stop. She leaves the house, with one of numerous explanations and protestations of innocence, and Patrick knows she is lying.

Even before he started therapy, Patrick had been struck by the similarity between how he feels now, waiting for his wife to come home, and how he felt as a child waiting for his mother.

PATRICK: *I wonder about it. Even though Francine doesn't drink, I'm going through the whole thing with my mother again. I don't understand it. I wait for Francine to come home, and it's that same lonely feeling.*

LINDSAY: THIRTY-TWO YEARS OLD. SHE HAS ONE RELATION-SHIP AFTER ANOTHER AND NEVER SETTLES DOWN.

Our first impression of Lindsay was that she was likable and intense. Most people take a while to warm up to us, but not Lindsay. She very quickly became emotionally involved with us. Within a few sessions we felt like we had been her therapists for years.

In the first session, Lindsay told us why she had come:

LINDSAY: *I wish I could find that right man, the one who will marry me and we'll stay together forever, but it never seems to happen.*
THERAPIST: *What happens instead?*
LINDSAY: *I go from one man to another.*

Lindsay's relationships are turbulent. She gets involved very intensely, very fast. She feels frightened but swept away. Sometimes even in the first weeks of a relationship, she is saying "I love you," wanting to be with the man every minute, and talking about being together forever. In fact, she scares most men away because she is too much too soon.

Lindsay is passionate. She has always had more intense feelings than the average person. In romantic relationships, she seems to lose all sense of reason and to get lost in her emotions. As soon as the man pulls away slightly, she begins accusing him of wanting to leave her. And she tests him, seeing how far she can go before he will leave her, sometimes doing outlandish things. For example, she once attended her boyfriend's birthday party and left with another man.

When a relationship ends and she is alone, she feels bored and empty. Negative feelings start to overwhelm her, and she rushes into another relationship. Her relationships are short, and they always end with the man abandoning her. In the end, all her boyfriends have left her.

THE ABANDONMENT QUESTIONNAIRE

This questionnaire will measure the strength of your Abandonment life-trap. Answer the items using the scale below. Rate each item based on the way you have felt or behaved *in general during your adult life*. If there has been a lot of variation during different periods of your adult years, focus more on *the most recent year or two* in rating an item.

1 Completely untrue of me
2 Mostly untrue of me
3 Slightly more true than untrue of me
4 Moderately true of me
5 Mostly true of me
6 Describes me perfectly

If you have any 5's or 6's on this questionnaire, this lifetrap may still apply to you, even if your score is in the low range.

SCORE	DESCRIPTION
	1. I worry a lot that the people I love will die or leave me.
	2. I cling to people because I am afraid they will leave me.
	3. I do not have a stable base of support.
	4. I keep falling in love with people who cannot be there for me in a committed way.
	5. People have always come and gone in my life.
	6. I get desperate when someone I love pulls away.
	7. I get so obsessed with the idea that my lovers will leave me that I drive them away.
	8. The people closest to me are unpredictable. One minute they are there for me and the next minute they are gone.
	9. I need other people too much.
	10. In the end, I will be alone.
	YOUR TOTAL SCORE (Add your scores together for questions 1–10)

INTERPRETING YOUR ABANDONMENT SCORE

10–19 Very low. This lifetrap probably does *not* apply to you.
20–29 Fairly low. This lifetrap may only apply *occasionally*.
30–39 Moderate. This lifetrap is an *issue* in your life.
40–49 High. This is definitely an *important* lifetrap for you.
50–60 Very high. This is definitely one of your *core* lifetraps.

THE FEELING OF ABANDONMENT

You have a fundamental belief that you will lose the people you love and be left emotionally isolated forever. Whether people will die, send you away, or leave you, somehow you feel that you will be left *alone*. You expect to be abandoned, and you expect it to last forever. You believe you will never regain the person you have lost. In your heart, you feel it is your destiny to live your life completely alone.

PATRICK: *There are times, when I'm driving or something, when it comes to me. I know Francine's eventually going to leave me. She'll fall in love with one of these guys, and that'll be it. And all I'll have left is missing her.*

The lifetrap gives you a sense of despair about love. You believe that no matter how good things seem, in the end your relationships are doomed.

It is difficult for you to believe that people will be there for you—and that they are still there for you in some way even when they are absent. Most people are not upset by short separations from their loved ones. They know the relationship will survive the separation intact. But with the Abandonment lifetrap there is no such security. As Abby says, "Whenever I see Kurt walking out the door, I feel like he is never coming back." You want to cling to people too much, and you become inappropriately angry or frightened at the possibility of any separation, no matter how slight. Particularly in romantic relationships, you feel emotionally dependent on the other person, and you fear the loss of that intimate connection.

Abandonment is usually a *preverbal* lifetrap: it begins in the first years of life, before the child knows language. (Abby is an exception. Her lifetrap began later, at seven, when her father died. Correspondingly, her lifetrap is slightly less severe than it might be otherwise.) In most cases, the abandonment starts early, before the child has words to describe what is happening. For this reason, even in adulthood there may be no thoughts connected to the experience of the lifetrap. However, if you try to talk about the experience, the words are something like, "I'm all alone," "No one is there for me." Because the lifetrap begins so early, it has tremendous emotional force. A person with a severe Abandonment lifetrap responds to even brief separations with the feelings of a small child who has been abandoned.

The Abandonment lifetrap is triggered primarily by *intimate* relationships. It may not be apparent in groups or in casual relationships. Separations from a loved one are the most powerful triggers. However, separations do not have to be real to trigger the lifetrap, nor do they have to occur on a physical level. If you have the lifetrap, you are overly sensitive and often read the intent to abandon you into innocent remarks. The most powerful triggers are real loss or separation—divorce, someone moving or going away, death—but often triggers are much more subtle events.

You often feel *emotionally* abandoned. Perhaps your spouse or lover acts bored, distant, momentarily distracted, or more attentive to another person. Or perhaps your spouse or lover suggests a plan that involves spending a brief time apart. Anything that feels disconnected can trigger the lifetrap, even if it has nothing to do with real loss or abandonment.

Lindsay, for example, once abruptly left a dinner party because her boyfriend ignored a remark she had made.

LINDSAY: *Greg and I were at a dinner party, and he was talking to the woman sitting next to him, and he didn't hear what I was saying to him. I got up and left. I felt totally crushed. When he called me the next day, I flew into a rage about it.*
THERAPIST: *What was it that upset you so much?*
LINDSAY: *I had seen him looking at this woman earlier. I was sure he was attracted to her.*

Greg, who had not even heard her remark, was naturally confused by her extreme reaction. This episode further convinced him that Lindsay was not the right person for him. In the end (as Lindsay had always known he would), he left her.

THE CYCLE OF ABANDONMENT

Once the lifetrap is triggered, provided the separation lasts long enough, the experience progresses through a cycle of negative emotions: fear, grief, and anger. This is the cycle of abandonment. If you have the lifetrap, you will recognize it.

First, you have a panicky feeling, as though you are a small child left alone, perhaps in a supermarket, and you cannot find your mother temporarily. You have a frantic, "Where is she, I'm all alone, I'm lost," kind of feeling. Your anxiety can build to the level of panic, and can last for hours, even days. But if the anxiety goes on long enough, it passes. Eventually it subsides, and yields to acceptance that the person is gone. Then you experience grief about your loneliness, as though you never will recover the lost person. This grief can evolve into depression. And finally, particularly when the person returns, you experience anger at the person for leaving you and at yourself for needing so much.

• TWO TYPES OF ABANDONMENT •

There are two types of abandonment, and they come from two types of early childhood environments. The first type comes from an environment that is too secure and overprotected. This type represents a combination of the Abandonment and Dependence lifetraps. The second type comes from an environment that is emotionally unstable. No one is consistently there for the child.

TWO TYPES OF ABANDONMENT

1. Abandonment based upon dependence
2. Abandonment based upon instability or loss

Many people who have the Dependence lifetrap also have the Abandonment lifetrap. In fact, it is difficult to imagine a person having the Dependence lifetrap and *not* having the Abandonment lifetrap. People who have the Dependence lifetrap believe that they cannot *survive* alone. They need a strong figure to guide and direct them through the activities of day-to-day life. They need *help*. Abby is an example of a person who has both lifetraps.

THERAPIST: *What do you imagine would happen to you if you actually lost Kurt?*

ABBY: *I don't know. I just couldn't* cope *without him. I couldn't live. I can't imagine my life without him.*

THERAPIST: *Would you be able to survive—to eat, clothe yourself, keep yourself sheltered?*

ABBY: *No. I can't function in the world alone. (Pause.) I guess I believe I would die without him.*

If you believe your life depends on another person, then the possibility of losing that person is terrifying. Certainly, anyone who has a strong Dependence lifetrap will also have an issue with abandonment.

However, the reverse is not true. Many people have a strong Abandonment lifetrap and do not have an issue with dependence. They belong to the second type, whose lifetrap arose from the instability of the child's emotional connections to the people who are most intimate—the mother, the father, sisters and brothers, and close friends. Both Patrick and Lindsay are afraid of being abandoned by the people they love, but they can function independently. They have a dependence of sorts on their partners, but it is an *emotional,* rather than a *functional,* dependence.

If your lifetrap arose from instability, then what happened was you experienced an emotional connection, and then it was lost. You cannot bear to be apart from the people you love because of the way you *feel* without them. It is a matter of feeling connected to the rest of humanity. When the connection is lost, you are thrown into nothingness.

LINDSAY: *After Greg left me, I was totally alone. I could feel it around me, like an ache. There was just nothing at all.*

You need other people to feel soothed. This differs from abandonment based upon dependence, in which you need someone to take care of you as a child needs a parent. In one case, you are looking for guidance, direction, and help; and in the other case, you are looking for nurturance, love, and a sense of emotional connection.

There is another difference: Dependent people often have a number of people lined up as backups in case their main person leaves. They have someone immediately available to take the person's place, or they find someone new, and quickly form another dependent relationship. Few lonely people have dependence underneath. Dependent people do not tolerate the loneliness. Most dependent people are quite talented at finding someone to take care of them. They go from one person to another, with rarely more than a month between.

This is not necessarily true of people who fear *emotional* abandonment. They can be alone for long periods of time. They might withdraw from close relationships out of hurt and out of fear of being hurt again. They have already faced the loneliness as children, and they know they can survive. That is not the issue. It is the process of loss that is devastating.

It is having that connection, and then losing it, and being thrown back into the loneliness one more time.

THE ORIGINS OF THE ABANDONMENT LIFETRAP

When we talk about the origins of lifetraps, we focus primarily on features of the child's *environment.* We know quite a bit about the dysfunctional family environments—such as abuse, neglect, and alcoholism—that seem to promote individual lifetraps. We downplay the contribution of *heredity,* in part because researchers know so little about the role of biology in determining our long-term personality patterns. We assume that heredity must make its mark in terms of our temperament, which in turn influences how we are treated as children and how we respond to that treatment. But we rarely have any way of guessing how a child's temperament influences the development of specific lifetraps.

Abandonment is an exception to this general rule. Researchers who study infants have observed that some babies react far more intensely to separation than do others. This suggests that *some* people may be biologically predisposed to develop the Abandonment lifetrap.

The way we respond to separation from a person who takes care of us seems at least partly innate. Separation from the mother is a vital issue in a newborn's life. Throughout the animal world, infants are totally dependent on their mothers for survival, and if an infant loses its mother, it usually dies. Infants are born prepared to behave in ways designed to end separations from their mothers. They cry and show signs of distress. They "protest," as John Bowlby called it in his classic book, *Separation.*

Bowlby wrote about infants and young children who were temporarily separated from their mothers. The babies were placed in nurseries along with other children. Observation of these children revealed three phases of the separation process, displayed by all the babies.

BOWLBY'S THREE PHASES OF SEPARATION

1. Anxiety
2. Despair
3. Detachment

First the babies "protested," as we have noted, and exhibited great anxiety. They searched for their mothers. If another person tried to comfort them, they were inconsolable. They showed flashes of anger at their mothers. But as time passed and their mothers did not come, they grew resigned and settled into a period of depression. In this phase they were apathetic and withdrawn. They were indifferent to attempts to connect with them emotionally by the staff. If enough time passed, however, the babies came out of this depression and formed other attachments.

If the mother then returned, a baby entered the third phase, detachment. The baby was cold to the mother and did not approach or show interest in her. As time passed, however, the baby's detachment broke, and the baby became attached to the mother once again. This baby was likely to be clingy and anxious when the mother was out of sight—to have what Bowlby calls "anxious attachment" to the mother.

Bowlby says this pattern of anxiety, despair, and detachment is universal. It is the response that all young children have to separation from their mothers. Furthermore, the response occurs across the animal kingdom. Not only human infants but infants of all animal species generally display the same pattern. Such universality of behavior strongly suggests a biological predisposition.

You might recognize the similarity between Bowlby's separation process and what we have called the cycle of abandonment: anxiety, grief, and anger. Some people, like Lindsay, seem born with the capacity to experience this cycle of emotions to an uncommonly strong degree. When a separation occurs, the anxiety, grief, and anger that they feel are so intense that they are unable to soothe themselves, and they feel totally disconnected and desperate. They can distract themselves from the feeling for only a short time. Without the person there, they cannot make themselves feel calm and secure. Such people are extremely sensitive to losing the ones they love. They connect deeply to other people—this is one of their gifts—but they cannot tolerate being alone.

People who are born with a tendency to respond to separation so intensely and who are unable to soothe themselves in the absence of a loved person are probably more likely to develop the Abandonment lifetrap. But this does not mean that everyone who has the biological predisposition develops the lifetrap. It depends in part on the early childhood environment.

If you had stable emotional connections as an infant, particularly to your mother but also to other important people, then even if you are biologically predisposed you may not develop the lifetrap. And certain environments are so unstable or filled with such loss that even if you are not at all predisposed you may develop the lifetrap.

Nevertheless, it is likely that the more a person has the biological predisposition, the less trauma is needed to activate the lifetrap, and we might look in vain through the past for the reasons that justify its intensity.

THE ORIGINS OF THE ABANDONMENT LIFETRAP

1. You may have a biological predisposition to separation anxiety—difficulty being alone.
2. A parent died or left home when you were young.
3. Your mother was hospitalized or separated from you for a prolonged period of time when you were a child.
4. You were raised by nannies or in an institution by a succession of mother figures, or you were sent away to boarding school at a very young age.
5. Your mother was unstable. She became depressed, angry, drunk, or in some other way withdrew from you on a regular basis.
6. Your parents divorced when you were young or fought so much that you worried the family would fall apart.
7. You lost the attention of a parent in a significant way. For example, a brother or sister was born or your parent remarried.
8. Your family was excessively close and you were overprotected. You never learned to deal with life's difficulties as a child.

Certainly, loss of a parent at an early age is the most dramatic origin of the lifetrap. This was the origin for Abby. Perhaps a parent became ill and had to be away from you for a long time. Perhaps your parents divorced, and one parent moved away and gradually forgot you. Death of a parent, illness, separation, and divorce are all in the same category of important relationships that end in separation. Loss of a parent is particularly devastating in the first years of life. Generally, the earlier the loss, the more vulnerable the child, and the more potent the lifetrap is going to be.

How deeply the loss of a parent affects you depends upon a number of other factors. Of course, the quality of your other intimate connections is important. Abby, for example, had a loving and stable relationship with her mother that helped sustain her and worked against the strength of her lifetrap. Her lifetrap is circumscribed. She reenacts it only in her romantic relationships with men. If you are able to establish a connection with a substitute for the lost parent, such as with a stepparent, that can help as well. And it can help if the lost parent is restored to you in some way, such as when an ill parent recovers and comes home, or separated parents reunite, or an alcoholic parent becomes sober. Many kinds of experiences can help heal your lifetrap. However, the memory of being abandoned still remains. If you have had a large amount of healing experience, it might require dramatic events to trigger your lifetrap, such as the actual loss of a loved person. If you lost a parent at a young age, you are acutely aware of what it can mean to suffer loss, and the prospect of being thrown back into that pain is frightening.

This is the crux of the difference between the Abandonment lifetrap and the Emotional Deprivation lifetrap. With Emotional Deprivation, the parent was always *physically* there, but the quality of the emotional relationship was consistently inadequate. The parents did not know how to love, nurture, and empathize well enough. The connection with parents was *stable, but not close enough*. With Abandonment, the connection once existed and it was *lost*. Or the parent would come and go *unpredictably*. Unfortunately, for some children, their parents were *both* emotionally inadequate and unpredictable. In this environment, which is quite common, children will usually develop both the Emotional Deprivation *and* Abandonment lifetraps.

Aside from the loss of a parent, another origin for Abandonment is the absence of *one* person who consistently serves as a maternal figure for the child. Children whose parents have no time for them, who are raised by a succession of nannies or in a succession of day-care centers, or who are raised in institutions where the staff constantly changes are examples of this origin. Particularly during the first years, the child needs the stable presence of one caretaker. The caretaker does not necessarily have to be the parent. However, if there is constant turnover in who serves as that person, it creates disruption. To the child, it can seem like living in a world of strangers.

The next origin is more subtle. You may have a stable mother figure, but there may be instability in the way she *relates* to you. For example, Patrick's alcoholic mother could be very loving and connected one moment, and then totally indifferent within a matter of a few hours. And Lindsay's mother, perhaps reflecting the same biological predisposition as Lindsay herself, was subject to intense mood swings. She was physically there, but the way she related to Lindsay was unpredictable.

LINDSAY: *My mother was there for me, or I should say she was present. Sometimes she was happy and excited and interested in me. Other times she was deep in depression, laying in bed all day and not responding, no matter what I did.*

This origin reflects the moment-to-moment interactions that pass between mother and child. If these interactions are unstable, then the child can develop the Abandonment lifetrap.

Patrick's mother was not abusive when she drank. She was indifferent. It is not necessarily abusive parents who give rise to the Abandonment lifetrap. If you have a parent who, because of drug abuse or temper problems, was alternately loving and abusive, you may or may not have developed the Abandonment lifetrap. It depends on whether you experienced the abuse as a loss of emotional connection. To a child who can get little else from a parent, even punishment can be experienced as a connection. Abusive parents can be either connected or withdrawn. This explains why Abuse and Abandonment are not necessarily the same issue.

There are other childhood situations that foster the development of the Abandonment lifetrap. Perhaps your parents were continually fighting, and you felt the family was unstable and might dissolve. Or perhaps your parents divorced and one or both remarried into families with other children. You may have experienced your parent's involvement with the new family members as an abandonment. Or perhaps your parent withdrew attention and nurturing from you to give it to a younger sibling. Of course, not all new births in a family are traumatic for the older child. These events do not *always* create the lifetrap. It depends upon the degree of disconnection. To create the lifetrap, the events must trigger powerful feelings of abandonment.

Often, a child who feels abandoned by a parent will follow that parent around. The child will shadow the parent, watch the parent, stay near the parent at all times. To an outside observer, it might seem as though the parent and child have a strong connection. In fact, the connection is not strong enough, so the child must always keep the parent in view to make sure the connection is still there. Maintaining the connection with the parent can become the most important thing in the child's life and can sap the attention the child has for other people in the world.

Finally, as we noted before, the Abandonment lifetrap can arise from an *over*protective environment and become mixed with Dependence. The dependent child fears abandonment. This is what happened to Abby with her mother.

ABBY: *After my father died, my mother didn't want me to leave her side. She was afraid something would happen to me, that she would lose me, too. I always wanted to be near my mother. I remember I didn't want to go to school, and I'd rather be home than out playing with friends.*

Abby's need to be close to her mother undermined her autonomy. She was not free to explore the world and develop confidence in her ability to take care of herself. She stayed dependent on her mother for guidance and direction. In truth, this was probably what her mother wanted as well. Her mother could not face another loss.

Other children respond to the loss of a parent by becoming more autonomous. Since no one is taking care of them, they learn how to take care of themselves.

ABANDONMENT AND INTIMATE RELATIONSHIPS

If you have the Abandonment lifetrap, your romantic relationships are seldom calm and steady. Rather, they often feel like roller coaster rides. This is because you experience the relationship as perpetually on the brink of catastrophe. Lindsay expressed what it was like for her in an image in therapy. She was talking about a fight she had had with Greg, which had ended in typical fashion—with her pleading and him being cold and aloof.

THERAPIST: *Close your eyes and give me an image of how you feel.*
LINDSAY: *I see myself falling backwards. It's like falling backwards into this dark cellar, where I'll be all alone forever. Greg is pushing me backwards into the cellar, and the door is going to shut, and I'm going to be all alone.*
THERAPIST: *What are you feeling?*
LINDSAY: *Terrified.*

If your lifetrap is severe, this is how you experience even minor disruptions in your intimate relationship. You feel that if your connection to the loved person were lost, you would be plunged into utter aloneness.

Some people who have the Abandonment lifetrap cope by avoiding intimate relationships altogether. They would rather remain alone than go through the process of loss again. Patrick was this way for many years before he married Francine.

THERAPIST: *You were alone a long time.*
KURT: *I just couldn't keep going through it. It was too painful. I could never find someone who would be there for me. I was better off alone. At least I had some peace.*

If you are willing to engage in intimate relationships, then you probably do not have peace. Your relationships feel unstable. The sense that you might lose them is always there.

You have difficulty tolerating any withdrawal in a relationship. You worry about even relatively small changes, exaggerating the probability the relationship will end. Lindsay interprets the slightest sign of dissatisfaction from her boyfriends as evidence that they want to end the relationship. Anytime a boyfriend is angry with her, upset with her, feeling disconnected—anything relevant to the possibility that he might abandon her—she feels certain it is the end. Jealousy and possessiveness are common themes. She perpetually *accuses* her boyfriends of wanting to leave her, a habit that can become quite irritating. In a self-fulfilling prophecy, her relationships are marked by frequent breakups and tumultuous reconciliations.

Similarly, every time her husband leaves on a business trip, Abby worries obsessively that his plane will crash and he will die. Other times she gets caught up in worrying that her mother will become sick and die or that her children will die. She goes through periods of thinking only about death and about how she will not be able to manage alone.

Early in your relationships, you become excessively clingy. Clinging reinforces your lifetrap because it reinforces the idea that you are going to lose the person. It keeps the possibility of abandonment *alive* in the relationship.

Your clinging has a desperate quality. Lindsay illustrates this well. As with her mother, her connection with her boyfriend never feels strong enough. She feels lonely and lost, so she pours her whole life into the relationship. Her absorption is total. As she says, she becomes obsessed, forgetting about the outside world. All her energy becomes invested in keeping the connection because it is so important.

DANGER SIGNALS IN THE EARLY STAGES OF DATING

You probably feel drawn to lovers who hold some potential for abandoning you. Here are some early warning signs. They are signs that your relationship is triggering your Abandonment lifetrap.

DANGER SIGNALS IN POTENTIAL PARTNERS

1. Your partner is unlikely to make a long-term commitment because he/she is married or involved in another relationship.
2. Your partner is not consistently available for you to spend time together (e.g., he/she travels a lot, lives far away, is a workaholic).
3. Your partner is emotionally unstable (e.g., he/she drinks, uses drugs, is depressed, cannot hold down a regular job) and cannot be there for you emotionally on a consistent basis.
4. Your partner is a Peter Pan, who insists on his/her freedom to come and go, does not want to settle down, or wants the freedom to have many lovers.
5. Your partner is ambivalent about you—he/she wants you but holds back emotionally; or one moment acts deeply in love with you and the next moment acts as though you do not exist.

You are not looking for partners who present *no* hope of a stable relationship, rather you are attracted to partners who present some hope for stability, but not complete hope—who present a mixture of hope and doubt. You feel as if there is a *possibility* that you might win the person permanently, or at least get the person to relate to you in a more stable fashion.

You are attracted most to partners who show some degree of commitment and connection, but not so much that you are absolutely sure that they will stay. Living in an unstable love relationship feels comfortable and familiar to you. It is what you have always known. And the instability keeps activating your lifetrap, generating a steady flow of chemistry. You stay passionately in love. Choosing partners who are not really there for you ensures that you will continue to reenact your childhood abandonment.

UNDERMINING GOOD RELATIONSHIPS

Even if you choose a partner who is stable, there are still pitfalls to avoid. There are still ways for you to reinforce your Abandonment lifetrap.

ABANDONMENT LIFETRAPS IN A RELATIONSHIP

1. You avoid intimate relationships even with appropriate partners because you are afraid of losing the person or getting too close and being hurt.
2. You worry excessively about the possibility that your partner will die or otherwise be lost, and what you would do.
3. You overreact to minor things your partner says or does, and interpret them as signs that he/she wants to leave you.
4. You are excessively jealous and possessive.
5. You cling to your partner. Your whole life becomes obsessed with keeping him/her.
6. You cannot stand to be away from your partner, even for a few days.
7. You are never fully convinced that your partner will stay with you.
8. You get angry and accuse your partner of not being loyal or faithful.
9. You sometimes detach, leave, or withdraw to punish your partner for leaving you alone.

It is possible that you are in a stable, healthy relationship, yet continue to *feel* that the relationship is unstable. This is the case with Abby. We have met with Kurt several times, and believe he is fully committed to the marriage. Objectively, there is no evidence that he intends to leave Abby. On the contrary, he seems very much in love. But Abby somehow can never be reassured of this. This frustrates Kurt, because he cannot win her trust.

KURT: *No matter what I do she doubts me. She drives me crazy. She is especially suspicious about my business trips. For absolutely no reason, she thinks I'm having affairs with other women. Sometimes I wonder if she's the one who wants to be with other men. Why does she talk about it so much?*

You might also fall into another Abandonment lifetrap—behaving in ways that tend to drive your partner away. Lindsay, for example, blows up even minor arguments to such proportions that they threaten to end the relationship. She exaggerates the meaning of fights just as Abby exaggerates the meaning of separations from her husband during his business trips.

Lindsay and Abby constantly say such things to their partners as: "You don't really love me," "I know you are going to leave me," "You don't miss me," "You are glad that we have to be apart." We know that Lindsay and Abby say these things to their partners, because they also say them to us; they keep waiting for us to throw them out of treatment or move away. Their accusations constantly suggest to their partners that they do *not* care, that they *will* eventually leave. Lindsay and Abby push the people they love away with one hand, while clinging desperately to them with the other.

Whenever the relationship feels threatened in any way, you have a strong emotional reaction. It could be anything that breaks the connection with your partner—a momentary separation, the mention of someone who incites your jealousy, an argument, or a change in your partner's mood. Your partner almost invariably feels you are overreacting, and might well express bewilderment. It seems like such a drastic response to a minor disruption. Kurt described what it is like:

KURT: *We get to the airport and suddenly Abby is all upset. She's crying like someone has died or something. I feel so confused by it all. Here I am, going on a two-day trip, and she's acting like our marriage is over.*

It feels like a tremendous overreaction to a partner who does not share the lifetrap.

You usually do not feel good when you are alone: you probably feel anxious, depressed, or detached. You need the feeling of connection to your partner. As soon as your partner leaves, you feel disconnected. Usually this feeling of abandonment does not go away until your partner returns. You can distract yourself from it, but the feeling of being disconnected is always there. It lurks in the background waiting to engulf you. Almost everyone who has the lifetrap has a limit to the amount of time they can distract themselves, and then they cannot do it anymore.

The better you are at distraction, the longer you can be alone. The worse you are at distraction, the quicker you experience the wanting, the sense of loss, and the need to reconnect.

ABBY: *I was gardening, trying to forget about Kurt being gone, and my neighbor came by. Talking to her, it occurred to me that from the outside, it looked as though I was enjoying myself, like I was a person who was really enjoying my solitude. But I wasn't enjoying myself. I felt more like someone who was running and running, and when I was too tired to run anymore, the bad feelings would catch up with me again.*

Detachment is the Counterattack for Abandonment. When you are detached, you are denying the need for connection. It is a defiant, "I don't need you." There is usually some anger mixed in with your detachment, and it is partly punitive. You punish your partner for withdrawing from you, for not giving you what you need. Although this helps you cope with your feelings of abandonment, you pay a price: you give up your feelings and exist in a chilly emotional numbness.

A real loss, such as the breakup of a relationship, is devastating to you. It confirms your sense that no matter where you turn, you will never find a stable connection. You might feel ambivalent about starting new relationships. Part of you wants to connect, and another part anticipates abandonment. Part of you wants the closeness, and another part is angry, usually before anything has happened to warrant it. The relationship may be just beginning, and at times you feel like the person is already gone.

FRIENDS

If your Abandonment lifetrap is strong, it probably affects other intimate relationships such as close friendships. The same issues come up in a close friendship as in a romantic relationship, although not as intensely.

You have an underlying view of friendships as unstable. You cannot count on them to last. People come and go in your life. You are hypersensitive to anything that might threaten the connection with a friend—the person moving away, separations, the person not returning phone calls or invitations, disagreements, or the person developing other interests or preferring someone else.

LINDSAY: *I'm really mad at my friend Valerie. I called her Monday, and it's Wednesday, and she still hasn't called me back. I'm thinking of calling her and telling her off. She has no right to treat me this way!*

CHANGING YOUR ABANDONMENT LIFETRAP

Here are the steps to changing your Abandonment lifetrap:

CHANGING ABANDONMENT

1. Understand your childhood abandonment.
2. Monitor your feelings of abandonment. Identify your hypersensitivity to losing close people; your desperate fears of being alone; your need to cling to people.
3. Review past relationships, and clarify the patterns that recur. List the pitfalls of abandonment.
4. Avoid uncommitted, unstable, or ambivalent partners even though they generate high chemistry.
5. When you find a partner who *is* stable and committed, trust him/her. Believe that he/she is there for you forever, and will not leave.
6. Do not cling, become jealous, or overreact to the normal separations of a healthy relationship.

---

1. Understand Your Childhood Abandonment. First, consider whether you have a biological predisposition to develop the lifetrap. Have you always been an emotional person? Did you have difficulty as a child separating from the people you love? Was it hard for you to start school or sleep at a friend's house? Did you become overly upset when your parents went out for the evening or away for short trips? Did you cling to your mother in new places more than the other children? Do you still have a lot of trouble coping with the intensity of your feelings?

If you answered "yes" to many of these questions, it may be that you can be helped by medication. We have seen many patients helped to contain their feelings through the use of medication. If you have a therapist, you might speak to him or her about this possibility, or make an appointment with a psychiatrist to be evaluated.

Whether or not you have a biological predisposition, it is important to understand the situations in your childhood that contributed to your lifetrap. When you have some quiet, peaceful time, let images of your childhood float to the top of your mind. When you first start, do not force your images in any direction. Let images emerge undisturbed.

The best place to start is with a feeling of abandonment in your current life. When something happens now in your life that triggers your feelings of abandonment, close your eyes and remember when you felt that way before.

LINDSAY: *Ever since Greg told me he was thinking of breaking up, I've been so upset I can't think about anything else. I've been snapping at people, even at work. I'm so angry. I can't believe he's doing this to me. And I keep calling him. I can't help it. He's starting to get really mad at me, but I can't help it.*

THERAPIST: *Close your eyes and get an image of Greg. What do you see?*

LINDSAY: *I see his face, looking at me like he's disgusted, like he thinks I'm so pathetic for trying to hold on to him.*

THERAPIST: *What are you feeling?*

LINDSAY: *Like I hate him and I want him at the same time.*

THERAPIST: *Give me an image of when you felt this way before, as far back as you can.*

LINDSAY: *(Pause.) What comes is visiting my mother in the hospital. I am eight years old, and my father is taking me to visit my mother in the hospital. My father tells me she took too many pills by mistake. But I know something more is going on. And I walk in the room and I see my mother, and I hate her so much, but at the same time I want her to come home so badly.*

Forge these links between the present and the past with imagery. Try to remember the beginnings of your feelings of abandonment.

2. Monitor Your Feelings of Abandonment. Become aware of your feelings of abandonment now in your life. Hone your ability to recognize when your lifetrap is triggered. Perhaps you are undergoing a loss somewhere in your life. You may have a parent who is ill, a spouse who is going away, a relationship that is ending, a lover who is unsteady—who keeps jerking you around—or you may be so sealed off from the possibility of loss that you are totally alone.

See if you can recognize the cycle of abandonment in your life. Abby, Patrick, and Lindsay all saw this cycle clearly once they looked for it.

PATRICK: *It really is the same thing every time. First, I realize Francine isn't coming home and I'm frantic. One minute, I'm terrified that something has happened to her, that she's had a car accident. The next minute, I'm so angry at her for doing this to me again that I feel I could kill her when she walks in the door.*

I go on like this for hours until I'm too tired to keep doing it. Then I lie down, and I feel so depressed. I just try to sleep.

When she finally gets home, most of the time I just don't care. But sometimes I get angry again when I see her, and it's hard for me not to hit her.

Allow yourself to experience all the feelings in the cycle. Become aware of the cycle whenever you ride it.

It is important for you to start spending time alone if you are not doing so. *Choose* to spend time alone instead of running away. This was something Abby learned to do. When Abby first came to therapy, she spent much of her time in a frantic effort to avoid being alone. She always had someone standing by, in person or by phone, who could take care of her if she needed it. Abby had to learn to tolerate being alone. Later she learned to appreciate solitude.

ABBY: *It feels good to stop scheming all the time about how to keep people near me. It took a lot out of me. I tell myself that I can function on my own, that I can take care of myself, that I can be okay alone.*

You can start a little at a time. Spend time alone. Make it special. Do things you enjoy. Your fears will pass. If you do it often enough, you can pass through the fears into a space of peace.

3. Review Past Romantic Relationships and Clarify the Patterns That Recur. List the Pitfalls of Abandonment. Make a list of the romantic relationships in your life. What went wrong with each one? Was the person overprotective, and did you hold on at all costs? Was the person unstable? Did you leave each person because you were too afraid the person would leave you? Do you keep picking people who are likely to leave you? Were you so jealous and possessive that you drove the person away? What pattern emerges? What are the pitfalls for you to avoid?

When Lindsay made her list, she saw that she had been through one unstable relationship after another. In fact, her relationship with us was the first time that someone was there for her on a consistent basis who would not go away. And we felt that our relationship stabilized Lindsay. It showed us once again how important a solid relationship can be, how the person can really settle down, become centered, more able to focus on living life.

4. Avoid Uncommitted, Unstable, or Ambivalent Partners Even Though They Generate High Chemistry. Try to form relationships with stable people. Avoid people who are going to take you on a roller coaster ride, *even though these are the exact people to whom you are most attracted.* Remember that we are not saying that you should go out with people you find unattractive, but an intense sexual attraction *may* be a sign that your partner is triggering your Abandonment lifetrap. If this is so, the relationship means trouble, and you should probably think twice about pursuing it.

In the middle of her second year of therapy, Lindsay started going out with a man she met at work (she is a high school art teacher). His name was Richard, and he was another teacher at her school. With Richard, Lindsay had her first stable relationship with a man. Richard was clear about his commitment to Lindsay. Near the end of our second year of therapy, he asked her to marry him. He was an alcoholic, but he had been in recovery for twelve years. He was consistently there for Lindsay emotionally. In fact, he was the unruffled type who seldom became moody or lost his cool. Emotional people and calm, rational people often form relationships with one another. Richard's steady love for Lindsay helped contain her intense emotions, just as her relationship with us did.

When Lindsay began the relationship with Richard, she only felt moderately attracted to him, but her attraction grew. Unlike most of her other relationships with men, Lindsay stayed friends with Richard for several months before they became lovers. This had the effect of stabilizing the relationship as well. Lindsay felt less vulnerable, and she did not cling as much nor make her usual accusations of infidelity.

Patrick ended his marriage to Francine. He finally understood that she was never going to change, no matter how much he tried to improve himself for her. Although he predicted he would never become interested in any other women, he is dating other women now. He is learning about himself in relationships. More importantly, he is learning to *keep* himself in relationships. Patrick has always given himself entirely away, so that he had nothing and the other person had everything. If you give everything to the other person, it *is* a catastrophe to lose that person. Patrick is learning to hold on to his power in relationships.

PATRICK: *I always thought the whole point of a relationship was to hold on to the other person. I would do anything to keep her. But now I see that I can let people go and survive. I can let people go and walk away, and eventually I'll be fine.*

5. When You Find a Partner Who is Stable and Committed, Trust Him/Her. Believe That He/She is There for You Forever, and Will Not Leave. After so much experience with abandonment, it is hard to learn to trust. But this is the only way to finally step out of the cycle and find fulfillment in love. Get off the roller coaster. Give up the wild, unstable love in favor of the strong and steady.

All three of our patients had to learn to trust. Abby had to learn that Kurt was really there for her, even when he was away.

ABBY: *It's funny, but I feel like the end of the* Wizard of Oz. *What I was looking for the whole time was in my own backyard. I already have with Kurt what I have always wanted most, someone who is there for me but who wants me to stand on my own.*

Similarly, Patrick and Lindsay had to learn to trust their partners in healthy, committed relationships.

6. Do Not Cling, Become Jealous, or Overreact to the Normal Separations of a Healthy Relationship. If you are in a good relationship with a stable, committed partner, learn to control your tendency to overreact to emotional slights. The best way is by working on yourself. Explore your own resources, and learn that you can be alone and flourish. To get by day-to-day, remember that you can make flashcards. Using a flashcard each time your lifetrap is triggered chips away at the lifetrap, weakening it.

We helped Lindsay write a flashcard (see the next page) to deal better with her relationship with Richard. She used it to stop clinging and making accusations, and to reaffirm her trust in him and in herself whenever that trust felt shaken.

AN ABANDONMENT FLASHCARD

Right now I feel devastated because Richard is withdrawing from me, and I am about to become angry and needy.

However, I know that this is my Abandonment lifetrap, and that my lifetrap is triggered by just the slightest evidence of withdrawal. I need to remember that people in *good* relationships withdraw, and that withdrawal is part of the natural rhythm of good relationships.

If I start behaving in an angry and clingy way, I will push Richard even further away. Richard has a right to pull away at times.

What I should do instead is work with my thoughts to try to take a longer view of the relationship as a whole. My feelings are way out of proportion to reality. I can tolerate my feelings and remember that in the big picture Richard and I are still connected, and the relationship is good.

To best help myself, I should turn my attention to my own life, and ways of developing myself. The better able I am to be on my own, the better I will be in relationships.

If your lifetrap is severe, and you cannot seem to form a good relationship, consider therapy. A therapy relationship can help get you to the place where you can bring good relationships into your life.

7

"I Can't Trust You"
The Mistrust and Abuse Lifetrap

FRANK: Thirty-two years old. He is mistrustful in his personal and work life.

Frank comes to therapy with his wife, Adrienne. They have been having marital problems.

FRANK: *Even though I know she loves me, I have trouble trusting her. It's like I keep expecting the whole thing to be a big trick. Like she's gonna turn around and say, "Okay, it's over, I never really loved you, I've been tricking you all along."*

ADRIENNE: *Like the other day. I went out to the grocery store. While I was there I ran into my friend Melinda. We went out for coffee for about half an hour.*

When I got home Frank was beside himself. "Where was I, who was I with, what was I doing." At one point he grabbed me and started shaking me. He was shouting at the top of his lungs. I felt really scared of him.

FRANK: *Yeah. I know. I don't want this to get out of control.*

Frank has a similar problem with us. He does not trust us. It took us a long time to gain his trust. Even after months of therapy, he was capable of great mistrust.

FRANK: *You know, I was at work yesterday, talking to my boss. And he started telling me that I come across too strong with customers. I don't want to sound paranoid or anything, but it sounded an awful lot like what we were talking about in our last session.*

I started wondering, "Is there any way you could know my boss? Is there any way you could have discussed me with him?"

THERAPIST: *We don't know your boss. And you know we would never speak to anyone about you without your written permission.*

FRANK: *It just seemed like such a coincidence. It seemed like my boss knew about our discussion when he was talking to me.*

THERAPIST: *We would never do that to you. We're on your side, remember?*

Frank and Adrienne have two children. In that first session we ask if he has any problem controlling his anger with his children. "No," they both tell us. Frank is wonderful with the children.

FRANK: *No. That's one thing. I had a really lousy childhood. My father used to beat me. I've always vowed that my children would have it better. I've never laid a hand on my children, and I never will.*

In fact, since he became an adult, Frank has only lost his temper once, and that was while he was drinking four years ago. He has not had a drink since.

We feel immediately sympathetic toward Frank. He is struggling hard to be a finer person than his childhood set him up to be.

MADELINE: TWENTY-NINE YEARS OLD. SHE HAS NEVER HAD A LONG-TERM ROMANTIC RELATIONSHIP.

Madeline comes to therapy because of problems with men.

MADELINE: *I guess I'm here because I'm worried if I'll ever have a normal relationship with a guy.*

In my early twenties I used to drink a lot and have sex with guys I barely knew. I was really promiscuous. But two years ago I stopped drinking. I haven't had a boyfriend since.

The other night I was at a party. I was talking to this guy. He seemed really nice. But later we were dancing, and he grabbed me and gave me a little kiss. I got really angry at him and left the party. That was the night I decided to come to therapy.

Madeline tells us that she always thinks men are out to use her or take advantage of her.

THERAPIST: *When did these feelings about men begin?*
MADELINE: *Oh, I know where they began. When I was nine and my mother married my stepfather. He sexually abused me for the entire three years they were married. (Starts to cry.) I'm sorry. This is something I don't usually talk about.*
THERAPIST: *Where was your mother?*
MADELINE: *Oh, she was too zoned out on tranquilizers to know what was going on.*

Madeline wants to marry and have children, but she is afraid that she will never let a man get close enough to make that happen.

THE MISTRUST AND ABUSE QUESTIONNAIRE

This questionnaire will measure the strength of your Mistrust and Abuse lifetrap. Answer the items using the following scale:

SCORING KEY

1 Completely untrue of me
2 Mostly untrue of me
3 Slightly more true than untrue of me
4 Moderately true of me
5 Mostly true of me
6 Describes me perfectly

If you have any 5's or 6's on this questionnaire, this lifetrap may still apply to you, even if your score is in the low range.

SCORE	DESCRIPTION
	1. I expect people to hurt or use me.
	2. Throughout my life people close to me have abused me.
	3. It is only a matter of time before the people I love will betray me.

	4. I have to protect myself and stay on my guard.
	5. If I am not careful, people will take advantage of me.
	6. I set up tests for people to see if they are really on my side.
	7. I try to hurt people before they hurt me.
	8. I am afraid to let people get close to me because I expect them to hurt me.
	9. I am angry about what people have done to me.
	10. I have been physically, verbally, or sexually abused by people I should have been able to trust.
	YOUR TOTAL MISTRUST AND ABUSE SCORE (Add your scores together for questions 1–10)

INTERPRETING YOUR MISTRUST AND ABUSE SCORE

10–19 Very low. This lifetrap probably does *not* apply to you.
20–29 Fairly low. This lifetrap may only apply *occasionally*.
30–39 Moderate. This lifetrap is an *issue* in your life.
40–49 High. This is definitely an *important* lifetrap for you.
50–60 Very high. This is definitely one of your *core* lifetraps.

THE EXPERIENCE OF ABUSE

Abuse is a complex mixture of feelings—pain, fear, rage, and grief. The feelings are intense, and they simmer near the surface. When we are with patients who have been abused, we are conscious of these strong feelings. Even if they appear calm, we can feel them in the room. They seem about to burst like water through a dam.

You may have volatile moods. You suddenly become very upset—either crying or enraged. It often surprises other people. Frank's fits of rage at his wife and Madeline's sudden bursting into tears are examples of this.

At other times you may be spaced out—what we call dissociated. You seem to be somewhere else. Things seem unreal to you. Your emotions are numb. This is a habit you developed as a kind of psychological escape from the abuse.

ADRIENNE: *When Frank doesn't want to talk about something, it's like he can click off. Like snap, he's gone. I don't even exist.*

FRANK: *I know what she means. I know I do that. I don't really mean to, it just happens. It's like I just don't want to deal with something and my feelings shut off.*

Your experience of relationships is a painful one. Relationships are not places to relax and become vulnerable. Rather, they are dangerous and unpredictable. People hurt you, betray you, and use you. You have to stay on your guard. It is hard for you to trust people, even the ones closest to you. In fact, it may be *particularly* the ones closest to you that you are most unable to trust.

You assume people secretly mean you harm. When someone does something nice for you, your mind searches for the ulterior motive. You expect people to lie to you and to try to take advantage of you.

MADELINE: *Usually I figure, no matter how nice a guy is, I know what he's really after.*

THERAPIST: *What's that?*

MADELINE: *Sex. Only sex.*

Mistrust and abuse bring about a state of *hypervigilance*. You are constantly on your guard. The threat can emerge at any time: you must be alert for the moment when the person turns on you. You watch and you wait.

This stance may be directed at the whole world or only at specific types of people. For example, while Frank tended to be suspicious of everyone, Madeline's suspiciousness was limited fairly well to men. (She had issues about women as well, but these centered more on abandonment.)

The way you *remember* your childhood abuse is important. You may remember everything, and your memories may haunt you. Things remind you of the abuse.

MADELINE: *Lots of times I hate having sex. Images keep popping into my head of my stepfather. And I get these waves of revulsion.*

On the other hand, you may have no clear memories of the abuse. There may be whole patches of your childhood that seem vague and foggy.

MADELINE: *There's a lot of things I don't know about those years. Like how long it went on. I have no idea. I say it was for the whole time, but I don't really know. I just have the feeling that it was for a long time.*

You may not remember anything directly. But you remember in other ways—dreams or nightmares, violent fantasies, intrusive images, suddenly feeling upset when something reminds you of the abuse. Your *body* can remember, even when you yourself do not.

FRANK: *Something funny happened the other day. I went into the storage closet I built, and when I switched on the light, the bulb was dead. I was standing there in the dark and all of a sudden I broke out into this cold sweat. I was petrified.*
THERAPIST: *Can you close your eyes and get an image of that moment?*
FRANK: *Okay.*
THERAPIST: *Now give me an image of when you felt that way before.*
FRANK: *I get an image of me as a kid, standing in the closet in the dark, shaking.*
THERAPIST: *Why are you afraid?*
FRANK: *My father's out there looking for me. It's funny. I didn't make the connection. That's why I was so scared.*

You may even have flashbacks—memories so strong that you feel as though the abuse were recurring. But perhaps the most dangerous way you remember is through your current relationships. You reenact your childhood abuse.

Anxiety and depression are common. You may have a deep sense of despair about your life. Certainly you have low self-esteem and feelings of defectiveness.

ORIGINS OF THE MISTRUST AND ABUSE LIFETRAP

The origins of this lifetrap are in childhood experiences of being abused, manipulated, humiliated, or betrayed.

ORIGINS OF THE MISTRUST AND ABUSE LIFETRAP

1. Someone in your family physically abused you as a child.
2. Someone in your family sexually abused you as a child, or repeatedly touched you in a sexually provocative way.
3. Someone in your family repeatedly humiliated you, teased you, or put you down (verbal abuse).
4. People in your family could not be trusted. (They betrayed confidences, exploited your weaknesses to their advantage, manipulated you, made promises they had no intention of keeping, or lied to you.)
5. Someone in your family seemed to get pleasure from seeing you suffer.
6. You were made to do things as a child by the threat of severe punishment or retaliation.
7. One of your parents repeatedly warned you not to trust people outside of the family.
8. The people in your family were against you.
9. One of your parents turned to you for physical affection as a child, in a way that was inappropriate or made you uncomfortable.
10. People used to call you names that really hurt.

All forms of abuse are violations of your boundaries. Your physical, sexual, or psychological boundaries were not respected. Someone in your family who was supposed to protect you willfully started to hurt you. And, being a child, you were largely defenseless.

With Madeline it was her sexual boundaries. Her mother and her stepfather had become estranged, and her mother was abusing tranquilizers. (Drugs and alcohol are often implicated somewhere in the abuse situation.) Her stepfather turned to her as a source of affection.

MADELINE: *It started as just normal stuff, hugging and kissing. At first I really liked my stepfather. He seemed to really care about me. At first I liked it when he hugged and kissed me.*

This is a common scenario. The parents have conflicts or drift apart, and a parent uses the child as a replacement. The child may welcome the attention—which can become a source of guilt later on.

Her stepfather's affection progressed to sexual abuse. At first Madeline was not sure that abuse was occurring.

MADELINE: *But there came a time when I knew it was wrong. I remember he started falling asleep on the couch with me. He'd have his arms around me, and he'd start accidently touching me or rubbing against me.*

It is important to note that the extent of abuse can range widely. With some people there is intensive sexual abuse, and with others it is limited to touching or fondling. The most important point is how you felt about it. If you felt very uncomfortable about the touching, then it was almost certainly sexual abuse.

Another source of guilt later is that the child *believes* that he or she allowed, encouraged, or even enjoyed the abuse. Madeline let her stepfather touch her.

MADELINE: *I would just lie there. Like I couldn't move.*
THERAPIST: *You had no sense of being able to protect yourself, and that was very frightening.*

The abuse also stirred sexual feelings in Madeline. This confused her, and made her feel bad and ashamed.

It is important to understand that you bear none of the responsibility. The fact that you may have allowed the abuse or even responded sexually to it in no way implies your guilt. The fact that you were a child absolves you. If there are people in your family who are bigger and stronger than you, and they want to violate your boundaries, there is little you can do. The situation is too complex. You were not expected to protect yourself. Rather, your family was supposed to be protecting you.

The fact that no one protected her is one of the greatest sources of pain for Madeline.

MADELINE: *They didn't care enough what happened to me. Neither one of them. They were my mother and my stepfather, and they didn't care what happened to me.*

Sexual abuse is a violation of your spirit as well as your body. No matter how you feel, you were innocent. Your innocence and your trust were betrayed.

The secrecy was another source of guilt and shame. Her stepfather would tell her it was their little secret.

THERAPIST: *Why didn't you tell your mother?*
MADELINE: *Well, first, because he told me not to. But I was also too ashamed to tell her. I mean, to this day, you're the first person I've ever really talked about it with. I couldn't talk about it with her. And also I was worried that it would break up the family.*

   I would try to get her to take fewer pills, though. He used to do it most when she was passed out on pills. I used to beg her not to take those pills. She should have seen that something was wrong. But she couldn't stop taking those pills.

The feeling of not being protected is part of most forms of abuse. One parent abused you, and the other failed to prevent or stop it. They both let you down.

   We all know what we should do when a stranger attempts to abuse us. We should fight back, we should get help, we should escape. All of these options become problematic when you are a child and the abuser is someone you love. At bottom, you tolerated the abuse because you needed the connection with the person. It was your parent or brother or sister. Indeed, it may have been the *only* connection you were able to get. Without it you would have been alone. To most children, *some* connection, even an abusive one, is better than no connection at all.

   In terms of the three types of abuse—physical, sexual, and verbal—the similarities are more important than the differences. They all involve that same strange mixture of love and hurt. Frank's psychological experience of abuse was similar to Madeline's. But because it was his natural father who abused him from an earlier age, and because it was more prolonged, Frank's lifetrap is more severe.

   Frank remembers living in a constant state of fear. His father's rages were unpredictable.

FRANK: *You never knew when he'd go off. One minute we'd be having a normal conversation, and the next he'd be shouting at the top of his lungs, or swinging his fists. Sometimes he'd yell at my brother and sometimes at me. It was like living in the house with a crazy giant.*

   Even when things seemed okay, they weren't. There were no real safety zones.

To this day, it is hard for Frank to feel safe. Safety issues absorb his attention and keep him from concentrating on other things. There is always part of him searching for that threat.

It is hard to convey how chaotic and dangerous the world seems when you are a child and someone close to you can invade you and hurt you. A basic sense of security that most people take for granted is simply *not there.*

In every instance of abuse we have encountered as therapists, the abuser makes the child feel worthless. The abuser *blames* the child, and the child accepts that blame.

FRANK: *At the time I thought it was happening because I was so* bad. *I was clumsy and would get into trouble. My father used to tell me I would rot in hell. I believed him. I just thought it was happening because I was such a lousy person.*

Abuse creates powerful feelings of defectiveness. It makes you ashamed of who you are. You are unworthy. You are not entitled to have any rights or to stand up for yourself. You have to let the person use you and take advantage of you. It feels to you as if abuse is *all you deserve.*

The last defense a child has is psychological. When reality is too terrible, there is the possibility of psychological escape. Depending upon the severity of your abuse, you may have spent portions of your childhood in a dissociated state. Particularly while the abuse was happening, you may have learned to dissociate. This was an adaptive response, as a child.

MADELINE: *While he was doing it I would pretend I was this orange balloon, floating up into space. Nothing was real and nothing could bother me.*

Dissociating may have been a way for you to remove yourself from the situation emotionally and just get through it.

Dissociating also gives an air of separateness to an event—it seems to be happening separately from the rest of your life. Thus you may have been able to relate to your abuser relatively normally in other situations.

MADELINE: *It was so strange, although I didn't think about it at the time. I would have sex with him at night, then get up and go downstairs and chat with him and my mother over breakfast. It was like the night before had happened in another world.*

In situations where the abuse is extreme, dissociating can lead to the formation of multiple personalities.

Frank's outbursts of anger are Counterattacks to cope with his expectations of abuse. Sometimes he becomes *like* his father. The child imitates the behavior of the abuser. This is a way for the child to feel more powerful.

FRANK: *I used to beat up on my younger brother. Man, I feel so bad about it now. I would beat up on him just like my father beat up on me.*

One of the most common Counterattacks for the Mistrust and Abuse lifetrap is to abuse somebody else. This is what perpetuates the chain of abuse. The abused sometimes become the abusers. In fact, most child abusers were abused themselves as children. Frank's father is a case in point:

FRANK: *I know why my dad did it to me. He was an abused child himself. His own dad used to beat up on him.*

It is important to realize that the reverse is not necessarily true. Most victims of child abuse *do not* grow up to become child abusers. Although he has outbursts of anger, Frank himself is not a child abuser. He has broken the chain.

Many victims of abuse who do not actually *behave* abusively do have *fantasies* of abusing or hurting people.

FRANK: *I remember when I was a kid, I had this teacher who was giving me a hard time. He would put me down in front of the whole class. Man, I hated him. I used to sit in his class and daydream about tying him up and hitting him in the stomach again and again until he* begged *for mercy.*

You may lash out at other people sporadically. You may enjoy seeing other people hurt. You may be manipulative or insulting. What we are describing is a *sadistic* part of you. It is a part you may find appalling—the part that Counterattacks by becoming like the one who hurt you.

Frank's father was also verbally abusive. The criticalness that gives rise to the Defectiveness lifetrap shades into verbal abuse when there is an *intent to hurt*. The person deliberately humiliates you and beats you down.

FRANK: *He loved to make me cry. He thought it was funny. I would try so hard not to cry, but he'd keep at me.*
THERAPIST: *What would he say to you?*

FRANK: *He'd call me names, call me a wimp, spastic, a loser. He'd do it in front of my brothers and in front of my friends. He really enjoyed making me squirm. I swear, he really did.*

Frank's father seemed to hate him. It is hard to understand how a parent could hate a child in this way. Frank's vulnerability was somehow unbearable to him. He needed to destroy that vulnerability, to stamp it out. Frank's father was under the sway of his own Mistrust and Abuse lifetrap. He had learned to compensate for his own childhood abuse by becoming the aggressor.

A child who has a sadistic parent is in serious trouble. It is difficult to emerge from this situation without significant scars. There are parents who can coldly use and hurt their children. Such a parent will almost always strike when the child is very young—below five, for example. The parent does not have to worry as much that the child will tell or that other people will find out.

Although it is not as severe a form of the lifetrap, it is possible to learn to be abusive and mistrustful by example. You may have had a parent who was unethical and manipulative in dealings with friends or in business. Or your parent may have manipulated you or betrayed your confidences. You learned that this is how people are, and therefore expect most people to be this way.

DANGER SIGNALS IN RELATIONSHIPS

The danger is that you will be attracted to abusive partners or to partners who do not deserve to be trusted. These are the signs.

DANGER SIGNALS IN PARTNERS

1. He/She has an explosive temper that scares you.
2. He/She loses control when he/she drinks too much.
3. He/She puts you down in front of your friends and family.
4. He/She repeatedly demeans you, criticizes you, and makes you feel worthless.
5. He/She has no respect for your needs.
6. He/She will do anything—lie or manipulate—to get his/her way.
7. He/She is somewhat of a con artist in business dealings.
8. He/She is sadistic or cruel—seems to get pleasure when you or other people suffer.

9. He/She hits you or threatens you when you do not do as he/she
    wants.
10. He/She forces you to have sex, even when you do not want to.
11. He/She exploits your weaknesses to his/her advantage.
12. He/She cheats on you (has other lovers behind your back).
13. He/She is very unreliable, and takes advantage of your generos-
    ity.

It is one of the most puzzling facts of life that we seem to keep repeating the same self-destructive patterns over and over. This is what Freud called the repetition compulsion. Why would someone who was abused as a child willingly become involved in *another* abusive relationship? It does not make sense. Yet that is what happens.

You may find that you are most attracted to abusive partners. People who use, hit, rape, or insult and demean you—are the lovers who generate the most chemistry. This is one of the most devastating consequences of your childhood abuse. It turned you into a person who is drawn to abusive relationships in adulthood—so you can never escape, even when you grow up—unless you get treatment.

Madeline's relationships with men in her early twenties were examples. Since she was taking a lot of drugs herself, several of her boyfriends were drug addicts.

MADELINE: *My longest relationship was with Richie. I still see him from time to time. He was hooked on coke and really strung out. He used to steal money from me, and once he tried to get me to sleep with this guy so he could get some coke.*

There are few people more likely than a drug addict to use you and take advantage of you. But even her straight boyfriends were sexually abusive in some way. The most common scenario was that "they used me for sex and then dumped me." For a period of years, Madeline became involved in one abusive relationship after another.

When we asked Madeline why she allowed this to happen, she said, "These were the guys I fell in love with. Besides, it was better than being alone." But we do not agree that it is better than being alone. At least alone you have the chance to heal and rebuild your sense of self-esteem, to find a partner who will treat you differently.

The chart on the next page lists your lifetraps in long-term intimate relationships. There are a lot of them because abuse is such a serious problem:

LIFETRAPS IN RELATIONSHIPS

1. You often feel people are taking advantage of you, even when there is little concrete proof.
2. You allow other people to mistreat you because you are afraid of them or because you feel it is all you deserve.
3. You are quick to attack other people because you expect them to hurt you or put you down.
4. You have a very hard time enjoying sex—it feels like an obligation or you cannot derive pleasure.
5. You are reluctant to reveal personal information because you worry that people will use it against you.
6. You are reluctant to show your weaknesses because you expect people to take advantage of them.
7. You feel nervous around people because you worry that they will humiliate you.
8. You give in too easily to other people because you are afraid of them.
9. You feel that other people seem to enjoy your suffering.
10. You have a definite sadistic or cruel side, even though you may not show it.
11. You allow other people to take advantage of you because "it is better than being alone."
12. You feel that men/women cannot be trusted.
13. You do not remember large portions of your childhood.
14. When you are frightened of someone, you "tune out," as if part of you is not really there.
15. You often feel people have hidden motives or bad intentions, even when you have little proof.
16. You often have sado-masochistic fantasies.
17. You avoid getting close to men/women because you cannot trust them.
18. You feel frightened around men/women and you do not understand why.
19. You have sometimes been abusive or cruel to other people, especially the ones to whom you are closest.
20. You often feel helpless in relation to other people.

Even when you are in a good relationship, you may do things to turn it into an abusive one. You may become the abuser or the abused. Either way you reenact your childhood abuse.

There are a lot of things you can do to make good partners *seem* like abusers. You can twist the things they say, so innocent remarks take on the cast of cuts and insults. You can set up tests that fail to convince you, even when your partner passes. You can accuse them of trying to hurt you when they are not. You can magnify their disloyalties and minimize their acts of love. Even when they truly treat you well, you can *feel* as though you are being abused.

Frank's attitude toward his wife is a perfect illustration. From everything we could gather, Adrienne was worthy of his trust.

THERAPIST: *Can you name times she deliberately set out to hurt you?*

FRANK: *Right before we got married she went out with this guy Joe behind my back.*

ADRIENNE: *Oh, this gets me so mad! We've gone through this a thousand times! Before we got married my ex-boyfriend Joe called me and asked me to meet him for lunch. He said it was important. I said I would go, and I didn't tell Frank because I knew he wouldn't understand. It meant nothing to me!*

THERAPIST: *What did Joe want?*

ADRIENNE: *He wanted to know if there was any chance we could get back together. There wasn't any chance at all and I told him so. And that was it! I didn't do anything! I was just trying to let Joe down easy. I loved Frank and I still do.*

THERAPIST: *So this is an incident you two have discussed many times.*

ADRIENNE: *You can't believe how many times he's brought it up and thrown it in my face.*

THERAPIST: *(to Frank) Can you name any other times she set out to hurt you?*

FRANK: *Nah. I mean, I know she's right. But still I can't take that chance. I can't trust her. I can't believe she won't let me down.*

Perhaps it hurt Frank too much as a child to hope and be disappointed. It was a long time before he was willing to take that risk again.

Depending upon the pervasiveness of your abuse, your whole world view may be based upon the idea that people cannot be trusted. Your basic sense of people is that they are out to hurt you and secretly enjoy your suffering. It is the emotional *tone* of your relationships—the feeling that surrounds you when somebody gets close.

You may also do things that encourage partners who might otherwise be good to treat you badly. You do this by *lowering your value* in the relationship: you give in too easily to whatever the person wants, put yourself down, allow your partner to take advantage of you, send out messages that you are not worth treating well.

MADELINE: *A lot of times with guys, they would sleep with me and then feel too good for me. I remember there was this one guy, Alan, that I really liked a lot. In that whole period where I was really sleeping around, he was the one guy I really cared about.*

I used to always tell him, "You just think you're too good for me because I slept with you the first night we met." Or I would tell him, "You think you're too good for me because I've slept around."

THERAPIST: *What happened?*

MADELINE: *I guess eventually he started to believe it because he ended up leaving me.*

It was not only that Madeline put herself down, but she also felt helpless to defend herself. When men behaved sadistically toward her, she had that old childhood feeling of not being able to move. She was not able to stand up for herself. As she says, "No matter what they did, I couldn't say *no.*"

You may swing to the opposite end and have a problem with aggressiveness. This is an example of Counterattack as a coping style. This is when you believe the saying, "The best defense is a good offense." Since you expect the other person to attack, you make sure you attack first. You do not notice that time passes and you are the only one attacking.

ADRIENNE: *He's always accusing me, but meanwhile he's the one who's always on me. He says I put him down, and I'm not, I'm really careful not to put him down. I know it really upsets him.*

The other night he tripped on the ice and almost fell down. When I asked him if he was all right, he yelled at me. He thought I was making fun of him. I swear, I wasn't! I just wanted to know if he was all right. I get so frustrated. He acts like I'm his enemy.

Sometimes when you are aggressive, the other person retaliates and becomes aggressive back. Your outbursts of anger paradoxically bring about the very situation you fear. Or they slowly drive the other person away.

You have a lot of anger at people for the way they have treated you.

Even in good relationships, this anger is bound to become an issue. Your anger comes out in destructive ways. It may be that you have been abusive or cruel to the people you love. This is the first thing that has to stop. It damages you almost as much as it damages them.

If you were sexually abused, the damage to your sexuality is bound to be an issue in romantic relationships. You are prone to feeling angry or emotionally dead during sex.

MADELINE: *Sometimes I think I wouldn't mind if sex weren't a part of life. I don't look forward to sleeping with men again. I just feel so shut-down during sex it makes me upset.*

Madeline also had sado-masochistic sexual fantasies that disturbed her. The whole issue of sex was fraught with negative emotions.

CHANGING YOUR MISTRUST AND ABUSE LIFETRAP

These are the steps to changing your Mistrust and Abuse lifetrap.

CHANGING YOUR MISTRUST AND ABUSE LIFETRAP

1. If at all possible, see a therapist to help you with this lifetrap, particularly if you have been sexually or physically abused.
2. Find a friend you trust (or your therapist). Do imagery. Try to recall memories of abuse. Relive each incident in detail.
3. While doing imagery, vent your anger at your abuser(s). Stop feeling helpless in the image.
4. Stop blaming yourself. You did not deserve the abuse.
5. Consider reducing or stopping contact with your abuser(s) while you work on this lifetrap.
6. If it is possible, when you are ready, confront your abuser face-to-face, or send a letter.
7. Stop tolerating abuse in your current relationships.
8. Try to trust and get closer to people who deserve it.
9. Try to become involved with a partner who respects your rights and does not want to hurt you.
10. Do not abuse the people close to you.

---

1. If At All Possible, See a Therapist to Help You with This Lifetrap, Particularly if You Have Been Sexually or Physically Abused. If your lifetrap is severe, we do not want you to tackle it alone. Mistrust and Abuse is one of the most powerful lifetraps. It leads to extreme symptoms and problems in relationships. It is also one of the most difficult to change.

An attempt to change through a self-help book will probably not be enough. Perhaps if you have a milder strain of the lifetrap, you can make headway just by reading this chapter. But if you were seriously abused as a child, you should seek help from a therapist.

In addition, if possible, join a self-help group for adult survivors of incest or abuse. There are groups like this all over the country. There are also some excellent books that are tailored specifically for survivors of abuse. One well-known book is *Courage To Heal,* by Ellen Bass and Laura Davis.

You need a safe place to remember. A therapist can give you that safe place.

2. Find a Friend You Trust (Or Your Therapist). Do Imagery. Try to Recall Memories of Abuse. Relive Each Incident in Detail. Remembering is the most painful part. It is the part for which you particularly need the support of a therapist or someone you trust. The images of being physically, verbally, and sexually abused are frightening. The feelings that come up can be overwhelming. A therapist or friend can contain your feelings and help make the experience a healing one.

You have powerful reasons for not wanting to remember. One is what it will mean about your parent.

FRANK: *It's so hard for me to accept that my dad was such a lousy parent. I always figured he had reasons for what he did. He was overworked, my mother was a nag, I kept getting into trouble.*
THERAPIST: *Your desire to believe you had a good father is very strong.*
FRANK: *Yeah. I mean, if I thought he did all this to me for no reason, how could I have anything more to do with him?*

For Frank to admit he had a bad parent was very upsetting. Viewing his father as good allowed him to maintain the relationship and was one of the things that enabled him to tolerate the abuse in the first place.

Another reason you do not want to remember is that the feelings are so painful. You may have gone to enormous lengths to tune out and numb yourself to your memories. It was emotional protection to keep yourself sane. To let that go is very scary.

It took Frank months of therapy to get to the point where he was willing to explore his abuse through imagery. But once he was willing, the images came right away.

THERAPIST: *Close your eyes and give us an image from your childhood.*
FRANK: *I see myself and my father. My father looks huge. I'm about seven years old. I'm standing there shaking. My father is yelling at me. (Imitates father's voice) "I'll teach you, you little brat!" He's got the belt out, and I'm so scared that I pee in my pants.*

At first Frank could not believe all his memories. "Maybe I made it up," he would say, or "Maybe they're just fantasies." It was a battle to get him to accept that his memories were true.

You will find that, once you feel safe, the images will come. You will remember it all, and experience that pain. And in experiencing the pain, you will start to heal.

3. While Doing Imagery, Vent Your Anger at Your Abuser(s). Stop Feeling Helpless in the Image. Strike back at your abuser. Imagine yourself stronger, older, or well-armed, so you can express your anger. Stop being that helpless child. Bang on a pillow or telephone books while you do this.

THERAPIST: *What do you see in the image?*
FRANK: *We're in the kitchen. My father is beating up on my younger brother. He's really out of control. My mother is standing in the corner screaming.*
THERAPIST: *I want you to freeze the image for a moment.*
FRANK: *Okay.*
THERAPIST: *Now turn to your father and tell him what he's doing that's wrong.*
FRANK: *I can't. It's too dangerous. (Seems to collapse into his chair.)*
THERAPIST: *I understand. You're not powerful enough. Let's do something to help you. I want you to grow up in the image, until you are as big as you are now.*
FRANK: *Okay.*
THERAPIST: *Now tell him. Tell him what he's doing wrong. You can hit the couch with your fists as you talk.*
FRANK: *Okay. I step between him and my little brother, and shove him back against the wall. I look down into his face. He looks nervous. (Punches the couch.)*
I tell him, "Hey, big man, beating up a five-year-old. You must be

a worm inside to get your kicks like this. A sleazy worm. You're vile. I hate you. (Punches the couch.) If you ever touch my brother again I'll beat you within an inch of your life."

THERAPIST: *How did that feel?*

FRANK: *(smiles) Great.*

This exercise is one of empowering yourself. It will help free you from the domination of your abuser. At some level you are still operating in the world as a frightened child. We want you to claim the power of an adult. You no longer have to submit to your abuser.

4. Stop Blaming Yourself. You Did Not Deserve the Abuse. Stop making excuses for your abuser. You were not at fault. You were a helpless child. You did the best you could under the circumstances. It is important to be crystal-clear on this issue. *No child deserves to be abused.*

MADELINE: *I know I shouldn't sleep with guys right away. It makes me feel dirty. But I feel dirty anyway, like I'm damaged goods. Who could really want me, except for a one-night stand?*

THERAPIST: *It upsets us to see you blame yourself this way. It was your stepfather who was dirty, not you.*

No matter what you were made to feel, the abuse did not happen because you were bad. That was just a convenient excuse. Victimizers always devalue their victims. Awake from your feelings of defectiveness. Find the good child within you. Feel sympathy for this wounded child.

THERAPIST: *I want you to bring yourself into the image as an adult, and help the child.*

MADELINE: *(sighs) I bring myself in. The child Madeline is lying on the couch with him. Her eyes look dead. I pick her up and carry her out of the room. I take her outside, far away. I sit down with her in my arms, and I just rock her.*

Get angry at the parent who did not protect you. This is part of the picture too. Direct the anger away from yourself. Stop dealing with your anger in self-destructive ways—by eating, or becoming addicted, or by feeling depressed and empty. Use your anger to make you stronger.

5. Consider Reducing or Stopping Contact with Your Abuser(s) While You Work on This Lifetrap. We find that patients generally make better progress when they cut off contact with their abusers. Some patients cut contact off temporarily, and others cut it off forever. The eventual relationship you want with your abuser is wholly your decision. It is also your decision whether you tell your abuser why you are stopping contact.

But, at least for a while, in the beginning stages of healing, it is often best to sever contact. Your abuser is a powerful reinforcer of your lifetrap. He or she gives you all the wrong messages—that you are helpless, a victim, defective, at fault.

FRANK: *When Adrienne and I had dinner with my parents, I felt like such a jerk. Right away. We sat down at the table, and I immediately knocked over my glass of water. My pants got soaked. My father started calling me spastic and laughing at me. I felt like a worm.*
THERAPIST: *What did you do when he said that?*
FRANK: *Nothing. I got kind of quiet. I was quiet for the rest of the meal.*

It is hard to heal in that toxic environment.

6. If It is Possible, When You Are Ready, Confront Your Abuser Face-to-Face, or Send a Letter. This exercise is also about empowering yourself. Until you confront your abuser, some part of you will remain a helpless child—unable to protect yourself in a world of malevolent adults. Part of you will still be afraid. But you are not a helpless child anymore. You *can* stand up to your abuser.

FRANK: *I did it Saturday. I invited my father over to my apartment. I figured it would go better on my turf. As soon as he got there, I started in.*
   I told him that he had abused me and my brother, and that his behavior showed him to be a bully and a coward. I told him that I hated him for what he had done, and did not want to speak to him again until I said so, maybe never. I told him he was a selfish, infantile, weak man. I told him it was a lie that I in any way deserved his abuse. I told him everything.
THERAPIST: *How did it feel?*
FRANK: *I never felt better in my life.*

State what the abuser did to you. Bring it out in the open. You will feel relief. Stand up and say, "You did this to me," "I won't permit it anymore," and "I'm furious at you."

Madeline was no longer in contact with her stepfather, but she wrote him a letter:

> *Dad,*
>
> *When I was a child you took advantage of my normal need for love and affection. I was especially vulnerable. My own father had died and my mother was hooked on drugs. There was no one to protect me.*
>
> *The thing that hurts me the most is that I really loved you. At first you were so wonderful to me. You gave me love and I was thirsty for love.*
>
> *It was so hard for me to believe that it was all fake, but it was. You were using me. If you cared about me, you could never have done what you did.*
>
> *Now I hate you. You have damaged my ability to love and robbed me of the joy of my sexuality. These are things that were rightfully mine and you took them. You made me hate myself.*
>
> *I don't ever want you to contact me again.*
>
> *Madeline*

Whether you intend to send it or not, writing such a letter is a good exercise. It can be a cleansing process. For one thing, it states your vision of the truth. This is an important validation of yourself. It can also be a rehearsal for a later face-to-face confrontation. In the letter, tell the person what they did that was wrong. Tell how it made you feel, and how you wished it could have been instead.

Madeline confronted her mother in person. Her mother was still addicted to drugs.

MADELINE: *I told her I considered her use of drugs a selfish act that had hurt me deeply. It had left me without a mother. I told her she had abandoned me when I was too young to take care of myself. And because of this I had been sexually abused by one of her husbands for many years.*

THERAPIST: *How did it feel?*

MADELINE: *It was upsetting but it was good. It made me feel better.*

Of course she just started making her usual excuses and denials. But I wasn't going to let her get to me. I just turned around and left the room.

I don't know when I'll call her again.

Get support from someone you can trust as you do this. This is most important, since in all likelihood your abuser will deny responsibility. In our experience, most of the time when there has been serious abuse, the parent denies it. *You must be prepared for this possibility.*

The important thing is that you are stating the truth. The success of the confrontation does not depend on how your abuser responds. Rather, the success is in what the confrontation does for you—how it makes you feel strong and good about yourself.

7. Stop Tolerating Abuse in Your Current Relationships. We have to combat your fatal attraction to abusive partners.

MADELINE: *I spent my whole early twenties going out with psychopaths, creeps, drug addicts, and liars.*

Look at your current relationships. Write down the ways in which you still permit yourself to be abused—hit, manipulated, put down, humiliated, raped. This all must stop. You cannot heal while your lifetrap is being reinforced. Starting this moment, we do not want you to allow anyone to abuse you ever again.

If your abuser is a partner or friend, there is a small chance he or she can change. You can give the person one chance. Stand up for your rights. Protect yourself. Stop blocking your anger—express it. Confront the person. Do not become aggressive yourself. Stay assertive and controlled.

But do not get sucked into denial. If your abuser will not change, you have to leave the relationship. We know this may be difficult for you, and again we emphasize that you should be in therapy. You need support for the hard decisions that lie ahead.

8. Try to Trust and Get Closer to People Who Deserve It. You may have difficulty trusting people, even when they are well-intentioned. This is one of the main ways you maintain the lifetrap. Take an objective look at your relationships. Focus on intimate ones—family, close friends, lovers, spouses, children.

For each person in your life that is not obviously abusive, write down all the evidence that he/she *can* be trusted. Next write down all the evidence that he/she *cannot* be trusted. If you do not really have much evidence of bad treatment, try trusting more. Let down your guard gradually. Try to get closer, and trust people who deserve it.

Patients are often surprised at how little objective evidence they have that various people are worthy of mistrust. This was certainly the case with Frank.

FRANK: *Seeing as how the only evidence I really have is that old-boyfriend episode years ago, I've decided to try to give Adrienne the benefit of the doubt. I've stopped checking up on her wherever she goes. I've stopped accusing her of cheating on me. (pause) I'm just so frightened to be wrong. It's frightening to me, but I'm doing it.*

THERAPIST: *What's the effect been on your relationship?*

FRANK: *It's definitely better. For one thing I don't feel on the verge of losing it all the time anymore. I'm not getting as angry. And Adrienne's definitely happier. She's getting more relaxed.*

I mean I still get flare-ups. Like the other day, she got this call from this guy Bill, whom she works with. I could hear her laughing on the phone, and it really started to bother me. I got into wanting to sneak and listen on the extension. I started getting all worked up, thinking I would hear some clue that Adrienne's messing around with him. But I stopped myself from doing it. And once I decided not to do it, I felt much better.

In the old days that would have been a fight for sure.

Unless you have surrounded yourself completely with abusive people, there are bound to be *some* people in your life that you can trust.

A therapy relationship may be the best place for you to begin. You can learn to trust in a safe place.

9. Try to Become Involved with a Partner Who Respects Your Rights and Does Not Want to Hurt You. Examine your intimate partners, past and present, for evidence of abuse. If you are in an abusive relationship, get help to stop the abuse or end the relationship. It is most devastating of all to remain with an abusive romantic partner.

Try to recognize the danger signals in choosing future partners. Knowing the danger signals can help you feel confident that you can pick a trustworthy partner. Even if the chemistry is weaker, get involved with men/women who respect your rights and do not want to hurt you.

The greatest stumbling block for Madeline was overcoming her avoidance of romantic relationships. Her conviction that men are untrustworthy was profound.

MADELINE: *I'd rather be alone than go through another bad relationship.*
THERAPIST: *So you don't believe a relationship with a man can be good.*
MADELINE: *No. It's how men are. Deep inside they all want to use you and then throw you away. They just pretend to care to get what they want.*
THERAPIST: *You sound very angry.*
MADELINE: *Yeah, I'm angry. I'm angry, I'm stuck, and I'm angry about being stuck.*

Madeline believed that the best she could hope for was another painful relationship. With that logic, it made sense to avoid relationships altogether. This is an example of Escape as a coping style.

However, the truth is that there are many people in the world who are kinder than the people in your family. You expect the whole world to be like your family, and you are wrong. You are over-generalizing.

Go through a period of just dating first. Work your way into relationships slowly. Keep a feeling of control. As you get into relationships, make sure you stand up for your rights. Protect yourself. Value yourself highly. It will encourage your partner to do the same.

10. Do Not Abuse the People Close to You. Do not act out the abusive behavior you experienced as a child on your partner, children, friends, or employees. There is no excuse for abuse.

FRANK: *The thing that made me change toward Adrienne most of all was realizing that even though I don't ever hit Adrienne or anything, my constant haranguing of her and outbursts really were a form of abuse.*

If you have been abusing someone you love, *stop right now.* If you cannot stop, get help right away. More than getting caught up in guilt and continuing the cycle, stopping will help you.

We want you to make amends to the people you have hurt. Tell them you realize you have been wrong, and ask their forgiveness. Outline specific ways you are going to change.

Remember your own inner child. It is the best way to keep yourself from becoming an abuser.

SOME FINAL WORDS

The road out of the Mistrust and Abuse lifetrap is long and difficult. But for that reason it can be one of the most rewarding. The road can bring you to what you have always wanted—to love and be loved. Do not live your whole life caught in the lifetrap. Get help to get out. The lifetrap arises from child abuse. You should have no shame about needing help. Reclaim the things that, as Madeline says, are rightfully yours—all the joys that are possible in supportive human relationships.

8

"I'll Never Get the Love I Need"
The Emotional Deprivation Lifetrap

JED: THIRTY-NINE YEARS OLD. WOMEN ALWAYS DISAPPOINT
HIM EMOTIONALLY.

Two things struck us about Jed as he walked into our office for the first time. One was how handsome he looked, and the other was how cold. There was a remote quality to him that was difficult to pierce in therapy. But in that first session he sat down and told us why he was there.

He had been through a series of relationships with women, starting when he was a teenager, but none had lasted longer than six months. The pattern was always the same. Each time he started a relationship, he felt a sense of hope and excitement. He believed that, at last, this was the woman for whom he had been looking so long. Despite his initial strong attraction, inevitably the relationship ended in disappointment. Jed expressed his frustration:

JED: *And now, it's happened again with Elaine. I was sure it was going to be different this time. It was so good at first. But just like with all the others, after a while I started to get bored and dissatisfied. She began to* irritate *me.*
THERAPIST: *What did Elaine do that made you angry?*
JED: Everything *she did made me angry. She didn't return my phone*

109

calls fast enough, she talked to other people too much at parties, she spent too much time with her friends, she spent too much time at work, she didn't give me an expensive enough birthday present. But mainly she just wasn't exciting enough. You know, I know she loved me. But she just wasn't enough. I needed more.

At the beginning of Jed's love relationships, the chemistry he feels is strong. But he gradually loses his passionate feelings until only a sense of disappointment remains. It is soon after this that the relationship ends.

DUSTIN: TWENTY-EIGHT YEARS OLD. HE FALLS IN LOVE WITH UNAVAILABLE WOMEN.

Dustin described his predicament:

DUSTIN: *The same thing keeps happening. I fall madly in love with someone. For some reason, it can't work out. Like this. (He begins to list on his fingers.) Anne was married, Jessica and Melinda both had other boyfriends who didn't know about me, Lisa lived too far away, and Gail had just broken up with someone else and wasn't ready to jump into another serious relationship.*

Dustin's lovers are usually a certain personality type. He is attracted to women who are cold and aloof: "When I meet a woman who is warm and giving, I seem to lose interest quickly." The women who keep Dustin's interest, indeed the women with whom he becomes *obsessed,* are narcissistic, self-centered, and expect much but give little in return. Although they might find it gratifying to be with Dustin because he is so attentive, they seldom want to form a close relationship, and never make a commitment.

Dustin's relationships are stormy. He goes through ecstasies and agonies. As he grows more angry and frustrated, gradually the woman begins to dislike spending time with him. Finally the relationship ends. Dustin goes through a period of dejection until the whole process starts again with the next woman.

ELIZABETH: FORTY YEARS OLD. EMOTIONALLY GIVING TO OTHERS, BUT MARRIED TO A MAN WHO CANNOT GIVE TO HER.

Elizabeth and Josh have been married for five years. They have a baby boy. Elizabeth is a warm and nurturant mother. In fact, she tends to spoil her son. She finds it painful to hear the sound of his crying, and rushes to fill even his slightest demands.

ELIZABETH: *Before the baby was born, I worked as a social worker. But I gave it up to stay home with Danny. My life revolves around that baby. My time with him is blissful.*

But I am so unhappy with Josh. He is so cold. It is like trying to get water from a stone. I knew he was like this when we got married, but I hoped he would change. But really it has just gotten worse.

Josh is an executive in a large corporation. He works long hours and travels all over the world. Elizabeth spends many nights and weekends home alone with the baby: "Even when Josh is home, it is not much better. He's preoccupied with his work and seems uninterested in spending time with me." Elizabeth suspects that he is unfaithful to her on his business trips. She is in a constant state of anger. On the rare occasions that they are together, she spends most of the time complaining and reproaching him. Ironically, her anger just serves to push Josh further away.

Jed, Dustin, and Elizabeth all have the Emotional Deprivation lifetrap. If you have this lifetrap, you have a deep and fixed belief that your needs for love will never be met.

THE EMOTIONAL DEPRIVATION QUESTIONNAIRE

The questionnaire below will help you decide how strongly you have this lifetrap. Rate each item using the following scale:

SCORING KEY

1 Completely untrue of me
2 Mostly untrue of me
3 Slightly more true than untrue of me
4 Moderately true of me
5 Mostly true of me
6 Describes me perfectly

If you have any 5's or 6's on this questionnaire, this lifetrap may still apply to you even if your score is in the low range.

SCORE	DESCRIPTION
	1. I need more love than I get.
	2. No one really understands me.
	3. I am often attracted to cold partners who can't meet my needs.
	4. I feel disconnected, even from the people who are closest to me.
	5. I have not had one special person I love who wants to share him/herself with me and cares deeply about what happens to me.
	6. No one is there to give me warmth, holding, and affection.
	7. I do not have someone who really listens and is tuned into my true needs and feelings.
	8. It is hard for me to let people guide or protect me, even though it is what I want inside.
	9. It is hard for me to let people love me.
	10. I am lonely a lot of the time.
	YOUR TOTAL EMOTIONAL DEPRIVATION SCORE (Add your scores together for questions 1–10)

INTERPRETING YOUR EMOTIONAL DEPRIVATION SCORE

10–19 Very low. This lifetrap probably does *not* apply to you.
20–29 Fairly low. This lifetrap may only apply *occasionally*.
30–39 Moderate. This lifetrap is an *issue* in your life.
40–49 High. This is definitely an *important* lifetrap for you.
50–60 Very high. This is definitely one of your *core* lifetraps.

THE EXPERIENCE OF EMOTIONAL DEPRIVATION

The experience of emotional deprivation is harder to define than some of the other lifetraps. Often it is not crystallized into thoughts. This is because the original deprivation began so early, before you had the words to describe it. Your experience of emotional deprivation is much more the *sense* that you are going to be lonely forever, that certain things are never going to be fulfilled for you, that you will never be heard, never be understood.

Emotional deprivation feels like something is missing. It is a feeling of *emptiness*. Perhaps the image that most captures its meaning is that of a *neglected* child. Emotional deprivation is what a neglected child feels. It is a feeling of aloneness, of nobody there. It is a sad and heavy sense of knowledge that you are destined to be alone.

When Jed first came into therapy, he could not really tell us what was disturbing him. At first he said things like, "I feel alone," "I feel detached." Later he told us that he has experienced such *intense* feelings of loneliness and disconnection that he has considered suicide.

JED: *I am emotionally dead. My lack of intimacy with women applies to all my relationships. I'm not close to anyone, not to any family members, not to friends.*

For Jed the world is an emotional desert. His only respite from isolation is in the very early stages of his relationships with women. And, as we have noted, these are short-lived.

Some people with this lifetrap show a tendency to be *demanding* in relationships. There is an *insatiable* quality to the lifetrap. No matter how much people give you, it never feels like enough. Ask yourself, "Do people keep telling me that I am too needy, or that I ask for too much?"

Jed is an example. Elaine arranged an elaborate birthday party for him at great effort and expense. Nevertheless, when he opened her present at the party, Jed felt a sharp pang of disappointment: "The one I gave her was *much* more expensive." It is this persistent feeling of deprivation in the face of clear evidence of caring that marks the person with an Emotional Deprivation lifetrap.

One way Elizabeth expressed her lifetrap was by choosing a field of work that involved meeting the needs of other people. She became a social worker. Perhaps you are in one of the healing or helping professions. Giving *nurturance* to others may be a way for you to compensate for your own feelings of unmet emotional needs. Similarly, you might exert great effort toward meeting the needs of your friends. Elizabeth said:

ELIZABETH: *I am always the listener. Other people tell me their problems, and I help them as best I can, but I don't tell anyone my problems. I guess that's why I came to see you. I understand people better than they understand me, or care to understand.*

Finally, it is a sign of the Emotional Deprivation lifetrap to feel chronically *disappointed* in other people. People let you down. We are not speaking about a single case of disappointment, but rather a pattern of experiences over a long period of time. If your conclusion as a result of all your relationships is that you cannot count on people to be there for you emotionally—that is a sign that you have the lifetrap.

THE ORIGINS OF EMOTIONAL DEPRIVATION

The origins of emotional deprivation lie in the person who serves as the maternal figure for the child—the person who is chiefly responsible for giving the child emotional nurturance. In some families this figure is a man, but in our culture it is usually a woman. The father figure is important also, but in the first years of life, it is usually the mother who forms the center of the child's world. That first relationship becomes the prototype for those that follow. For the rest of the individual's life, most close relationships will bear the stamp of that first experience with mother.

With emotional deprivation, the child received a less than average amount of maternal nurturance. The term *nurturance* has a number of dimensions, as you can see from the table below outlining the origins of this lifetrap. We use the word *mother* to refer to the maternal figure.

THE ORIGINS OF EMOTIONAL DEPRIVATION

1. Mother is cold and unaffectionate. She does not hold and rock the child enough.
2. The child does not have a sense of being loved and valued—of being someone who is precious and *special.*
3. Mother does not give the child enough time and attention.
4. The mother is not really tuned into the child's needs. She has difficulty empathizing with the child's world. She does not really *connect* with the child.

> 5. Mother does not soothe the child adequately. The child, then, may not learn to soothe him/herself or to accept soothing from others.
> 6. The parents do not adequately guide the child or provide a sense of direction. There is no one solid for the child to rely upon.

Jed's deprivation was severe. He was almost totally neglected. Jed's mother was seventeen when she became pregnant. His father was much older and married, and refused to acknowledge Jed as his son. His mother had hoped that once Jed was born, his father would relent and assume his place beside her. This is not what happened, however.

JED: *My father showed no more interest in her after I was born than he had shown before. As soon as she realized I was useless as bait to win him back, she lost all interest in me. She expected her life to return immediately to normal, so she could resume dating rich older men. She really never should have had me.*

We often hear phrases like these from patients with Emotional Deprivation: "I don't know why she had me," or "They never should have had me." Jed remembers from the time he was very young, having no one to take care of him.

JED: *Most of the time she wasn't around. But even when she was with me it was no different. Whenever I wanted something from her, she would say, "Be quiet, go to sleep, you need a nap," and go on with what she was doing as if I wasn't there.*

For Elizabeth, the deprivation was more subtle. Her mother was a responsible person and would not *neglect* her child. However, like Jed's mother, she was *narcissistic*. Instead of viewing her child as a separate person with needs of her own, she viewed her child as an extension of herself. She saw Elizabeth as an *object,* to be used for her own gratification.

What Elizabeth's mother wanted, what she had failed to achieve in her own life, was to be rich. She wanted Elizabeth to marry a rich man.

ELIZABETH: *She taught me to be pretty and charming. It was the price of her love. She taught me to perform for company. She took me shopping. She dressed me up like a doll. But when we were done shopping and the company was gone, she ignored me. I just wasn't relevant anymore.*

As we know, Elizabeth grew up to fulfill her mother's wishes. She married a rich man. Now she is the executive's wife. He expects her to be pretty and charming for company. When the company is gone, he ignores her.

Dustin, the man who keeps falling in love with unavailable women, seemingly had a good mother. She did all the right things. She gave Dustin the best toys, the best clothes, the best schools, the best vacations. Yet there was a sense of coldness. Dustin's mother was a successful lawyer. She had built a career at a time when it was a rarity to find women working in the professions. She focused her attention almost exclusively on her work. At home she was self-absorbed and withdrawn.

Although she did not admit it to herself, in her heart she regarded Dustin as a nuisance, as a demanding child who distracted her from matters of true importance. And she was simply not a warm woman. She had difficulty showing affection, even to people whom she appreciated more than Dustin. Secretly, she blamed Dustin for the low intensity of her feelings toward him. It was not *her* fault that he aroused so little love.

Dustin grew up with a core of grief over the absence of a nurturing mother. He covered his grief with a hard shell of anger. This is an example of the Counterattacking coping style we discussed in Chapter 4. On the surface, he seemed very much the spoiled, petulant boy.

Now, as an adult, Dustin reenacts his Emotional Deprivation lifetrap in his numerous romantic relationships with unavailable women. He pursues one doomed relationship after another. Inevitably, each woman frustrates him and he becomes increasingly demanding. It always ends with the woman breaking his heart.

DUSTIN: *Before I started therapy I really had no idea I was caught in this process. Each time I thought I just* happened *to fall in love with a woman who just* happened *to be unavailable.*

Although his mother was emotionally depriving, Dustin was fortunate in one respect. He had a loving father. If not for the relationship with his father, Dustin might have sealed himself off forever from intimate human contact. The love Dustin's father gave him partly healed the damage done by his mother, so that the lifetrap developed in a more limited way. He was able to form other healthy relationships outside the family.

Dustin's lifetrap has a restricted range in his adult life. He does not view *everyone* as depriving—only the women with whom he falls in love. Dustin has satisfying relationships with many people. He has many good friends, both male and female, to whom he pours out the misery of his stormy love affairs.

Dustin's case illustrates the important role the father plays in the child's early life. If a child has an emotionally depriving mother, but a father who is not depriving, the father can become a bright spot in the child's otherwise dark psychic life. The father's love can serve as partial remediation of the child's emotional deprivation. If the child is lucky, the father will sense the inadequacy of the mother and assume a greater portion of responsibility for providing nurturance. As Dustin said, "My father helped me keep hope in the world." Similarly, children who have a depriving father but a mother who is not depriving, may reenact their emotional deprivation as adults in certain relationships but not in others. For example, girls with depriving fathers may reenact this lifetrap in love affairs with men, but not so much in other types of relationships.

It sometimes takes us a while to realize that a patient has the Emotional Deprivation lifetrap. Unlike most of the other lifetraps, where the parent does something *active* that damages the child, emotional deprivation results from the *absence* of certain mothering behaviors. Behaviors of the parent such as the criticalness that gives rise to the Defectiveness lifetrap, or the domination that gives rise to Subjugation, are highly visible. The parent commits actions the child can remember. But emotional deprivation is not always like this. Emotional deprivation is something *missing,* something the child never knew.

Emotional deprivation, therefore, can be a difficult lifetrap for you to recognize. Unless you experienced extreme neglect, it might take some exploration to determine whether you were deprived as a child. You might recognize the lifetrap in yourself only after you have asked yourself specific questions: "Did I feel close to my mother, did I feel she understood me, did I feel loved, did I love her, was she warm and affectionate, could I tell her what I felt, could she give me what I needed?"

In therapy, many people with the Emotional Deprivation lifetrap at first say things like, "Oh, I had a normal childhood. My mother was always there." Dustin began therapy saying, "My mother gave me everything. I had everything I wanted." However, when people with this lifetrap describe their past and current relationships, something is wrong. A disturbing pattern emerges. There is a feeling of disconnection. Perhaps the person is hypersensitive to being deprived or is chronically angry. It is only when we work our way backwards that we understand the origin. Although Emotional Deprivation is one of the most common lifetraps, it is often one of the hardest to detect.

ROMANTIC RELATIONSHIPS

In our culture, it is romantic relationships that are usually the most intimate. For this reason, some people who have the Emotional Deprivation lifetrap avoid romantic relationships altogether, or only get into them for a short time. This is typical of the Escape coping style. However, if you are willing to become involved in romantic relationships and do not simply remain alone, it is probably in these relationships that your lifetrap is most visible.

Perhaps you, like Jed, have a history of breaking off relationships when the person starts to get too close. You conveniently find reasons to end the relationship. Or, like Dustin, you protect yourself from closeness by choosing partners who are unavailable. Or, like Elizabeth, you choose someone who is there, but is cold and ungiving. No matter what path you take, the final outcome is the same. You wind up in a situation that is emotionally depriving, thus replicating your childhood deprivation.

The next table lists some of the danger signals to avoid in the early stages of dating. They are signals that you are about to repeat the pattern again and become involved with someone who is emotionally depriving.

DANGER SIGNALS IN THE EARLY STAGES OF DATING

1. He/She doesn't listen to me.
2. He/She does all the talking.
3. He/She is not comfortable touching or kissing me.
4. He/She is only sporadically available.
5. He/She is cold and aloof.
6. You are much more interested in getting close than he/she is.
7. The person is not there for you when you feel vulnerable.
8. The less available he/she is, the more *obsessed* you become.
9. He/She does not understand your feelings.
10. You are giving much more than you are getting.

When several of these signals are occurring at once, *run*—particularly if the chemistry is very strong. Your lifetrap has been triggered full force.

We know it will be hard for you to take this advice. All your yearning will be directed toward staying in the relationship. This is what happened to Dustin. Dustin began dating Christine in the course of therapy. Christine was beautiful; she was a successful model in New York City. Dustin was just one of a throng of men who pursued her. Although he knew the affair was doomed, he could not stop himself. His lifetrap fought for the relationship's survival. We watched the whole process spin itself out, from the height of Christine spending the weekend with him at his country house, to the depth of her final refusal to see him or to return his increasingly desperate phone calls.

Even if you choose an appropriate partner who is emotionally giving, there are still pitfalls to avoid as your relationship progresses.

EMOTIONAL DEPRIVATION LIFETRAPS IN A RELATIONSHIP

1. You don't tell your partner what you need, then feel disappointed when your needs are not met.
2. You don't tell your partner how you feel, and then feel disappointed when you are not understood.
3. You don't allow yourself to be vulnerable, so that your partner can protect or guide you.
4. You feel deprived, but you don't say anything. You harbor resentment.
5. You become angry and demanding.
6. You constantly accuse your partner of not caring enough about you.
7. You become distant and unreachable.

You might reinforce your deprivation by *sabotaging* the relationship. You might become hypersensitive to signs of neglect. You might expect your lover to read your mind and almost magically to fill your needs. Although, as we will discuss next, some people who have the lifetrap Counterattack by becoming demanding in relationships, most do not ask for what they want. It probably does not occur to you to spell out your needs. Most likely you do not ask for what you want, and then become very hurt, withdrawn, or angry when your emotional needs are not met.

DEMANDINGNESS IN RELATIONSHIPS

Some people with the Emotional Deprivation lifetrap *counterattack;* they compensate for their feelings of deprivation by becoming hostile and demanding. These people are *narcissistic*. They act as if they are *entitled* to get all their needs met. They demand a lot, and often get a lot, from the people who become their lovers.

Jed is like this. Regardless of how much nurturing he receives from a woman, he still feels that his needs are not being met. However, instead of acting hurt or rejected about not getting enough, he becomes *angry*. This is very different from Elizabeth, who is also hypersensitive to emotional slights, but instead remains *silent* about her needs. Jed and Elizabeth illustrate two different styles of coping with Emotional Deprivation: Jed's anger and demandingness are typical of the Counterattack coping style, while Elizabeth's silence is characteristic of Surrender as a way of coping.

Why do some people react to Emotional Deprivation by becoming narcissistic? The answer lies in a combination of the Emotional Deprivation lifetrap and the Entitlement lifetrap. Although as children their *emotional* needs were not met in important ways, narcissists have learned to fight the feelings of deprivation by becoming very demanding about other, more *superficial* needs.

For example, you might be very demanding about what you eat, or how you dress, or whom you are with, or where you go. You might be very demanding about *material* things. You might be demanding about anything except the true object of your craving, which is emotional nurturance. Unfortunately, these material demands are ultimately a poor substitute for love and understanding, and so you are not satisfied. You go on craving tangible rewards, never addressing the underlying issue, and are *never* satisfied.

As a child, you were not allowed to be demanding about emotional needs. Your mother (probably) did not respond. But if she allowed you to be demanding about other needs, it was at least a way for you to get *something*. This is what happened to Dustin. Although Dustin's mother was cold, she was excellent at filling other types of needs. She was lavish with material gifts, so Dustin developed a sense of entitlement about material things. Unlike Dustin, some children are neglected in both domains, emotionally and materially. No matter where they turn, they encounter deprivation. These children usually just give up and learn to expect nothing (the Surrender coping style).

There is an *inauthentic* quality to a relationship with a narcissist. Intimate encounters, even with the people they are closest to, remain superficial. If this is you, at some level you feel a sense of despair at the shallowness of your relationships. It is because you are so seldom demanding about the needs that are most pressing, the primary emotional needs, that your encounters strike a note of falseness.

The following list outlines the steps to change the Emotional Deprivation lifetrap:

CHANGING EMOTIONAL DEPRIVATION

1. Understand your childhood deprivation. Feel the deprived child inside of you.
2. Monitor your feelings of deprivation in your current relationships. Get in touch with your needs for nurturance, empathy, and guidance.
3. Review past relationships, and clarify the patterns that recur. List the pitfalls to avoid from now on.
4. Avoid cold partners who generate high chemistry.
5. When you find a partner who is emotionally generous, give the relationship a chance to work. *Ask* for what you want. Share your *vulnerability* with your partner.
6. Stop blaming your partner and demanding that your needs be met.

Let us explore each step in more detail.

1. Understand Your Childhood Deprivation. Feel the Deprived Child Inside of You. Understanding is always the first step. You must come to terms with the truth of what happened to you as a child. As we have noted, with Emotional Deprivation this can be more difficult than with some of the other lifetraps. You may not even know that you were deprived.

Jed knew when he came to therapy that he had been deprived. Such blatant deprivation is easily recognized. Even early in therapy Jed was able to generate images of his neglect—of being the only child without a mother present at countless occasions, from receiving a Cub Scout medal all the way to his high school and college graduations. He remembered forging his mother's signature on his report cards because she could not bother to sign them.

Jed could easily access his anger about the deprivation, but he had difficulty accessing the pain (typical of Counterattackers). Elizabeth, on the other hand, was in touch with the pain, with how lonely she felt as a child (typical of Surrenderers). It was harder for her to access the anger. You have both anger and grief about your deprivation. As we shall see, it is important to try to feel both.

For Dustin and Elizabeth, understanding the past was more difficult. They were uncovering a more subtle process. Actually, we believe that there are three distinct types of emotional deprivation. Breaking it down this way may help you to clarify exactly what it was that happened to you as a child. You may have been deprived in one or two of these areas but not the others.

THREE KINDS OF EMOTIONAL DEPRIVATION

1. Deprivation of Nurturance
2. Deprivation of Empathy
3. Deprivation of Protection

Each kind of deprivation refers to a different aspect of love. *Nurturance* refers to *warmth,* attention, and physical affection. Did your parents hold and rock you? Did they comfort and soothe you? Did they spend time with you? Do they hug and kiss you when you see them now?

Empathy refers to having someone who *understands* your world and *validates* your feelings. Did your parents understand you? Were they in sync with your feelings? Could you confide in them when you had problems? Were they interested in listening to what you had to say? Would they discuss their own feelings with you if you asked them to? Could they communicate with you?

Finally, *Protection* refers to providing *strength, direction,* and *guidance.* Did you have someone you could go to as a child when you needed advice, and who was a source of refuge and strength? Was there someone who looked out for you, who made you feel *safe?*

Jed experienced severe deprivation in all three areas. He was so damaged that, as an adult, he could neither give nor receive any of the three—nurturance, empathy, or protection. For Elizabeth and Dustin, the situation was more complex.

Dustin felt *protected* by his mother, and she was a good person to go to when he needed sensible, unemotional advice. And Dustin had an almost magical belief that his family's name and wealth could shelter him from all adversity. But Dustin's mother was neither nurturing nor empathic. However, he had a nurturing and empathic father who healed some of the damage done by his mother and acted to weaken his lifetrap.

Elizabeth seemingly got a lot of love and affection as a child. She generated a number of images of her mother hugging and kissing her. Here is a typical memory: "I am sitting on my mother's lap. We are at a party. I'm wearing a pretty dress. I feel pretty and special." As the superficiality of this image suggests, her mother's love was a false love. It happened only when company was there to witness it. At bottom, Elizabeth had deprivation of nurturance. But, like Dustin, she did feel protected as a child; in fact, she probably took *too* much advice and guidance from her mother. However, Elizabeth clearly experienced deprivation of empathy. For example, she generated this image in therapy:

THERAPIST: *What's happening?*
ELIZABETH *(eyes closed): I am at a birthday party with my mother. My mother is telling me to go over and kiss this other little girl. I tell my mother I don't like that little girl. But my mother wants me to like her, and she says to me, "That's nonsense, of course you like her."*
THERAPIST: *How do you feel?*
ELIZABETH: *Invisible.*

Her mother did not *mirror* Elizabeth's feelings back to her. Her mother neither knew nor seemed to care how she felt.

The first step toward understanding your childhood deprivation is to create images. Go to a quiet, private place and allow images of your childhood to float to the top of your mind. Experience the memories fully, with all the emotions that you felt at the time. Experience the images, then study them. Generate images for each parent. As with Dustin, one parent can offset the damage done by the other. And include all other close members of your family to get a full picture.

2. Monitor Your Feelings of Deprivation Now. Get in Touch with Your Needs for Nurturance, Empathy, and Guidance. Become more aware of your feelings of deprivation in your current life. Teach yourself to *notice* when your lifetrap is triggered. It might be a time that you feel slighted, lonely, or empty, or that no one understands how you feel. You might feel sad that your lover is unavailable, or cold and ungiving. You might feel angry that you always have to be the strong one, that you are always the one who takes care of your partner, and it is never the other way around. Any strong feeling of deprivation can serve as a cue that your lifetrap is triggered and that you should pay attention to what is going on.

It is important that you allow yourself to feel all the emotions that get triggered along with your lifetrap. Try not to block any feelings. Explore the whole spectrum of emotions, as fully as you can.

You can use imagery to connect even further with your feelings. When some event in your current life provokes strong feelings of deprivation, relive the experience again through imagery. Allow all your feelings to emerge. Get in touch with your needs for nurturance, empathy, and protection. Then connect the image to an image in the past when you were a child and felt the same way. If you repeatedly alternate between the present and the past in this manner, you will be able to deepen your awareness of the ways you reenact your childhood deprivation in your current relationships.

Dustin did this imagery exercise in a therapy session with us. He was describing an incident with Christine that had upset him greatly. They had already broken up and had run into each other at a party. We asked Dustin to get an image of Christine.

THERAPIST: *What do you see?*
DUSTIN: *I see Christine. She's there in the middle of the image, dressed in white—like she was in that magazine ad. She looks frozen and perfect. She's surrounded by glass.*
THERAPIST: *Where are you?*
DUSTIN: *I'm outside the glass. I'm trying to tell her something, but she can't hear me through the glass. I can't get her to look at me. I'm waving my arms and I'm yelling, but she can't hear me through the glass.*
THERAPIST: *Tell me what you're feeling.*
DUSTIN: *I'm alone.*

We then asked Dustin to get an image of when he felt this way before, as a child. The memory that came was of his mother: "I see her sitting on the couch reading, and I'm walking on the other side of the room very quietly because I know she'd be annoyed if I disturbed her while she was reading her book."

3. Review Your Past Relationships. Clarify the Patterns That Keep Repeating. List the Pitfalls to Avoid from Now On. Make a list of the most important relationships in your life. You may want to focus on romantic relationships, or you may want to focus on family or close friends. Think about what went wrong with each relationship. Was the person unable or unwilling to meet your needs? Did you drive him/her away with your incessant demands, which, when filled, never made a difference anyway? Did you grow bored with someone who was treating you well? Were you in fact getting more from the relationship than you acknowledged at the time?

It was in making this list that Dustin's pattern became glaringly obvious to him. He clearly saw that, with each woman that he had been attracted to, there were clues *from the beginning* that she was emotionally unavailable in some important way. Of course, in each case, he had ignored these early warning signs. It was painful for him to recognize in therapy that his most powerful love relationships had been doomed from the start.

The pattern that emerged from the list Elizabeth made was that she gave a lot to each person, but got little in return. And for Jed, it was that he had been dissatisfied with every woman, regardless of what she gave him. In his characteristic blaming way, he said, "It's a list of women who were one disappointment after another." What is the unifying principle of your list? What are the pitfalls for you to avoid?

4. Avoid Cold Partners Who Generate High Chemistry. This is that simple rule that is so hard to follow. *Do not get involved with depriving partners.* The rule is so hard to follow because these are *precisely* the partners who attract you the most. We often give patients this rule-of-thumb: If you meet someone for whom you feel a high degree of chemistry, rate how much chemistry on a 0 to 10 scale. If you rate the person a 9 or 10, then *think twice about becoming involved with this person.* Occasionally, such relationships work out, after a great deal of turmoil. But, more often, the strong chemistry you feel will be based on lifetraps that they trigger in you, rather than positive qualities that will make the relationship last.

We are not saying that you have to settle for spending the rest of your life with a partner who only generates a response of 0–5 in you. We feel that there has to be *some* chemistry for the relationship to work. But, if there is *only* romantic chemistry, it almost certainly will *not* work in the long run. There are plenty of 6's, 7's, and 8's out there. One of them might bring you the deep fulfillment of an intimate, loving relationship, perhaps for the first time in your life.

5. When You Find a Partner Who is Emotionally Generous, Give the Relationship a Chance to Work. Ask for What You Want. Share Your Vulnerability with Your Partner. When you get into a healthy relationship, give it a chance. Many times people with this lifetrap feel bored and dissatisfied in healthy relationships, and they want to walk away. Do not walk away so fast, even if the relationship seems unexciting. Maybe you just need to get used to the strange sensation of having your emotional needs met.

After the fiasco with Christine, Dustin became involved with a woman named Michelle, who was warm and caring. Dustin was *very* attracted to her at first, but this changed. As they got deeper into the relationship, the chemistry he felt for her faded. He began coming to sessions saying he was bored with Michelle, that he was not attracted to her anymore, and that maybe the relationship was a big mistake. However, we were still hopeful. Good things were happening between them at the same time. Dustin was allowing Michelle to care for him. Despite Dustin's feelings that he might want to end the relationship, we thought it was possible that it still might work out.

There were many good signs about Dustin's relationship with Michelle that kept us hopeful. First of all, he was *once* attracted to her. We do not believe that you can create chemistry when there was never any there. But, if there is at least a moderate degree of chemistry at the start, it is worth an attempt to recapture it if it fades. It is worth trying to address your problems in the relationship in the hope that you can get some of the chemistry back. It may be more a matter of allowing yourself to connect with the person, of your making yourself vulnerable and asking for what you want.

As we talked in our sessions, Dustin realized that most of the time, in fact, he was not really bored with Michelle but irritated. He was angry that she was not giving him what he needed. Of course, Dustin was not *telling* Michelle what he needed. This is a common pattern with Emotional Deprivation. You keep what you want a secret, then get angry when you do not get it. Keeping your needs secret is a way of surrendering to your lifetrap. You make sure that even though your partner is a warm person, your needs *still* will not get met. If you are with a loving partner, tell the person what you need. Allow your partner to take care of you, protect you, and understand you.

We realize that this can be frightening. It means making yourself *vulnerable* to your partner. You have become very invested in doing the opposite, keeping yourself invulnerable to protect yourself from disappointment. As a child you had a good reason for this. You have probably had good reason to keep up this wall in many relationships since childhood. But ask yourself, "This time, is it different? Can I trust this person?" If the answer is "yes," perhaps you should take a chance.

6. Stop Blaming Your Partner and Demanding That Your Needs Be Met.
As Dustin said: "My anger builds. I get to the point that *all* I feel is resentment, and all I'm doing is telling Michelle off." Do not harbor resentment. Express your needs directly to your partner. When you are angry, tell your partner how you feel. Do it calmly, without blame. Below the

anger is a feeling of hurt, of vulnerability. Share that with your partner. If you show only the angry, demanding surface, you will drive your partner away and make it less likely that he or she can meet your needs. Becoming angry and demanding is self-defeating. It rarely works. You almost *never* end up feeling better—things just get worse and worse.

Much of what we are saying comes down to communication. If you want a relationship to work, you have to be willing to communicate your thoughts and feelings to your partner. You have to share yourself. You have to connect.

THE OUTLOOK FOR CHANGE

It is not easy to change. As we have said before, it is in your hands. To a large extent, how much you change is a function of how hard you work and persist. Your Emotional Deprivation lifetrap will not fall away suddenly. It is a matter of slowly chipping away at the lifetrap—of countering the lifetrap each time it is triggered. You must throw your whole being against the lifetrap—your thoughts, feelings, and behavior.

It is sad that the more you were damaged as a child, the harder you will have to work. This is one more unfairness in the string of unfairnesses against you. If you were seriously damaged as a child, you may need professional help. The last chapter in this book tells you how to begin to find the help you need.

It took a long time for Jed to begin to change in therapy. He had a great deal of difficulty making himself *vulnerable* to the people in his life and to us. His stance had always been that he would rather lose everything than take that risk. The armor that protected him best in childhood as an adult had become his enemy, sealing him off from connection and intimacy.

Jed could easily access his anger about his past, but it was very difficult for him to feel the pain. He felt anger rather than pain, and anger was what he expressed. Jed never saw himself as responsible for *creating* relationships. He always focused on how the other person was disappointing *him,* how the other person was letting him down.

At first this was the theme of therapy. We discussed how we were letting him down, we were not helping him, how there must be other kinds of therapy that are better. But something kept him in therapy. At some level he knew that, if he left, he would just move on to another empty, short-lived relationship. He started to express the pain of his loneliness.

JED: *I was having a cup of coffee in a sidewalk cafe, and this couple walked by. The man had his arm around the woman and was looking at her. It's hard to describe, but all of a sudden I remembered a time my mother picked me up and hugged me, and I felt like crying.*

Jed began to share his vulnerability and pain with others. Recently, for the first time, he passed the six-month mark in a romantic relationship. He is engaged to marry a woman named Nicole.

Elizabeth left her husband Josh in the course of our therapy. Although we did not attempt to sway her decision, we supported her in this. We believe a person should leave a hopelessly unsatisfying relationship. Elizabeth tried very hard for a long time to improve the relationship with Josh, but to no avail. If she stayed, she would probably have remained frustrated and dissatisfied for the rest of her life. Josh did not love her enough to change.

Once divorced, Elizabeth immediately repeated the pattern twice more, with two other cold, ungiving men. "It's almost as though I had to live the pattern again in order to recognize it," she said. She still finds herself attracted to narcissistic men but now she resists them. Recently Elizabeth has become involved with Mark. It is the first time in a relationship with a man that she not only gives love, but gets love in return. As she says: "I let Mark take care of me. I guess it seems funny that I would have to learn how to *take,* but that's exactly what's happening. I'm learning how to take."

Dustin stayed with Michelle. They got married and have a child. He described his life in one of our last sessions:

DUSTIN: *I still have times when I feel discontent, like it isn't enough. But more of the time I feel connected. It's like I look up, and Michelle and the baby are there, and I suddenly remember that I'm not alone anymore.*

9

"I Don't Fit In"
The Social Exclusion Lifetrap

DEBRA: TWENTY-FIVE YEARS OLD. SHE FEELS ANXIOUS AND
INFERIOR IN SOCIAL SITUATIONS.

In our first session, Debra tells us that she is unhappy with her social life.
Ever since college ended, she has had trouble meeting people.

DEBRA: *I haven't had a date in seven months. I haven't really met anybody
who wants to date me.*
THERAPIST: *Where do you usually meet people?*
DEBRA: *That's part of the problem. I really hate going to a lot of the places
to meet people. I'm really shy. I can't talk to people. I don't expect them
to like me.*

It surprises us that Debra feels this way, because we find her very person-
able. Once again we are reminded that a person is not necessarily the same
with us as they are in social situations. People can be infinitely more shy
and awkward in a group.

As we explore further, it turns out that Debra avoids most social
situations: "They make me too anxious." When she is so anxious, she "can't
think of what to say" and says "stupid things." She considers herself
unattractive and does not expect men to be sexually attracted to her. (Once
again we are surprised, because Debra is quite pretty.)

With tears springing to her eyes, Debra tells us that sometimes she feels "like a failure in adult socializing."

ADAM: THIRTY-FIVE YEARS OLD. HE HAS PROBLEMS WITH LONELINESS.

From the beginning we sense a quality of apartness in Adam. He seems to hold himself back, to stay detached. He is less able than Debra to say what is wrong, but his problem, too, is loneliness.

Adam feels *different* from other people. "I don't seem to fit in anywhere," he tells me. He has a few close friends he sees occasionally, but less frequently through the years.

ADAM: *I am afraid I am going to end up entirely alone. I don't really fit in with the people at work, and my personal life is getting sparser and sparser. I just don't feel like I belong anywhere. I'm always on the outside, looking in.*

Adam is able to connect on an intimate level. In the past he has had intimate relationships with lovers and friends. However, he has stopped meeting people, and, aside from work, is not attached to any organization. Like Debra, he avoids most social and group situations.

THE SOCIAL EXCLUSION QUESTIONNAIRE

This questionnaire will measure your Social Exclusion lifetrap. Answer the questions using the following scale:

SCORING KEY

1 Completely untrue of me
2 Mostly untrue of me
3 Slightly more true than untrue of me
4 Moderately true of me
5 Mostly true of me
6 Describes me perfectly

If you have any 5's or 6's on this questionnaire, this lifetrap may still apply to you, even if your score is in the low range.

SCORE	DESCRIPTION
	1. I feel very self-conscious in social situations.
	2. I feel dull and boring at parties and other gatherings. I never know what to say.
	3. The people I want as friends are above me in some way (e.g., looks, popularity, wealth, status, education, career).
	4. I would rather avoid than attend most social functions.
	5. I feel unattractive—too fat, thin, tall, short, ugly, etc.
	6. I feel fundamentally different from other people.
	7. I do not belong anywhere. I am a loner.
	8. I always feel on the outside of groups.
	9. My family was different from the families around us.
	10. I feel disconnected from the community at large.
	YOUR TOTAL SOCIAL EXCLUSION SCORE (Add your scores together for questions 1–10)

INTERPRETING YOUR SOCIAL EXCLUSION SCORE

10–19 Very low. This lifetrap probably does *not* apply to you.
20–29 Fairly low. This lifetrap may only apply *occasionally*.
30–39 Moderate. This lifetrap is an *issue* in your life.
40–49 High. This is definitely an *important* lifetrap for you.
50–60 Very high. This is definitely one of your *core* lifetraps.

THE EXPERIENCE OF SOCIAL EXCLUSION

The primary feeling is loneliness. You feel excluded from the rest of the world because you feel either *undesirable* or *different*. These are the two types of social exclusion. Of course, they often come mixed together, and you may well have both.

Debra is the first type. She feels inferior in social situations, and consequently experiences a great deal of social *anxiety*.

DEBRA: *I was invited to a party last Saturday night, and I dreaded it all week. What is it with me? Other people look forward to a party, but all week I couldn't get it off my mind. I couldn't relax. I was always on the verge of tears.*

THERAPIST: *What were you imagining would happen?*

DEBRA: *Oh, you know, I would get there and be so nervous, and not know what to say. I would act like a jerk. And everyone would seem better than me, better looking or smarter or more successful, and I'd have nothing to offer.*

And you know, that's exactly what happened. The party was like a nightmare. I couldn't wait to leave, and when I got home, I cried and cried.

Debra feels excluded because of surface qualities. Something about the way she presents herself does not feel good enough. However, Debra does not have the Defectiveness lifetrap. Once she breaks through, meets people, and begins to get close, she is fine. She is comfortable in intimate relationships, and although she has no boyfriend she has many close friends. Debra's friendships offer her some relief from her feelings of inferiority and loneliness. Social Exclusion is about *outward,* or external, qualities; Defectiveness is about *inner,* or internal, qualities.

It may be that you have both Social Exclusion and Defectiveness, with Defectiveness the more core lifetrap. If this is so, things are more difficult for you. You may have no connections at all. Right down the line, you are alone. As difficult as Social Exclusion is, Social Exclusion plus Defectiveness is much worse.

In a circular way, a prime characteristic that makes Debra feel inferior is her anxiety itself.

DEBRA: *I know when I walk in that I'm going to be anxious. It's embarrassing to be so anxious. I'm uncomfortable, and I make other people feel uncomfortable. As soon as I get in, I know I'm going to screw up somehow. I'll say the wrong thing or do the wrong thing. I just want to crawl into a hole.*

Debra constantly compares herself to other people. This one is better looking, that one is smarter and more interesting. One large focus of her anxiety is her inability to carry on a conversation. She wants to respond appropriately—to speak freely, smile, laugh, and ask questions. But she is too inhibited to do so.

DEBRA: *It's so frustrating, because as soon as I know the person, I can carry on normal conversations. But when I meet a stranger, I can't do it. I freeze up.*
THERAPIST: *It's almost like stage fright.*

This kind of performance anxiety is a fundamental part of your experience. You fear being scrutinized, evaluated, judged negatively. You are obsessed with what other people think of you. Depending upon where your sensitivity lies—your looks, career, status, intelligence, or conversational ability—you fear being exposed as inadequate.

Debra's anxiety makes her socially awkward. Although she has good social skills when she is comfortable, in most social situations she is too nervous to use them. She loses her poise. She becomes shy and withdrawn. It is not that she feels particularly different from other people. It is that she feels socially inept.

In contrast, Adam's problems are not related to social skills. In fact, he can have very good social skills. Adam feels fundamentally different from other people. His primary feeling is one of detachment. He comes across as aloof rather than anxious. He has an aura of being "untouchable."

ADAM: *It's like I'm alone even when I'm in a crowd. In fact, I feel most alone when I'm in a crowd.*
THERAPIST: *Your loneliness becomes more glaring.*

Adam experiences his life as though he were walking through a crowd of strangers. There is no place where he belongs.

For most people this feeling of being different is painful. Although some see themselves as better, or feel good about being different, most see it as a source of unhappiness. Most of us want to fit in, and we feel pain, hurt, and loneliness when we do not.

Unlike Debra, who feels *rejected* in social situations, Adam feels a kind of nothingness, a disconnection. For him, social situations trigger a feeling of *isolation*.

THERAPIST: *So if you didn't really talk to people at the party, what did you do?*

ADAM: *I just went off into my own little world.*

Adam is not angry at the world for rejecting him. Rather, he just feels like an outsider. He is different. He does not fit in.

Social exclusion has many faces. You may be the person everyone teases or bullies. Or you may be the one who is an outsider—the loner or social outcast. You stay on the sidelines, not quite a member of any club or group. Or you may be someone whose lifetrap is largely invisible. It is hard to spot. You go through the motions of social interchange, but inside you feel alone.

Whatever your type, you are probably prone to a whole range of psychosomatic symptoms. Loneliness is often linked to heart and stomach problems, sleep problems, headaches, and depression.

These are some of the reasons you may have felt undesirable or different as a child:

THE ORIGINS OF SOCIAL EXCLUSION

1. You felt inferior to other children, because of some observable quality (e.g., looks, height, stuttering). You were teased, rejected, or humiliated by other children.
2. Your family was different from neighbors and people around you.
3. You felt different from other children, even within your own family.
4. You were passive as a child; you did what was expected, but you never developed strong interests or preferences of your own. Now you feel you have nothing to offer in a conversation.

One origin is growing up in a family that is different from other people. Your family may have been different in many ways—race, ethnic background, religion, social status, educational level, material possessions. Perhaps your family's daily habits were different, their manners and customs. Or perhaps there was a language barrier. Or there may have been mental illness in your family, such as alcoholism or schizophrenia. Your family may have moved from place to place, never staying long enough to form roots, such as with military "brats."

Another origin may have been something about *you* that may have set you apart, so that you felt different even from the children in your own family. Gifted children sometimes experience this. Their interests are different from other children their age. They enjoy reading or listening to music more than playing with other children. You also may have had interests that were atypical for your gender, such as a boy who likes to play with dolls, or a girl who likes rougher, boy games. Your sexual identity may have isolated you—gay men and women often have the Social Exclusion lifetrap. Your personality may have been different—shy, emotional, introspective, intellectual, or inhibited. Or you may have developed faster or slower than other children, physically, sexually, or in your level of independence, intelligence, or social skills.

Something about you may have caused you to feel inferior to other children. You may have been teased or humiliated. Patients have told us many reasons they became the targets of such attacks:

SOURCES OF CHILDHOOD AND ADOLESCENT UNDESIRABILITY

Physical
> Fat, thin, short, tall, weak, ugly, acne, physical handicap, small breasts, big breasts, late puberty, poor at sports, uncoordinated, not sexy.

Mental
> Slow at school, learning disabilities, bookworm, stuttering, emotional problems.

Social
> Awkward, socially inappropriate, immature, unable to carry on conversations, weird, dull, uncool.

As a result of appearing different or undesirable, other children excluded you from their groups. They would not play with you. They teased and humiliated you. You withdrew into the background to avoid being teased. Whenever you went into a social situation, you felt self-conscious. You stopped trying to make friends in order to avoid rejection. You may have associated with other children who were different, but longed to be part of the in-group. You became increasingly lonely and isolated. You developed solitary interests, such as reading or computer games. You may have developed expertise in non-social arenas to compensate for your feelings of inferiority.

Any and all of these things may have happened to you. Most of them happened to Debra.

DEBRA: *I was fat as a child. I was disgusting. In the playground other kids made fun of me. They would chase me and try to get me to fall down. When I got older, none of the boys wanted to go out with me. It wasn't till I lost weight before college that I had my first date.*

Debra's social exclusion involved a lot of shame. Her shame about her weight kept her from wanting to be near other children. She felt that as soon as they saw that shameful part of her, they would exclude her.

To compensate for her lack of social success, Debra excelled at school. In fact, she developed Unrelenting Standards in regard to her school performance. It is fairly common for children who feel socially undesirable to develop Unrelenting Standards as a compensation. Part of Debra's problem is that she has such high standards for how she must come across in a social situation—how poised, how intelligent, how attractive—that she feels that anything less is going to be unacceptable to other people. She anticipates criticism. This is one reason she feels so anxious.

As we noted above, you may have developed Social Exclusion as part of a more core Defectiveness lifetrap. You had such a global sense of being unlovable in your own family that it naturally transferred to your social life. You were uncomfortable in intimate situations and social situations. Now, whenever you interact with another person, you expect your personal unacceptability to become an issue, and you either feel anxious or avoid the situation. You do not expect to be loved or valued. Your lifetrap is part of a more fundamental sense of being defective.

Adam grew up in an alcoholic household. Both parents drank. He was the oldest son, and took over management of the house. By the age of twelve he was effectively functioning as both father and mother to his four younger brothers and sisters.

ADAM: *My home life made my life at school seem unreal. Other kids would be worrying about what to wear to a party, or making some team, or who to ask to the prom, and I'd be worrying about paying the monthly bills and keeping us off the street.*

Although Adam acted normal at school, he felt far from normal inside—"I felt like another species of life entirely." He never felt he could bring friends to his house, and became very anxious whenever a friend had contact with either of his parents. He tried to keep his school and home lives separate. His family was like a secret he kept from the other children.

Throughout Adam's childhood, the financial status of the family progressively declined. This made matters worse for Adam. Not only did they move a lot, but they also lived in neighborhoods where they felt they did not fit in.

ADAM: *My parents always considered us above everyone around us. They acted as though we were really different—as though we still belonged in a fancy house in a fancy neighborhood. In fact they would make it seem like our neighbors were kind of bad to be around, a bad influence, so I was encouraged to be kind of different and to stay away from the other kids.*

Adam's parents made him reluctant to get involved with the people around them.

Sometimes overly critical parents can foster social exclusion. We had one patient whose parents constantly criticized him for social imperfections—the way he looked, the way he talked, the way he carried himself. They led him to feel he was socially inadequate. He became inhibited in social situations. He was afraid of being criticized, and therefore avoided connecting with other people.

Another origin of Social Exclusion is related to the Dependence and Subjugation lifetraps. An important aspect of learning to socialize is developing a sense of ourselves as active and self-directed: we are encouraged by our parents to develop our own unique identity, interests, and preferences. We have a unique *personality*. This personality provides us with the energy and ideas to carry on conversations with other people.

Some children are either passive by nature or their parents discourage the development of their children's individuality. When your uniqueness is squashed, you do what is expected by other people. You take their lead and become a conventional follower. But you fail to develop ideas, interests, or preferences of your own. When you are in a conversation, you then feel that you have nothing to say. Your passivity makes you feel as if you have nothing of your own to offer other people. Carrying on conversations becomes a burden. You are very comfortable listening, but you cannot initiate a topic. You cannot contribute your own opinions. You do not have suggestions about what to do or where to go. After a while, you may decide to avoid socializing altogether rather than be with others and have nothing to contribute. This pattern, like the other origins we have already discussed, leads you to feel socially anxious and isolated.

Almost everyone has a certain degree of the Social Exclusion lifetrap. We have a certain part of ourselves that is insecure, unsure of being accepted. Who has not experienced *some* social rejection? It is a question of how pervasive it was, and how traumatic. Similarly, the earlier the social exclusion started, the more powerful the lifetrap.

Many people develop the lifetrap during the adolescent years. Adolescence is the time when peer pressure is at its height. It is easy *not* to fit into a peer group. Many teenagers feel different, isolated, alienated. In fact, it is so common, it is almost normal. However, most of us come out of this alienation when we reach college and thereafter. We find a relationship, or a group of friends who are more like us, or we just become less concerned about being part of the most popular group.

But, for some people, the sense of Social Exclusion continues through the rest of their lives. These are usually the people whose lifetrap originated earlier, in childhood. As far back as the person remembers, there was always a sense of being excluded by peers.

LIFETRAPS IN WORK AND LOVE

These are the ways you maintain your Social Exclusion lifetrap.

SOCIAL EXCLUSION LIFETRAPS

1. You feel different or inferior to the people around you. You exaggerate differences and minimize similarities. You feel lonely, even when you are with people.
2. At work you are on the periphery. You keep to yourself. You do not get promoted or included in projects because you do not fit in.
3. You are nervous and self-conscious around groups of people. You cannot just relax and be yourself. You worry about doing or saying the wrong thing. You try to plan what to say next.

> You are very uncomfortable talking to strangers. You feel you have nothing unique to offer other people.
>
> 4. Socially, you avoid joining groups or being part of the community. You only spend time with your immediate family or with one or two close friends.
> 5. You feel embarrassed if people meet your family or know a lot about them. You keep secrets about your family from other people.
> 6. You pretend to be like other people just to fit in. You do not let most people see the unconventional parts of yourself. You have a secret life or feelings that you believe would lead other people to humiliate you or reject you.
> 7. You put a lot of emphasis on overcoming your own family's deficiencies: to gain status, have material possessions, sound highly educated, obscure ethnic differences, etc.
> 8. You have never accepted certain parts of your nature because you believe other people would think less of you for them (e.g., you are shy, intellectual, emotional, too feminine, weak, dependent).
> 9. You are very self-conscious about your physical appearance. You *feel* less attractive than other people say you are. You may work inordinately hard to be physically attractive, and are especially sensitive to your physical flaws (e.g., weight, physique, figure, height, complexion, features).
> 10. You avoid situations where you might seem dumb, slow, or awkward (e.g., going to college, public speaking).
> 11. You compare yourself a lot to other people who have the hallmarks of popularity that you lack (e.g., looks, money, athletic ability, success, clothing).
> 12. You put too much emphasis on *compensating* for what you feel are your social inadequacies: trying to prove your popularity or social skills, win people over, be part of the right social group, have success in your career, or raise children who are popular.

You may feel a lot of romantic chemistry with many types of people. You may be drawn to people who are the *opposite* of you—who have the outward signs of belonging that you lack. Depending on what your particular Social Exclusion issues are, you may pursue partners who are good-looking, high status, popular or part of the in-group, comfortable in social situations, or normal and conventional. In this way, you can feel as though you belong.

There are advantages and disadvantages to choosing a sociable partner. It might act as a force that keeps you socializing. Eventually you might learn to feel more comfortable and connected. On the other hand, there is a danger that you might become excessively dependent on such a partner to smooth the way for you in social situations. You may even become more shy than before, and rely totally on your partner to carry on conversations and to conduct social encounters. In this way selecting such a partner can reinforce your view of yourself as socially incompetent.

You might also feel attracted to other outsiders. You might feel a special bond with other socially excluded people. You can bolster one another in feeling different.

ADAM: *My girlfriend Susan was an outcast also. She was this arty type who always wore black and painted these weird pictures. When we were together, we made fun of everyone else. We felt sorry for everyone else for being so pathetically and boringly normal.*

This kind of partner can comfort you about feeling different and make you value your uniqueness more. Instead of feeling *alone* and different, you can feel *together* and different—that you are both better than people who are conventional.

People who feel different often band together in groups: the arty types, the nerds, the punks, the greasers. In unity there is strength. A group of outcasts can often elevate their status and feel quite superior and special. Cult groups display this phenomenon. The members consider themselves as having a secret, which only they possess. This fact puts them above outsiders. *They* are now the insiders, and the rest of the world are the ones left out.

However, some people with this lifetrap do not even feel part of a significant subculture. You may be alienated from all groups.

ADAM: *I don't fit in anywhere. I'm athletic, but I'm not a jock. But I'm not an intellectual either. I'm not a bohemian, but I'm not a yuppie. I'm torn between all these worlds, and I don't really identify with any of them.*

Even if you overcome your Social Exclusion in adulthood, you may at times still *feel* undesirable or different. The old feelings persist. You magnify the differences between yourself and others, making it hard for you to connect. These differences set up a barrier. As soon as you start to get close, you become highly sensitive to areas of dissimilarity.

The lifetrap can have a profound effect on your choice of career. You are probably drawn to activities that do not involve much meaningful social interplay. In fact, becoming good at some solitary activity that can be later turned into a career is often a side-benefit of the lifetrap. You might be an artist. You might be a scientist or a freelance writer. You might be a reporter. You might choose a job that involves a lot of travel, or allows you to work at home. Computers is a common field for people with this lifetrap. You might even start your own company, so that you can have relationships on your own terms. You do not have to worry about other people accepting you. But the last thing you are likely to choose is a job in which your upward mobility depends on having to make contacts and connections with other people. You are not the corporate type who works your way up the ladder through political expertise.

If you *do* work within a corporation or other organization, you probably feel inferior, or that you do not fit in. You may be excellent at your work, but your lifetrap holds you back.

DEBRA: *I have the kind of work where I'm supposed to be entertaining clients, taking them out to dinner and for cocktails, but I avoid it. It's really hurting me. I don't keep my clients.*

You might even present yourself as odd, eccentric, or aloof.

Escape is your primary means for coping with your lifetrap. It is the rock upon which your Social Exclusion is built. Your avoidance of social situations ensures that nothing can change for you. Your skills cannot improve. Your beliefs cannot be disconfirmed. You are more comfortable, but you are stuck. Changing requires a basic shift from a stance of Escape to one of confrontation and mastery. The people who overcome social exclusion are the ones who make this shift.

On the following page are the steps to overcoming social exclusion.

CHANGING SOCIAL EXCLUSION

1. Understand your childhood social exclusion. Feel the isolated or inferior child inside of you.
2. List everyday social situations in which you feel anxious or uncomfortable.
3. List group situations that you *avoid.*
4. List ways that you *Counterattack,* or *overcompensate,* for feeling different or inferior.
5. Drawing on steps 1–4, above, list the qualities in yourself that make you feel alienated, vulnerable, or inferior.
6. If you are convinced that a flaw is *real,* write down steps you could take to *overcome* it. Follow through gradually with your plans of change.
7. Reevaluate the importance of flaws that you cannot change.
8. Make a flashcard for each flaw.
9. Make a hierarchy of social and work groups you have been avoiding. Gradually move up the hierarchy.
10. When you are in groups, make a concerted effort to initiate conversations.
11. Be yourself in groups.
12. Stop trying so hard to *compensate* for your perceived areas of undesirability.

1. Understand Your Childhood Social Exclusion. Feel the Isolated or Inferior Child Inside of You. The first thing to do is to remember. Let the memories come of yourself as a child, feeling different or excluded by other children. When you have some time alone, darken the room and sit back in a comfortable place. Remember not to force the images. Just close your eyes and let them come. Remember when you felt different or inferior. You can start with an image of a *current* situation that triggers feelings of Social Exclusion.

Often the memories that come are of being laughed at, humiliated, teased, or bullied, or of being alone, apart from the others, not fitting in. Here is an illustration of Debra's imagery. In one session she was telling us about another miserable party. We asked her to close her eyes and get an image of it.

DEBRA: *I'm standing next to this guy, who's talking to me. I'm so relieved that someone is talking to me, that I don't have to stand there alone, but I'm so nervous I can't talk to the guy. I'm talking really fast, and I know my eyes look really anxious. I just feel really pressured. He starts to look uncomfortable, and then he finishes the conversation and walks away.*

I left right after that. I haven't gone to a party since.

THERAPIST: *Stay with it, and let an image come of when you felt the same way as a child.*

DEBRA: *Okay. I'm at my friend Gina's house. There are a bunch of kids there. We're picking sides for a game of kickball, and no one is picking me. I'm the last kid to be picked, and, when the team gets me, they all start to groan.*

Adam's images focused more on being on the outside of groups. One session he told us about a camping trip he took as a child. They swam in a waterfall.

ADAM: *There were about five of us swimming right near the falls. At one point I dove into the falls and stood there, letting them fall right on top of me. I could see the other kids sort of blurry, and I could hear them muffled through the roar of the falls. All of a sudden I felt so alone. I had the thought that it was always like this, with everyone coming at me from far away. And I'm watching, like through a window. Everyone else is out there playing and being normal with each other, and I'm outside looking in.*

Memories of social exclusion are painful. We want you to comfort that excluded child. Imagine yourself as an adult, comforting the child you were. Social exclusion is a cold, lonely feeling. Do not leave your inner child in that cold place. Before you leave the image, bring yourself in as an adult, and give support to your inner child.

ADAM: *I bring myself in, and I dive into the falls where my childhood self is standing, and I tell him that he is not alone anymore. I am here, and I will help him connect with other people.*

2. List Everyday Social Situations in Which You Feel Anxious or Uncomfortable. Write down the situations that make you uncomfortable, but which you do not avoid. Your list might include parties, meetings, eating in public, talking in front of a group, dating, talking to people in authority, being assertive, or having a conversation. Here is Debra's list.

SOCIAL SITUATIONS THAT MAKE ME ANXIOUS BUT THAT I DO NOT ESCAPE FROM

1. Greeting my doorman.
2. Calling prospective clients.
3. Lunch at the cafeteria at work.
4. The coffee-hour at church.
5. Meetings with coworkers.
6. Talking to people I don't know well.
7. Getting to know the people in my apartment building.

Now make two more columns on the chart. In the second column, for each situation, write down the ways you feel undesirable, different, or inferior. For example, for parties, Debra wrote, "not good-looking, bad conversationalist, look anxious." For meetings at work, she wrote, "say stupid things when put on the spot, can't relax and chat before and after, don't have the professional look of the others."

Finally, in the last column, write down your worst-case scenario of what could go wrong. Let yourself get a vivid image. What is the catastrophe you fear? Will people laugh at you, or reject you? Will you be exposed as inferior? Or will you fail to fit in, again?

3. List Social Situations That You Avoid. Here list the situations that you *avoid.* These are the activities that you would rather, and usually do, avoid. Here is Debra's list.

SOCIAL SITUATIONS I AVOID

1. Most parties.
2. Taking clients out to dinner.
3. Dates.
4. Asking my boss for favors.
5. Inviting people I don't know well to get together with me.
6. Going out after work with coworkers.
7. Giving presentations at work.

When you have completed your list, make two more columns and go through the same steps as in 3, for each situation. In the second column, write down the ways you feel different or inferior. In the last column, write your worst-case scenario.

4. List Ways That You Overcompensate for Feeling Different or Inferior. These are the ways you try to prove that the *opposite* of the lifetrap is true. This is a form of Counterattack. You try to combat the lifetrap by doing everything possible to show that you are *not* different. You are *not* undesirable. Here is Adam's list:

WAYS I OVERCOMPENSATE FOR FEELING DIFFERENT

1. I pretend to be like whoever I'm with, just to fit in. I keep my thoughts to myself.
2. I don't let people see the strange parts of me (liking foreign films, my short stories, my family).
3. When I have a girlfriend, I don't let my friends or family spend time with her. I try to keep my worlds separate.
4. I dress more conservatively than I would like to.
5. I try to impress people with how popular I am.
6. I try to have friends who are popular.

Similarly, you might overcompensate for feelings of inferiority by becoming inordinately focused on your appearance, or becoming successful in your career, or struggling to be in, or hiding your flaws.

Overcompensations like these are fragile. They easily collapse. We want you to build a more solid base. We want you to become open to experiencing social situations anew. You will find they can be quite different from the nightmare experiences of your childhood. Adults are generally more accepting of differences than children and adolescents. They are much less likely to humiliate or reject you.

5. Drawing on Steps 1–4, Above, List the Qualities in Yourself That Make You Feel Alienated, Vulnerable, or Inferior. Take one sheet of paper for each quality. Make up a title for each sheet (e.g., "The Fat Child," "The Dumb Child"). Then, on each sheet do the following:

1. Define the quality in specific terms (e.g., fat = over 200 pounds).
2. List all the evidence in your *adult* life that *substantiates* your feeling that this is a real flaw.
3. List any evidence that *refutes* your feeling.
4. Ask friends and family for their opinions about how you fare on each quality.
5. Write a paragraph summarizing the *objective* evidence. How valid is your self-criticism?

The qualities Margaret listed included "not good-looking," "can't carry on an interesting conversation at parties," "not successful enough," "anxious at social occasions," "I get flippant and say stupid things," and "I make a terrible first impression." Here is the sheet she drew up for "I make a terrible first impression."

"I MAKE A TERRIBLE FIRST IMPRESSION"

1. Definition
> People don't like me when they first meet me.

2. Evidence in My Adult Life That This is a Real Flaw
> I never meet guys at parties. People who don't know me lose interest in talking to me fast at parties. I don't do well at job interviews. People have made fun of the first impression I made on them (for example, Ellen, Bill). I have a lot of trouble meeting new people. People in my apartment building don't seem to like me. They are much friendlier to other people.

3. Evidence from My Adult Life That Refutes the Feeling
> I have made *some* new friends since I've been an adult. In fact I have a lot of good friends. When I was in college, the mothers of my boyfriends seemed to like me.

4. Ask My Friends and Family
> I asked my sister, mother, and two friends. All of them pretty much agreed except my mother. My sister said that I come off as uptight at first. My friends said pretty much the same thing.

5. Summary of the Objective Evidence
   Although there is evidence that I can sometimes make a good
   first impression, the majority of the evidence is that this is a real
   flaw.

Doing this for her other qualities, Margaret admitted that she was probably
good-looking and successful enough, but that the other flaws were real.
   The qualities Adam listed included:

WAYS I AM DIFFERENT FROM MOST PEOPLE

1. I don't talk about the same things other people talk about.
2. I'm strange.
3. People don't want to get to know me.
4. I'm too serious. I can't seem to lighten up.
5. I dress differently from other people.
6. I have unusual interests that other people don't seem to have.
7. I act so aloof that it puts people off.

After doing his sheets, he decided that "I don't talk about the same things
that other people talk about," "I'm too serious. I can't seem to lighten up,"
and "I act so aloof that it puts people off," were real flaws.
   One thing became clear as we evaluated whether Adam's flaws were
real or imagined. This was that Adam *exaggerated* differences between
himself and other people. This was one important way he reinforced his
lifetrap. He constantly maximized differences and minimized similarities.

THERAPIST: *Why didn't you feel you could talk to that new manager at
   work?*
ADAM: *I just felt like we had nothing in common.*
THERAPIST: *But you are in the same field. That is something already.*
ADAM: *But we're different in so many other important ways.*
THERAPIST: *Like what?*
ADAM: *Oh, he dresses different, and drives an expensive car.*
THERAPIST: *But didn't you hear that he's a foreign film buff too?*
ADAM: *Yeah. But that car of his really put me off. I just figured he's a really
   materialistic person. And I'm not like that.*

The very way he saw the world—in terms of differences rather than similarities—reinforced Adam's lifetrap.

6. If You Are Convinced That a Flaw or Difference Is Real, *Write Down Steps You Could Take to* Overcome *It. Follow Through Gradually with Your Plan of Change.* You might write things like working to improve your social skills, becoming warmer and more friendly to people, losing or gaining weight, taking a class in public speaking, going back to school, learning to look your best, or any number of other self-improvement strategies. Gradually do these things. Sometimes when we have a flaw, we shrink from overcoming it. We feel so ashamed that we do not even want to think about it. Resist falling into this trap. Attack your deficiencies head-on.

Debra developed a plan to deal with her "terrible first impression." First, she tried to get direct feedback about what aspects of her behavior were problematic. She did this by observing herself when meeting people, asking friends and family, and doing role-plays of first meetings with us in sessions.

THERAPIST: *So what can we conclude from all this?*

DEBRA: *I guess I have two main problems with making a good first impression. The first is that, because I'm so anxious, I make flippant comments that the other person doesn't know are meant as jokes. And the second is that, when people ask me about myself, I don't know what to say.*

Once Debra identified her tendency to be flippant, it was fairly easy for her to stop doing it. She stopped herself from making jokes, at least until she knew the person a little better. In terms of the second problem, knowing what to say when asked about herself, we practiced this in sessions. We *prepared* Debra to talk about herself in various areas—her work, her family, her interests. Many social skills can be learned through preparation. Planning in advance how to handle various scenarios will reduce your anxiety.

Imagery can also play a large role in your preparation. Instead of spending time before an event imagining catastrophic situations and making yourself even more afraid—spend time imagining yourself performing well. Imagine yourself performing exactly as you wish. Have dress rehearsals of success rather than failure.

DEBRA: *Before I went to the company Christmas party, I lay down and relaxed myself, and I imagined the party going very well. I pictured myself walking in and looking around, smiling, and picking one person to go up to and talk to. I imagined walking up and saying, "hi," and feeling composed. I imagined starting to talk, the things I would say.*

7. Reevaluate the Importance of Flaws That You Cannot Change. Alcoholics Anonymous has a saying: "God grant me the serenity to accept the things I cannot change, courage to change the things I can, and wisdom to know the difference." There are some things you can change about yourself, and some things you cannot. Beyond self-improvement lies acceptance of yourself.

You may have flaws that you can never change, or never change enough. You will always be too short or tall, you may always be too fat, you may never be successful enough, or tell great stories at parties. However, people with this lifetrap almost always *exaggerate* the importance of their flaws. Consider this. How significant really are your flaws relative to your other good qualities?

List your good qualities and your flaws. Do the same for people you know. Are you really that much worse, or different, overall? Try to put your flaws *in perspective*. Debra may be awkward in social situations, but she is also an intelligent, sensitive, and sweet human being. The same for Adam. He is a funny, interesting person whose differences often make him quite charismatic. Our experience of patients with this lifetrap is overwhelmingly that their flaws pale against the backdrop of the person as a whole.

You probably believe that other adults regard your flaws in the same light as the children who made fun of you in childhood. But you are wrong. Adults are usually much more tolerant of differences than children. Adults appreciate differences more. It is only children—or immature adults—who feel that pressure to be exactly the same.

DEBRA: *When I'm at a party I feel the same as back on the playground at school. I feel like it's recess, and everybody's making fun of me. I half expect people to start ganging up on me and start chanting songs about how fat I am.*

Finally, you may have flaws that you do not *want* to change. Some of your so-called flaws may be valued parts of yourself. This is how Adam finally felt about the way he dressed. He enjoyed buying clothes and creating outfits. He was not about to give it up. The way he dressed was distinctive but not outrageous. Debra had a similar issue about makeup. She was not willing to wear it, even if it would enhance her chances of meeting a man.

How much you are willing to change yourself is ultimately your decision. But you must be aware of the consequences of what you do. If fitting in is your goal, then *flaunting* your uniqueness is not going to help you reach it. One of the most challenging tasks in life is finding a balance between fitting in or being normal, and expressing our unique, individual natures. If we go too far toward conformity, we lose a sense of who we really are; if we go to the extreme of individual expression and uniqueness, we cannot fit in with the rest of the community.

8. Make a Flashcard for Each Flaw. Make flashcards to carry around with you. Read them each time your lifetrap is triggered. In this way you can chip away at the lifetrap.

When you are writing a flashcard, emphasize ways you are exaggerating the flaw. Mention your good qualities. Include ways you can improve.

We will give you some examples. Here is the card Debra wrote for the flaw, "I am anxious at social occasions."

SOCIAL EXCLUSION FLASHCARD #1

I know that right now I feel anxious, as if everyone is looking at me. I feel like I can't talk to anyone. But it is just my lifetrap being triggered. If I look around, I will see that people are not looking at me. And even if someone is, it is probably a friendly look. If I start talking to people, in a little while my anxiety will grow less. People can't really tell I'm anxious. Besides, other people are anxious too. Everyone is a little anxious in social situations. I can start by relaxing my body, looking around the room, and finding one person to talk to.

Here is the card Adam wrote for the flaw, "I act so aloof that it puts people off."

SOCIAL EXCLUSION FLASHCARD #2

I'm starting to feel different from the people I'm with. I'm feeling like an outsider, alone in the crowd. I am holding myself back, becoming aloof. But this is my lifetrap kicking in. In fact I'm exaggerating how different I am. If I become friendlier, I will find that we have things in common. I just have to give myself a chance to connect.

A flashcard can help break the spell of the lifetrap, and get you back on the right track.

9. Make a Hierarchy of Social and Work Groups You Have Been Escaping. Gradually Move Up the Hierarchy. This is the most crucial step. Stop escaping! Of all the factors that maintain your lifetrap, avoidance is the most important. As long as you keep running away, your lifetrap cannot change.

By the time we reach adulthood, the likelihood of people rejecting us is lower than it was in childhood. As most people get older, they become more tolerant and accepting. But you do not see this. You are frozen in childhood, unaware that the world has changed around you. You ascribe the mentality of a child to the adults around you. So you avoid situations where you might get exactly the positive feedback that you need. You never find out that you might actually be accepted.

We realize this step will be difficult for you. We will make it as easy as we can. The reason you try to escape is that you experience such high anxiety in social situations. You will do almost anything to avoid experiencing this anxiety. And what is more, with the Social Exclusion lifetrap, it is *possible* to live your life avoiding almost all social situations. You can still get by, even though your life lacks an important dimension of gratification.

Take the list you made in step 3, of group situations that you avoid. Rate how difficult it would be to complete each item, using the following scale. (Use any number from 0 to 8.)

SCALE OF DIFFICULTY

0 Very Easy
2 Mildly Difficult
4 Moderately Difficult
6 Very Difficult
8 Feels Almost Impossible

For example, Debra rated the items on her list as shown on the following page.

SOCIAL SITUATIONS I AVOID	DIFFICULTY RATING
1. Most parties.	8
2. Taking clients out to dinner.	5
3. Dates.	6
4. Asking my boss for favors.	4
5. Inviting people I don't know well to get together with me.	7
6. Going out after work with coworkers.	3
7. Giving presentations at work.	8

Start with the *least* difficult item. (Make sure you have included some relatively easy items—some 1's, 2's, and 3's.) Do this item over and over until you have achieved a sense of mastery over that level of difficulty. Debra's easiest item was "going out after work with coworkers." She did this several times a month for five months before she moved up to her next hierarchy item.

Debra made up other items at level 3 difficulty, and did those too. She chatted with people she knew in passing, such as doormen and store clerks. She struck up conversations with men she found moderately attractive. By the time she got to level 4, she felt ready. We want you to do the same. At each level of difficulty, make up other items and do those. And plan carefully how you will complete each item. Think everything through in advance. Work out solutions to many possible eventualities. Use positive imagery to practice performing well.

Gradually move up your hierarchy. Your successes will sustain you as you go. The hardest part is getting started. Take a chance and start growing socially again. You might even find that you enjoy it.

10. When You Are in Groups, Make a Concerted Effort to Initiate Conversations. When you attend a social event, set yourself a goal of starting a certain number of conversations to initiate, then try to meet your target. Orient yourself toward the outside world. People with this lifetrap spend too much social time staying in their own head. They do not connect. Even though they have entered the social situation, they are still escaping real contact. They are there, yet not really there. You have to overcome this more subtle form of Escape as well.

When Debra and Adam practiced their hierarchy items, they would agree to talk to a specific number of people. Going to a party, they would say something like, "I'll talk to at least two people that I don't know." This is what we want you to do. You will be surprised to find out that setting a specific goal will often *reduce* your anxiety rather than increase it. Once the anticipatory anxiety has passed, you will probably find that walking up and talking to people greatly decreases your anxiety. This is how it usually works with avoidance. You predict that you will be much more anxious than you actually are.

DEBRA: *It really wasn't bad at all. I talked to two people during the coffee break, and it wasn't that bad. And next time I go, it will be much better, because now I have some people I can talk to.*

Try to make friends with *one* person in the group, then expand to other group members gradually. This is a strategy which we have found helpful. Focusing on the group as a whole is too overwhelming. You feel the group's eyes on you. Break the group down into manageable units. Conquer it one or two people at a time.

11. Be Yourself in Groups. There is another more subtle form of avoidance. This is to hide parts of yourself. You talk to people, but you are secretive or careful to avoid certain topics, so that your defect or difference will not be exposed. Perhaps it is that you are gay, or unsuccessful, or from a certain family background. Or maybe it is a physical characteristic, or some aspect of your status—such as education or income.

You pay too high a price for keeping these secrets. Meeting people becomes fraught with tension and loneliness. As one of our patients once said, "Having a secret is isolating." Try, as much as possible, *not* to hide your flaws or perceived differences. We are not saying to be *outrageously* different. We are simply saying to be yourself. Let people know that you are gay or from a certain family background. Stop hiding it. As you get to know people better, share some of your vulnerabilities and insecurities. It is the only way for you to find out that you are acceptable nevertheless.

12. Stop Trying So Hard to Overcompensate for Your Perceived Areas of Undesirability. Allow yourself to see that *most* people will accept you for who you are—not for trying to impress them with your accomplishments or possessions. Resist that pressure. You will find that it is a relief to give up this pressure.

ADAM: *Having to prove all the time that I was a popular guy was a burden. I was always lying about who I was. I really don't want to have to do it anymore.*

Debra had a similar issue about her lack of success. Because she was ashamed of her work situation, she constantly tried to prove to people how smart she was. If the subject of work came up at all, her conversation would grow strained and artificial.

DEBRA: *I would almost start bragging really. No matter what we were talking about, I'd manage to drop in some comment about how I won an award in college or something. Maybe start talking about some complicated theory. Or all of a sudden become really* condescending. *It would sound really hollow. I mean the other person would know exactly how I really felt.*

Not only is counterattacking like this a burden, but your behavior is transparent as well. Other people see right through you. They know you feel ashamed inside. The showing off is false. You know it, and they know it too. Replace the person that you pretend to be with the person you really are. People will like you better, and you will like yourself better as well.

We are not saying that you should start talking yourself down. Rather, we are saying to calm down, to stop trying so hard to impress people.

SOME FINAL WORDS

The journey out of Social Exclusion is a journey from loneliness to connection. Try to see it in this positive light. If you are willing to apply these change strategies, you will find that there are many rewards. Debra is now dating, enjoying herself at parties, going out several nights a week. She comes to her sessions happy. Adam has made some new close friends with whom he shares the truth about himself. The ultimate reward is a satisfying social life. You can feel part of a group or the community. This is a vital part of life, of which you are now deprived. Why miss out in this way?

10

"I Can't Make It on My Own"
The Dependence Lifetrap

MARGARET: TWENTY-EIGHT YEARS OLD, FEELS TRAPPED IN
HER MARRIAGE TO AN ABUSIVE HUSBAND.

When Margaret first walks into our office there is a frightened look in her eyes. It raises a protective impulse in us and we move to take care of her. When we tell her she seems frightened, she tells us that she does not even like to think about her problems, let alone talk about them.

Margaret feels trapped in a relationship that she is too afraid to leave. She is afraid to be alone. Anthony, her husband, is verbally abusive. He has been unemployed for two years and blames her. In fact, he blames her for all his problems. Margaret is agoraphobic: she has panic attacks and avoids many situations for fear that she will have an attack—trains, restaurants, grocery stores, shopping malls, crowds, movie theaters. On some days she is so anxious that she is afraid to leave her home. She has come to therapy because coping with her marriage and her phobias has become too much for her.

As you might imagine, aside from making day-to-day functioning difficult, Margaret's agoraphobia sharply decreases her pleasure from her leisure time. Activities that other people find enjoyable, she experiences as onerous tasks.

MARGARET: *Anthony is mad at me. He wants me to meet him at the restaurant tomorrow night. He doesn't want to have to come home first and get me. But I just can't do it. I can't get on the train.*
THERAPIST: *What are you afraid of?*
MARGARET: *What if something happens to me and there is no one to take care of me?*
THERAPIST: *What might happen to you?*
MARGARET: *What might happen to me? My panic might get so bad that I'd collapse on the street.*

When Margaret is home, if Anthony has to leave for some reason, she, too, finds herself rushing out of the house. Or she starts to make telephone calls: "My telephone is my lifeline to the world." Although Anthony complains angrily about the cost to him of baby-sitting her, whenever she strikes out on her own, he seems to discourage her. In a strange way, Margaret feels he *wants* to keep her dependent.

WILLIAM: THIRTY-FOUR YEARS OLD, IS STILL DEPENDENT ON HIS PARENTS TO TAKE CARE OF HIM.

William, too, has a frightened look when he walks into our office. He seems to be a shy, quiet man. He has an air of timidity. And he also moves us to take care of him, to try to make him comfortable. We find we are *gentle* with him.

William is still living with his parents. He had left home for an extended period of time only once, when he went to college. It lasted one year: after that, he transferred to a small school close enough that he could live at home and commute. William became an accountant like his father, and he works in his father's firm. He is extremely anxious about his work. He has been dating a woman named Carol for a long time, but somehow finds it hard to make a commitment. He cannot decide if she is the right person for him.

WILLIAM: *I keep thinking, "What if I'm making a mistake, what if she's not the one? What if there's someone better? How do I know if she's the right one, or if I'm just settling for less?"*
We get along, but there just aren't fireworks. And what if I can't support her? She wants to have a lot of kids. How do I know that I can support a wife and kids? I can barely support myself. Sometimes I think I should just break up with her now, and get it over with.

William has been trying to make up his mind about Carol for two years. He has come to therapy because she has finally given him an ultimatum— either marry her or end the relationship. William feels paralyzed.

CHRISTINE: TWENTY-FOUR YEARS OLD, IS SO INDEPENDENT THAT SHE CANNOT ACCEPT HELP, EVEN WHEN SHE NEEDS IT.

Christine does not look frightened when she walks into our office. On the contrary, she looks very capable of taking care of herself. Her manner is assured and competent.

Christine prides herself on her independence. She is self-reliant: "I do not need anyone," she tells us. She has been supporting herself and living on her own since she started college. For the past year she has worked as a social worker in a drug treatment center. She walks through the most dangerous city neighborhoods without fear.

Eight months before she came to see us, Christine broke her leg in a skiing accident. She is still using a cane to walk. Right after the accident, she had to return temporarily to her parents' home. Her parents and two younger sisters had to bring her meals, help her wash, and dress her. They had to take care of her. The stress of having people take care of her, particularly family members, was so intense that she entered therapy.

CHRISTINE: *I'm just not the kind of person who likes to be taken care of. I just don't like it. I found myself getting really depressed and upset about it.*

I guess I realized that I shouldn't *get so upset about it. And now I'm back in my apartment, and I'm having a hard time letting my friends do the things I need to have done for me. And the funny thing is, I know I would do the same for them in a flash, without even thinking about it.*

Why can't I accept help from people?

THE DEPENDENCE QUESTIONNAIRE

Take this test, rating each item using the scale on the following page.

1 Completely untrue of me
2 Mostly untrue of me
3 Slightly more true than untrue of me
4 Moderately true of me
5 Mostly true of me
6 Describes me perfectly

If you have any 5's or 6's on this questionnaire, this lifetrap may still apply to you, even if your score is in the low range.

SCORE	DESCRIPTION
	1. I feel more like a child than an adult when it comes to handling the responsibilities of daily life.
	2. I am not capable of getting by on my own.
	3. I cannot cope well by myself.
	4. Other people can take care of me better than I can take care of myself.
	5. I have trouble tackling new tasks unless I have someone to guide me.
	6. I can't do anything right.
	7. I am inept.
	8. I lack common sense.
	9. I cannot trust my own judgment.
	10. I find everyday life overwhelming.
	YOUR TOTAL DEPENDENCE SCORE (Add your scores together for questions 1–10)

INTERPRETING YOUR DEPENDENCE SCORE

10–19 Very low. This lifetrap probably does *not* apply to you.
20–29 Fairly low. This lifetrap may only apply *occasionally*.
30–39 Moderate. This lifetrap is an *issue* in your life.

40–49 High. This is definitely an *important* lifetrap for you.
50–60 Very high. This is definitely one of your *core* lifetraps.

THE EXPERIENCE OF DEPENDENCE

If you have the Dependence lifetrap, life itself seems overwhelming. You feel that you cannot cope. You believe that you are incapable of taking care of yourself in the world, and that therefore you have to turn to other people for help. It is only with such help that you can possibly survive. At the core of your experience of dependence is the sense that it is a constant struggle to fulfill the normal responsibilities of adult living. You simply do not have what it takes. It is a feeling of something *lacking,* of *inadequacy.* An image that captures the essence of dependence is that of a small child who feels that suddenly the world is too much and starts crying for mommy. It is a feeling of being a small child in a world of adults. Without an adult to take care of you, you feel lost.

Your typical thoughts reflect your sense of incompetence: "This is too much for me," "I can't handle this," "I'm going to fall apart," "I'm not going to be able to handle my responsibilities." Other typical thoughts reflect your fear of abandonment—your fear that you will lose the people upon whom you are most dependent: "What would I do without this person?," "How will I get by on my own?" These thoughts are usually accompanied by a sense of desperation and panic. As Margaret says, "There are so many things I can't do. I have to have someone there to do them for me." You dwell on this necessity. It drains a great deal of your mental energy. You plot and scheme to be sure someone will be there. Left on your own, you have a global sense of everything being overwhelming.

You often betray a complete lack of trust in your own judgment. You have little sense of your ability to make good judgments. Difficulty trusting your judgment is a core feature of dependence. You are *indecisive.*

WILLIAM: *I wish I could make up my mind about Carol. I don't know why I waver back and forth so much. It's like I believe that I can't possibly make the right choice.*

When you have a decision to make, you solicit the opinions of others. In fact, you probably rush from person to person seeking advice. You change your mind a hundred times. The whole process just leaves you confused and exhausted. If you finally manage to make a decision, you have to keep asking for reassurance that your decision was right.

Alternately, you might seek the advice of one person in whom you have great confidence, and rely solely on that. That person is often a therapist. In the beginning of therapy, our dependent patients always try to get us to make their decisions for them. This is not always easy to resist. Because it can be so painful for us to watch a patient vacillating endlessly, it is tempting to jump in and make the decision. We have to try hard to resist this temptation because it really does not help these patients. It increases their dependence on us, when the goal of therapy is their eventual independence.

Dependent people do not like change. They like everything to stay the same.

MARGARET: *When I first met Anthony at school, I used to tell him that I wished we could stay in school forever, that it never had to end. He couldn't wait to get out, for school to end, but I wanted it to go on and on.*
THERAPIST: *What was it that you were going to lose?*
MARGARET: *I guess it was that I felt so safe there. I knew what to expect.*

It is your lack of faith in your judgment that makes you so afraid of change. Your confidence is low in new situations, because you have to rely on your own judgment. In situations that are familiar to you, you have already gotten the judgments of other people and you have already established some knowledge of the best approach to take. But when you confront a new situation, unless you have someone to advise you, you have to rely on your own opinions, and you do not trust those.

We would like to say that your sense of incompetence is more imagined than real, but unfortunately this is often not the case. Often dependent people lack competence exactly because they have so successfully avoided the tasks of adulthood. They have gotten other people to do these tasks for them. This avoidance leads to some realistic deficits in skills and judgment. However, most dependent patients *exaggerate* their incompetence. They doubt themselves more than the situation warrants.

When you consistently act in ways designed to keep people doing things for you, you are *surrendering* to your lifetrap. Having people do things for you reinforces the idea that you are not capable of doing these things on your own and keeps you from developing a sense of competence. However, it is almost certainly true that, if you were living on your own, you would eventually be able to learn the things that are required for competence in daily living. Your dependence is one large untested hypothesis. You have never found out that you actually can function alone.

Escape is another way of reinforcing your lifetrap. You avoid the tasks you believe are too difficult for you. There are certain tasks dependent people commonly avoid. These include driving, attending to financial matters, making decisions, taking on new responsibilities, and learning new areas of expertise. You avoid breaking apart from a parent or partner. You rarely live alone or travel alone. You rarely go to a movie alone or out to eat alone. By continually running away from these tasks, you confirm your sense that you cannot accomplish them on your own. Margaret says, "Anthony takes care of all the money. I could never keep our checkbook balanced." William says, "I could never get a job with another firm. What if I was a miserable failure? Other bosses wouldn't be as lenient with me as my dad."

DEPENDENCE AND ANGER

Although you find change frightening and resist it, you often feel trapped even as you feel secure. This is the negative side of the Dependence lifetrap. This is the price you pay. Dependent people often allow themselves to be abused, subjugated, or deprived in order to maintain the dependence. They will do almost anything to keep the person with them.

You probably accept a subordinate role in your relationships with family members, lovers, and friends. Undoubtedly this gives rise to anger (although you may not be aware of it). You like the security of these relationships, but you feel angry toward the people who provide it. And usually you do not dare express your anger openly. That might drive people away, and you need them too much. The dark side of this lifetrap is that you feel trapped in your dependent role.

THERAPIST: *Close your eyes and give me an image of your marriage.*
MARGARET: *I'm in a dark place that I can't get out of, and there is no air, and I can't breathe. It's claustrophobic. Anthony is yelling at me about something. I hear him going on and on, and I hate him so much that I feel like I'm going to explode.*
THERAPIST: *What do you do?*
MARGARET: *I apologize to him, and I promise I'll never do it again.*

Many of Margaret's panic attacks occur when she is angry at Anthony and trying to keep it inside. Dependence exacts a high price in terms of freedom and self-expression.

Some dependent people do express their anger more openly. These are people who have what we call "dependent entitlement." Some dependent people feel *entitled* to have their dependence needs met. Carol expressed this about William in one of our sessions (at William's request, Carol attended some of our sessions).

CAROL: *Yesterday, William was really nasty and critical. He gets that attitude. I was cooking dinner, and he starts hovering over me and correcting me. It's like I can't do anything right.*
THERAPIST *(to William): What was happening with you?*
WILLIAM: *It really started after I got home from the doctor. I was really mad that she didn't want to go to the doctor with me for my allergy shots. She made me go by myself.*
CAROL: *I had an economics test!*
WILLIAM: *You could have made it up later.*

It may be that you have a combination of the Dependence and Entitlement lifetraps. In this case you get angry when people do not meet your needs. You *punish* them by sulking, acting irritated, or getting overtly angry.

DEPENDENCE AND ANXIETY

Panic attacks and agoraphobia are common. In many ways agoraphobia is a drama of dependence. The core feature of autonomy is the ability to venture into the world and have the resources to function independently. Agoraphobia is the exact opposite. Margaret feels *helpless*. When she ventures into the world, she has no confidence that she can handle what happens. She would rather avoid the world altogether. She wants to stay home where she feels safe.

Margaret feels like a child in the world—as if she can no more survive alone than a child. Her only hope is to latch onto someone who will take care of her. Ultimately what she fears is death, insanity, poverty, homelessness—the extremes of helplessness. Each time she has a panic attack, she becomes convinced that she is having a heart attack or losing her mind. Like most agoraphobics, she also has Vulnerability, the other lifetrap in the Autonomy realm.

Even if you do not have panic attacks, you undoubtedly have tremendous anxiety. All the natural changes of life seem overwhelming, even the positive changes. A promotion at work, the birth of a child, graduation, marriage—any new responsibility can trigger anxiety. Occasions most people regard as causes for celebration throw you into a state of dread.

You may also feel a chronic sense of depression along with the anxiety. At heart you may despise yourself for your dependence on others. As William says, "I feel like an inadequate person." Low self-esteem is an integral and painful part of the Dependence lifetrap.

COUNTERDEPENDENCE

Christine, the social worker who broke her leg, is an example of a counterattacker. She copes with her Dependence lifetrap by putting all her energy into achieving at a high level and being *completely* independent. She overcompensates by constantly fighting against her core feelings of incompetence. She must *continually* prove to herself and to others that she can get by on her own. She suffers from hidden dependence.

Christine *is* competent. Her competence is one of her most salient features. But underneath she feels a tremendous amount of anxiety. She is constantly afraid that she will not perform adequately. Each time she gets a promotion, which is often, she fears she will be unable to handle the job. When her friends put her into leadership positions, which they often do, she fills the role competently but with great trepidation. Christine's fears pressure her to ever higher levels of competence, as she drives herself to master every task. But she never gives herself credit. She believes she is fooling people. She always discounts her accomplishments and magnifies her errors or deficiencies.

Christine overcompensates for her feelings of dependence by behaving as though she does not need help from anybody. Christine is *too* independent. No matter how anxious she feels, she forces herself to face things alone. This tendency to go to the other extreme—to act as though she does not need anybody for anything—is called counterdependence, and is a strong indication of the presence of the Dependence lifetrap. Counterdependent people refuse to turn to others for help, even when it is reasonable to do so. They refuse to ask for advice, assistance, or guidance. They cannot allow themselves to get a normal amount of help from other people, because it makes them feel too vulnerable.

CHRISTINE: *It is like if I turn to anyone at all I might become totally dependent. Right after the accident, when I was at home, it really scared me to become dependent on my parents again.*

If you are counterdependent, even though you do not acknowledge your feelings of dependence, at your *core* you feel the same as other dependent people. You may appear to be functioning well, but you do so at a high level of anxiety. It is the feeling underneath that gives you away.

THE ORIGINS OF THE DEPENDENCE LIFETRAP

The Dependence lifetrap can originate either in parents who are over-protective or parents who are underprotective.

Overprotective parents keep their children dependent. They reinforce dependent behaviors and discourage independent behaviors, *smother* their children, and do not give their children the freedom or support to learn to be self-sufficient.

Underprotective parents fail to take care of their children. From a very young age, their children are on their own in the world and have to function at a level beyond their years. Such children can give the illusion of being autonomous, but in fact have strong dependence needs.

We are born totally dependent upon our parents. When our parents meet our physical needs—when they feed us, clothe us, and keep us warm—they establish a safe base from which we can venture into the world. There is a clear developmental process with two steps.

THE STEPS TOWARD INDEPENDENCE

1. Establishing a safe base.
2. Moving away from this base to become autonomous.

If either of these two steps is missing, the person may develop a Dependence lifetrap.

If you never had a safe base, if you never were allowed to rest securely in that dependent state, then it is hard for you to move toward independence. You always long for that dependent state. As Christine says, "I feel like a child who is acting as *if* I am an adult." Your competence and independence do not feel real to you—you are waiting for the base to collapse.

Aside from providing a safe base, our parents must gradually allow us to move away from them toward independence. They must provide us with just enough help. It is a delicate balance; there cannot be too little or too much. Fortunately, most parents fall somewhere in the middle, and most children develop a normal degree of autonomy. But parents on either extreme often produce children who develop Dependence lifetraps.

In the best of all possible worlds, our parents give us the freedom to explore the world, communicate that they are there if we need them, provide help when we truly need it, and convey trust in our ability to succeed on our own. They give us the safety and protection to feel secure, and the freedom and encouragement to go out on our own.

The Dependence lifetrap is formed early. Parents who fail to meet the child's dependence needs or who suppress the child's independence will probably start doing so early in the child's life—usually by the time the child begins to walk. By the time a child starts school, the lifetrap is probably firmly in place. What we see later, for example in adolescence, is simply the continuation of a process that started long before.

ORIGINS IN OVERPROTECTIVENESS

The most common origin of Dependence is parents who are overprotective. This was the origin for both Margaret and William.

THE ORIGINS OF DEPENDENCE IN OVERPROTECTIVENESS

1. Your parents are overprotective and treat you as if you are younger than you are.
2. Your parents make your decisions for you.
3. Your parents take care of all the details of your life so you never learn how to take care of them yourself.
4. Your parents do your schoolwork for you.
5. You are given little or no responsibility.
6. You are rarely apart from your parents and have little sense of yourself as a separate person.
7. Your parents criticize your opinions and competence in everyday tasks.
8. When you undertake new tasks, your parents interfere by giving excessive advice and instructions.
9. Your parents make you feel so safe that you never have a serious rejection or failure until you leave home.
10. Your parents have many fears and always warn you of dangers.

Overprotectiveness usually involves two dimensions. The first is *intrusiveness*. The parent jumps in and does things for the child before the child has a chance to try alone. The parent might well have good intentions; he or she may want to make life easier for the child or spare the child the pain of making mistakes. But when the parent does everything, the child never has the chance to learn to function competently. When we try and fail and try again, we learn to master aspects of our world. This is learning, and, without firsthand experience, little learning occurs. All we learn is that we *must* have our parent there.

William's childhood provides a typical example. His father was over-involved.

WILLIAM: *It was very important to my father that I do well in school. Whenever I had trouble with a problem or assignment, he would do it for me. He wrote my papers and did my science projects.*

You know, I can't remember a single aspect of my schoolwork that I handled alone. Over and over again, my father did the bulk of my work.

Despite all his father's attention, by the time he entered junior high school, William was only an average student. He did well on work done at home, such as papers and projects, but he did not do well on tests. He had tremendous test anxiety. Tests were the one thing that he had to face alone. Even though his father spent hours with him the night before, coaching him, and even though he was intelligent, he did poorly on tests. His poor test-taking ability was probably the result of being so *anxious*. As time went on, his grades suffered. William developed a view of himself as a poor student who only did as well as he did because of his father's help.

WILLIAM: *I secretly thought of myself as lazy. Why else would I let my father do so much of my work?*

His father was deeply involved in far more than his schoolwork. He was involved in William's social life, athletics, leisure time, and day-to-day activities. His father's presence *permeated* William's life. He made William's decisions. He gave guidance and direction. In almost every area of life, William's ability to function on his own was impaired.

The second dimension of overprotectiveness occurs when the parent *undermines* the child's efforts to act independently. The parent is critical of the child's judgment and belittles the decisions the child makes.

MARGARET: *The statement I heard most often from my mother was, "If only you had listened to me." She was really into, "I told you so's." To this day I still feel that if I don't take her advice, I'm going to fail.*

William remembers telling his father once that he wanted to write a history essay alone. His father pushed his chair back abruptly from the table and said, "Fine. Just don't come crying to me when you can't think of anything good to say."

William's father blatantly undermined him. This was painful for William; even today, he is hypersensitive to any hint of criticism, particularly from authority figures. However, with most parents who foster dependence, the undermining process is more subtle. Margaret's mother rarely criticized her. On the contrary, she was supportive and loving. But she herself was a fearful woman and became anxious whenever Margaret left her side. Margaret would sense her mother's anxiety and become anxious herself. Like her mother, she became afraid of the world.

Many of our dependent patients view the world as unsafe because a parent was excessively worried about danger. In forming her daughter's dependence, Margaret's mother also passed down her Vulnerability lifetrap. "Don't go!" she would say. "Don't go out, it's too cold. You'll get sick. Don't go out, it's too dangerous. Don't go out, it's too dark."

As Margaret's mother illustrates, parents who foster dependence in their children are not usually emotionally depriving. Their problem is not providing too little love or affection. Quite the opposite, overprotective parents are often very loving and affectionate. But typically they are also frightened, nervous, anxious, or agoraphobic. They may keep the child near them as protection from their own fears of abandonment; in doing so, they undermine the child's autonomy. They are frequently too insecure to give their children a sense of security. They often give love, but not the specific kind of support and freedom that is necessary for a child to become independent.

We have found that Dependence differs from other lifetraps in an interesting way when the origin is overprotectiveness. Generally, overprotected patients do not have painful memories. Often, their images are of an extremely safe, secure family environment. Many dependent people were fine as children, until they had to leave that secure family environment and deal with the adversity, rejection, and loneliness of the real world.

Sometimes these patients' early memories are of being held back, particularly if the Dependence was combined with the Vulnerability lifetrap.

MARGARET: *I remember once going to the beach at Ocean City, and I wanted to stay out and swim. I was swimming in the ocean in water over my head, and suddenly my mother was there, looking really scared and saying, "Come on back, it's too deep."*

I remember telling her, "No, I'm having fun, let me swim," but she kept insisting, "You're going to drown, it's too deep," until finally I got scared too and swam back in. Afterwards, I remember I felt depressed.

This memory conveys the sense of what Margaret felt as a child. She felt constricted, with her mother always looming to protect her: "There were so many times that I wanted to do something on my own, but my mom wouldn't let me, so I gave up and felt depressed afterwards."

When patients who were overprotected as children generate images in therapy, often they are images of a small child in a big world of adults. Margaret saw an image of herself as "little, surrounded by all these tall people, all these grown-ups." William generated an image of himself as a child, "sitting on a tiny chair, with my father pacing back and forth with giant steps."

Often the images convey a sense of passivity. In William's image of himself in the chair, he is writing down what his father is saying. Another prominent theme is the anxiety of trying new things. These images convey more pain, as each time the person starts something new, he or she feels dependent and incompetent.

Often the Dependence and Subjugation lifetraps go together. Subjugation is an effective way to keep a person dependent. William's father subjugated him. The parent who is overprotective is often overcontrolling.

WILLIAM: *Sometimes I feel like I never should have been an accountant. It was my father who wanted it, not me. He wanted me to be like him.*

William's father forced his own image onto his child, and forced William to fit it, no matter what his natural inclinations might have been. What William wanted was of no importance, and he gradually lost his sense of self. He once described himself as an empty hole inside. If you have no sense of self, you are totally dependent. There is an emptiness inside, and the only way to fill it is to rely on someone else, someone who has a sense of self.

Enmeshment often accompanies overprotectiveness. "Enmeshment" and "fusion" refer to the sense that you and another person have become like one. It is hard to tell where your identity starts and the other person's begins. Both William and Margaret are enmeshed in their families of origin, with William the more dramatic example. Because William believes that he cannot function in the world, he has trouble separating from his family for even short periods of time. He cannot grow up and leave home. He has a fused self.

There are many dependent people, most in their twenties, who are at the point in their lives when they should be breaking away from home. But they are still too enmeshed and dependent on their mother and father to leave. Their friends have all gone off into separate lives, and they are still at home. Their situation is usually more difficult because their parents continue to encourage their dependence. Their parents still give advice about everything, still improve upon all their decisions, still undermine their judgment. One might expect more women than men to have this kind of dependence. In our culture, women are protected more as children. But, in our experiences with patients, this has not been true. We see as many dependent men as women.

ORIGINS IN UNDERPROTECTIVENESS

Underprotectiveness is the other origin of the lifetrap. This is the origin of the Counterdependent person. Because these parents are so weak and ineffectual, beset with their own problems, or simply absent and neglectful, they fail to provide adequate guidance or protection for their children. These patients have a combination of the Dependence and Emotional Deprivation lifetraps. From very early, the child senses the lack of protection and feels unsafe. The child never stops longing for that dependent role.

THE ORIGINS OF DEPENDENCE IN UNDERPROTECTIVENESS

1. You do not get enough practical guidance or direction from your parents.
2. You have to make decisions alone beyond your years.
3. You have to be like an adult in your family, even when underneath you still feel like a child.
4. You are expected to do things and know things that are over your head.

This was the origin for Christine.

CHRISTINE: *My mother was addicted to alcohol and prescription tranquilizers. She could not take care of herself, let alone take care of me. And my father was never around. He had his buddies, his clubs.*

There was no one to give Christine the sense of guidance and protection that she needed. Her mother was not strong enough to take care of her, and her father did not care enough.

Christine's mother was anxious, lacked confidence, and was very dependent herself. She made her child into her parent. Christine was a "parentified child." She had to become self-sufficient to take care of herself *and* her mother, so she became competent and independent. But underneath she did not feel secure and wished for the normal dependence of a child.

Christine grew up making decisions that were too much for a child to handle. She did not have the judgment or experience that were necessary.

CHRISTINE: *I always had the feeling that I was swimming out of my depth. I always had the feeling that my decisions weren't good ones, that I wished there was someone I could ask.*

Children such as this long for someone upon whom they can depend, to relieve the weight of responsibility. They question their decisions, feel a lot of anxiety about their competence, and yet have no choice but to continue making them.

Often this yearning is totally out of awareness. The child is only aware of chronic anxiety, pressure, or fatigue—when the number of responsibilities gets too great or when the child feels fraudulent while undertaking a difficult new task.

DEPENDENCE AND INTIMATE RELATIONSHIPS

The people upon whom you depend can include parents, brothers, sisters, friends, lovers, spouses, mentors, bosses, therapists, or others. The person upon whom you depend might even be a child. You might be the dependent parent who makes your child into your parent. Margaret is this way with her five-year-old daughter, Jill.

MARGARET: *I know it sounds strange, but my daughter is one of my safe people. I can do a lot of things with Jill that I can't do alone, like go to the supermarket. I don't know what it is I think Jill could do if something happened, but I still feel safer with her there.*

One reason Margaret started therapy is that Jill started kindergarten, leaving Margaret stranded at home.

DANGER SIGNALS IN THE EARLY STAGES OF DATING

Your Dependence lifetrap is bound to appear in your romantic relationships. You are drawn to lovers who foster your dependence. This ensures that you will continue reenacting your childhood situation. Here are some warning signs that your partner is triggering your Dependence lifetrap:

DANGER SIGNALS IN POTENTIAL PARTNERS

1. Your partner is like a father/mother figure, who seems strong and protective.
2. He/She seems to enjoy taking care of you and treats you like a child.
3. You trust his/her judgment much more than your own. He/She makes most of the decisions.
4. You find that you lose your sense of self around him/her—and that your life goes on hold when he/she is not around.
5. He/She pays for almost everything, and takes care of most financial records.
6. He/She criticizes your opinions, taste, and competence in everyday tasks.
7. When you have a new task to undertake, you almost always ask his/her advice, even if he/she has no special expertise in that realm.
8. He/She does almost everything for you—you have almost no responsibility.
9. He/She almost never seems frightened, insecure, or vulnerable about him/herself.

If this list describes your relationship, then you are still living in the dependent state of your childhood. You might note that all the characteristics of your partner, listed above, are characteristics of your parents also.

Nothing has changed for you. You have managed to prolong your dependence into your adult life. You have few responsibilities, few worries, few challenges. Although this may seem to be a satisfactory arrangement for you, it is time for you to consider the price you pay to maintain your dependence. It costs you your will, your freedom, and your pride. It costs you your very *self*.

SURRENDERING TO YOUR DEPENDENCE LIFETRAP

Even if you find a partner who would like to support your autonomy, there are pitfalls to avoid. You can twist a healthy partner until he or she fits the shape of your Dependence lifetrap.

In fact, you tend to twist almost all your relationships to fit your lifetrap. To a lesser extent, are you not also dependent on your friends? Do you not make yourself dependent on *strangers* in certain situations, where strangers are all that are available?

THERAPIST: *Tell me what happened once you got to the grocery store.*
MARGARET: *Well, the first thing I did was look for someone I could turn to if I needed help. There was this woman shopping a little ahead of me, and I thought she looked nice, and would maybe take care of me if things got really bad.*
THERAPIST: *Is that usually the first thing you do, look for someone to take care of you?*
MARGARET: *Yes. I make sure someone is there who might help me.*
THERAPIST: *Have you ever used such a person to help you?*
MARGARET: *No. Never. I have never had to yet. But you never know.*

The Dependence lifetrap can also influence the way you approach your job. It leads you to avoid taking the responsibility and initiative you need to get ahead.

Here are the ways you maintain your Dependence lifetrap in work and in love.

DEPENDENCE LIFETRAPS

1. You turn to wiser or stronger people all the time for advice and guidance.
2. You minimize your successes and magnify your shortcomings.
3. You avoid new challenges on your own.
4. You do not make your own decisions.
5. You do not take care of your own financial records or decisions.
6. You live through your parents/partner.
7. You are much more dependent on your parents than most people your age.
8. You avoid being alone or traveling alone.
9. You have fears and phobias that you do not confront.
10. You are quite ignorant when it comes to many areas of practical functioning and daily survival skills.
11. You have not lived on your own for any significant period of time.

If you are *counter*dependent, like Christine, you reinforce your lifetrap in other ways. You shape things so that you are always swimming out of your depth.

THE SIGNS OF COUNTERDEPENDENCE

1. You never seem to be able to turn to anyone for guidance or advice. You have to do everything on your own.
2. You are always taking on new challenges and confronting your fears, but you feel under constant pressure while doing it.
3. Your partner is very dependent on you, and you end up doing everything and making all the decisions.

You ignore the part of you that wants a little *healthy dependence,* that just wants to stop coping for a while and rest. Christine's imagery expresses this yearning for normal dependence:

THERAPIST: *What image do you see?*
CHRISTINE: *I see myself as a child. My mother's sitting on the couch, and*

all I want to do is go across the room, sit down, and lay my head in my mother's lap.

CHANGING YOUR DEPENDENCE LIFETRAP

Here are the steps to changing your lifetrap:

CHANGING DEPENDENCE

1. Understand your childhood dependence. Feel the incompetent/dependent child inside of you.
2. List everyday situations, tasks, responsibilities, and decisions for which you depend on other people.
3. List challenges, changes, or phobias that you have avoided because you are afraid of them.
4. Systematically force yourself to tackle everyday tasks and decisions without asking for help. Take on challenges or make changes you have been avoiding. Start with the easy tasks first.
5. When you succeed at a task on your own, take credit for it. Do not minimize it. When you fail, do not give up. Keep trying until you master the task.
6. Review past relationships and clarify the patterns of dependence that recur. List the lifetraps to avoid.
7. Avoid strong, overprotective partners who generate high chemistry.
8. When you find a partner who will treat you as an equal, give the relationship a chance to work. Take on your share of responsibilities and decision-making.
9. Do not complain when your partner/boss refuses to help you enough. Do not turn to him/her for constant advice and reassurance.
10. Take on new challenges and responsibilities at work, but do it gradually.
11. If you are counterdependent, acknowledge your need for guidance. Ask others for help. Do not take on more challenges than you can handle. Use your anxiety level as a gauge of how much you are comfortable taking on.

---

1. Understand Your Childhood Dependence. Feel the Incompetent/Dependent Child Inside of You. You must first understand how you got this way. Who fostered your dependence in childhood? Was it your mother, who was afraid to let you try things on your own? Was it your father, who criticized the things you did without him? Or perhaps you were the youngest in the family and were babied by the rest. What was it that happened to you?

Explore your images of childhood. Remember, a good place to start is with a feeling of dependence. Any time that you feel your Dependence lifetrap in your current life can serve as an opportunity for an imagery exercise. Find a quiet place to summon that feeling back.

MARGARET: *I went to the mall with Anthony to practice controlling my panic, and he left me. We were sitting on a bench, and I wanted to practice walking around the mall alone, and I told him to wait at the bench. I walked across to the drug store and came back, and he was gone. Right away I started to panic, and I was running around looking for him. When I found him, he was standing behind a column, laughing at me. He was watching me the whole time and laughing. He thought it was funny, just a joke. I could have killed him.*

THERAPIST: *Close your eyes and bring that moment back with imagery.*

MARGARET: *Okay (closes eyes). Okay, I can see him, behind the column, looking at me.*

THERAPIST: *What are you feeling?*

MARGARET: *Like I always do. Like I hate him, but at the same time I'm so relieved he's there.*

THERAPIST: *Now give me an image of when you felt this way before, as a child.*

MARGARET: *(Pause.) Okay. I can remember standing at the door of my house. My mother and father are about to go out for the night, and they are leaving me with Lisa, the baby-sitter. I'm watching them leave, crying, and begging them not to go. Lisa is trying to pull me back into the house, and my parents are going out the front door and down the steps. My mother turns back and gives me this worried look.*

This image reflects how the Dependence and Abandonment lifetraps work together.

Other events can serve as sources of imagery. William told us about a dream he had that captured the dependence of his childhood. He was talking about how frightened it made him to think of breaking up with Carol, and he remembered this dream.

WILLIAM: *I was walking up the stairs with my parents. My parents were walking, holding my hand on either side of me. I was a little boy. But then they were letting go of my hand and moving away, and the stairs started getting steeper and steeper, and I was having trouble climbing them alone.*

When you have an image, try to remember what you felt as a child. That child is still alive in you. It is a frightened child. Try to comfort that child. Encourage that child. Support that child's efforts to tackle things alone. The dependent child within you needs a certain type of help that you *can* give. Learn to support your own efforts to move toward independence.

2. List Everyday Situations, Tasks, Responsibilities, and Decisions for Which You Depend on Other People. Make explicit the extent of your dependence. This will give you a more objective view. For example, here is a list William made in reference to his dependence on his parents.

WAYS I DEPEND ON MY PARENTS

1. Provide me with a place to live.
2. Provide me with a job.
3. Get my car fixed.
4. Meals.
5. Laundry.
6. Investing my money.
7. Planning vacations.
8. Planning holidays.

Your list is a blueprint of what you have to master. These are the tasks of life, and almost everyone can do them.

3. List Challenges, Changes, or Phobias That You Have Avoided Because You Are Afraid of Them. List challenges you have avoided. Some will be relatively easy, while others will be difficult. Here is a list Margaret composed with us.

TASKS I HAVE AVOIDED

1. Being more assertive with Anthony.
2. Riding the subway.
3. Going shopping alone.
4. Staying home alone.
5. Driving on the highway.
6. Going to a movie with Anthony.
7. Going out dancing with Anthony.
8. Going out to lunch with girlfriends.
9. Going to see a lawyer about options for ending the marriage.
10. Talking to Anthony about marriage counseling.

Try to include items from all spheres of your life. Margaret did not have a job when she first came into therapy—this was something she tackled much later. But your list should include items about work. For example, one aspect of William's job that we addressed in therapy was his tendency to run to his father whenever he had even the slightest question or doubt about how to do something. (As you will remember, his father is his boss at the accounting firm.) William had to learn to tolerate the anxiety and solve problems himself. He made mistakes at first, but he improved and gradually took on more responsibility. After about a year, he left his father's firm and took a job elsewhere. This was after considerable struggle and effort on his part that slowly built his confidence.

4. Systematically Force Yourself to Tackle Everyday Tasks and Decisions Without Asking for Help. Take on Challenges or Make Changes You Have Been Avoiding. Start with the Easy Tasks First. Use the two lists you have just constructed to map out a plan for yourself. Sit down and rate how difficult each item would be for you to complete, using the following scale:

SCALE OF DIFFICULTY

0 Very Easy
2 Mildly Difficult
4 Moderately Difficult
6 Very Difficult
8 Feels Almost Impossible

For example, Margaret rated the items on her list as follows:

TASKS I AVOID	DIFFICULTY LEVEL
1. Being more assertive with Anthony.	6
2. Riding the subway.	5
3. Going shopping alone.	3
4. Staying home alone.	6
5. Driving on the highway.	4
6. Going to a movie with Anthony.	5
7. Going out dancing with Anthony.	7
8. Going out to lunch with girlfriends.	3
9. Going to see a lawyer about options for ending the marriage.	7
10. Talking to Anthony about marriage counseling.	8

Begin with the easy items. Make sure that you have included items that will be relatively easy for you to complete. In addition, it is important to do a lot of planning before you actually attempt an item, even an easy one. We want you to be ready.

The first item Margaret chose was going shopping alone. She decided to go to the grocery store. We spent a long time talking about how she would handle different scenarios. If she started to panic, she would do deep-breathing exercises to control her physical symptoms. If she started having catastrophic thoughts, she would challenge and correct them. If she wanted to run out, she would tell herself that she could handle the situation without running, and she would stay. Examine every possibility, and plan what you would do if it occurred.

You might want to do several items at the same level of difficulty before you move on to a more difficult item. If you need to, add to your list. Margaret added a number of level 3 items to her list before moving to level 4—going to an uncrowded department store alone, exercising, balancing the checkbook. We want you to feel that you have attained a level of mastery before going onto more difficult tasks. We want you to feel that you are building mastery and competence in a systematic fashion. We want you to feel a sense of *control*.

5. When You Succeed at a Task on Your Own, Take Credit for It. Do Not Minimize It. When You Fail, Do Not Give Up. Keep Trying Until You

Master the Task. It is important to give yourself credit when you have earned it. You may have a tendency to feel that you do not deserve credit because you *should* be able to do these things already. When Margaret successfully completed her first item, going to the grocery store alone, she expressed this feeling:

MARGARET: *I didn't feel too good about it really. After all,* everyone *goes to the grocery store. What's the big deal really?*
THERAPIST: *But to someone with panic attacks, going to the grocery store is a big deal.*

Be realistic when you appraise how competently you completed an item. There will be some things you did well, and some things you did not do well. Try to recognize your achievements and learn from your mistakes.

You may have the tendency to criticize yourself if you had a critical parent. If you start to disparage yourself, stop. Support yourself instead. This is part of the nurturing of yourself that you must learn to do. It enables you to move on, even if you are not perfect, to keep strengthening yourself and to build your competence.

6. Review Past Relationships and Clarify the Patterns of Dependence That Recur. List the Lifetraps to Avoid. Make a list of the people who have been most important in your life. Include your family, friends, lovers, teachers, bosses, and coworkers. Look at each relationship in turn. Look at your dependence. What was it about that person, and what was it in your behavior, that fostered your dependence? What are the lifetraps for you to avoid?

Here is the list that Margaret made:

DEPENDENCE LIFETRAPS

1. Acting like a child instead of an adult.
2. Staying with people no matter how they treat me.
3. Acting clingy.
4. Picking people who like to take over my life and take care of me.
5. Giving up my old life to be with somebody. Living their life instead of my own.
6. Not making my own decisions.
7. Not making my own money.
8. Not pushing myself to see what I can achieve.

This is a list of what may have gone wrong in your relationships. By being aware of your lifetraps, you can start to correct them.

Margaret did this in her relationship with us. With our support, she was able to become stronger in our relationship and assert herself. It showed us once again how *one* relationship can help heal a person. Asserting herself with us mobilized Margaret to assert herself with Anthony. Once she saw what it was like to be autonomous in a relationship, she did not want to go back. You will not want to go back either. It is a relief and a pleasure to give up the desperation of dependence for the calm and strength of independent functioning. As Margaret said, "It feels good not to need him so badly."

7. Avoid Strong, Overprotective Partners Who Generate High Chemistry. This is that tricky principle—avoid the very partners to whom you are most attracted. Remember, the chemistry is usually highest with partners who trigger your lifetrap. You are undoubtedly prone to falling for partners who like to dominate and protect you. You are probably most attracted to partners who encourage you to collapse into your dependent role.

There was a high degree of chemistry in the relationship between Margaret and Anthony. They were perfectly matched for triggering lifetraps. Through therapy, Margaret dared to become more assertive in the relationship. She became more able to stand on her own, and so no longer feared losing him more than anything else.

MARGARET: *The only way I'll stay with Anthony now is if he changes. I can't just allow him to treat me badly. I'd rather be alone than continue being abused by him.*

When Anthony saw that he really might lose Margaret, he agreed to enter therapy. As is typical of most narcissists, the threat of abandonment motivated him to change. As of this writing, they are working in therapy to create their relationship anew in a way that satisfies both of them. Whether or not they are successful as a couple, Margaret has chosen to give up the trap of Dependence.

8. When You Find a Partner Who Will Treat You as an Equal, Give the Relationship a Chance to Work. Take on Your Share of Responsibilities and Decision-Making. You may find there is little chemistry with partners who foster independence and autonomy, or that the chemistry fades with time. We were convinced that the reason William felt so few fireworks in his relationship with Carol was that she challenged his dependence. You might find that it is worth trying to give such relationships a chance. If you once felt chemistry with this partner—if there was some period, maybe at the beginning, when you were attracted—the chemistry might come back as you grow more confident.

When you find a partner who wants you to stand on your own, try to make the relationship work. Resist undermining the relationship. When William first started dating Carol, he was attracted to her. But it soon became apparent that Carol was resisting William's efforts to turn himself into a child in the relationship, and to turn her into a parent. She wanted him to be strong. She wanted a peer, a companion. She refused to take over his life. As time went on, William's attraction faded. He began telling us that she just was not right for him, that he was not in love with her and was more interested in other women.

With our encouragement, William stayed with Carol. He gradually took on more responsibility for his life. He moved into his own apartment, took a job at another firm, started managing his own money, buying his meals, and planning his time. As he grew more comfortable with these new roles, his attraction to Carol returned. He was able to restore much of the chemistry he had lost.

9. Do Not Complain When Your Partner/Boss Refuses to Help You Enough. Do Not Turn to Him/Her for Constant Advice and Reassurance. This advice is for entitled Dependents. You must realize that people do not owe it to you to take care of you. People have a right to expect you to take care of yourself. Right now, your first impulse at work when you face a problem is to run for help. You probably do not even try to solve the problem yourself. We want your response to be to try it on your own first. If you try hard, if you truly do your best to solve the problem, and you still cannot do it, *then* ask for help.

WILLIAM: *When I was learning the computer system that handled our accounts, I would go to my father every time I had a question. He would get mad at me, but he would tell me the answer. I never even tried to use the manual.*

But once I started trying to learn it, once I started trying to understand the manual, I found I could do it. I rarely go to him with questions anymore, and when I do, he often has trouble answering them himself.

When you try things on your own, you will have the urge to seek reassurance that your approach is right. Seeking reassurance is like a drug for you—it tranquilizes your anxiety about functioning alone. You need to withdraw from this drug. You need to tolerate the anxiety of functioning alone. The anxiety will pass. Have faith—there will come a time when you will function alone with minimal anxiety.

10. Take On New Challenges and Responsibilities at Work, but Do It Gradually. Expand your skills at work *systematically.* Do not set yourself up to fail—do not take on too much at once. Stay in control of the process of your growth.

You can use an approach like the one we described above, which Margaret used to overcome her fears. Make a list of the responsibilities at work that you have been avoiding. Include both solitary tasks and interpersonally oriented items, ranging from easy to difficult. Rate the difficulty of each task on a 0 to 8 scale, with 0 being not at all difficult, and 8 being as difficult as you can imagine. Start with the tasks you rated lowest. Do these tasks again and again until you are comfortable with that level of difficulty. Attain a sense of mastery before you move to higher items on the list.

If you find that you cannot complete even the items you rated lowest, it is because even the lowest items are too hard. Come up with easier items. We have found that even the most dependent people can come up with *some* items they feel they can complete easily.

11. If You Are Counterdependent, Acknowledge Your Need for Guidance. Ask Others for Help. Do Not Take On More Challenges Than You Can Handle. Use Your Anxiety Level as a Gauge of How Much You Are Comfortable Taking On. There is a saying in psychotherapy: "It is the relationship that heals." With Christine, this seemed to be the case. Our relationship helped heal her. We became the first people from whom she accepted help. She allowed herself to be vulnerable with us. She shared the part of herself that is weak and uncertain, the damaged and overtaxed child within. This made her extremely anxious at first. But after assessing that she could trust us, she took a risk and made herself dependent. We nurtured and supported that healthy, dependent part of her, and Christine learned to nurture that part of herself with imagery exercises.

THERAPIST: *What image do you see?*
CHRISTINE: *I see myself as a child, maybe eight years old. I'm in my living room. My mother is lying on the couch, half passed out watching soaps.*

I'm trying to iron the clothes I'm wearing to school because one of the kids made fun of me because my clothes were wrinkled.

THERAPIST: *I want you to bring yourself into the image as an adult and intercede to help that child.*

CHRISTINE: *That's hard for me to do. I don't know what to say. I guess I would say, "Here, I'll show you how to iron, it's not so hard. I'm sorry that you have to do everything yourself. I know it's too much for you. But I'm here for you when the going gets tough. You can come to me when you need help."*

Christine gradually allowed herself to turn to other people for help. If there is someone in your life that you would like to trust in this way, make sure it is a person who is worthy of your trust. Do not pick your partners foolishly. Do not pick people unless you are confident they will be there for you when you need them. Christine had to change the type of man she typically pursued. She had been drawn to weak, fragile men who often were substance abusers. Changing your Dependence lifetrap may require a profound shift in the way you choose romantic partners.

The other aspect of changing your lifetrap is gaining control over how much you take on in life. We want you to *regulate* how much you take on at home, at work, in the community, and with friends. Use your anxiety level as a gauge. When your anxiety climbs above comfortable levels, you have taken on too much, and you must let go of some responsibilities. For example, when Christine feels overly anxious with a friend or coworker, she views it as a sign that she is too involved in trying to help and give advice to that person. She steps back and focuses on her own life.

Christine expressed what she gained from treatment:

CHRISTINE: *I feel like it was a matter of bringing some balance into my life, so that I take care of other people and they take care of me. I never had that before. I feel calmer now, like I'm not always struggling out of my depth.*

SOME FINAL WORDS

The journey out of the Dependence lifetrap is a movement from childhood to adulthood. It is a trading of fear and avoidance for a sense of mastery— for the sense you can function independently in the world. Give up the exhausting struggle to get people to take care of you. Learn to take care of yourself. Learn to believe in your *own* ability to cope by mastering the tasks of life.

11

"CATASTROPHE IS ABOUT TO STRIKE"
THE VULNERABILITY LIFETRAP

ROBERT: THIRTY-ONE YEARS OLD. SUFFERS FROM PANIC AT-
TACKS.

Robert is visibly upset when he walks into our office. He can barely sit still
to tell us what is wrong.

ROBERT: *I really don't know if this is where I belong, but I've been told to
come here. I've been going from doctor to doctor, and no one can find
what's wrong with me. They keep telling me it's anxiety, that I need to
see a shrink.*
THERAPIST: *What do you think?*
ROBERT: *I think there really is something physically wrong with me. They
just haven't found it yet.*

Robert has been having panic attacks.

ROBERT: *Usually how it goes is that all of a sudden, out of the blue, this
feeling comes over me. It's like a feeling of doom. I get dizzy and
light-headed and feel like I can't breathe. My heart starts pounding. And
everything feels unreal.*
THERAPIST: *What does it feel like to you? What do you think is happening?*

184

ROBERT: *It feels like I'm having a nervous breakdown. Like I'm going to go crazy on the spot.*

Other times Robert believes that he has a brain tumor or a heart problem.

ROBERT: *For a long time I would run to the emergency room every time it happened. I thought I was having a heart attack or brain aneurysm or something. Those were the worst ones. I really thought I was dying.*
THERAPIST: *So you don't think that anymore?*
ROBERT: *Well, sometimes I still do. Sometimes I get this funny pressure in my head and I get scared that it's an aneurysm. But I've pretty much learned that I'm going to be all right, that I'm not going to die. I mean, it's happened so many times. It has to be a really bad one now for me to believe I'm dying. Mostly I worry now about losing my mind.*
THERAPIST: *What do you mean by "losing my mind"?*
ROBERT: *Suddenly I'll start screaming or raving or hearing voices, and it will never stop.*

When we ask Robert if any of these things have ever happened, he tells us "no." He is just afraid that they are *going* to happen.

HEATHER: FORTY-TWO YEARS OLD. HER FEARS ARE CAUSING HER MARITAL PROBLEMS.

Heather comes to therapy with her husband, Walt. When we ask them what the problem is, they tell us Heather has phobias.

WALT: *She won't do anything. We can't go on vacation because she won't get on the plane, and she won't go in the water, and she won't get in the elevator. We can't go into the city on a weekend night because it's too dangerous. And besides, we can't spend the money because we have to save every cent. Living with her is like living in prison. It's driving me crazy!*

Heather agrees that her phobias place a lot of restrictions on their activities. But she resents being pushed to do things.

HEATHER: *I prefer to spend my time around the house. It won't be fun for me to do the things he wants. What kind of vacation would it be for me if I had to spend the whole time worrying about the plane trip back or the trips up in the elevator? Or if I had to spend the whole evening in the city worrying about getting mugged? I would rather not go!*

Over the years Heather's fears have grown worse, and they have become an increasing source of conflict in her marriage.

THE VULNERABILITY QUESTIONNAIRE

This questionnaire will measure the strength of your Vulnerability lifetrap. Answer the items using the following scale:

SCORING KEY

1 Completely untrue of me
2 Mostly untrue of me
3 Slightly more true than untrue of me
4 Moderately true of me
5 Mostly true of me
6 Describes me perfectly

If you have any 5's or 6's on this questionnaire, this lifetrap may still apply to you, even if your score is in the low range.

SCORE	DESCRIPTION
	1. I cannot escape the feeling that something bad is about to happen.
	2. I feel that catastrophe can strike at any moment.
	3. I worry about becoming a street person or vagrant.
	4. I worry a lot about being attacked by a criminal, mugger, thief, etc.
	5. I worry about getting a serious illness, even though nothing has been diagnosed by a physician.
	6. I am too anxious to travel alone on planes, trains, etc.
	7. I have anxiety attacks.
	8. I am very aware of physical sensations in my body, and I worry about what they mean.

	9. I worry I will lose control of myself in public or go crazy.
	10. I worry a lot about losing all my money or going broke.
	YOUR TOTAL VULNERABILITY SCORE (Add your scores together for questions 1–10)

INTERPRETING YOUR VULNERABILITY SCORE

10–19 Very low. This lifetrap probably does *not* apply to you.
20–29 Fairly low. This lifetrap may only apply *occasionally.*
30–39 Moderate. This lifetrap is an *issue* in your life.
40–49 High. This is definitely an *important* lifetrap for you.
50–60 Very high. This is definitely one of your *core* lifetraps.

THE EXPERIENCE OF VULNERABILITY

The primary feeling associated with the Vulnerability lifetrap is *anxiety.* Catastrophe is about to strike, and you lack the resources to deal with it. This lifetrap is two-pronged: You both exaggerate the risk of danger and minimize your own capacity to cope.

What you fear varies depending upon the type of the lifetrap. There are four types of Vulnerability. You can be more than one type.

TYPES OF VULNERABILITY

1. Health and Illness
2. Danger
3. Poverty
4. Losing Control

• HEALTH AND ILLNESS •

If you belong to the Health and Illness type of Vulnerability you may be a hypochondriac. You worry obsessively about your health. Despite the fact that physicians keep telling you nothing is seriously wrong, you are convinced you are ill, that you have AIDS, cancer, multiple sclerosis, or some other dread disease.

Most people who have panic attacks belong to this type. You constantly scan your body for signs that something is wrong. You are *sensitized* to your body. Any strange sensation, no matter how naturally caused, can trigger panic. Hot weather, cold weather, exercise, anger, excitement, caffeine, alcohol, medication, sex, heights, motion—all can cause sensations that trigger a panic attack.

ROBERT: *I had a bad panic yesterday, out of the blue. I was on the train, just sitting there reading a magazine.*
THERAPIST: *What were you reading about?*
ROBERT: *Just this article. I don't remember.*
THERAPIST: *What exactly were you thinking about when the attack began?*
ROBERT: *Actually I was thinking about Parkinson's disease. I was noticing that my hand was trembling holding the magazine, and I was thinking, "What if I had Parkinson's disease?"*

These are the famous words of a panicker: *"What if."*

You are hypervigilant to anything in your environment that is relevant to the possibility of illness. You may read everything you can get on the subject, or you may avoid any mention of illness entirely. Similarly, you may run to the doctor continuously, or you may avoid doctors altogether because you are afraid of finding out that something is wrong. Either way, you are constantly preoccupied with thoughts of illness.

You may avoid activities that give rise to panic. Robert was avoiding all forms of exercise, including sex, when he first came to therapy. The sensations made him too anxious—they were too similar to panic. He had given up playing tennis, which he loves. By trying to Escape his Vulnerability lifetrap, Robert was putting a serious dent in his lifestyle.

It is possible that you have this lifetrap because you actually are physically frail. Perhaps you were sick a lot as a child, so now you have an exaggerated fear of sickness. Or perhaps you had a parent who was sick. However, in order to qualify for this lifetrap, your fears must be excessive and unrealistic *in the present.*

• DANGER •

If you fit this type, you have an exaggerated concern for your personal safety and the safety of your loved ones. You see the world as fraught with danger at every turn.

WALT: *She sits home at night reading all the crime stories in the newspaper. She won't even go out onto our own driveway at night.*

HEATHER: *It's really dark on our driveway. I don't like to go out at night.*

WALT: *We have this really expensive burglar alarm system, which she made me get, but she still worries about people breaking in.*

HEATHER: *People who know what they're doing can get by burglar alarms. I keep telling him to put window bars on all the downstairs windows but he won't listen to me.*

WALT: *It's ridiculous! We live in a safe neighborhood. We don't need window bars!*

You have a general feeling of unsafety when you are out in the world that is out of proportion to the real level of danger. You are alert to anyone who looks suspicious or dangerous. At any moment you feel that someone might attack you.

You are also afraid of disasters such as car accidents and plane crashes. These are things beyond your control that can happen suddenly. Hence, like Heather, you may avoid traveling. You are afraid of natural catastrophes such as floods and earthquakes. Despite all reasonable odds, you believe something will happen *to you*.

WALT: *During the Gulf War she wouldn't even go into the city during the day because she was afraid of a terrorist attack.*

HEATHER: *They said New York was a prime target!*

WALT: *Right. So, of all the millions of places and times, they were going to hit us.*

This lifetrap is very draining. You are continually tense and vigilant. You believe that if you relax your guard, something bad will happen.

• POVERTY •

This is the so-called depression mentality, named for people who were children during the Great Depression of the 1930s. You are always worried about money. You are unrealistically afraid you will go broke and end up on the street.

HEATHER: *I know I worry a lot about money. It's just that I can see us getting older and losing everything. Sometimes I worry that I'll end up like some bag lady.*

No matter how financially secure you become, it still seems like a small step from your current financial situation to utter ruin.

You often think in terms of safety cushions. You feel that you have to have a certain amount of money to be safe. This gives you the assurance that you are not going to collapse below a certain point. You are likely to save a certain amount, and to become extremely anxious if it drops below that amount.

You find it difficult to spend money and you go to extreme lengths to save even a few dollars.

HEATHER: *I have to laugh at myself. The other day I went all the way out on Long Island to buy pants because I had a coupon for ten dollars off. Of course I got there and they didn't have my size. Meanwhile, I had taken a bus and a cab to get there, costing four dollars each way.*

You worry needlessly about having enough money to pay your bills (even when you have more than enough money available). You anxiously scan the news for signs of economic recession (even when the economic climate is excellent). These signs serve as evidence that you are right to feel as you do. You worry about people in your family losing their jobs (even when there is no logical reason). Perhaps you buy excessive amounts of disability and other insurance.

Controlling money is a big issue for you. You believe that if you relax your grip you will lose control and spend everything. Your financial practices are very conservative. You do not like buying things on credit. You are unwilling to take *any* risks with money because you are afraid of losing it.

You need the money *in case something happens.* Some catastrophe might wipe out everything you have and leave you with nothing. You have to be prepared.

• LOSING CONTROL •

This type fears a catastrophe of a more psychological nature—having a nervous breakdown. You fear going crazy or losing control. It also includes many panic attacks.

ROBERT: *When I get that unreal feeling, I get afraid that I'll just keep drifting further and further away, that I'll never come back, and I'll turn into one of those people who talk to themselves and hear voices. It terrifies me. And I feel totally out of control. I might do anything. I might start running, screaming through the streets, or something.*

Perhaps you fear losing control of your body in some way—fainting or getting sick. Whatever you fear, the mechanism is basically the same as in all panic attacks. You seize upon an internal sensation and interpret it in a catastrophic way.

Catastrophic thinking is at the core of all types of the Vulnerability lifetrap. You immediately jump to the worst possible case, and you feel as powerless to cope as a weak, helpless child.

For those of you who suffer from panic disorder, catastrophic thinking *drives* your panic attacks. A panic attack in itself should only last one or two minutes. Your catastrophic thinking makes it last much longer. "What if I am dying, going crazy, losing control?"—*anyone* who thinks that these things are happening is going to have a panic attack.

Escape is of crucial importance in reinforcing this lifetrap. Almost everyone with the Vulnerability lifetrap avoids many situations. Most likely, your avoidance robs you of many of life's most enjoyable activities.

These are the possible origins of the lifetrap:

ORIGINS OF VULNERABILITY

1. You learned your sense of vulnerability from observing and living with parents with the same lifetrap. Your parent was phobic or frightened about specific areas of vulnerability (such as losing control, getting sick, going broke, etc.).
2. Your parent was overprotective of you, particularly around issues of danger or illness. Your parent continuously warned you of specific dangers. You were made to feel that you were too fragile or incompetent to handle these everyday issues. (This is usually combined with Dependence.)
3. Your parent did not adequately protect you. Your childhood environment did not seem safe physically, emotionally, or financially. (This is usually combined with Emotional Deprivation or with Mistrust and Abuse.)
4. You were sick as a child or experienced a serious traumatic event (e.g., a car crash) that led you to feel vulnerable.
5. One of your parents experienced a serious traumatic event and perhaps died. You came to view the world as dangerous.

The most common origin is having a parent with the same lifetrap. You learn through modeling.

ROBERT: *My mother was a hypochondriac herself. She was always running to the doctor with this complaint or that complaint. I think she had panic attacks also. There were a lot of times she wanted to leave places suddenly, and there were a lot of times she wouldn't go. I know she didn't like crowds. She was always warning me about everything: "It's cold, put a sweater on, don't go out, you'll catch your death." She was always checking me, checking my temperature, looking at my throat. And she was always dragging us to the doctor.*

THERAPIST: *What about the "going crazy" stuff? Did you learn that from her also?*

ROBERT: *I guess so in the sense that she was very superstitious. She used to talk about evil eyes and that kind of stuff. I remember when I was a teenager, I was going to the planetarium. You know, to the laser light show. And she told me not to go, that she had heard about a girl who went into a hypnotic trance at the light show and never came out of it. I remember I ended up not going. She freaked me out.*

This is a kind of direct transmission of the lifetrap. You learn to feel vulnerable from a parent who feels that way.

A related origin is parental overprotectiveness. Parents who have the Vulnerability lifetrap are likely to be overprotective as well. They see danger everywhere. They give the child the message that the world is a dangerous place.

ROBERT: *My mother thought that the world was teeming with germs. She was always cleaning and disinfecting. She would give me dire warnings about sharing food with my friends. Once she found me and my friend Mikey about to become blood brothers. She really flipped out! You would have thought Mikey had the bubonic plague.*

This message was compounded by the idea that Robert was not equipped to handle the danger. He was too fragile and he needed his mother to protect him. Without her there to guide him, he was convinced that something bad would happen. He could catch some dread disease or accidentally go into a trance from which he would never return.

Heather had a more unusual pathway to her lifetrap. Both her parents were Holocaust survivors. In their teens, they had been in a concentration camp together.

HEATHER: *I grew up in a world in which the Holocaust was a possibility, you know what I mean? It could always happen again. I used to lie awake in my bed and worry that the Nazis were going to break into the house.*

Almost everyone in both my parents' families was killed. They had an album of pictures, and almost everyone in it was dead. I used to look at the pictures. There were pictures in it of children just my age.

As you might imagine, Heather's parents were very protective of her. They taught her to fear people, particularly non-Jews.

HEATHER: *They would always tell me not to trust people who weren't Jewish, even friends and neighbors. I remember when I was in sixth grade, my best friend wasn't Jewish. My mother used to tell me not to trust her, not to get too close. She told me that when she was a girl in Germany, she saw neighbors turn against her family and suddenly become enemies.*

Heather is unable to feel *safe*. The world is too dangerous, people are too dangerous. She walks through the world hypervigilant to danger.

Vulnerability can attach to a number of other lifetraps. If your parents abused you, deprived you, or abandoned you, certainly you felt vulnerable. These events were an assault on your basic sense of safety. Underneath, you are always worried about the bad thing happening again.

DANGER SIGNALS IN RELATIONSHIPS

You are most attracted to people who can take care of you. By selecting a partner who protects you, you Surrender to your Vulnerability lifetrap and thus reinforce it. On the following page are the signs that your choice of partner is lifetrap-driven:

DANGER SIGNALS IN RELATIONSHIPS

1. You tend to select partners who are willing and eager to protect you from danger or illness. Your partner is strong, and you are weak and needy.
2. Your prime concern is that your partner is fearless, physically strong, very successful financially, a doctor, or otherwise specifically equipped to protect you from your fears.
3. You seek people who are willing to listen to your fears and reassure you.

You want someone strong who is solicitous of your problems. You want someone who will pamper and overprotect you. You want someone who will make you feel safe.

VULNERABILITY LIFETRAPS

1. You feel anxious much of the time as you go about daily life because of your exaggerated fears. You may have generalized anxiety.
2. You worry so much about your health and possible illnesses that you: (a) get unnecessary medical evaluations, (b) become a burden to your family with your constant need for reassurance, and (c) cannot enjoy other aspects of life.
3. You experience panic attacks as a result of your preoccupation with bodily sensations and possible illness.
4. You are unrealistically worried about going broke. This leads you to be unnecessarily tight with money and unwilling to make any financial or career changes. You are preoccupied with keeping what you have at the expense of new investments or projects. *You cannot take risks.*
5. You go to exorbitant lengths to avoid criminal danger. For example, you avoid going out at night, visiting large cities, traveling on public transportation. *Therefore, your life is very restricted.*
6. You avoid everyday situations that entail even a slight degree of risk. For example, you avoid elevators, subways, or living in a city where there could be an earthquake.

7. You allow your partner to protect you from your fears. You need a lot of reassurance. Your partner helps you avoid feared situations. You become overly dependent on your partner. You may even resent this dependence.
8. Your chronic anxiety may, in fact, make you more prone to some kinds of psychosomatic illnesses (e.g., eczema, asthma, colitis, ulcers, flu).
9. You limit your social life because, as a result of your fears, you cannot do many of the things other people do.
10. You restrict the lives of your partner and family, who have to adapt to your fears.
11. You are likely to pass on your fears to your own children.
12. You may use a variety of coping mechanisms to an exaggerated degree to ward off danger. You may have obsessive-compulsive symptoms or superstitious thinking.
13. You may rely excessively on medication, alcohol, food, etc., to reduce your chronic anxiety.

Escape from Vulnerability is one of the greatest dangers. You avoid so many activities that it damages the quality of your life—and the lives of your partner and family. The lifetrap limits and restricts you.

HEATHER: *Sometimes I feel like I'm living inside of this dark cloud, and outside the world is going on bright and sunny. And I'm missing it all.*

You experience so much anxiety that it is hard for you to feel other things.

HEATHER: *I was at my son Robby's school concert, and there was one moment when I was sitting there with Walt and looking at Robby play, and I just felt so happy. It just struck me that I am so seldom happy. It was just a moment when the happiness broke through and the anxiety was blessedly gone.*

You can be in such a protective mode that you become closed to life.
Robert felt trapped in a job he did not like because he was afraid to take risks. He worked as a computer programmer.

ROBERT: *My job is really dull and boring, way below my level. I really could be an analyst. It's really depressing for me to go to work. All day, I sit there and do the same repetitive things.*
THERAPIST: *Why don't you look for another job?*

ROBERT: *I know. I think about that myself. It's just that the money's good and the job is really secure. I mean, they're not about to fire me.*

When you weigh the costs and benefits of taking a risk, the overwhelming factors you consider are safety and security. They are more important than any possible gain. Life for you is not a process of seeking fulfillment and joy. Rather, life is a process of trying to contain danger.

The Vulnerability lifetrap damages you socially as well. Your constant need for reassurance is a drain on the people you love. Trying to reassure you is exhausting. (We know. Before we learned better, we went this route with a number of Vulnerability patients.) You can never be reassured *enough*. It is a bottomless pit.

The Vulnerability lifetrap also drains you of time and energy you might otherwise devote to social activities. Instead of socializing, you are running to the doctor or installing burglar alarms. You are beset with symptoms, such as panic attacks and psychosomatic disorders, that further distract and debilitate you. And, of course, there are many places socially that you just cannot go. You might get attacked or spend too much money. And you require the people you love to restrict *their* lives as well.

Dependence often goes along with Vulnerability. If you deal with the Vulnerability lifetrap by picking a strong partner and constantly asking for reassurance, you never learn that you can cope on your own. Alone, you feel completely exposed to that feeling of vulnerability. You need your partner there. Obviously, this situation can create anger on both sides.

WALT: *She gets angry at me when I won't go places with her. Angry at* me. *It boggles my mind. Like I'm supposed to go trotting after her wherever she goes.*

You are prone to superstitious thinking. You may use magic rituals to ward off perceived dangers.

HEATHER: *Before I go to sleep I have to go around the house and check everything five times. I check the iron, the stove, the microwave, the toaster oven, the hair dryer, the children's room, the car, and the garage.*
THERAPIST: *That sounds pretty tedious. Why five times?*
HEATHER: *It's what I have to do to be able to relax and go to sleep.*
THERAPIST: *What happens if you don't do the checking?*
HEATHER: *I lie in bed and worry. I just can't go to sleep until I've checked everything five times.*

Counting, checking, washing, cleaning—these are all examples of obsessive-compulsive rituals you may engage in to make life magically safe. Such rituals are a further drain on your life energy.

All of these patterns reinforce your exaggerated sense of the world as dangerous. You never learn that with *reasonable* precautions, the world can be a safe place.

These are the steps to changing your lifetrap:

CHANGING YOUR VULNERABILITY LIFETRAP

1. Try to understand the origins of your lifetrap.
2. Make a list of your specific fears.
3. Develop a hierarchy of feared situations.
4. Meet with the people you love—your spouse, lover, family, friends—and enlist their support in helping you face your fears.
5. Examine the probability of your feared events occurring.
6. Write a flashcard for each fear.
7. Talk to your inner child. Be a strong, brave parent to your child.
8. Practice techniques for relaxation.
9. Begin to tackle each of your fears *in imagery*.
10. Tackle each fear in real life.
11. Reward yourself for each step you take.

---

1. Try to Understand the Origins of Your Lifetrap. Were your parents phobic? Overprotective? Underprotective? In what areas did you learn to feel vulnerable? Was it illness? Traveling? Money? Dangers in your environment? Losing control?

The origin of the lifetrap is usually obvious. You may know it already. Insight into the origin is important. However, it does not usually have as powerful an effect on this lifetrap as it does on some others. It is a good place to start, but it will not get you far in terms of change.

2. Make a List of Your Specific Fears. We want you to take an objective look at your fears. Look at the ways you Surrender to your Vulnerability (by overprotecting yourself) and the ways that you Escape (through avoiding situations).

Use the following chart. List the situations that you fear—the subway, the streets at night, spending money, places where there are germs, etc. Now rate each fear along a number of dimensions. Use a scale from 0 to 100, with 0 meaning "not at all" and 100 meaning "as much as you can imagine." How strong is the fear? How much do you Escape, or avoid, the situation? Finally, how do you and your family overprotect yourself?

Here is the chart, filled out by Robert, for "Being alone in my house at night." Robert feared this because "something bad might happen. I'll be alone without distractions, and my mind will start going off on a track." Ultimately, what Robert feared was having a panic attack and losing his mind.

FEARED SITUATION	LEVEL OF FEAR	DEGREE OF AVOIDANCE	HOW I OVERPROTECT MYSELF	HOW I ALLOW MY FAMILY TO OVERPROTECT ME
Being alone in my apartment at night.	75%	80%	Invite friends over, call friends, go out at night all the time, work late, get girlfriends to stay over.	Talk on the phone with me constantly.

Do this for all your feared situations. Become aware of how the Vulnerability lifetrap manifests itself in your life.

3. Develop a Hierarchy of Feared Situations. We want you to develop a hierarchy for each feared situation on your chart. Break each fear into small steps you could take to overcome it. Next, rate the steps from 1 to 100 in terms of how anxious you are about each one. Finally, arrange the steps in order, listing the easiest step first and working your way up to the most difficult step. For example, here is Heather's list of hierarchies:

FEARED SITUATION	ANXIETY RATING
1. SWIMMING	
1. Swimming in shallow water	20
2. Swimming in water over my head	65
2. ELEVATOR	
1. Going on elevator five floors or less *with someone*	25
2. Going on elevator five floors or less *alone*	40
3. Going on elevator more than five floors *with someone*	60
4. Going on elevator more than five floors *alone*	80
3. GOING TO THE CITY	
1. Going to the city for a day activity *with someone*	30
2. Going to the city for a day activity *alone*	50
3. Going to the city for a night activity *with someone*	75
4. Going to the city for a night activity *alone*	100
4. ALONE IN THE HOUSE	
1. Alone in the house during the day *with phone calls*	30
2. Alone in the house during the day, *no phone calling*	45
3. Going onto the driveway at night alone	50
4. Alone in the house during early evening	55

FEARED SITUATION	ANXIETY RATING
5. Alone in the house at night *with phone calls*	80
6. Alone in the house at night, *no phone calling*	95
5. SPENDING MONEY	
1. Spending some money from savings on fun activity	35
2. Looking for a bigger house	55
3. Selling some insurance policies	75
4. Spending money on fancy family vacation	85
6. GOING PLACES ALONE	
1. Going to the supermarket without Walt or the children	40
2. Driving to visit friends alone	60
3. Going to the mall alone	85
7. TRAVELING	
1. Planning trips	30
2. Going on a day trip with family	50
3. Going on a day trip by train alone	85
4. Going away overnight with family	95
5. Getting on an airplane	100

List as many steps for each situation as you like. The crucial factor is that the hierarchy be *do*-able. There should always be an item easy enough to do at the top of your list.

The hierarchies involve gradually stopping both your escapes (e.g., going places you usually avoid) and your overprotections (e.g., taking more risks alone). Be sure to include both. Use the first chart you made as a reference.

4. *Meet with the People You Love—Your Spouse, Lover, Family, Friends—and Enlist Their Support in Helping You Face Your Fears*. Let the people around you know what you are doing. Tell them you are trying to overcome your feelings of vulnerability. Ask them to start protecting you less and reassuring you less. You can ask them to gradually phase these things out.

Encourage people to express more of their own vulnerability to you. Most likely, they will be relieved.

WALT: *It's nice not to have to be the strong one all the time. It was wearing on me. I mean, I have problems too. I'd like to discuss them with Heather without her falling apart. I have some problems at work especially that I really would like to talk out.*

Most partners will jump at the opportunity to give up such an overprotective role. Usually partners are weary of being so solicitous. Besides, they do not have to give up the role entirely. They just have to reduce it to a normal level.

You have chosen many of the people around you because they reinforce your lifetrap. You have to get them to stop if you want to overcome your Vulnerability lifetrap.

5. *Examine the Probability of Your Feared Events Occurring*. Many people with the Vulnerability lifetrap exaggerate the probability that feared events will occur.

THERAPIST: *What do you think the odds are of your airplane crashing?*
HEATHER: *I don't know. I guess about one in a thousand.*
THERAPIST: *And when you are on an airplane, what do you think the odds are then?*
HEATHER: *When I'm on the plane, the odds seem higher. Maybe six out of ten.*
THERAPIST: *Do you know that the odds really are closer to one in a million?*

Right now you use *intuition* to judge the odds of feared events occurring. You *feel* that the likelihood of danger is high. The problem is that your intuition is simply wrong because it is under the sway of your lifetrap.

We want you to conduct a more objective assessment of the odds. Start gathering information. Solicit the opinions of other people. Read about the subject. Educate yourself. Greater accuracy will decrease your anxiety.

For each feared situation, write down the odds of each fear happening *as it feels to you when you confront it*. Then write down the *realistic* odds of your fear happening, based on the opinions of the people close to you who do not share your Vulnerability lifetrap.

Use this chart. This is a sample entry filled out by Robert.

FEARED SITUATION	HOW LIKELY I FEEL THIS IS TO HAPPEN WHEN I'M IN THE SITUATION	MORE REALISTIC ODDS OF MY FEAR HAPPENING (BASED ON OTHER PEOPLE'S OPINIONS)
Losing my mind during a panic attack	99%	25%

In fact, the 25 percent figure Robert wrote here is too high. The odds of someone losing their mind while having a panic attack are *practically zero*. This is because, as far as we know, it has never happened. Panic Disorder is a vastly studied subject, but there is not one reported case of a person going crazy during a panic attack. The same is true of dying and losing control. These things do not happen during panic attacks. You are just *afraid* they will happen.

To put it another way, the odds that you will die, go crazy, or lose control during a panic attack are no higher than they are at any other time, when you are not having a panic attack. The panic attack does not make it any more likely.

Exaggerating the odds is part of your tendency to catastrophize. You jump to the worst possible conclusion and consider it to be the most likely one. In fact, the likelihood of most catastrophic events happening to you is extremely low.

6. Write a Flashcard for Each Fear. Write a flashcard for each one of your fears. Remind yourself of how the lifetrap leads you to catastrophize. Encourage yourself to face what you are escaping, and give up your overprotectiveness.

Here is a card Heather wrote for her fear, riding the elevator.

A VULNERABILITY FLASHCARD

I know that right now I am afraid to ride the elevator. I am afraid of some catastrophe, like the building catching fire, and the elevator getting stuck. I feel this is very likely to happen.

But what really is happening is that my Vulnerability lifetrap is getting triggered. I'm probably exaggerating the degree of risk. Therefore, I will force myself to go into this situation anyway, in spite of my fears, to see that it's not really dangerous.

I know I want to count the floors five times before I get on the elevator. I feel that the checking will make me feel safer. But I don't need to do the checking. I am safe enough without it. The checking is just a superstition. Besides, it's a burden and I want to give it up.

Use the flashcards whenever your lifetrap is triggered. It can counter your tendency to catastrophize. Keep reassessing the odds. Enter the situation. Eventually, your anxiety will pass and you will feel comfortable.

7. Talk to Your Inner Child. Be a Strong, Brave Parent to Your Child. The feelings connected to your lifetrap are *child* feelings. They are the feelings of your vulnerable inner child. You need to develop an inner parent to help this inner child. You can use imagery.

THERAPIST: *Get an image of a time as a child that you felt vulnerable. Don't force it. Just tell me the first one that comes into your mind.*
HEATHER: *I am in the kitchen with my mother and our new neighbor. Her name is Blanche and she's very nice.*

I'm about six. I was almost six when Blanche moved into the neighborhood. I'm sitting at the table eating a sandwich, and I hear Blanche ask my mother about the numbers on her arm. She has just noticed my mother's tattoo. My mother starts to tell Blanche that she was in a concentration camp. "A long time ago," she says, "when I was a child."

This is the first time I have really heard of it. I mean, I already know something terrible happened, but this is the first time I start to understand what it was.

THERAPIST: *How do you feel?*
HEATHER: *I feel this chill rush over me. I'm scared, very scared.*

Once you are in touch with the image and the feeling of vulnerability, bring yourself into the image as an adult to comfort your frightened child. Try to make the vulnerable child feel safer.

HEATHER: *I bring myself into the image as an adult. I sit down at the table with the child Heather. I say: "You don't have to be afraid. You're safe. You're in your own house and I am here and you're safe. No one will hurt you. There are no Nazis here. If you want to go out and play, I will come with you. I'll protect you. I'll help you face what you fear."*

We want you to bring in this adult whenever your lifetrap is triggered. Reassure yourself that there is nothing to fear. Help your inner child feel safe enough to confront the situation.

8. Practice Techniques for Relaxation. Relaxation techniques can help center both your body and your mind. They can control the physical symptoms of anxiety and keep your mind from galloping away into catastrophizing.

Here is a simple meditation. It has two parts: a breathing part and a meditation part. Breathe slowly and from your diaphragm. That is, you should breathe no more than eight breaths a minute, and when you breathe, only your stomach should move. Your chest should be totally still. Breathing this way will prevent you from hyperventilating, the major cause of most physical anxiety symptoms, particularly panic attacks.

The meditation part follows the rhythm of your breathing. As you breathe in, slowly think the word *relax*. As you breathe out, think the word *breathe*. Just keep mentally repeating these words, slowly in time to your breaths.

Use this relaxation technique whenever your Vulnerability lifetrap is triggered. You will find it can help immeasurably.

ROBERT: *At first, when I started using the breathing meditation, it made me nervous. It took me a while to really get going with it. I didn't like focusing on my breathing.*
THERAPIST: *I know, you have to get through that with this technique.*
ROBERT: *But I did get through it and now it really helps. Whenever I start getting panicky I use it, and it calms me down and helps me stay in the situation.*

9. Begin to Tackle Each of Your Fears in Imagery. Imagery plays a major role in the triggering of this lifetrap. If you pay attention, you will realize that you are not only having catastrophic thoughts, but you are also having catastrophic images. You are vividly picturing the worst possible outcome. Naturally, this scares you.

We want you to start using imagery to make things better, not worse. We want you to rehearse *good* outcomes—in which you give up your overprotections, enter situations, and cope well.

Use the hierarchies you developed. Start with the easier steps first. Sit down in a comfortable chair, and relax yourself with your breathing meditation. Once you are relaxed, get an image of the feared situation. Imagine yourself going through the situation exactly as you would wish.

THERAPIST: *What are you imagining?*

HEATHER: *I'm standing at the elevator. Walt is with me, and the adult Heather is there too. It makes me feel safe to have them there.*

I want to count all the floors five times, but I resist. Once I decide not to do the counting, I get this wave of anxiety, but it passes through me and leaves. I feel fine. I feel strong and confident.

The elevator comes and the doors open. We get in. I stand calmly and do my relaxation. Before you know it, the elevator stops and we get out. We have gone five floors and I feel fine.

Gradually work your way up your hierarchies. Use imagery to gain a sense of mastery over all your fears. You have had many imagery rehearsals of bad outcomes. It is time to have some imagery rehearsals of success and safety.

10. Tackle Each Fear in Real Life. Behavioral change is the culmination of everything you have done so far. It is the most powerful way to change your lifetrap. Once you actually experiment with overcoming avoidance and start proving to yourself you were distorting, then it becomes like a loop. The more you enter situations and see that the bad thing does not happen, the safer you feel, and the safer you feel, the more you enter situations.

Again, use your hierarchies and start with the easier steps. Keep doing a step until you can do it comfortably. Gain a sense of mastery over one step before you move to the next one. Gradually work your way up until you are doing everything. Use the flashcards, breathing meditation, and reparenting techniques to help you confront each situation.

11. Reward Yourself for Each Step You Take. Remembering to reward yourself will cement the gains you have made. After you complete a hierarchy step, take a moment to congratulate yourself. Give your inner child credit for confronting these fears. You deserve praise—what you did took courage. It is not easy for you to confront your fears.

Point out to yourself how each fear does not actually come true. This will reinforce the sense that your feelings of vulnerability are greatly exaggerated.

SOME FINAL WORDS

The real reward for overcoming your Vulnerability lifetrap is the expansion of your life. There is so much that you miss because of your fears. After using the steps described here, both Heather and Robert found their lives vastly improved.

ROBERT: *I think the thing that really got me moving was realizing how much I was missing out. I mean, I was really depriving myself of so much. It was a life devoted to anxiety.*

If you find you cannot overcome the lifetrap alone, consider therapy. Why continue to restrict your activities and deny yourself? The journey out of the Vulnerability lifetrap is a journey back to life.

12

"I'M WORTHLESS"
THE DEFECTIVENESS LIFETRAP

Alison looks frightened when she walks into our office. It is obvious she is uncomfortable talking about herself. We try to put her at ease. After a while, we ask her why she has come. She tells us she is depressed.

ALISON: *I guess I get down on myself a lot. I'm always thinking, "Why would anyone want to be with me?" Like there's this guy I've gone out with for a few months. Almost a year actually. His name is Matthew. The other day I called him and left a message on his machine. Waiting for him to call back, I kept thinking, "I know he won't call, he doesn't want to see me anymore." Like he's found me out or something. It's like I keep waiting for the moment that he finds me out.*

And even when he called back, the whole time I kept thinking, "He doesn't want to talk to me, he wants to get off the phone."
THERAPIST: *It's hard for you to believe that he really cares.*

As we talk more, I realize that Alison is considering marrying Matthew: "He asked me to marry him a few weeks ago. He's really good to me. I know I'd be crazy not to marry him." But for some unaccountable reason she finds herself frightened at the idea of marriage.

ALISON: *Maybe I just haven't had too many good relationships. The last guy I thought about marrying was not exactly the nicest guy in the world. In fact he was emotionally abusive. He was on my back about something all the time.*

THERAPIST: *But it doesn't sound like Matthew is like that. Just the opposite.*

ALISON: *No, I know. It's something different. I think I'm just afraid to let anyone get close to me. And Matthew's a person who is trying to get close to me.*

And that is why Alison has come to therapy. She is having a "crisis of intimacy."

ELIOT: FORTY-THREE YEARS OLD. HE COMES TO THERAPY WITH HIS WIFE FOR MARITAL PROBLEMS.

Our first impression of Eliot is one of tight self-control. Throughout the session, we glimpse a kind of cold anger underneath. Eliot has come to therapy with his wife, Maria, to focus on marital problems.

Eliot and Maria have been married for seven years and have one child. Maria has just found out that Eliot has been having an affair. She threatened to leave the marriage unless he agreed to come to therapy. In that first session, he told us, "I really don't think that *I* need to be here," and "If you ask me, *she's* the one who has problems." It is almost as if he expected us to work with him to solve *her* problems.

Throughout the session, Eliot is critical of Maria and critical of us. It is difficult to connect with him. He keeps a distance. After we explain lifetrap therapy to them, he says, "It sounds incredibly simple-minded," and "Is that all there is to this therapy?" We know he is testing us, and we tell him so. "You want to make sure we can handle you." He wants to see if he can put us one-down—if he can make us defensive. When he sees that he cannot, we gain some of his respect.

Although we are feeling irritated, we remain empathic. We know that, underneath, Eliot is frightened of us. He is afraid we can see through him.

THE DEFECTIVENESS QUESTIONNAIRE

This questionnaire will measure the strength of your Defectiveness lifetrap. Use this scale to answer each of the items:

1 Completely untrue of me
2 Mostly untrue of me
3 Slightly more true than untrue of me
4 Moderately true of me
5 Mostly true of me
6 Describes me perfectly

If you have any 5's or 6's on this questionnaire, this lifetrap may still apply to you, even if your score is in the low range.

SCORE	DESCRIPTION
	1. No man or woman could love me if he/she really knew me.
	2. I am inherently flawed and defective. I am unworthy of love.
	3. I have secrets that I do not want to share, even with the people closest to me.
	4. It was my fault that my parents could not love me.
	5. I hide the real me. The real me is unacceptable. The self I show is a false self.
	6. I am often drawn to people—parents, friends, and lovers—who are critical and reject me.
	7. I am often critical and rejecting myself, especially of people who seem to love me.
	8. I devalue my positive qualities.
	9. I live with a great deal of shame about myself.
	10. One of my greatest fears is that my faults will be exposed.
	YOUR TOTAL DEFECTIVENESS SCORE (Add your scores together for questions 1–10)

INTERPRETING YOUR DEFECTIVENESS SCORE

10–19 Very low. This lifetrap probably does *not* apply to you.
20–29 Fairly low. This lifetrap may only apply *occasionally*.
30–39 Moderate. This lifetrap is an *issue* in your life.
40–49 High. This is definitely an *important* lifetrap for you.
50–60 Very high. This is definitely one of your *core* lifetraps.

THE EXPERIENCE OF DEFECTIVENESS

The emotion that is most connected to the Defectiveness lifetrap is *shame*. Shame is what you feel when your defects are exposed. You will do almost anything to avoid this feeling of shame. Consequently you go to great lengths to keep your defectiveness hidden.

You feel that your defectiveness is *inside* you. It is not immediately observable. Rather, it is something in the essence of your being—you feel completely unworthy of love. In contrast to the Social Exclusion lifetrap, which concerns superficial or *observable* characteristics, Defectiveness is an inner state. While we usually know fairly quickly whether someone has a Social Exclusion lifetrap, Defectiveness is not so obvious. Certainly it is one of the most common lifetraps, but it is often hard to detect. Because your imagined defect is internal—unseen—you suffer even more from the terror of being exposed.

Almost half our patients have Defectiveness as one of their primary lifetraps. However, on the surface, these patients look very different. Each copes with feelings of shame in different ways. Some lack confidence and look insecure (Surrender). Some look normal (Escape). And some look so good you would never believe they had the lifetrap (Counterattack).

Alison is an example of someone who *surrenders* to her sense of defectiveness. She is in touch with feelings of being inherently flawed.

ALISON: *I have always felt there is something wrong with me, deep inside where no one can see. And that I would live my whole life without anyone loving me.*
THERAPIST: *When you think of someone loving you, how does it feel?*
ALISON: *It makes me* cringe.

Alison feels that there is something about her—some secret—which, if known, would make her utterly unacceptable. She cannot say what that secret is.

There is a strong sense that, whatever Alison's secret is, she believes she cannot change it. It is what she *is*, her very being. The best she can do is hide it, and try to postpone the inevitable moment when someone gets close enough to find out.

Alison believes strongly that no one could possibly care about her. She constantly discounts evidence that people like her and want to be with her.

ALISON: *I told Matthew that I didn't want to go to his brother's wedding.*
THERAPIST: *Why did you do that? I thought you wanted to go.*
ALISON: *Yes, but I knew Matthew didn't really want me to go.*
THERAPIST: *Didn't he ask you?*
ALISON: *Yes, but I just knew he really didn't* want *me there.*

She also magnifies evidence that people dislike and reject her, even with us; she tries to twist what we say to imply we do not really care about her.

THERAPIST: *We wanted to ask you if we could switch your session time next week to an hour earlier.*
ALISON: *Do you mean you don't want to have our session? If you don't, it's okay. I mean, if there's something you have to do.*
THERAPIST: *No, not at all. Of course we want to have our session. We just want to know if it's possible for you to move it back an hour.*

Alison is very self-punitive. At various times we have heard her say, "I'm no good," "I'm a jerk," "I'm worthless," "I'm good-for-nothing," "I have nothing to offer." At the beginning of therapy, her thinking was filled with put-downs of herself. And there were a few extremely painful moments in therapy when her self-criticism rose to self-hatred. At these moments, she experienced herself as "a vile, disgusting person."

Alison's Defectiveness lifetrap makes her much too vulnerable in relationships. The other person has *so* much power to hurt her. She does not protect herself or defend herself. Eliot is at the opposite end of the spectrum. He has a quality of *invulnerability*. No one can touch him. He has developed the Counterattacking style of coping so effectively that most people never suspect; in fact, Eliot himself is largely unaware of his own deep feelings of shame.

Eliot is an example of a fragile narcissist. A narcissist is someone who lacks empathy, blames others for problems, and has a strong sense of *entitlement*. People like Eliot have developed this narcissism to fight back against their underlying feelings that no one will ever love or respect them. It is as if they are saying to the world: "I will be so demanding, act so superior, and become so special that you will never be able to ignore or criticize me again." (This is an example of the Counterattack coping style we describe in Chapter 4. You can read more about narcissism and how it can be changed, in the chapter on Entitlement.)

Narcissists will hold onto their self-centeredness at almost all costs. Eliot was watching his marriage to a woman he loved deeply disintegrate, yet he was unable to admit that he had problems. He would rather lose everything than risk making himself vulnerable. This is often the case. Until their backs are against the wall, narcissists will not change. As with Eliot, the threat of abandonment is one thing that can sometimes motivate a narcissist to change.

MARIA: *No matter how much he hurt me, no matter how much pain I was in, it didn't make any difference. I could cry a thousand tears, and he would keep seeing that woman. It was only when he saw I was really leaving that he agreed to stop seeing her.*

Eliot and Maria *both* have the Defectiveness lifetrap. He *counterattacks* his underlying shame through narcissism, while she *surrenders* to her sense of worthlessness. He rejects her, and she is the victim of rejection. Together they reenact their original drama of rejection by the parent.

If you have the Defectiveness lifetrap, you probably lie somewhere between the two extremes represented by Alison and Eliot. Perhaps you allow yourself to be quite vulnerable in some areas but not in others. We have many patients like this. They come in very willing to talk about their lives, but when certain topics arise, they skirt the issue. These topics make them feel ashamed or defective.

It is relatively unusual for patients to come in knowing that they feel defective. Most patients mask or avoid these feelings in some way because it is so painful to experience the extraordinary self-hatred and shame connected with this lifetrap. Without realizing it, people strive to keep themselves unaware of their feelings of shame. They come to therapy complaining of other things, of relationship problems or depression.

You may experience a chronic, vague unhappiness without being able to explain why. You do not realize that your depression is a function of your negative view of yourself. Feeling unworthy and angry at yourself is a large part of depression. You may feel that you have been depressed your whole life—a kind of low-level depression lurking in the background.

If your primary coping style is Escape, you may have addictions or compulsions. Drinking, drugs, overworking, and overeating are all ways of numbing yourself to avoid the pain of feeling worthless.

THE ORIGINS OF THE DEFECTIVENESS LIFETRAP

1. Someone in your family was extremely critical, demeaning, or punitive toward you. You were repeatedly criticized or punished for how you looked, how you behaved, or what you said.
2. You were made to feel like a disappointment by a parent.
3. You were rejected or unloved by one or both of your parents.
4. You were sexually, physically, or emotionally abused by a family member.
5. You were blamed all the time for things that went wrong in your family.
6. Your parent told you repeatedly that you were bad, worthless, or good-for-nothing.
7. You were repeatedly compared in an unfavorable way with your brothers or sisters, or they were preferred over you.
8. One of your parents left home, and you blamed yourself.

The Defectiveness lifetrap comes from feeling *unlovable* or *not respected* as a child. You were repeatedly rejected or criticized by one or both of your parents.

ALISON: *I once read this book that said that the purpose of a woman's life was to inspire love. It always struck me that that's what I've been unable to do. Inspire love.*

Defectiveness is a global feeling. It is the sense of being unworthy of love. You felt so flawed or inadequate that even your parent could not love you or value you for who you are.

You almost certainly felt that your parent was *right* to criticize you, devalue you, reject you, or not give you love. You felt that you deserved it. As a child, you blamed yourself. Everything happened because *you* were so worthless, inadequate, flawed, and defective. For this reason, you probably did not feel angry about the way you were treated. Rather, you felt ashamed and sad.

Alison's lifetrap is largely the result of her father's criticalness. He made it clear very early that she was a disappointment.

ALISON: *I just wasn't what he wanted in any way, really. I felt that every-thing about me was wrong. We used to sit at the dinner table, and, when I was quiet, he would criticize me for not talking; when I talked, he would tell me how boring I was.*

She *incorporated* her father's criticalness. Her father's view of her became her view of herself.

ALISON: *I just keep thinking, why would Matthew want to marry me? I have nothing to offer. I'm so immature. I just don't have what it takes to keep a man interested. I'm not particularly special in any way. My looks are mediocre, my mind is mediocre. I don't have a great personality.*
THERAPIST: *Whose voice is this? Whose voice is it in your head that's saying all this?*
ALISON: *Well, it's Eric. My old boyfriend.*
THERAPIST: *Is it anyone else?*
ALISON: *(Pause.) It's my father's voice.*

Like Alison, you internalized the voice of your critical parent and it became part of you. In a sense, the voice of your critical parent *is* your lifetrap—this voice that constantly criticizes, punishes, and rejects you in your mind.

Shame may have dominated your childhood. Each time your defec-tiveness was exposed, you felt ashamed. This shame cut deep. It was not about superficial things. Rather it was about who you were.

ALISON: *I remember when I was a teenager, I once spent the whole after-noon reading up on this political event, it was Watergate I think, just so I could talk about it at dinner. And, when I opened my mouth, he said, "Is that all you can think to say about it?"*
THERAPIST: *What did you feel?*
ALISON: *I felt so ashamed that I tried to be interesting, and that I failed so abysmally.*
THERAPIST: *Yes, like you were* exposed *as wanting to be something you could never be.*
ALISON: *What was that?*
THERAPIST: *Loved by him.*

We might ask *why* Alison's father was so cold and rejecting. One strong possibility is that he had a Defectiveness lifetrap himself. However, he coped with his lifetrap by Counterattacking. He made himself feel better by putting Alison down and making her feel that she was the defective one. He scapegoated her. Perhaps in Alison he saw a reflection of his own defectiveness. We feel this is often the case. Many times it seems that the parents have defectiveness issues themselves, which they pass along to their children. This is how the lifetrap is passed down through the generations.

Parents who give rise to the Defectiveness lifetrap are usually punitive and critical. There may be physical, emotional, or sexual abuse. Defectiveness and Abuse often go hand-in-hand. While it is *possible* for a child who is abused to feel that it is unfair and to be angry without feeling defective, this is seldom the case. Far more often, the child accepts responsibility. The child feels guilt and shame.

Many children find some way to make up for their feelings of defectiveness. This is where the lifetrap starts to blend with Entitlement and Unrelenting Standards. Many people who have grown up being criticized and made to feel defective *compensate* by trying to be superior in some area. They set high standards and strive for success and status. They may act arrogant and entitled. With money and recognition, they try to allay that inner feeling of defectiveness.

This is what happened to Eliot. On the surface, he looks very much like a success. He is the owner of a popular nightclub frequented by stars. Each night he walks through the club bestowing favors on important people. He decides who gets a table, who gets free drinks, who gets an invitation to the V.I.P. room. He tells stories with obvious glee about denying special favors to celebrities. However, the defective feeling is still there underneath.

ELIOT: *Only one person has ever made me squirm at my club. That was [a popular male movie star]. He pranced in, acting like he owned the place, and I decided to put him in his place. I showed him to this really mediocre table. As I walked away, I looked at him, and he was giving me this look. Man, it was a withering glance.*
THERAPIST: *What did you feel at that moment?*
ELIOT: *I felt like he could see right through me. Like I wasn't fooling him one bit. Like I was an impostor.*

The sense that it all might collapse is always with Eliot. This is the fragility of his narcissism. His *persona* can collapse, suddenly exposing the worthless person he believes he is underneath.

Both of Eliot's parents were consistently critical and demeaning. What made it more difficult was that his parents adored his older brother.

ELIOT: *My problem was that my brother was such a hard act to follow. He was better looking, smarter, funnier. And he treated me like dirt. Just like my parents did. He'd pick on me and they'd laugh. He always got the best of everything and I was left with hand-me-downs. Well, he doesn't have the best of everything now. I have it now, and he's nothing.*

Defectiveness is often formed through comparisons with a favored sibling. Older siblings often foster this lifetrap. It is easy for them to be better at everything because they are older. They are smarter, faster, stronger, or more competent. Older siblings are often critical of their younger, less talented siblings.

Humiliation was a prominent theme in Eliot's childhood. Again and again, his shortcomings were the object of ridicule.

ELIOT: *I remember one time my dad was going to take me and my brother to a ball game. Then my brother got sick and couldn't go. The day we were supposed to go, I got dressed and was waiting by the door. I was all excited. My father came down and looked at me, and asked me where I thought I was going. I said the ball game, and he said he'd have to be crazy to go all the way to the game just for me.*

I never let him know I wanted anything from him again.

Eliot learned to hide his true thoughts and feelings. His true self became a secret, known only to him. This way, he felt less vulnerable. He could maintain a sense of pride. It was too dangerous to reveal himself. Anything he offered was met with a critical eye. Revealing himself meant risking exposure to shame, and the worst shame was being exposed as wanting love.

We pay a high price for burying our true self in the way Eliot did. It is a great loss, like a death. Spontaneity, joy, trust, and intimacy are all lost, and they are replaced by a guarded, shut-down shell. The person constructs a false self. This false self is harder, less easily wounded. But no matter how hard the exterior, deep inside there is pain about losing one's true self.

The advantage of building this protective shell is that you often feel better day-to-day. At least on the surface, you seem to be doing well. But it is an illusion. Inside you still *feel* defective and unloved. The problem with the shell is that you never really address the core issue. A true self that stays hidden cannot heal. You have to stop settling for illusion and start going for the real thing.

It is very important to realize that the Defectiveness lifetrap is *not usually based on a real defect*. Even people who have serious physical or mental handicaps do not necessarily develop this lifetrap. The crucial factor is not the presence of a defect, but rather how you are made to feel about yourself by your parents and the other members of your family. If you are loved, valued, and respected by your family members—regardless of your actual strengths and weaknesses—you will almost certainly not feel worthless, ashamed, or defective.

DANGER SIGNALS WHILE DATING

1. You avoid dating altogether.
2. You tend to have a series of short, intense affairs, or several affairs simultaneously.
3. You are drawn to partners who are critical of you and put you down all the time.
4. You are drawn to partners who are physically or emotionally abusive toward you.
5. You are most attracted to partners who are not that interested in you, hoping you can win their love.
6. You are only drawn to the most attractive and desirable partners, even when it is obvious that you will not be able to attain them.
7. You are most comfortable with partners who do not want to know you very deeply.
8. You only date people you feel are below you, whom you do not really love.
9. You are drawn to partners who are unable to commit to you or to spend time with you on a regular basis. They may be married, insist on simultaneously dating other people, travel regularly, or live in another city.
10. You get into relationships in which you put down, abuse, or neglect your partners.

You may cope with your Defectiveness lifetrap by avoiding long-term, intimate relationships altogether. You may have no relationships at all, only short relationships, or multiple relationships. By avoiding long-term commitment, you make certain that no one gets close enough to see your inner flaws.

Another way you might avoid intimacy is by becoming involved with someone else who does not want to be intimate. Even though you are dating, you lead parallel lives where you never get too close.

Eliot had a series of affairs throughout his marriage; he was always involved with at least one other woman, sometimes two. However, only once did he ever meet a woman that he thought he could love. Interestingly, *he did not ask her out.* Like Eliot, you might avoid dating people who really interest you. You only date people you know you could never love.

You might have a relationship with a person who lives at a distance, or who is traveling all the time. You can only see the person on weekends. There are many ways you can set up relationships to escape the intimate contact you fear.

Alison is more willing than Eliot to become intimate; she gets involved with men and falls in love. But she is most attracted to men who criticize and reject her. Her previous boyfriend was this way. She stayed with him for years even though he was nasty and insulting the entire time.

Many people who get into masochistic relationships—in which they tolerate being badly mistreated—have Defectiveness lifetraps. They basically feel that this is all they deserve. When we asked Alison why she stayed with her previous boyfriend for so long, she said, "I felt I was lucky to have someone who wanted to be with me at all."

If you have the Defectiveness lifetrap, be careful when there is very strong chemistry. You probably have the most powerful attraction to partners who criticize and reject you. They reinforce your feelings of defectiveness. Critical partners will feel *familiar* because they echo your childhood environment. We strongly recommend that you stop dating partners who do not treat you well rather than try to win them over and gain their love.

DEFECTIVENESS LIFETRAPS

1. You become very critical of your partner once you feel accepted, and your romantic feelings disappear. You then act in a demeaning or critical manner.
2. You hide your true self so you never really feel that your partner knows you.

3. You are jealous and possessive of your partner.
4. You constantly compare yourself unfavorably with other people and feel envious and inadequate.
5. You constantly need or demand reassurance that your partner still values you.
6. You put yourself down around your partner.
7. You allow your partner to criticize you, put you down, or mistreat you.
8. You have difficulty accepting valid criticism; you become defensive or hostile.
9. You are extremely critical of your children.
10. You feel like an impostor when you are successful. You feel extremely anxious that you cannot maintain your success.
11. You become despondent or deeply depressed over career setbacks or rejections in relationships.
12. You feel extremely nervous when speaking in public.

If you do form a relationship with a partner who loves you and whom you could love, there are many ways you can reinforce your Defectiveness lifetrap within the relationship.

Your criticalness can be a major problem. If you are narcissistic, you may be more comfortable with a partner you can see as one-down. Then you do not have to worry so much about being found out, judged, or rejected. Eliot illustrated this pattern in his marriage to Maria:

MARIA: *Eliot picks apart everything I do. When I'm with him, I feel like I'm always doing something wrong.*

In sessions alone with us, Eliot would recount his sexual exploits. And, as he described each woman, there was always something wrong. This one had the wrong texture of hair, that one had legs that were too short, this one had too menial a job. In fact, Eliot had exact specifications for his perfect woman.

THERAPIST: *What is it that you want from a relationship?*
ELIOT: *What I want most is a woman with blonde hair, tall but not too tall, like not above 5'7", tan skin. Slim and athletic. Not too big breasts. I want her to dress kind of preppy. You know, that clean look, but with*

an arty edge. And I want her to be successful, but not too successful. Not more successful than I am (laughs).
THERAPIST: *Have you ever found her?*
ELIOT: *Not even close.*

Eliot criticizes his partners for failing to meet his specifications. In this way, he keeps himself from caring too much about how they feel toward him. If you have the Defectiveness lifetrap, you may also try to devalue your partners. You believe that a truly desirable partner will see your flaws and ultimately reject you.

The person Eliot criticizes most is the person he loves most—his wife Maria. In fact, the vehemence with which he criticizes her is one of the signs of his love. When Eliot feels his love for her, it increases her value, and almost reflexively he lashes out at her.

You may feel that anyone who could love *you* must be low in value anyway. This is the old Groucho Marx line, "I never would want to belong to a club that would have me as a member." It is as if, in loving you, your partner does something wrong.

ELIOT: *Each of my relationships is a conquest for me. I get all excited about the pursuit, but when I finally win her, I lose interest.*
THERAPIST: *At what point do you win her?*
ELIOT: *(Pause.) I guess it's when she starts to care about me.*

Romantic relationships are the most intimate, so your false self moves into full gear. As Alison puts it, "I always feel like I'm putting on an act with Matthew." The failure to be genuine is a common pattern with this lifetrap. You believe that only your false self is worthy of love. By hiding your true self, you never believe that your partner loves the real you. By not being completely open, you reinforce your sense that the real self is shameful and unlovable. Your greatest terror may be of being exposed: that eventually your partner will see through your act to the defective person beneath.

ALISON: *I just know that I'll marry him and one day he'll turn around and tell me that it's all been a mistake, that he doesn't really love me. I don't really understand why he hasn't done it yet. But he's gonna do it sometime.*
THERAPIST: *And you're just waiting.*
ALISON: *Yes. It's only a matter of time.*

You may even, like Alison, consider ending the relationship. The situation is so fraught with anxiety that you feel that you cannot stand it anymore.

Envy and jealousy are almost always facets of the Defectiveness lifetrap. You are constantly comparing yourself unfavorably to other people.

ALISON: *Whenever we go out, like to a bar or a party, I always feel like he wants to be with the other women more than with me. He tells me I'm crazy, and in a way I think I am. I mean he doesn't flirt or anything. It's just that I start thinking that the other women are prettier or sexier or more interesting. I would rather be with them if I were him. If he even so much as talks to another woman, I get very upset.*

Alison idealizes other women and exaggerates her own flaws. When she makes comparisons, it is hard for her to win. She spends much of the time feeling that other women are more desirable than she.

To reassure herself that Matthew still cares, Alison barrages him with questions: "You want to be with her, don't you?" "Don't you think that girl's prettier than me?" She hangs onto Matthew, afraid to leave him alone. Her attempts to insulate him from her rivals usually backfire. She comes across as needy and insecure, which drives Matthew away. This tends to lower her value in his eyes.

Matthew described this process in one of our couples sessions.

MATTHEW: *The other night we went out dancing with my friend, Kevin, and his new girlfriend, Elyssa. Alison got all sulky, and started saying that I'd rather be with Elyssa. For no reason. It was a real drag.*

I really love Alison, but I don't want to be with someone where I can't even go to the bathroom for five minutes without being accused of trying to play around.

You may not be as obvious as Alison. Like Eliot, you may have learned to hide your feelings of jealousy, but inside you probably feel as they do: that the world is filled with more desirable competitors for your lover.

You may also find it difficult to tolerate criticism. You are probably hypersensitive to it. Even a slight criticism can lead you to feel enormous shame. You may vehemently deny that you have done anything wrong, or put down the person who is criticizing you. This is because to acknowledge any flaw is to let in a flood of painful feelings related to Defectiveness. Thus, you protect yourself by denying any flaw, mistake, or error. Your defensiveness and inability to take criticism can be a serious problem.

As we have noted, you are likely to feel the most chemistry toward partners who trigger your Defectiveness lifetrap. The flip side is that you tend to get bored with people who treat you well. This is your paradox: you want love so much, but the more your partner gives you love, the less attracted you feel. This is exactly what happened with Eliot and Maria.

ELIOT: *When we first met, I was madly in love with her. I really thought this was it for me, I would never need anybody else. But, after we got married, I just lost it for her. I stopped wanting to sleep with her. We haven't slept together in over a year.*

You have the most chemistry in situations that reinforce your defectiveness. It is consistent with your self-image. It somehow feels alien to have someone you value value you.

These are the two sides of the swing for you. At one extreme you pursue someone you desire highly. You feel one-down. The chemistry is high and the fear is high. At the other extreme, you pursue someone who loves and accepts you. You are less afraid, but you soon devalue your partner and lose the chemistry.

Defectiveness is present in other close relationships as well. One danger we mentioned earlier is that you may try to allay your own feelings of shame by becoming critical and rejecting of your own children. You do to them what was done to you. You scapegoat them. They are vulnerable and innocent and cannot stop you.

MARIA: *Eliot picks on the children all the time. He harps on every possible little flaw. Every little thing. He doesn't realize how much it hurts them.*

Putting down your children makes you feel better about yourself, at least temporarily.

Many people who attain quick success and then become self-destructive (for example, through drugs or alcohol) have underlying Defectiveness lifetraps. This is often true of celebrities, actors, and entrepreneurs: success is so discrepant from what they really feel that they are unable to maintain it. The pressure to maintain the success when they feel so bad about themselves becomes overwhelming, and many fall apart.

If you use success in your career to make up or compensate for feelings of defectiveness, then your sense of well-being may be quite fragile. Your whole sense of worth becomes built on your success. Any small deflation or failure may be enough to make you nervous. If something serious happens—if you get fired, go bankrupt, have a business reversal, or get snubbed by a higher-up—it throws you back into that shameful feeling. You may operate only at extremes: either you are successful and feel wonderful about yourself, or you fail and collapse utterly into feelings of worthlessness.

Jobs that require public speaking may be a particular problem for you. You feel exposed. Public speaking anxiety is particularly common among people with Defectiveness lifetraps. The sense is that somehow people will see through you. Perhaps, through your anxiety symptoms—sweating, shaking, your voice cracking—they will sense your defectiveness.

CHANGING YOUR DEFECTIVENESS LIFETRAP

1. Understand your childhood feelings of defectiveness and shame. Feel the wounded child within you.
2. List signs that you might be coping with Defectiveness through Escape or Counterattack (i.e., avoiding or compensating).
3. Try to stop these behaviors designed to Escape or Counterattack.
4. Monitor your feelings of defectiveness and shame.
5. List the men/women who have attracted you most and the ones who have attracted you least.
6. List your defects and assets as a child and teenager. Then list your current defects and assets.
7. Evaluate the seriousness of your current defects.
8. Start a program to change the defects that are changeable.
9. Write a letter to your critical parent(s).
10. Write a flashcard for yourself.
11. Try to be more genuine in close relationships.
12. Accept love from the people close to you.
13. Stop allowing people to treat you badly.
14. If you are in a relationship where you are the critical partner, try to stop putting your partner down. Do the same in other close relationships.

---

1. Understand Your Childhood Defectiveness and Shame. Feel the Wounded Child Within You. The first step is to re-experience your early feelings of defectiveness and shame. Where did the lifetrap come from? Who criticized and shamed you? Who made you feel invalid and unloved? Was it your mother? father? brother? sister? The answer almost certainly lies in your early family life.

Try to remember as much as possible about specific events. You can use photographs to help you. You can return to familiar places from your childhood, and you can utilize imagery.

When you have some time to yourself, sit in a darkened room in a comfortable chair. Close your eyes and let images of your childhood come. Do not force them. Just let them float to the surface of your mind. If you need somewhere to begin, start with something in your current life that triggers a feeling of defectiveness.

ALISON: *I remember when I was little, maybe about seven, my uncle put a $50,000 bond in my name. Of course, he really did it for my mother, but somehow at the time I was confused and thought he did it for me. Because he liked me or something. I remember being really embarrassed to see him after I found out.*

THERAPIST: *Can you get an image of it?*

ALISON: *(Closes eyes.) I see myself in my room. I'm getting dressed. My mother has just told me that we're going to my uncle's house. I'm getting dressed really carefully. I want to look good for my uncle.*

When I finally come out, I ask my father how I look. He tells me I might as well get undressed, I'm not going to my uncle's. He and my mother are going without me. He says that's just what my uncle wants, a whining brat hanging around.

I get mad and I tell him my uncle does so want to see me, or else why would he give me so much money?

My father laughs, saying do I actually think the gift has anything to do with me.

THERAPIST: *How do you feel?*

ALISON: *I feel that same way. Exposed. Like all of a sudden I realize the gift wasn't really for me. I'm embarrassed that I got all dressed up, and the gift wasn't really for me. I'm standing in the hall, and I feel so exposed. I'm trying really hard not to cry.*

We want you to feel that child who wanted love but instead got disapproval and rejection. Picture yourself as a child wanting those things. And picture the people you love not giving them to you. Allow yourself to relive that original pain.

Bring yourself in as an adult and comfort that child in the images. Comfort, love, praise, and support can heal shame.

ALISON: *I bring myself into the image. I take that little girl's hand, and lead her away from her father. We go outside the house and far away. I take her on my lap and rock and kiss her. I tell her that I love her, that it will be okay, that if she wants to cry she can.*

Link these early feelings with your Defectiveness lifetrap today. Can you feel the wounded child who wanted approval and validation?

2. List Signs That You Might Be Coping with Defectiveness Through Escape or Counterattack (i.e., by avoiding or overcompensating). Are you hypercritical of other people? Are you defensive about criticism? Do you devalue the people you love? Do you overemphasize status or success? Do you try to impress people? Do you ask for reassurance incessantly? These are the ways you Counterattack or overcompensate.

Do you abuse alcohol or drugs? Do you overeat or overwork? Do you avoid getting close to people? Are you very closed about discussing personal feelings? Are you hypervigilant about rejection? These are the ways you Escape or avoid.

Make explicit the ways you Escape or Counterattack to cope with your feelings of defectiveness. Watch yourself and write them down.

3. Try to Stop These Behaviors Designed to Escape or Counterattack. This will allow your feelings of defectiveness to surface more readily. You cannot deal with your lifetrap until you are in touch with it.

For example, you may place too much emphasis on success as a way of compensating for your feelings of worthlessness. You try to disprove your defectiveness by proving you are of value. But the problem is, you overdo it. It becomes your sole focus, and your life starts to revolve around success. Eliot displayed this pattern:

ELIOT: *I always maintain that the main reason I don't spend more time with my family is time. I don't have the time. I'm at the club from eleven in the morning till three or four in the morning at least five nights a week.*
MARIA: *And he spends the days he is home recovering. He really doesn't want to do much but lie in bed or watch television.*
THERAPIST: *All you do is work or recover from work.*

Eliot's life is devoted to gaining success and status. He does it to impress people. When he is with a woman, it is all he talks about. This is his way of proving himself worthy of love. The end result, though, is that he has status and success, but he still does not have love. He is looking for love but settling for admiration. His success never touches his core feeling of defectiveness. It just provides temporary relief.

Success and status often become addictions. You try to get more and more, but you can never get enough to make you feel good. Success is a pale substitute for finding one person who really knows and loves you.

Similarly, if you are always running away from your feelings of defectiveness—if you are always drinking, avoiding close relationships, or hiding your real thoughts and feelings—your lifetrap cannot change. Your feelings of defectiveness remain frozen.

Eliot avoided intimacy with his family in many ways. On days that he was home, he smoked marijuana and drank beer. Most of the time, he stayed isolated in his bedroom watching television. At dinner he spent most of the time bragging about his success or criticizing his children. Some evenings he made excuses to leave so he could meet one of his lovers.

We made an agreement that he would stop trying to escape in these ways for one month. We want you to do the same. We want you to stop engaging in patterns that keep you from facing your feelings of defectiveness. We want you to get in touch with your defectiveness feelings so that we can begin to work on them.

4. Monitor Your Feelings of Defectiveness and Shame. Observe situations that trigger your lifetrap. Become aware. List situations in which you feel defective or ashamed. These feelings are cues that your lifetrap has been triggered. Here is Alison's list:

SITUATIONS THAT TRIGGER MY DEFECTIVENESS

1. Alone on a Saturday night with nothing to do. Matthew is away. I feel that no one wants to be with me.
2. Out to lunch with my best friend, Sarah. I feel that she is better than I am—smarter, prettier, more interesting. Instead of talking about myself, I fade.
3. Talking to my mother on the phone. She gets down on me for not being able to make up my mind about getting married. She sounds desperate, like if I don't say "yes" now, no one will ever ask me again.

List all the ways your lifetrap manifests itself: when you feel insecure, inadequate, or worried about rejection; when you compare yourself to others or feel jealous; when you feel sensitive to slights or defensive about criticism; when you allow yourself to be mistreated because you believe you do not deserve anything better. List all the situations that trigger Defectiveness for you.

We realize that this will be hard. We all devote considerable energy in life trying *not* to feel painful things. Try to maintain hope throughout this process by reminding yourself that acknowledging these feelings is the first step toward overcoming a problem that is bringing you great unhappiness.

In addition, write down the complaints various partners have made about you. See if there are patterns. Have you been accused repeatedly of being too jealous, insecure, or oversensitive? Have you been told that you need too much reassurance, or that your feelings are too easily hurt? These complaints may provide important clues about how you reinforce your lifetrap.

5. List the Men/Women Who Have Attracted You Most, and the Ones Who Have Attracted You Least. We want you to take a look at your choice of partners. List all the lovers you have had. Group them into the ones that excited you most and the ones that excited you least. Compare the two groups. Were you most excited by partners who were more critical of you? More rejecting? More aloof or ambivalent toward you? Are you most attracted to partners before you have won them over? Does your interest drop off afterward? Were you bored by partners who loved you?

6. List Your Defects and Assets as a Child and Teenager. Then List Your Current Defects and Assets. We want you to get a more objective view of yourself. The view you have now is not objective. It is biased against you. Your cognitive style is to exaggerate your flaws and discount your positive features. Take a more scientific approach. List your defects and assets, both when you were a child and teenager, and now.

Here is Alison's list:

ASSETS AS A CHILD OR TEENAGER

1. I was smart.
2. I was sensitive.
3. I was pretty good to other people.
4. I could sing.
5. I had leadership qualities. (I was head cheerleader and class representative of my junior and senior class.)
6. I was good to my younger brother and sister.
7. I was popular with other girls.

DEFECTS AS A CHILD OR TEENAGER

1. It's hard for me to say what my defects were. I just didn't have much to offer anyone. No one really wanted to be with me. I have always felt that there is something about me that people don't like. I can't really say what it is. It is something about me that other people can see. Boys in particular didn't like me. When I was a teenager, boys didn't ask me out.

It was interesting for Alison to see how much trouble she had writing this list.

ALISON: *It's funny, but writing the positive parts made me upset. It was hard for me to just say what was good about me.*
THERAPIST: *It's so alien to you.*
ALISON: *And writing the negative part was hard too. At first it surprised me that I couldn't think of any defects. But then I realized it wasn't any one thing about me. It was who I was.*

Alison had a similar experience writing the list for herself now. Although it was not easy, she was able to generate many positive qualities. But she had difficulty listing any significant defects. Her only evidence was that she *felt* defective.

These lists represent the evidence that you are defective versus the evidence that you have value. Examine the evidence. Writing the lists helped Alison to see that there were positive things about her that she tended to discount.

You can also turn to family and close friends for help developing your lists. (Of course, do not ask the people in your family who gave you the lifetrap in the first place.) At first Alison could not generate any positive qualities at all. She was just unaccustomed to thinking that way.

ALISON: *You know, each positive quality that people told me about, my first reaction was that I knew that, but I just didn't think it was very important. I mean, I know I'm a nice person, I know there were good things about me. I just didn't think that it mattered in terms of my total worth.*

THERAPIST: *You automatically devalue everything you do well.*

When you think of good qualities, do not minimize them and leave them off the list. If people give you positive feedback that you find hard to believe, include it anyway. Include everything, without passing judgment.

Play down qualities that are success-oriented—assets that may be part of your false self. And when you ask people what they value about you, be sure to get specifics. Do not settle for general comments like "You're great," or "I like you." Unless they specify what they like, you will assume they are describing only your false self and not the real you.

You will be surprised to find that people are happy to give you feedback. We have seen amazing changes in patients' feelings about themselves just by being willing to ask for positive feedback from their friends and loved ones.

7. Evaluate the Seriousness of Your Current Defects. When your list is finished, ask yourself how you would feel about someone else who had these assets and liabilities. Keep in mind that everyone has flaws. Everyone has both good and bad qualities.

ALISON: *I have to admit I would think this was an okay person. Maybe someone who has problems with men, but an okay person. But I still feel that I'm not okay. I mean I know I'm okay, but I still feel like I'm not.*

Like Alison, you may not feel better at this point. But we want you to recognize, intellectually at least, that you are a worthwhile person. And we want you to be able to say why.

Review your assets list daily. Try not to discount them anymore. Chip away at the lifetrap. This will help you make the gradual transition from intellectual knowledge to emotional acceptance.

8. Start a Program to Correct the Flaws That Are Changeable. Which of your limitations could you change? Many people find that their defects are situational or changeable, not inherent or immutable. Start a program to correct the limitations you can change.

We often find that the defects patients list are the *result* of their lifetrap, not the cause. That is, they are the manifestations of the lifetrap itself. Both Alison and Eliot found that a lot of their flaws were actually mechanisms they had developed to cope with their feelings of defectiveness.

For example, we tried to piece together Alison's defect, that "boys didn't like me" (which translated into "Men don't find me attractive" on her adult list). She asked some of her male friends, and they confirmed she had some attributes that might be unattractive to men. Basically, she came across as too eager and too insecure. We could confirm this as well, based on her relationship with us. But, *all of these behaviors are lifetrap-driven.* In fact, Alison could not name a single defect that was independent of her lifetrap. Clearly, her defectiveness reflected how she had been treated as a child, and not anything about who she was.

Once Alison became aware of these lifetrap-driven behaviors, it was fairly easy for her to stop them.

ALISON: *When I'm with Matthew, and I feel all needy and jealous, I tell myself it won't help at all to start bugging him about it. I tell myself it will just make me feel worse.*
THERAPIST: *How will it make you feel?*
ALISON: *Weak and kind of worthless. Plus it gets him mad at me. It just doesn't help. I do the same thing when I'm at work, and I get the urge to call him to make sure he still cares. I stop myself. I tell myself it won't help at all. I feel much better since I've stopped making those frantic phone calls.*
THERAPIST: *So, if you don't start acting needy, what do you do instead?*
ALISON: *I talk to myself. I tell myself it's okay, he loves me. I tell myself I'm worthy of his love.*
THERAPIST: *Good. You comfort yourself.*

Similarly, Eliot's flaws were mostly forms of counterattack or ways he overcompensated: his criticalness, his need to impress people, his workaholism, his infidelity. As we noted before, Eliot agreed to stop these behaviors for one month.

ELIOT: *The odd thing is that I feel more relaxed and more in control. Especially at work. Nobody's throwing me off at all.*
THERAPIST: *It's a feeling of being more centered.*

What was hard for Eliot was spending time with his wife and children being himself. Suddenly he was face-to-face with them, with his mask off.

ELIOT: *I feel nervous around them. Like I don't quite know what to talk about. And I feel ashamed of how I treated them. Especially the kids.*
THERAPIST: *The important thing is that you're treating them well now.*
ELIOT: *It's true. Maria and the kids seem happier.*
THERAPIST: *What about you?*
ELIOT: *Yes. At some level I'm happier too. Like the other day, my younger daughter threw her arms around me and gave me a kiss. It startled me. She hadn't done that in a long time.*

9. Write a Letter to Your Critical Parent(s). We want you to write letters to the people in your family who criticized you when you were a child. *You are under no pressure to send these letters.* In fact, you probably will not want to send them. The important thing is for you to feel totally free to express your feelings in the letters. We want you to vent the anger and the sadness in response to the people who treated you badly. We want you to *talk back.*

Tell them what they did to you when you were a child. Tell them how it felt to be criticized and invalidated. Explain why you did not deserve to be treated this way. Stress the good qualities you had that they overlooked or downplayed.

Tell them how you wished it could have been. Tell them about the support and approval you needed—what it would have meant to you and how it would have changed your life. And tell them what you want from them now.

Do not make excuses for these family members, or rationalize their criticisms. You can do that *later,* if you choose. The road to healing is long; at the end, you may forgive them, when you do not feel defective anymore. But first you must stand up for yourself and vent the feelings you have buried.

We understand that you may have a strong impulse to defend your parents, even if they were the ones who hurt you. You want to see your parents as good people. So you say things like, "They didn't know any better," or "They had problems themselves," or "They were doing it for my own good." In this letter, try to stop defending them and just focus on being honest about what happened and how it made you feel.

Here is the letter Eliot wrote to his father:

Dear Dad,

You were cruel to me when I was a child. You acted as though I had nothing worthwhile about me, nothing special or great. I just didn't matter to you. You didn't care that I had feelings, that I could feel pain or get hurt. You couldn't be bothered to give me love.

What hurt most was how you always compared me to [my brother] Rick. You made me feel like nothing next to him. When you were around Rick, you'd act all happy and excited. But when you were around me, you were mean and disgusted. Like I was such a disappointment.

You criticized everything about me. I had no part of me I felt safe to show you. Anything I loved, I kept hidden from you. When I remember my childhood, the thing that stands out most is feeling ashamed.

Despite how you treated me, I had some great qualities as a kid. I was smart. I could wheel and deal. By the time I was sixteen, I had a little business going in baseball cards. I had my own interests (not that you cared), different from Rick's. Maybe I wasn't perfect, but it was wrong to treat me the way you did.

I hate you for what you did to me. My wife is threatening to leave me, my kids are miserable, and I'm working myself sick trying to just feel like a worthwhile person. I've shut out the ones I love, and instead I spend all my time boosting my ego with cocaine or trying to pick up chicks I couldn't care less about. And all these things are happening because I have such low self-esteem, because you and the rest of the family were so crummy to me.

All of you let me down. Did you ever think what it would have meant for me to have you once seem happy about me, once seem proud or pleased with who I was? It made me shut down. It made it so I didn't want to show anyone who I was.

I am trying now to grope towards a more meaningful life. Part of this is that it's no longer acceptable for you to insult me in any way. If you want to maintain a relationship, you are going to have to change how you treat me. And if you can't, our relationship is over.

Eliot

It was not easy by any means for Eliot to get to the point where he could write this letter. It took courage and strength on his part. But one thing was certain. He felt markedly better afterwards.

You will find the same. Writing a letter like this can be a healing process. It is a statement of what happened to you. "Your truth shall set you free."

10. Write a Flashcard for Yourself. Make a flashcard that you can take out and read whenever your Defectiveness lifetrap is triggered—whenever, as Alison says, "the voice of my father starts yammering in my head." We want you to chip away at the critical parent within you.

ALISON: *I want to be better to myself, but getting down on myself is a hard habit to break. I keep deciding not to do it, but then find myself doing it a minute later.*
THERAPIST: *Yes. And, like every habit, the way to stop is to catch yourself, and to stop yourself every time.*

The flashcard is a weapon against the voice of the lifetrap. It keeps you aware that there are two sides. There is the critical or unloving parent you have internalized, who is always putting you down, ignoring you, and making you feel defective and ashamed. But there is also the vulnerable child inside, who wants love, acceptance, approval, and validation. The flashcard helps you push the critical parent out, so your healthy side can give the child what he or she wants. Ultimately this healing process is about self-love. The flashcard helps you remember to give yourself love.

The flashcard should have on it all of the qualities in you that are good. It should invalidate your parents' criticisms—why the things they said were either wrong or less important than they made them out to be. Use objective evidence. Tell yourself to use a *constructive* tone with yourself, not a *punitive* tone.

Here is the card Alison wrote:

A DEFECTIVENESS FLASHCARD

Right now I feel humiliated and inadequate. I feel surrounded by people, especially women, who seem superior to me in every way—looks, brains, personality. I feel their presence diminishes me totally.

But this is not true. What is really going on is that my lifetrap is being triggered. The truth is that I am worthy too. I am sensitive, intelligent, loving, and good. The truth is that many people have found me to be worthy of love: [lists their names]. Generally I have not given people a chance to get close enough to really know and appreciate me. But believing what I say on this card will help me move in this direction.

Carry the card around. Use it to review your good points. Refute your constant put-downs of yourself. It is another way to fight the feeling of shame and unlovability.

11. Try to Be More Genuine in Close Relationships. Alison and Eliot are at opposite extremes of the lifetrap. Alison is too vulnerable, while Eliot is not vulnerable enough. Alison had to learn to protect herself better, and Eliot had to learn to reveal more of who he was.

If you are more like Eliot, try to be more genuine in close relationships. Stop trying to give the impression that you are perfect. Be vulnerable. Share some of your secrets. Acknowledge some of your flaws. Let other people inside more. You will find that your secrets are not as humiliating as they feel to you. Everyone has flaws.

ELIOT: *I did something that surprised me. The other night Maria and I went to a party. One of her friends from college, this guy Richard, was there.*

They were talking and I got jealous. I always get jealous when they're together, because they seem so into talking to each other. They look so happy. Like Maria and I never are.

My usual maneuver would have been to start hitting on some chick. But I didn't do that. Instead I told Maria. I told her I felt jealous.

THERAPIST: *What happened?*

ELIOT: *Her reaction was, "So you care? I didn't think you cared!"*

Because he was so afraid of looking insecure, Eliot withheld from Maria the signs of his caring. He was afraid to show her he loved her. In this case, showing a normal and appropriate amount of jealousy was actually helpful.

You can pace how much you reveal of yourself. Reveal yourself little by little. Keep a sense of control. In the early stages of a relationship, exposing too much insecurity can, in fact, turn the other partner off. There is an inevitable strategic element during the first few months. However, as you become more intimate and you sense that your partner seems genuinely to care for you, you can disclose more and more. It can be a risk to expose everything all at once.

Sometimes patients say, "But I don't know what a normal rate of showing vulnerability is." If this is the case, one solution is to pace yourself according to your partner. As your partner shows more vulnerability, you show more. Try to keep a balance in the relationship.

If you have secrets—humiliating things that happened to you, for example—gradually tell them to people close to you. There is an expression, "You are only as sick as your worst secret." Many things that we hide from people are not as bad as we think. Once we share them with someone, we see that they are not so shameful. We see that the person still loves us, and we feel better about ourselves.

You may have so much shame that you have always hidden yourself. You need to find out that you can actually be yourself and be loved for that.

12. Accept Love from the People Close to You. One of the hardest things for you is to let people love you. You are very uncomfortable being treated well. It is so alien. You are much more comfortable being mistreated or ignored. It is hard for you to tolerate situations where people take care of you, praise you, and support you. You try to push it away or discount it.

ALISON: *It's funny, but one of the hardest things for me has been to let Matthew give me compliments. To just accept them without denying them. Like the other night, we were going out to dinner, and he told me I looked beautiful. I started to say, "No, I don't," and then I stopped myself.*
THERAPIST: *What did you say?*
ALISON: *"Thank you."*

Both Alison and Eliot had to learn to accept love. Surprisingly, the experience brought up a lot of grief for both of them.

MARIA: *Something strange happened the other night. Eliot came home from the club and he was all upset. He had had a bad night.*

I lay down in bed with him, held him in my arms, and just comforted him. I was stroking his face.

All of a sudden he started to cry. These deep sobs.

THERAPIST: *It put him in touch with what he'd been missing for so long.*

MARIA: *I never felt closer to him or loved him so much.*

We want you to accept love as well. Stop pushing away the people who love you.

13. Stop Allowing People to Treat You Badly. As we have noted, there is a tendency for you to choose partners, and perhaps close friends, who are critical or rejecting. Examine your close relationships today. Do you allow people to put you down or criticize you unfairly?

ALISON: *Well, you know Matthew isn't a problem that way. But there is someone who is a problem. That's my best friend Lynn. She's been my best friend since we were little. She lived next door to me.*

She was always mean to me when we were little. She would say she didn't want to play with me, or she would make fun of me.

To this day she puts me down. Like the other day she said to me, "You better let Matthew get you that ring before he changes his mind."

That was such a bitchy thing to say.

THERAPIST: *What did you do when she said it?*

ALISON: *Nothing. I got upset.*

Start standing up for yourself. Assert your rights. Tell the person that you will no longer tolerate abusive criticism. Demand that you be accepted as you are. Remember the principles of assertiveness. Do not talk to the person in an angry and aggressive manner. You will be much more effective if you remain calm. Stand up straight and look the person in the eye. Be direct. Be specific. And above all, do not get into defending yourself. Just keep restating your point in a calm and controlled manner.

ALISON: *I invited Lynn to dinner and she came two hours late. We had finally started eating, so it meant I had to get up and start getting her courses. All the food was either cold or overcooked. I was really annoyed.*

At one point we were alone at the table. I told her that I was angry she had come so late, that it had made it hard for me and ruined my dinner. I told her I had worked hard on the dinner.

She started saying I had some nerve to get down on her when she was so upset about Lenny. Lenny is her boyfriend. They had had a fight and that was why she was late.

I didn't fall for it. I started to defend myself, but I stopped myself. I just told her again that it wasn't right for her to be so late for dinner.

Be careful not to go too far in the other direction. Try to accept *occasional* criticism that is not demeaning. Recognize the difference between fair criticism and excessive or unreasonable criticism.

If your friend or partner will not change after a while, you must consider ending the relationship. You can try everything; you can give the person every opportunity to change. If it is a romantic partner, you might consider couples therapy. Perhaps through therapy you can solve the problem. But ultimately you must stand up for yourself and either get the person to change or leave the relationship. It is going to be almost impossible for you to heal the Defectiveness lifetrap without ending unhealthy relationships. It is too difficult to fight this lifetrap when the people closest to you are continually reinforcing it.

We have found that the majority of patients with this lifetrap are in relationships that *can* be saved. They can stand up to their partners and get their partners to change. The partners are often able to stop being so critical. In fact, some partners welcome the change. They prefer to be with a person who has some backbone.

Occasionally we run up against partners who cannot tolerate being in a relationship on an equal basis. Most often this is because the partner's issue is Defectiveness as well. They put down other people as a form of Counterattack, to ward off their own feelings of worthlessness and shame. Such partners are not healthy enough to work on their own insecurities and change.

Some patients continue as adults to live or work with the critical or unloving parents who were responsible for the lifetrap developing in the first place. We have found this to be extremely destructive to the change process, and strongly advise you not to continue such close contact with a critical parent.

14. If You Are in a Relationship Where You Are the Critical Partner, Stop Putting Your Partner Down. Do the Same in Other Close Relationships. Stop criticizing your partner. Your partner does not deserve it. Remember, you cannot feel *basically* better about yourself by putting others down.

This is equally true with your children. They are innocent and vulnerable, and you are betraying them. Break the chain. Do not pass on your own Defectiveness lifetrap to them.

At some level you feel guilty about what you have done to your spouse or children. Resist getting lost in that guilt. The important thing is to change *now*.

ELIOT: *When I let myself think about it, I get very upset about things I've said to the children. But I know I didn't* choose *my lifetrap; I know I didn't bring it on myself. Now I have to get out of the lifetrap for the sake of my children.*

THERAPIST: *If you can fight your own feelings of defectiveness, you won't have to keep venting them on your children.*

You have to face what you have done, forgive yourself, and change, starting right now.

Try praising the ones you love. You love them for a reason. They have qualities that are valuable and deserve credit. Aim for a relationship of equals—beyond the see-saw of one-up, one-down.

SOME FINAL WORDS

How quickly you can change your Defectiveness lifetrap depends in part on how punitive your parent was. The more punishing and dramatic your parent's rejection was, and the more hatred and violence there was connected to it, the harder it is to change. You may need help from a therapist. Get help if you need it; there is no shame involved in getting help to treat your problem.

Changing your lifetrap involves gradually improving how you treat yourself, how you treat others, and how you allow others to treat you. With the exception of patients who are in truly abusive relationships, changing does not usually involve sudden, dramatic shifts. Rather it is an incremental process. Patients gradually feel better about themselves. They become less defensive and more able to take in love. They feel closer to people. They feel more valued and more loved.

Keep in mind that this is not a short-term issue. You will be working on it for years to come but there will be progress all along the way. Gradually you will come to accept that your defectiveness was something that was taught to you, and not something inherently true about you. Once you can open yourself up to the idea that your defectiveness is not a fact, the healing process can begin to work.

13

"I Feel Like Such a Failure"
The Failure Lifetrap

KATHLEEN: THIRTY-EIGHT YEARS OLD. CONSIDERS HERSELF A
FAILURE IN HER PROFESSIONAL LIFE.

When Kathleen first walks into our office, she has a tense, crestfallen appearance. She tells us that she has considered coming to therapy for quite some time, but has put it off.

KATHLEEN: *Lately I've been feeling really depressed.*
THERAPIST: *How did it start?*
KATHLEEN: *Well, I've really been depressed for a long time. Sometimes I think I've been depressed my whole life.*
    But something happened a few weeks ago that really upset me. My husband and I were out to dinner and we ran into my friend Ronnie. We went to college together. We got to talking, you know, and I found out that she just had been made a partner in her law firm.
THERAPIST: *And that bothered you?*
KATHLEEN: *Yeah, it bothered me. I mean, look at me. Thirty-eight years old and all I have to show for it is a job as a production assistant. I mean, I'm basically a go-fer, and have been for fifteen years.*

Kathleen works as a production assistant in television. It is basically an entry-level job, which she has held since she started in the business after graduating from college. She has made almost no progress up the ranks. "I feel like such a failure," she says.

BRIAN: FIFTY YEARS OLD. FEELS LIKE A FAILURE EVEN THOUGH HE IS A SUCCESS.

Brian has the impostor syndrome. People with this problem do not feel that their successes are justified. They believe that they fool people into seeing them as more competent than they really are. Although Brian has a good job as a press secretary for a prominent politician, he still *feels* like a failure.

BRIAN: *I'm not crazy. I know I have a great job, that people think I'm great. People think I'm doing well. But still I feel worried constantly. It's like I'm an approval junkie. If my boss tells me I did a great job, I'm on cloud nine, but if he makes one tiny correction I start worrying that he doesn't like me anymore, he's gonna fire me.*
THERAPIST: *Like he's found you out.*
BRIAN: *Yeah, like I've just been faking it all along, and he's finally found me out.*

Brian's sense of success is fragile. He is afraid he will be exposed as fraudulent and his entire career will collapse.

THE FAILURE QUESTIONNAIRE

This questionnaire will measure the strength of your Failure lifetrap. Use the following scale to answer the items. Rate what you *feel* more than what you *think* intellectually.

SCORING KEY

1 Completely untrue of me
2 Mostly untrue of me
3 Slightly more true than untrue of me
4 Moderately true of me
5 Mostly true of me
6 Describes me perfectly

If you have any 5's or 6's on this questionnaire, this lifetrap may still apply to you, even if your score is in the low range.

SCORE	DESCRIPTION
	1. I feel I am less competent than other people in areas of achievement.
	2. I feel that I am a failure when it comes to achievement.
	3. Most people my age are more successful in their work than I am.
	4. I was a failure as a student.
	5. I feel I am not as intelligent as most of the people I associate with.
	6. I feel humiliated by my failures in the work sphere.
	7. I feel embarrassed around other people because I do not measure up in terms of my accomplishments.
	8. I often feel that people believe I am more competent than I really am.
	9. I feel that I do not have any special talents that really count in life.
	10. I am working below my potential.
	YOUR TOTAL FAILURE SCORE (Add your scores together for questions 1–10)

INTERPRETING YOUR FAILURE SCORE

10–19 Very low. This lifetrap probably does *not* apply to you.
20–29 Fairly low. This lifetrap may only apply *occasionally*.
30–39 Moderate. This lifetrap is an *issue* in your life.
40–49 High. This is definitely an *important* lifetrap for you.
50–60 Very high. This is definitely one of your *core* lifetraps.

THE EXPERIENCE OF FAILURE

You feel like a failure relative to other people you consider your peers. Most of the time, you are probably in touch with your lifetrap, and your sense of failure is close to the surface.

KATHLEEN: *I'm just a stupid person. I don't have what it takes to get ahead. Over and over, I watch younger people get jobs at my level and then pass by me.*

I mean, I'm thirty-eight years old and I'm competing for promotions with twenty-two and twenty-three-year-olds. It's humiliating. You can't get much worse than that.

As with Kathleen, your feelings of failure are painful.

Most of the people with this lifetrap are more like Kathleen than Brian. That is, their actual level of achievement is lower than their potential. Their outward status generally matches their inner sense of failure. Occasionally, we see people like Brian, who have achieved a great deal but feel fraudulent.

BRIAN: *I feel really out of place where I work. I feel like everyone around me is top-shelf. I don't belong there. Somehow I've deceived everyone into thinking I'm more intelligent and competent than I am. And it's only a matter of time before they all discover the truth.*

In any case, no matter what your actual status or degree of accomplishment, the inner world is the same. Whether you *appear* to be a success or not, most of the time you experience yourself as a failure. Both Kathleen and Brian feel that because of their own shortcomings, they are doomed to fail.

You reinforce the Failure lifetrap primarily through Escape. Your avoidance is what holds you back. You avoid taking the steps necessary to widen your knowledge and advance your career. You let opportunities for success pass you by. You are afraid that if you try you will fail.

KATHLEEN: *A few weeks ago I went and talked to my boss about letting me be in charge of scheduling for this one project. It's really rare for me to make that kind of move, but I just felt like I had to do it.*

Anyway, my boss told me to write up a proposal. You know, a plan, whatever. Well, three weeks have gone by and I still haven't done it. The project is starting tomorrow and now it's really too late.

   With the Failure lifetrap, the degree to which you use Escape as a coping style is often massive. People avoid developing skills, tackling new tasks, taking on responsibility—all the challenges that might enable them to succeed. Often the attitude is, "What's the use?" You feel there is no point in making the effort when you are doomed to fail anyway.

   Your avoidance may be subtle. You may *appear* to tackle your work but still do things to avoid. You procrastinate, you get distracted, you do the work improperly, or you mishandle the tasks you take on. These are all forms of *self-sabotage*.

BRIAN: *This last project my boss gave me to do, I've been so anxious about it that I didn't get started until this week. I'm really under pressure now. I can't possibly do the job the way it should be done at this point. The whole thing has got me so frazzled.*

   Your tendency to run away from the possibility of failure undermines your ability to do a good job. You may suffer real penalties, such as getting demoted or fired.

   Another way you surrender to your lifetrap is by constantly twisting events and circumstances to reinforce your view of yourself as a failure. You exaggerate the negative and minimize the positive.

BRIAN: *I know I blow things out of proportion. Like yesterday, my boss gave me this really positive feedback about a press release I had written. But he criticized one tiny detail about it. And of course I went home and fretted about that detail all night.*

   You may also have feelings of depression.

KATHLEEN: *I just feel like I'm at a certain point in my life, and I haven't gotten to where I want to be. And I feel like I'm never gonna get there.*

You feel depressed about your failures, and see little hope for change.

   The Failure lifetrap is usually an easy lifetrap to assess. You are probably well aware of your painful feelings of failure.

   The origin of this lifetrap lies in feelings of failure in childhood. This can happen a number of different ways:

ORIGINS OF THE FAILURE LIFETRAP

1. You had a parent (often your father) who was very critical of your performance in school, sports, etc. He/She often called you stupid, dumb, inept, a failure, etc. He/She may have been abusive. (Your lifetrap may be linked to Defectiveness or Abuse.)
2. One or both parents were very successful, and you came to believe you could never live up to their high standards. So you stopped trying. (Your lifetrap may be linked to Unrelenting Standards.)
3. You sensed that one or both of your parents either did not care about whether you were successful, or, worse, felt threatened when you did well. Your parent may have been competitive with you—or afraid of losing your companionship if you were too successful in the world. (Your lifetrap may be linked to Emotional Deprivation or Dependence.)
4. You were not as good as other children either in school or at sports, and felt inferior. You may have had a learning disability, poor attention span, or been very uncoordinated. After that, you stopped trying in order to avoid humiliation by them. (This may be linked to Social Exclusion.)
5. You had brothers or sisters to whom you were often compared unfavorably. You came to believe you could never measure up, so you stopped trying.
6. You came from a foreign country, your parents were immigrants, or your family was poorer or less educated than your school-mates. You felt inferior to your peers and never felt you could measure up.
7. Your parents did not set enough limits for you. You did not learn self-discipline or responsibility. Therefore you failed to do homework regularly or learn study skills. This led to failure eventually. (Your lifetrap may be linked to Entitlement.)

As you can see, the Failure lifetrap may be associated with other lifetraps—Defectiveness, Abuse, Unrelenting Standards, Emotional Deprivation, Dependence, Social Exclusion, or Entitlement.

Kathleen had a number of forces propelling her toward failure as a child.

KATHLEEN: *One thing that hurt me was that my parents didn't really care about school. It was part of their general not caring about me really. I mean, other kids would be scared to death to bring their report cards home. I never worried about it because they just didn't care. My problem was getting them to look at it long enough to sign it.*

    It's weird, but I used to be jealous of kids who were scared to bring their report cards home. I remember once being in the girls' room at school with my friend Meg. She was in the stall, crying and carrying on, "I can't go home, my father's gonna kill me," on and on. And as upset as she was, I felt jealous of her. Isn't that weird?

THERAPIST: *She had someone who cared.*

KATHLEEN: *Yeah. But the other thing that happened was that I was sick a lot. I had asthma. I missed a lot of school in those early years. I fell behind and just never caught up. It's a miracle, really, that I ever made it through college.*

There was no one to help Kathleen when she fell behind. Nobody pushed her to catch up. Instead she began her lifelong pattern of escape.

KATHLEEN: *I would try to get out of going to school by playing sick. If there was a test or a paper due, I would get sick that day. I just couldn't face the humiliation of failing again.*

THERAPIST: *Would you try to learn the stuff?*

KATHLEEN: *Nah. I would just watch television. I spent my childhood watching television.*

Kathleen failed to develop the skills and discipline necessary to get ahead. Her approach was to try to do as little as possible and hide it as best as she could.

    Kathleen's lifetrap was an outgrowth of Emotional Deprivation. For Brian the issue was more one of Defectiveness.

BRIAN: *My father was always criticizing me about everything, not just about school. Actually achievement was the one area where I could sort of do okay. But I never trusted it, I never trusted that I really knew what I was doing.*

Brian had been feeling fraudulent about success for a long time. As a child, he did well in school, but he felt so defective generally that he could not believe in himself.

Upon reflection it seemed that his father felt competitive with him. He put Brian down as a way of feeling better about himself.

BRIAN: *Particularly after he lost his job and we had to move to a smaller house, when I was eight, he would really light into me. He would boost himself up by humiliating me.*

His father was threatened by Brian's success at school. He was afraid that Brian would surpass him, so he punished Brian for succeeding. His father undermined his self-confidence and damaged Brian's ability to believe in himself.

The Failure lifetrap feeds on itself in such a way that the entire arena of work becomes a disaster for you. Your expectation of failure becomes a self-fulfilling prophesy. Here are many of the ways you sabotage yourself and make sure that you remain a failure.

FAILURE LIFETRAPS

1. You do not take the steps necessary to develop solid skills in your career (e.g., finish schooling, read latest developments, apprentice to an expert). You coast or try to fool people.
2. You choose a career below your potential (e.g., you finished college and have excellent mathematical ability, but are currently driving a taxicab).
3. You avoid taking the steps necessary to get promotions in your chosen career; your advancement has been unnecessarily halted (e.g., you fail to accept promotions or to ask for them; you do not promote yourself or make your abilities widely known to the people who count; you stay in a safe, dead-end job).
4. You do not want to tolerate working for other people, or working at entry-level jobs, so you end up on the periphery of your field, failing to work your way up the ladder. (Note the overlap with Entitlement and Subjugation.)
5. You take jobs but repeatedly get fired because of lateness, procrastination, poor job performance, bad attitude, etc.
6. You cannot commit to one career, so you float from job to job, never developing expertise in one area. You are a generalist in a job world that rewards specialists. You therefore never progress very far in any one career.

---

7. You selected a career in which it is extraordinarily hard to succeed, and you do not know when to give up (e.g., acting, professional sports, music).
8. You have been afraid to take initiative or make decisions independently at work, so you were never promoted to more responsible positions.
9. You *feel* that you are basically stupid or untalented, and therefore feel fraudulent, even though objectively you have been quite successful.
10. You minimize your abilities and accomplishments, and exaggerate your weaknesses and mistakes. You end up *feeling* like a failure, even though you have been as successful as your peers.
11. You have chosen successful men/women as partners in relationships. You live vicariously through their success while not accomplishing much yourself.
12. You try to compensate for your lack of achievement or work skills by focusing on other assets (e.g., your looks, charm, youthfulness, sacrificing for others). But underneath you still feel like a failure.

Many of these patterns boil down to the issue of Escape: you avoid taking the steps necessary to advance yourself. Through your avoidance, you constantly twist events to reinforce your view of yourself as stupid, untalented, and incompetent.

Excelling in other roles is a way of compensating for the lifetrap. Men might excel in sports or seducing women; women might excel in their looks or ability to give to others. But, particularly for men, it is hard to develop an effective compensation. What does society value more in a man than achievement? A man who feels like a failure in his career is likely to feel like a failure as a person. Of course, this difference between men and women is changing as careers become more central to women's lives.

As a teenager Brian compensated for his lifetrap by adopting the image of a rebel. He dressed outlandishly and rode motorcycles. He became skilled at chasing women. He found a way to feel good about himself without tackling the prime issue. He compensated for his feelings of failure by carving out an area of success.

One way Kathleen compensates is by choosing a partner who is successful. Wayne, her husband, is the head writer on a top-rated television show. When she goes to job functions, such as cocktail parties and conventions, she moves in the highest circles.

You may be drawn to other roles or to partners who are successful to compensate for your feelings of failure. This is really another avoidance strategy on your part. It is another way for you to escape facing the challenges of achievement.

These compensations are fragile. They easily collapse, and yield to the feeling of failure. You need to deal with the issue of achievement more directly.

These are the steps to changing your lifetrap:

CHANGING YOUR FAILURE LIFETRAP

1. Assess whether your feeling of failure is accurate or distorted.
2. Get in touch with the child inside of you who felt, and still feels, like a failure.
3. Help your inner child see that you were treated unfairly.
4. Become aware of your talents, skills, abilities, and accomplishments in the area of achievement.

If you have, in fact, failed relative to your peers:

5. Try to see the pattern in your failures.
6. Once you see your pattern, make a plan to change it.
7. Make a flashcard to overcome your blueprint for failure. Follow your plan, step-by-step.
8. Involve your loved ones in the process.

---

1. Assess Whether Your Feeling of Failure Is Accurate or Distorted. The first thing to do is assess the accuracy of your feeling of failure. As we have noted, most of the time, like Kathleen, you will have a lot of realistic evidence. You have in fact failed relative to your peers. But sometimes, like Brian, your perception of failure is inaccurate, and you will find little evidence to support your view.

List a range of people with whom you went to high school, college, or graduate school. Be sure to choose people from the bottom, middle, and top of your class. Write down what each person has accomplished within their chosen fields. How far have they progressed? How much are they paid?

How much responsibility do they have at work? Where do you stand in comparison?

2. Get in Touch with the Child Inside of You Who Felt, and Still Feels, Like a Failure. Try to recall memories of being criticized, humiliated, compared, or discouraged by your family or peers. Understand the origins of your lifetrap.

When something happens in your current life to trigger your Failure lifetrap, take some time to explore the event through imagery. Sit in a dark, quiet room and close your eyes. Get an image of the current event. Make the image as vivid and emotional as possible. Then let an image come of when you felt the same way as a child. Do not force the image. Just let it float to the top of your mind.

Here is an example from a session with Kathleen.

KATHLEEN: *Oh, I really messed up. I feel so bad. I can't believe it. I told my boss the wrong time the moving men were coming with the set pieces. He hired all these guys to come in and work overtime to help move the stuff, and they all came at the wrong time. My boss had to pay them anyway. He was really mad at me. Oh my God, I feel so bad about it. I can't stop thinking about it. (Starts to cry.)*

THERAPIST: *Do you want to do imagery about this?*

KATHLEEN: *Okay. (Cries.)*

THERAPIST: *Then close your eyes and get an image of this situation that just happened with your boss.*

KATHLEEN: *All right. I see myself in my boss's office. He's about to come in to talk to me about what happened.*

THERAPIST: *How do you feel?*

KATHLEEN: *Oh, I feel frantic, really panic-stricken. I'm pacing around, I don't know what to do with myself. My heart is pounding. Oh, man. I'm so scared.*

THERAPIST: *Okay. Now give me another image of when you felt that way before, as a child.*

KATHLEEN: *All right. I'm in my sixth-grade classroom. My teacher's there, and she's going around the room, and each person's presenting this book report. We had all had to read part of this book on Africa the night before and make up a little presentation. Only of course I didn't do it. I didn't do it, and now she's going around the room and she's gonna come to me, and I'm gonna have nothing to say.*

Your images can help you understand the origins of your lifetrap. That child who felt like a failure is still very much alive in you.

3. Help Your Inner Child See That You Were Treated Unfairly. Many times when we fail as a child, it is because we are being pushed in a direction that is not naturally ours. Some parents have their own agendas, and want a child to excel in certain areas regardless of what the child's particular talents and inclinations might be.

Brian's father was a first-generation immigrant who worked hard to give his children a good education. He wanted Brian to be a doctor. Even when Brian was quite small, his father would tell people that he was going to be a doctor.

BRIAN: *The trouble was that science and math were not my thing. I was into more creative things—art and writing. My father always looked down on my interest in art. "That and fifty cents will get you a ride on the subway," he used to say.*

I mean, I did try going pre-med at college. But I just couldn't cut it. That was a really bad time for me. No matter how I tried, I couldn't get more than a "C" in any of my courses. I almost had a nervous breakdown.

When I switched to creative writing, my father was furious at me. He stopped paying for my education. I had to take out loans. He was really mad. (Imitates his father's voice:) "It's so impractical, you'll never make a living."

To this day my father criticizes my job. Even though I have a good job, I'm respected, I'm mentioned in the newspapers, I make a lot of money, he still gets down on what I do. He'll talk about our neighbor's son, who became a surgeon, and makes some real *money.*

What were some of your strengths and talents as a child? Were people's expectations of you realistic? How well could you have done if you had been praised, supported, and guided in areas of achievement where you had potential?

Get angry at the people who made you feel like a failure. Talk back to your lifetrap. Stand up for yourself. You can do this by writing letters, talking to people directly, or through imagery.

THERAPIST: *Tell your father how you feel in the image. Tell him how his attitude affects you.*
BRIAN: *Okay. Dad, when you put me down for my career and talk about*

how successful doctors are all the time, it really bothers me. First, it's really frustrating for me to be a success in everyone else's eyes but yours. Every time I see you, I end up feeling like a failure. And this is crazy! I'm doing well! Can't you understand that?

Get an image of a parent or a peer, and tell the person how you feel.

It is up to you whether you confront the person directly, in real life. But if you decide to confront someone, make sure you are emotionally prepared for the person to respond by denying your accusations. Do not have false hope that the person is suddenly going to change because of what you say. If this is what happens, great—but do not count on it.

The important thing is for you to confront the person in a way that makes you proud of yourself. Behave well. Stay calm and composed. State your points simply and briefly. If the person argues, just keep restating your position until you have had your say. Tell the person how they make you feel, and how you wish they could be instead.

THERAPIST: *What did you say to your father?*

BRIAN: *I told him that his criticism of me was unfair, that I was really far more talented and competent than I was given credit for as a child. I told him that he did a lot of damage to me by making me feel incompetent. He kept trying to interrupt me, but I just kept asking him politely to let me finish. I told him I wanted him to be more supportive in terms of my work from now on. I wanted him to give me some credit for what I've accomplished.*

THERAPIST: *How did it feel?*

BRIAN: *Well, it was hard to do, but it felt good afterwards. I still feel good when I think about it.*

You will find that it feels good to confront people if you can do it in this controlled, assertive way.

Regardless of whether you confront people directly, it is vital for you to confront them in your own heart. Write letters that you do not plan to send, or do imagery exercises. Give a voice to the strong part of you that can reject the label of failure.

4. Become Aware of Your Talents, Skills, Abilities, and Accomplishments in the Area of Achievement. Remember an important principle: there are many kinds of intelligence. The intelligence you need to do well in school is not the only kind. There is verbal intelligence, mathematical intelligence, visual-spatial intelligence, musical intelligence, physical intelligence, mechanical intelligence, interpersonal intelligence, etc. All kinds are valid.

What are your special abilities? Do you have a flair for drawing? Are you mechanical or logical? Do you have a gift for sports or dance? Are you creative in some way? Do you get along well with people? It is the rare person who truly has no talents.

Review what you have achieved in each of your talented areas. Try as much as possible to view yourself objectively. We know this will be hard for you—you have a strong tendency to minimize your achievements and maximize your failures. Resist doing this. Stop accentuating the negative. Recognize your own value as accurately as possible.

We need an accurate picture to see whether you have been capitalizing on your own talents. We believe that the people who are most successful are those who can find their natural talents and capitalize on them.

Make a list of your talents, skills, abilities, and accomplishments in the area of achievement, especially your natural talents. Review this list each day to remind yourself of your potential. Get help from friends or significant others in making this list.

Here is the list Brian made:

MY TALENTS AND ACCOMPLISHMENTS

1. I am a good writer.
2. I have good ideas. I am creative.
3. I can argue persuasively.
4. I am highly self-educated about politics.
5. I have a good sense of humor, especially about politics.
6. When my anxiety isn't too high, I accomplish a lot at work.
7. I am a prominent figure in the New York political scene.

For those of you like Brian who have an *inaccurate* sense of failure, steps one to four should be sufficient. These steps should bring about a change in the way you think and feel about yourself.

But this will not be true of most of you. Most of you have a more accurate sense of failure. You will go through steps one through four, and your cumulative conclusion after everything will still be that you are a failure. You can recognize your talents and abilities, you can confront the people who hurt you, you can learn compassion for your inner child, and you can accurately assess what you have achieved thus far. But the conclusion from it all may still be that you feel overwhelmingly like a failure.

Most of you need more. You need *behavior change.* You have to change your fundamental stance of escape and avoidance into one of confrontation and mastery. Even Brian had areas that he had not developed—he liked to write fiction and never pursued it because of his father's attitude. And even Brian procrastinated and delayed when faced with anxiety-provoking tasks.

If you *have,* in fact, failed relative to your peers, continue with the following steps.

5. Try to See the Pattern in Your Failures. Take a focused life history. Start from the very beginning. Go through your school and career life. Were you a failure from the start? Or were there indications of potential at the beginning that faded from lack of support?

How did your parents deal with your success and failure? Were they critical, supportive, reinforcing? As a child, did you avoid tasks or did you follow through on them? Did you avoid taking on challenges?

Try to see what your pattern has been in your career. Have you chosen an impossible career? Have you failed to commit to one career? Are you in a career that vastly underutilizes your potential? Have you been afraid to take responsibility, show initiative, or ask for a promotion? Have you procrastinated, shown a poor attitude, performed poorly at jobs? Have you avoided the discipline necessary to develop skills, get credentials, or receive adequate training?

Most likely, your pattern will boil down to the issue of Escape. You will find that your failure is the direct consequence of your tendency to avoid—rather than the result of some innate deficiency, lack of talent, or ineptness.

Kathleen found a lot of evidence of Escape in her history. Because she was sick a lot, she fell behind at school and never caught up. School became a humiliating experience for her.

KATHLEEN: *I remember so many times being called on by the teacher and not knowing the answer. I would get so embarrassed. Kids made fun of me. They used to call me "dumb" in the playground.*

The more aversive school became, the more Kathleen avoided it. Her frequent sicknesses and her failure at school were like the chicken and the eggs. Each one caused the other in a spiraling vicious cycle.

Kathleen's natural talent was for art. She had a good visual sense and a good sense of design. As a child, for example, she used to redecorate her room, and draw and paint. But she was unable to capitalize on this ability at school. School was too fraught with anxiety.

KATHLEEN: *I remember once, in high school, this teacher asked me to design the sets for this school play they were doing. We had had a homework assignment to design something, and he liked the job I did.*
    But I told him, "No." I wanted to, but I was really just too scared to do it.

It is true that there were subjects at school for which Kathleen had little aptitude. But she could have worked around her weaknesses and played on her strengths, and she did not. The trauma of failure at school led her to avoid everything.

6. Once You See Your Pattern, Make a Plan to Change It. At its most basic level, this will involve taking steps to overcome your avoidance. You must start to face challenges instead of running away. Acknowledge your real talents, accept your limitations, and pursue areas that play on your strengths.

Think through how you can begin to pursue the areas where you are most competent. You may have to start a new career to do this. Or you may merely have to change direction slightly in your current career.

What do you have to do to meet your goal? List the behaviors to change in the future. Develop a timeline for change. What is the first step? Stop making excuses and commit yourself to stop Escaping. Risk failure. It is the only way to succeed.

Set up small tasks for yourself. We believe the old cliché, "A journey of ten thousand miles begins with a single step." Develop a manageable hierarchy. Make each step reasonable and achievable one after the other. Start with a task you can do; if you start with a task that is too overwhelming, you are unlikely to succeed.

You have potential, but you have not actually developed it. Because you have avoided so much, you may have some real gaps in your learning. You may have to start at the beginning of your field and develop basic skills. You may even have to go back to school.

Take credit for the progress you make. Reward yourself. Reinforce yourself. Acknowledge the progress you make.

Since Kathleen's strengths are her visual and design abilities, she set a goal to become a television set designer. Oddly enough, she had never pursued this field, even though that was where her interests most lay. Instead she pursued administrative roles, such as scheduling and personnel management. These areas drew upon her weak organizational and administrative skills. She would mishandle her administrative tasks as she jealously watched the set designers proceed with their work.

Kathleen began by observing set designers. She stayed extra hours in order to do this. She slowly developed relationships with the design staff and became a volunteer. She supplemented this by taking some design courses to build basic skills. Eventually she was hired as an apprentice to a designer. This process involved a loss of pay in the short-term, but Kathleen knew she was working her way up.

She made a concerted effort to focus on tasks that used her visual aptitude. She allowed others to perform administrative functions. She stopped setting herself up to fail.

We know this is a hard part of the change process. You will have to push yourself. As your career starts to improve, the positive effects will sustain you. The process will become self-perpetuating. Confronting avoidance almost always has a marked beneficial effect on a person's life.

Starting is the hardest part. After that it will become easier.

7. Make a Flashcard to Overcome Your Blueprint for Failure. Acknowledge your Failure lifetrap and your history of escape. But list the evidence that you have the *potential* to succeed. Instruct yourself to take the next small step toward success. Remind yourself of the consequences of continuing to avoid.

On the following page is a flashcard we wrote with Kathleen.

A FAILURE FLASHCARD

Right now I am filled with feelings of failure. This is a familiar feeling. I have felt it all my life. All my life I have avoided taking chances to become a success. All my life I have ignored my design potential, even though teachers pointed it out and I did well in these kinds of classes and enjoyed them. Instead I kept setting myself up to fail by going after things I wasn't good at.

My avoidance developed when I was sick and lonely as a child. When I fell behind, no one helped me to catch up. No one noticed. Running away helped me cope as a child, but it isn't helping me now.

But now I'm on track. I'm trying to become a set designer. I have a good chance to succeed. I just have to keep myself focused on my path and on the fact that I'm making progress.

Don't start avoiding again. That leads only back to failure. What is my next step? This is what I should be doing. Working on taking my next step.

As you begin to make changes, take credit for each small success. Add it to your flashcard.

8. Involve Your Loved Ones in the Process. Try to create an interpersonal environment that counters, rather than supports, your Failure lifetrap. If your parent or partner discourages and criticizes you, fight back. Ask for support and encouragement as you take steps to change. If your partner is highly successful, emphasize the importance of succeeding for *yourself*— even if you do not need a career for financial reasons.

SOME FINAL WORDS

As we have noted, the Failure lifetrap is often connected to other lifetraps. To truly fight the Failure lifetrap, you will probably have to deal with these other issues as well. Brian had to work on his Defectiveness lifetrap, and

Pamela had to work on her Emotional Deprivation. Read the chapters on any linked lifetraps. Work to overcome them as well.

The Failure lifetrap is one of the most rewarding to overcome. A whole area of life that is now fraught with shame and tension can become a source of self-esteem. But you have to be willing to fight. You have to be willing to close off your escapes and capitalize on your strengths.

14

"I Always Do It *Your* Way!" The Subjugation Lifetrap

CARLTON: THIRTY YEARS OLD, PUTS EVERYONE'S NEEDS BEFORE HIS OWN.

The first thing that struck us about Carlton is that he seemed anxious and eager to please. He had a way of jumping to agree with whatever we said. Most patients spend at least some part of the first session sizing us up—trying to decide if we are what they want in therapists. But not Carlton: he seemed much more concerned with what *we* thought of *him,* with whether he was what we wanted in a patient.

Carlton is married and has two small children. He is what you might call henpecked. Erica, his wife, is very demanding. He tries to make her happy but seldom seems to succeed. She makes all the decisions about the family. He has difficulty setting limits with his children. Whenever he tries to discipline them, he feels guilty. He works in the textile business started by his father. Although he never wanted to work in his father's business, he is resigned that it is what he has to do. He does not enjoy his work.

Carlton feels trapped in his life. He has started therapy because he is depressed. Sometimes he dreams of running away to a different place and becoming whatever *he* wants to be.

MARY ELLEN: TWENTY-FOUR YEARS OLD, FEELS TRAPPED IN HER MARRIAGE TO A DOMINEERING HUSBAND.

The first impression Mary Ellen gave us was of surface cheerfulness with a hint of resentment simmering underneath. She was immediately on the defensive, and seemed to expect us to try to dominate her.

THERAPIST: *It sounds like you're pretty unhappy in your marriage.*
MARY ELLEN: *Are you telling me that I should end it?*

We found ourselves becoming careful about making any statements she might construe as controlling.

Mary Ellen was still a teenager when she married and had her first child. She has been married seven years and has two children.

MARY ELLEN: *My biggest problem is Dennis, my husband. He's very picky. I'm always running around waiting on him. I feel like a slave. When he wants something, he expects me to jump. And it's not only that. He wants everything done a certain way. If it's not exactly right, he throws a fit. He can get pretty nasty. He just goes on and on. Yesterday he yelled at me for hours because I woke him up ten minutes late.*

Mary Ellen feels that living with Dennis is intolerable. To make matters worse, he forbids her to spend time away from the family with her own friends. Once, he caught her sneaking out to see friends and hit her. Soon afterward, she decided to start therapy.

Mary Ellen feels desperately unhappy, but she is afraid of what Dennis might do if she left. She also believes she should stay for the sake of the children. The relationship is even more appalling to Mary Ellen because it mirrors so closely her relationship with her father. In fact, the primary reason she married in the first place was to escape from the house where she lived with her father. Now, living with her husband seems even worse.

Both Carlton and Mary Ellen have the Subjugation lifetrap. They allow other people to control them.

THE SUBJUGATION QUESTIONNAIRE

This questionnaire will measure how strongly you have the Subjugation lifetrap. Use the scale on the following page.

SCORING KEY

1 Completely untrue of me
2 Mostly untrue of me
3 Slightly more true than untrue of me
4 Moderately true of me
5 Mostly true of me
6 Describes me perfectly

If you have any 5's or 6's on this questionnaire, this lifetrap may still apply to you, even if your score is in the low range.

SCORE	DESCRIPTION
	1. I let other people control me.
	2. I am afraid that if I do not give in to other people's wishes they will retaliate, get angry, or reject me.
	3. I feel the major decisions in my life were not really my own.
	4. I have a lot of trouble demanding that other people respect my rights.
	5. I worry a lot about pleasing people and getting their approval.
	6. I go to great lengths to avoid confrontations.
	7. I give more to other people than I get back in return.
	8. I feel the pain of other people deeply, so I usually end up taking care of the people I'm close to.
	9. I feel guilty when I put myself first.
	10. I am a good person because I think of others more than of myself.
	YOUR TOTAL SUBJUGATION SCORE (Add your scores together for questions 1–10)

INTERPRETING YOUR SUBJUGATION SCORE

10–19 Very low. This lifetrap probably does *not* apply to you.
20–29 Fairly low. This lifetrap may only apply *occasionally*.
30–39 Moderate. This lifetrap is an *issue* in your life.
40–49 High. This is definitely an *important* lifetrap for you.
50–60 Very high. This is definitely one of your *core* lifetraps.

THE EXPERIENCE OF SUBJUGATION

To a large degree, you experience the world in terms of control issues. *Other* people in your life always seem to be in control—you feel controlled by the people around you. At the core of your subjugation is the conviction that you must *please* others, that you must please parents, brothers, sisters, friends, teachers, lovers, spouses, bosses, coworkers, children, and even strangers. In all likelihood, the only exception to this rule of pleasing people—the only person you do not feel obliged to please—is yourself. It is what the other person wants that comes first.

One common theme in the lives of Carlton and Mary Ellen is the feeling of being *trapped* in their lives. The feeling of subjugation is oppressive. It is a burden to live life under the weight of that feeling. Constantly meeting the needs of other people is so much responsibility. It is exhausting. Life loses much of its joy and freedom. Subjugation deprives you of your freedom because the choices you make are dictated by their effects on other people. Your focus is not on yourself. It is not, "What I want and feel," but rather, "What you want and what I can do to make you happy with me."

Subjugation robs you of a clear sense of what *you* want and need—of who you are. Carlton, who was hounded by his father since childhood to go into the family business and who obeyed, knows inside that he does not want to be a businessman, but has no idea of what he *does* want to be. He has never taken the appropriate steps to find out. You are *passive*. Life *happens* to you.

CARLTON: *I just feel like I can't get what I want in life. I don't know how to get it.*

THERAPIST: *You feel like all you can get is what other people deign to give you. You don't go after what you want.*

You feel that you cannot shape the course of events in your life. You feel trapped by circumstances or swept along by fate. Rather than an actor, you are a *re*actor. You feel there is little you can do to solve your problems. You merely wait and hope that suddenly, miraculously, everything will get better.

You probably think of yourself as the kind of person with whom it is easy to get along. Since you are so agreeable and eager to please, and tend to avert conflict, naturally you get along with others. You see yourself as someone who is willing to accommodate. You even might consider this one of your assets: that you are flexible and able to adjust to many types of people. But you have difficulty setting limits on the demands other people make of you. When people ask you to do things that are unreasonable, such as more than your share of the work, you say "yes." And you find it extremely difficult to ask other people to change their behavior, no matter how much their behavior disturbs you.

Similarly, you might feel proud that you are able to serve others—that you are able to help other people and be attentive to other people's needs. And you are right. The ability to be there for other people is a strength of self-sacrificing people. You probably have developed exemplary skills in helping others, and may be in one of the helping professions. However, one of your weaknesses is that what *you* want often gets lost. Too often you are unassertive and silent about your needs.

Your subjugation lowers your self-esteem. You do not feel *entitled* to the legitimate rights of all people in relationships. Everyone has rights except you. Erica expressed this about Carlton in one of our marital sessions.

ERICA: *I was so mad at Carlton the other night.*
THERAPIST: *What happened?*
ERICA: *We went out to eat, and when Carlton got his food, it was cold. But he wouldn't tell the waitress to take it back. He kept the food, and he ate it. And meanwhile he complained about it to me the whole night.*
CARLTON: *It just seemed like such a* trivial *thing to make a big fuss over.*

We hear this argument often from subjugated patients: that they do not fight for what they want because their desires seem so trivial. But in the end, when you add all the trivial desires together, you are left with a life in which few of your needs are met.

When we first pointed out his subjugation to Carlton, he argued that he was not subjugated, he was simply easygoing. However, Carlton was *passive* more than easygoing. Easygoing people have *some* areas in which they have strong feelings, and will assert what they feel. In minor matters, they will not express opinions, but in major matters they usually will express themselves. They will stand up for certain things. In subjugation, there are almost no strong opinions across the board. Whether the issues are big or small—no matter what is at stake—in subjugation there is no strong sense of self. Unexpressed anger is another clue that you are subjugated rather than easygoing.

Because you lack a strong sense of self, of *who* you are, there is the danger that you might lose yourself in your subjugator. You can become so immersed in trying to meet the needs of other people that you begin to blend or merge into these people. The boundary between who you are and who they are becomes blurred. You might adopt other people's goals and opinions as your own. You might adopt other people's values. You might lose yourself in the other. There is a chance that you might subjugate yourself to a group, particularly a group with a charismatic leader. You might even find some attraction to cult groups.

In our work, we have identified two major reasons why subjugated patients allow other people to control them. The first is that they subjugate themselves out of *guilt,* or because they want to relieve the pain of others; and the second is that they subjugate because they anticipate rejection, retaliation, or abandonment. These reasons correspond to two types of subjugation.

TWO TYPES OF SUBJUGATION

1. Self-Sacrifice (subjugation out of guilt)
2. Submissiveness (subjugation out of fear)

Carlton subjugates himself out of guilt. He wants to gain *approval.* He wants everyone to *like* him. Gaining approval is his primary motivation. In addition, Carlton feels the pain of others very deeply. When he feels that another person is suffering, he is moved to take care of that person. He tries to meet other people's needs. Whenever he believes he has failed, he feels guilty. He finds the experience of guilt very uncomfortable, and his self-sacrifice helps him avoid this guilt.

Mary Ellen, on the other hand, subjugates herself out of fear. She submits because she is afraid of being punished. This fear is certainly realistic: Dennis is cruel and domineering. However, one wonders what it is about Mary Ellen that caused her to flee from one subjugated relationship with her father into another one with her husband. In her marriage, Mary Ellen reenacts her childhood subjugation.

• SELF-SACRIFICE •

Self-sacrificers feel responsible for the well-being of others. As a child, you may have experienced too much responsibility for the physical or emotional welfare of a parent, sister, brother, or of some other close person. For example, you may have had a parent who was chronically ill or depressed. As an adult, you believe it is your responsibility to take care of others. In doing so, you neglect yourself.

Your self-sacrifice is a virtue that has become excessive. Taking care of others has many admirable qualities:

CARLTON: *I may be self-sacrificing, but I do a lot of good. All my friends come to me to discuss their problems. When my mother is sick, it's me she calls. I'm the one who takes her to the doctor, who gets her what she needs.*

Plus, I volunteer at a men's homeless shelter. I belong to Greenpeace and Amnesty International. People like me make the world a better place.

You are *empathic;* perhaps this is part of your innate temperament. You feel the pain of others and want to ease their pain. You try to fix things, to make everything better.

It is important to note that your subjugation is mostly *voluntary.* Whoever subjugated you as a child did not *force* you to do what he or she wanted. Rather, because they were in pain or especially weak, you felt that their needs took precedence over yours.

Although self-sacrificers are somewhat less angry than other subjugated types, you are bound to have some anger. The give-get ratio is out of balance in your life—you are giving much more than you are getting. Although the people you give to may not be to blame for taking more from you than they give back, you are almost certain to have *some* anger, even though you may not acknowledge any resentment.

Your lifetrap gets its strength primarily from the emotion of guilt. You feel *guilty* whenever you put yourself first. You feel guilty whenever you become angry about having to subjugate yourself. You feel guilty whenever you assert yourself. You feel guilty whenever you fail to alleviate pain. Guilt *drives* your subjugation lifetrap.

Whenever you step out of your subjugated role, you feel guilty. Each time you feel guilty, you revert back to self-sacrifice. Largely to relieve guilt, you subjugate yourself with renewed vigor and bury your anger one more time. You are going to have to learn to tolerate this guilt in order to change.

Carlton displays this pattern of anger and guilt in his relationship with his wife. He constantly tries to please her, yet, the more he tries, the more she seems to demand. Of course, her demands make him angry. But, whenever Carlton feels angry, he immediately feels guilty and tries to please his wife twice as hard. In this way, he alternates between anger at his wife and guilt about his anger.

• SUBMISSIVENESS •

Submission is the second form of the Subjugation lifetrap. You submit to the subjugation process *involuntarily*. Whether you actually have a choice or not, you *feel* as though you have no choice. As a child, you subjugated yourself in order to avoid punishment or abandonment, probably by a parent. Your parent threatened to hurt you or to withdraw love or attention. There was *coercion* in the subjugation process. You are almost always angry, even if you do not recognize your anger.

Mary Ellen is the submissive type of subjugator. Throughout her childhood and adolescence, Mary Ellen's father was strict.

MARY ELLEN: *When I left the house, he had to know where I was going. When I got back, he had to know where I'd been. He didn't let me date until I was seventeen, much later than everyone else. I was not allowed to wear makeup or tight clothes. I wasn't allowed out on weeknights, and had to be home early on weekends. It was a drag.*
THERAPIST: *What happened when you disobeyed?*
MARY ELLEN: *He grounded me, or yelled. Sometimes he hit me. I hated him.*

She felt that her house was a prison. Outwardly, she obeyed her father because she was afraid. Inwardly, she was filled with rage.

If you have this type of subjugation, you have a false belief: you attribute more power to the people who currently subjugate you than they actually have. Whoever subjugates you now—a husband, wife, or parent—in truth has little power over you. You have the power to end your subjugation. There may be exceptions, such as your boss, but even there you have more control than you think. You may have to be willing to leave the person, but, one way or another, your subjugation *can* end. You do not have to stay with someone who is dominating or abusing you.

At one time, your subjugation really was involuntary: as a child. In relation to the adults who subjugated you, you were dependent and helpless. A child cannot withstand the threat of punishment or abandonment. Your subjugation was adaptive. But as an adult, you are no longer dependent and helpless. As an adult, you have a choice. This is something you must realize before you can begin to change.

THE ROLE OF ANGER

Although you probably have an easygoing manner, many strong feelings press upon you. Anger in particular builds up from having to surrender your own needs to the needs of others, time after time. When your needs constantly are frustrated, anger is inevitable. You might feel that you are being used or controlled, or that people are taking advantage of you, or you might feel that your needs do not count.

Although you may be chronically angry, you are probably only dimly aware of your anger. You probably would not use the word *angry* to describe yourself.

CARLTON: *I was a little annoyed that Erica insisted I pick her up on the way to dinner. I had to go so far out of my way, and she was right near the train.*

You believe that it is dangerous and wrong to express your anger to others, so you deny and suppress these feelings.

You may be surprised to hear this, but anger is a vital part of healthy relationships. It is a signal that something is wrong—that the other person may be doing something unfair. Ideally, anger motivates us to become more assertive and correct the situation. When anger produces this effect, it is adaptive and helpful. However, since you typically hold back your anger and refrain from self-assertion, you ignore your body's natural signals and fail to correct situations.

Often, you are unaware of the ways in which you express your anger to others. You might blow up at some seemingly minor incident in a manner that is markedly disproportionate. Mary Ellen, whose usual manner is one of quiet passivity, suddenly became enraged when her daughter, Kathy, was ten minutes late for dinner. She unleashed an angry outburst that surprised her and her daughter equally.

MARY ELLEN: *I was standing by the door when Kathy walked in. All of a sudden, I started yelling at her. I had never yelled at her like that before. I couldn't believe it. She looked at me like she was shocked, and then she started to cry. I rushed over to her and told her I was sorry. I remember thinking then that I really needed to go into therapy.*

It is not unusual for such sudden, strong outbursts of anger to surprise the subjugated person as much as the recipient. This type of pent-up anger almost always seems excessive in light of the circumstance that set it off.

Although there may be times when you display your anger directly, it is more common for you to express it *indirectly,* in a disguised fashion—*passive-aggressively.* You get back at people in subtle ways, like procrastinating, being late, or talking about them behind their backs. You may do this unknowingly. When pressed, you deny that you meant to express anger. For example, when she had that angry outburst at her daughter, Mary Ellen was, on more careful analysis, actually mad at her boss.

THERAPIST: *Why did you get so angry at Kathy right then?*
MARY ELLEN: *It was just that I had gotten home late from work, and I was rushing to get dinner ready before Dennis got home, and Kathy was supposed to help me and she was late. I was in a really bad mood when I got home from work. My boss made me stay late* again.

It turned out that Mary Ellen's boss was requiring her to work excessively long hours. She never expressed anger directly toward her boss, nor did she assert herself appropriately. Instead, she was chronically late for work and chronically missed work deadlines. In this manner she got revenge on her boss, but indirectly. Her boss could not be sure about what was happening, that the lateness was hostile.

Passive-aggressive behaviors—procrastinating, talking behind other people's backs, agreeing to do something and not following through, making excuses—all share the feature that they irritate other people, but it is difficult for other people to know whether the passive-aggressive person *intends* the irritation.

Whether through therapy or for other reasons, subjugated people sometimes begin to become more assertive. When this happens, they often experience intense guilt. It is part of the subjugation lifetrap for you to believe it is somehow *wrong* for you to express your needs. It is best for you to learn to tolerate the guilt and continue the assertiveness nevertheless. Until you become more assertive, anger will continue to be a significant problem for you, even if you are not always aware of its harmful consequences.

"I'LL NEVER GIVE IN": THE REBEL

Subjugated people are generally most comfortable in a passive role. However, some people with Subjugation lifetraps learned to cope through Counterattack. Instead of submitting, they take on the *opposite* role. They become aggressive and domineering. By *rebelling,* they overcompensate for their feelings of subjugation.

Unlike Carlton and Mary Ellen, rebels tend to act as though only they are important and only they have needs. If you fit here, you deal with subjugation issues by adopting the role of someone who is aggressive, defiant, and self-centered. You *rebel.* Even so, inside you *feel* the same as other subjugated people: that you are less important and that other people are actually in control. Your aggression is just a mask, and you wear it with a sense of falseness. You feel driven to extremes of assertiveness. You might even seem insolent. People may accuse you of being bossy and overly controlling. Underneath your bravado exterior, you actually feel intimidated by other people.

Anger is close to the surface with rebels. In fact, you may be irritable much of the time, and you are probably prone to angry outbursts. As a child or teenager, you responded to attempts by your parents to subjugate you by becoming disobedient and unruly. You may have had temper tantrums or have been a behavior problem at school. You probably *still* have problems with authority figures. You tend to lose your poise too easily and to express your anger inappropriately. You constantly *battle* authority: you have great difficulty tolerating anything you perceive as external control—any suggestion, order, pressure, or command.

Rebels typically have lifelong battles with their parents. They never seem to leave these conflicts behind and settle into an adult role. In some ways, they remain rebellious adolescents, pursuing career interests or relationships that are the *opposite* of what their parents have wanted for them.

Rebels are not actually any more free than other subjugated people. They do not freely choose their interests or relationships; choices are made for them by the people they are rebelling against. Through an insistence on disregarding the rules, they are just as bound to them as the person who obeys them. They fit the punch line of that joke, "Why did the teenagers cross the road?"—"Because somebody told them *not* to."

ROSE: NINETEEN YEARS OLD, EXERTS SUCH TIGHT CONTROL OVER HER EATING THAT SHE IS ANOREXIC.

Some people make up for their feelings of subjugation by engaging in excessive *self*-control. Because they feel out of control of most areas of their lives, they seize control of some aspect of themselves. This is what happened to Rose, who has the eating disorder known as *anorexia nervosa*. Rose has starved herself until she has become excessively thin, all the while insisting that she is still too fat.

When we look at her family, we see that her mother has always dominated her and treated her like a child. Rose has learned to ignore her own needs and to conform to the wishes of her mother.

ROSE: *I've always been a "good girl." I've always been obedient. No one in my family can believe I'm causing problems.*
FATHER: *It's really true. If anything, she's always been too perfect.*

Rose has suppressed her own needs so often that she is no longer aware of what they are. She has great difficulty identifying her feelings and finds many of her inner states confusing.

The one area in which Rose feels in charge—the one area in which she exerts control—is her weight. She controls her weight with a vengeance. She and her mother are locked in battle constantly about how much food she eats. Rose is Counterattacking against her mother's control of her life by maintaining rigid control over her intake of food. Food becomes the battleground for control between Rose and her mother. Through the symptoms of anorexia, she rebels against her mother, and unknowingly reenacts her Subjugation lifetrap.

ORIGINS OF THE SUBJUGATION LIFETRAP

1. Your parents tried to dominate or control almost every aspect of your life.
2. Your parent(s) punished, threatened, or got angry at you when you would not do things *their* way.
3. Your parent(s) withdrew emotionally or cut off contact with you if you disagreed with them about how to do things.
4. Your parent(s) did not allow you to make your own choices as a child.
5. Because your mother/father was not around enough, or was not capable enough, you ended up taking care of the rest of the family.
6. Your parent(s) always talked to you about their personal problems, so that you were always in the role of listener.
7. Your parent(s) made you feel guilty or selfish if you would not do what they wanted.
8. Your parent(s) were like martyrs or saints—they selflessly took care of everyone else and denied their own needs.
9. You did not feel that your rights, needs, or opinions were respected when you were a child.
10. You had to be very careful about what you did or said as a child, because you worried about your mother's/father's tendency to become worried or depressed.
11. You often felt angry at your parent(s) for not giving you the freedom that other children had.

When you were a child, the people close to you subjugated you. They might have been parents, siblings, peers, or others. However, if Subjugation is one of your primary lifetraps, it was probably your mother or father, since parents are the most important figures in a young child's life.

As a child, you may only have had a vague awareness of your subjugation. You may have sensed that you were resentful toward one or both your parents, or that you felt oppressed. Even as an adult you may not fully realize the extent of your childhood subjugation. Sometimes, through therapy, patients with this lifetrap begin to understand the subjugation process, and gain insight into how much they were subjugated as children. They often become very angry. If this happens to you, it is important to realize that there is a great deal of variation in the motivations of parents who subjugate their children.

At the extreme negative end, there is the abusive parent who subjugates the child out of selfishness, such as Mary Ellen's father. Such parents try to maintain total control of their children through punishment or withdrawal of love. The child must subjugate in order to survive.

MARY ELLEN: *The other night, I was watching [my father] with my daughter. I was watching and knowing that he had done the same exact thing to me. He was making her ask to be excused from the table over and over. He didn't like the way she had asked to be excused. And she was only four! My daughter was crying, and the more she cried, the more he yelled at her.*

If you were brought up by a parent who was abusive, used drugs or alcohol, was mentally ill, or had other serious problems, you may have been subjugated in this extreme fashion. Such parents place their needs first, above the needs of their children, and lack empathy. They do great damage to their children. If you were a child of such a parent, it is almost certain that you have a strong Subjugation lifetrap. You might consider therapy as a way to overcome it.

Near the middle of the Subjugation continuum, one of your parents may have criticized or reprimanded you whenever you expressed any individuality. This is what happened to Carlton. Whenever Carlton made demands, his father called him weak and selfish.

CARLTON: *I really don't know what I would like to do if I left my father's business and went out on my own.*
THERAPIST: *Was there anything you liked as a child, something that was special to you?*
CARLTON: *There was something. As a child I loved to play the piano. But my father didn't like it. He thought it wasn't macho enough. He made fun of me. He wouldn't let me take lessons. What he wanted was for me to play sports. He used to force me to try out for the teams. I never made any. He used to get so mad at me for being such a lousy athlete.*

Carlton's father wanted a son formed in his own image. When Carlton resisted, he criticized him. After a while, Carlton learned that he was bad to have needs of his own. He carried this feeling with him so that later, as an adult, he became intensely self-critical whenever he wanted to assert himself.

Carlton married a woman similar to his father. Erica also has her ideas about what he should be. She scolds him whenever he deviates. In a familiar vein, she complains if he sits down to play the piano and pushes him to be more aggressive at work. Although Carlton is angry at her, he does not display it. Instead, he acts apologetic all the time and meekly submits. He does the same with other people. Carlton allows other people to subjugate him, and thus continues the process started by his father long ago.

Carlton's self-sacrifice originated in his relationship with his mother as well. Throughout much of Carlton's childhood, his mother was sick and confined to bed. She was depressed and needy.

CARLTON: *I tried to keep her company, keep her happy. She was so down all the time. I would stay with her instead of going outside to play. I remember I could hear the other kids playing outside as I sat in her room.*
THERAPIST: *What would you do for her?*
CARLTON: *Oh, read to her, or talk. Bring her food and try to get her to eat.*
THERAPIST: *It must have been hard for you to give up playing with your friends.*
CARLTON: *Oh, I don't remember minding it that much.*

Carlton did not develop a tremendous amount of anger at his mother because she did not *force* him to sacrifice for her. He did it because she needed him. But underneath he had a strong sense of deprivation.

The histories of Carlton and Mary Ellen express just a few of the forms subjugation can take in childhood. Since this is such a common lifetrap, we will tell you about a few more.

SHANNON: TWENTY-FOUR YEARS OLD. SHE IS A "GOOD GIRL" WHO DOES WHAT HER MOTHER AND HUSBAND TELL HER.

Shannon's parents seemed to mean well, but were overprotective. Her mother wanted to shield her from the consequences of making any wrong decisions.

SHANNON: *My mother made all my decisions for me. And, like a good girl, I went along. She decided who my friends were, who I dated, where I went to school, what I wore, what games I played, everything you could think of.*

Her mother controlled her, but in a subtle way. When Shannon rebelled and asserted herself, her mother undermined her confidence by implying that she was not capable of making her own choices.

In addition to Subjugation, she also developed a Dependence lifetrap (see Chapter 10). Her inability to make decisions reflects both Dependence and Subjugation. As an adult, Shannon still allows others to make all her decisions. Anthony, her husband, complains:

ANTHONY: *She has no initiative. I'm always the one who decides where to go for dinner, what show to watch, where to go on vacation, and what projects to do in the house. When we sit around with a bunch of friends trying to decide what to do for the evening, it's never Shannon who finally says, "Let's go to the movies." And when I ask her what she wants to do, she always says, "I don't care, whatever you want is fine."*
SHANNON: *Well, I really don't care. I really have no preference.*

As in her relationship with her mother, when Shannon does make a suggestion, her husband ridicules her. When this happens, she collapses back into her subjugation.

WILLIAM: THIRTY-SEVEN YEARS OLD. AS A CHILD, HE SERVED AS A PARENT TO HIS OWN ALCOHOLIC MOTHER.

In an all-too-common scenario in cases of children of alcoholics, William devoted much of his life to taking care of his alcoholic mother. As a very young child, he developed self-sacrifice as a means of preserving an attachment to his mother—by keeping her intact, he could insure that she would be available to him. He took care of his mother. He was the parentified child.

WILLIAM: *I did the shopping. I cooked the meals. I called her boss and made up lies to cover for her when she was too hung over to go to work. There were a lot of times that I told them I was sick at school, when I was just staying home to nurse my mother. I tried so hard to get her to stop drinking. I hid her scotch. I measured how much she was drinking. I used to mark the bottles before I went to bed. I begged her to get help.*
THERAPIST: *Didn't anyone try to help you?*

WILLIAM: *No. Once in a while my aunts and uncles would ask what was going on, but I would lie and tell them everything was fine. I knew they didn't really want to know.*

As an adult, William still tries to save other people. He is a doctor. He has learned to channel his talent for self-sacrifice productively into his work.

In his personal life, William has more trouble. He is co-dependent. His pattern is to seek out needy people, particularly alcoholic women, and form self-sacrificing relationships with them. He has helped himself to overcome this self-destructive pattern by joining a support group for children of alcoholics. His relationship with his current girlfriend is healthier. He is able to assert his needs, and, when he does, his girlfriend is responsive. William is learning that it is healthier for him to form relationships in which his needs have a chance of being met.

Perhaps you have seen yourself in one of these stories. Perhaps your story is somewhat different. There are many childhood paths that lead to the development of a Subjugation lifetrap. The crucial factor is that, for reasons that were beyond your control at the time, you were subjugated. And now in adulthood, though your circumstances have changed, you continue to subjugate yourself to the people in your life, either through submission or self-sacrifice.

DANGER SIGNALS IN POTENTIAL PARTNERS

1. Your partner is domineering and expects to have things his/her way.
2. Your partner has a very strong sense of self and knows exactly what he/she wants in most situations.
3. Your partner becomes irritated or angry when you disagree or attend to your own needs.
4. Your partner does not respect your opinions, needs, or rights.
5. Your partner pouts or pulls away from you when you do things your way.
6. Your partner is easily hurt or upset, so you feel you have to take care of him/her.
7. You have to watch what you do or say carefully because your partner drinks a lot or has a bad temper.
8. Your partner is not very competent or together, so you end up having to do a lot of the work.

9. Your partner is irresponsible or unreliable, so you have to be overly responsible and reliable.
10. You let your partner make most of the choices because most of the time you do not feel strongly one way or the other.
11. Your partner makes you feel guilty or accuses you of being selfish when you ask to do something your way.
12. Your partner becomes sad, worried, or depressed easily, so you end up doing most of the listening.
13. Your partner is very needy and dependent on you.

You have the strongest feelings of attraction and attachment to partners who trigger your lifetrap. These relationships become intense for you because they unlock the emotions of your childhood subjugation. Again and again, you turn relationships into reenactments of your childhood subjugation. Even if you are the rebel type and have selected a passive partner to dominate and control, the process is still one of subjugation.

One common pattern among subjugated people who are submissive is to seek out relationships with aggressive, dominant figures—with leaders. In your passivity you require a strong figure. You need someone to tell you what to do and how to feel about things. You may become dependent on others to make decisions for you. This is what happened to Shannon, whose mother made all her decisions for her. She was always "the good girl," exactly the daughter her parents wanted: she was polite and obedient, did well at school, and was the perfect daughter. Shannon married just the kind of man her parents wanted. Now she is the perfect wife.

SHANNON: *I guess I'm not really that happy about everything, but Anthony gets mad if I say anything. He gets really annoyed.*
THERAPIST: *What is so bad about Anthony getting mad at you?*
SHANNON: *Oh, the thought of him getting mad really scares me. What if he decided he didn't want to be with me anymore?*

Shannon feels totally dependent upon her husband. She feels anxious if they are apart even for a few hours. She does everything right to avoid his anger. What she fears most is that in his anger he might abandon her; she feels certain that she could never survive on her own. She subjugates herself totally. Her dependence maintains her subjugation, and her subjugation maintains her dependence.

If you are self-sacrificing, you may be drawn to needy and dependent partners. You rush to fill their needs. You might try to save or rescue them. Sometimes subjugated people choose narcissistic partners, who are demanding but give little in return, and who really do not care about others' feelings. You are comfortable in the role of the one who is giving all the time. If you are a rebel, you might pick someone who is even more subjugated than you, so you can be the one in control.

SUBJUGATION LIFETRAPS

1. You let other people have their own way most of the time.
2. You are too eager to please—you will do almost anything to be liked or accepted.
3. You do not like to disagree openly with other people's opinions.
4. You are more comfortable when other people are in positions of control.
5. You will do almost anything to avoid confrontation or anger. You always accommodate.
6. You do not know what you want or prefer in many situations.
7. You are not clear about your career decisions.
8. You always end up taking care of everyone else—almost no one listens to or takes care of you.
9. You are rebellious—you automatically say "no" when other people tell you what to do.
10. You cannot stand to say or do anything that hurts other people's feelings.
11. You often stay in situations where you feel trapped or where your needs are not met.
12. You do not want other people to see you as selfish so you go to the other extreme.
13. You often sacrifice yourself for the sake of other people.
14. You often take on more than your share of responsibilities at home and/or at work.
15. When other people are troubled or in pain, you try very hard to make them feel better, even at your own expense.
16. You often feel angry at other people for telling you what to do.
17. You often feel cheated—that you are giving more than you are getting back.
18. You feel guilty when you ask for what *you* want.
19. You do not stand up for your rights.

---

20. You resist doing what other people want you to do in an indirect way. You procrastinate, make mistakes, and make excuses.
21. You cannot get along with authority figures.
22. You cannot ask for promotions or raises at work.
23. You feel that you lack integrity—you accommodate too much.
24. People tell you that you are not aggressive or ambitious enough.
25. You play down your accomplishments.
26. You have trouble being strong in negotiations.

These are pitfalls for you to avoid in love and work. Even if you find a partner who wants a relationship based on equality, you may still find ways to reinforce your lifetrap. And even if you have a job that offers you the opportunity to become a major participant, you can twist it until it conforms to your subjugated role.

Whatever relationship you form, you are bound to have anger simmering below the surface. The build-up of anger is something that threatens the stability of subjugated relationships. Early in relationships, you suppress anger and avoid conflict. This helps keep the relationship intact, but it is hard to keep up. After a period of years, your anger may build up to such a point that you rebel, completely upsetting the balance of the relationship, or you may withdraw or retaliate. Often there are sexual difficulties. In addition, as the years pass, you may grow and develop a stronger sense of identity. If you become more assertive and no longer willing to stay in a subjugated relationship, your relationship must either change to adapt to your greater maturity or it must end.

WORK

Since the Subjugation lifetrap can have such a powerful effect upon your life at work, we will spend some time discussing this aspect.

Subjugated people often work in one of the helping professions, particularly if they are self-sacrificing. You may be a doctor, nurse, homemaker, teacher, minister, therapist, or other kind of healer. It is natural that you would gravitate toward a career of service to others; the Subjugation lifetrap takes a lot away from you, but one of its gifts is acute sensitivity to the needs and pain of others. In all likelihood, you are in a profession that exploits your ability to be there for others.

Although you probably shun the limelight, it is possible that you are the right hand of a more powerful person to whom you are devoted and who finds you very useful. In many ways, you are just the type of person a boss wants to hire. You are obedient, loyal, and demand little. It is probably a rare event for you to ask for a raise. You try hard to please everyone, especially your superiors, and you have trouble setting limits on the amount of sacrifice you will make. Here is an example from one of Carlton and Erica's marital sessions.

ERICA: *Another thing I'm mad about is that Carlton won't take a vacation with me. He won't ask his father for the time. We haven't gone on a vacation together in six years!*

CARLTON: *You just don't understand. They need me too much at the office. I know Dad would be disappointed. I just can't let him down that way.*

Although Carlton wants a vacation and feels torn that he cannot spend more time with his family, his work is always a higher priority than his own desires.

You might be too much of a yes person. You might agree with your boss or coworkers just to please them, rather than because you think they are right. Helen is this way.

HELEN: THIRTY-FOUR YEARS OLD. HER SUBJUGATION PREVENTS HER FROM FULFILLING HER POTENTIAL AT WORK.

Helen has a middle-management position in a large corporation. She did extremely well in business school, but has not advanced as quickly in the business world as her peers.

Helen tends to say what people at work want to hear, rather than what she views as the truth, especially when she deals with authority figures. She refrains from making suggestions or disagreeing, even when she has something important to offer. Many of her valuable opinions and ideas remain hidden because she is silent when she should speak.

When her superiors ask her about the status of her projects, she presents an overly optimistic view of things because she wants to please them. She also accepts too much work. It is not surprising that she keeps winding up in the position of being unable to deliver what she has promised.

Unlike Helen, who has strong opinions but does not express them aloud, many subjugated people feel that they lack strong opinions about work-related issues. When asked to comment on issues, they feel confused about where they stand. Shannon, who has both the Dependence and Subjugation lifetraps, is this way. Rather than thinking for herself, she simply conforms to whatever the group seems to want. Although she is a hard worker, her work does not bear the stamp of her individuality.

SHANNON: *I was a mess the other day at work. I had to decide whether to include these certain figures in my report to the Safety committee, and my boss was out for the day. I almost had a panic attack.*

THERAPIST: *How did you go about making the decision?*

SHANNON: *I went around to everyone I could find and got advice. It made me crazy, really. I would talk to one person, and they would make sense, but the next person would say something completely different, and they would make sense too.*

THERAPIST: *It sounds like the whole process just left you more confused.*

Shannon lacks a clear sense of her identity as a professional in her company. This detracts from the quality of her work. She is resentful that other people in her company who work less have risen faster on the promotional ladder.

You probably are too passive at work, and this damages your chances for advancement. You lack the initiative and ambition it takes to get ahead. You avoid leadership roles that require you to take independent action. You are most comfortable with an authority figure to direct and guide you.

KATHERINE: THIRTY YEARS OLD. SHE DID WELL IN SCHOOL, BUT CANNOT FUNCTION INDEPENDENTLY IN THE WORKPLACE.

Katherine is a lawyer working in a small firm. She had an excellent record as a student in law school, where she was closely tied to the professor who served as her mentor. Once she left school, she began to have problems. Her job demanded more autonomy and self-direction than she was able to supply.

KATHERINE: *I know I'm supposed to take on my own cases, but I find myself avoiding it. I really better get it together. I'm under so much pressure to produce.*

Accustomed as she is to the passivity of subjugation, Katherine is uncomfortable with her newfound independence.

ELIZABETH: TWENTY-EIGHT YEARS OLD, *UNDERSELLS* HERSELF AT WORK.

Elizabeth illustrates another characteristic of subjugation that can hurt your chances to get ahead. She works for an advertising agency as part of a team of six people that creates proposals for advertising campaigns. She is very bright and imaginative. However, she has the marked tendency to play down her importance.

ELIZABETH: *I work hard. I contribute a lot to the team. But I'm not confident enough. I don't like being the center of attention. Like the other day, when Greg took credit for my cake mix idea, I had trouble speaking up, setting the record straight.*
THERAPIST: *I thought you were going to present your cake mix idea.*
ELIZABETH: *At the last minute, I let Greg do it. And he ended up taking the credit.*

Furthermore, Elizabeth is not a strong negotiator; she backs down too easily. She even has assertiveness problems with subordinates because she tries too hard to please them and has difficulty exerting the proper authority. She praises their work when it is not up to par and allows them too many liberties. She does tedious work herself that she should delegate. When her subordinates make unreasonable requests, she finds it hard to say "no." Naturally, people take advantage of the situation.

It is inevitable that you will become angry about your subjugation at work. But you rarely express your anger directly. You keep your anger bottled up inside. By suppressing it, you increase rather than decrease your anger, and make it more likely that you will express your anger in self-defeating ways.

You might find that you restrain your anger for long periods, then suddenly erupt in what is usually an inappropriate expression of anger. Perhaps you have difficulty setting limits on the amount of work you accept from your boss. You might simmer with anger below the surface for a while, and then have an angry outburst at a meeting, or be overly aggressive in your dealings with a client or subordinate. Such behavior is unprofessional and damages your image.

However, the most likely scenario is that you express your anger passive-aggressively. This is what Carlton does.

CARLTON: *My father makes way too many demands on me. He takes advantage of my willingness to go the extra mile.*
THERAPIST: *Do you ever tell your father that the work is too much?*
CARLTON: *No. He should know. To his face I say it's just fine, but he should know from the way that I say it that I don't mean it.*

Carlton causes trouble in hidden ways. He acts out his anger rather than expressing it directly. He walks through the office with a sullen expression on his face. He complains to the other employees behind his father's back and encourages others to complain. He procrastinates, and then apologizes or makes excuses for not having his work done.

THE REBEL AT WORK

Rebels display the *opposite* pattern: they are domineering and controlling.

TIMOTHY: FORTY-THREE YEARS OLD. HE IS SERVILE TO HIS BOSS, BUT ACTS LIKE A BULLY WITH HIS SUBORDINATES.

You might subjugate yourself to some people at work, and then take it out on others. Timothy does this. He manages the men's clothing department of a large store. He subjugates himself to the general manager, trying ceaselessly to gain this manager's approval, but to no avail.

TIMOTHY: *The general manager seems to dislike me for some reason. He sometimes embarrasses me. The other day he scolded me in front of some customers and employees. He ordered me to stand there and fold clothes, like a menial clerk.*
THERAPIST: *What did you do?*
TIMOTHY: *I did it. I stood there and folded the clothes.*

Naturally, this state of affairs kindles anger. Timothy takes out his anger on the salespeople and other employees below him.

TIMOTHY: *I'm like a tyrant in the department. I snap out commands, and people better step to. And if they mess up, they are going to hear it from me, loud and clear all through the department.*
THERAPIST: *That's revenge. You treat them even worse than your boss treats you.*

Timothy has two extremes. At one extreme, he is servile and eager to please. At the other, he is demanding and furious. At one extreme, he appears anger-less; at the other, his anger is completely out of control.

Here are the steps to changing your Subjugation lifetrap:

CHANGING YOUR SUBJUGATION LIFETRAP

1. Understand your childhood subjugation. Feel the subjugated child inside of you.
2. List everyday situations at home and at work in which you subjugate or sacrifice your own needs to others.
3. Start forming your own preferences and opinions in many aspects of your life: movies, foods, leisure time, politics, current controversial issues, time usage, etc. Learn about yourself and your needs.
4. Make a list of what you do or give to others, and what they do or give to you. How much of the time do you listen to others? How much of the time do they listen to you?
5. Stop behaving passive-aggressively. Push yourself systematically to assert yourself—express what you need or want. Start with easy requests first.
6. Practice asking other people to take care of you. Ask for help. Discuss your problems. Try to achieve a balance between what you give and get.
7. Pull back from relationships with people who are too self-centered or selfish to take your needs into account. Avoid one-sided relationships. Change or get out of relationships where you feel trapped.
8. Practice confronting people instead of accommodating so much. Express your anger appropriately, as soon as you feel it. Learn to feel more comfortable when someone is upset, hurt, or angry at you.
9. Do not rationalize your tendency to please others so much. Stop telling yourself that it doesn't really matter.
10. Review past relationships and clarify your pattern of choosing controlling or needy partners. List the danger signals for you to avoid. If possible, avoid selfish, irresponsible, or dependent partners who generate very high chemistry for you.
11. When you find a partner who cares about your needs, asks your

---

opinions and values them, and who is strong enough to do 50 percent of the work, give the relationship a chance.

12. Be more aggressive at work. Take credit for what you do. Do not let other people take advantage of you. Ask for any promotions or raises you might be entitled to get. Delegate responsibilities to other people.

13. (To the Rebel.) Try to resist doing the *opposite* of what others tell you to do. Try to figure out what *you* want, and do it even if it is consistent with what authority figures tell you.

14. Make flashcards. Use them to keep you on track.

1. Understand Your Childhood Subjugation. Feel the Subjugated Child Inside of You. Your Subjugation lifetrap has great emotional strength. In part, this is because the emotions of childhood are strong. Children are less able than adults to modulate their emotions with their intelligence, so childhood emotions have a primitive force. When your Subjugation lifetrap is activated, these emotions are unleashed, and you are filled with negative feelings—anger, guilt, fear.

Ordinarily, you try to *escape* this kind of intense activation of your lifetrap. You try to avoid experiencing these painful feelings. You deny and suppress your feelings. Then, without knowing what you are doing, you blindly act out your subjugation. You repeatedly play a subjugated role in your relationships. In order to change, you must be willing to acknowledge and tolerate some painful feelings.

The best way to feel the subjugated child inside of you is through imagery. Start with an instance of subjugation in your current life. Take a moment to close your eyes, and let an image come into your mind of when you felt the same way before. Try to remember far back into childhood. Do not *force* the image to come. Simply allow it to float to the top of your mind. Who were you with? Was it your mother or father? Was it your brother, sister, or a friend?

MARY ELLEN: *I was giving Dennis the silent treatment the other night, and he didn't even notice.*

THERAPIST: *Were you mad at him?*

MARY ELLEN: *Mad? I kept trying to tell him something, and he wouldn't listen. He kept interrupting me and talking about* himself. *So I decided not to talk to him at all. And he didn't even notice.*

THERAPIST: *Let's do an imagery exercise about this. Close your eyes and bring back what happened the other night, when Dennis wouldn't listen. Can you do that?*

MARY ELLEN: *Yes. I'm back there, trying to get Dennis to listen to me.*

THERAPIST: *Okay. Now let an image come of when you felt that way before, as a child.*

MARY ELLEN: *Well (pause). I get an image of my father. I'm trying to tell him that all the girls are staying out late the night of the prom, but he won't listen to me. He just keeps yelling at me, telling me that no daughter of his is going to stay out until all hours. I am so frustrated I could scream.*

Imagery exercises such as these are capable of stirring up a great deal of emotion. What happens might surprise you. Try to accept your feelings, and to learn what they have to teach you. You might find that you experience intense anger at the ones who subjugated you. Try to tolerate this experience of anger. Your anger is part of your *healthy* side. It is serving a useful purpose, telling you that you need to change the way you relate to other people. Your anger can help you to get in touch with the part of yourself that wants something different—that wants to change and grow. One powerful way to get in touch with this sense of yourself is through your anger. Your anger may be your only clue that there is something else that you want.

Through imagery, you can trace the history of your Subjugation lifetrap. Follow the path of its development through your childhood. Note how your experiences reinforced your lifetrap and made it somehow inevitable that you would adopt a subjugated style of relating. Continue until you shift to a more realistic perspective of your early family life. By the end, we hope you will experience sadness or anger about what happened to you in your childhood, but stop viewing these early experiences as proof of your need to subjugate yourself.

2. List Everyday Situations at Home and at Work in Which You Subjugate or Sacrifice Your Own Needs to Others. Begin to watch yourself. Become an observer of yourself, standing outside of yourself and maintaining a detached view. Observe each instance of your subjugation. Make a list of the situations that tend to be difficult for you. They should be situations that you want to master.

Here is an example of a list constructed by Mary Ellen.

STEPS TO "UN-SUBJUGATE"

1. Tell the paper boy to bring the paper to the door when it's raining.
2. Tell a salesperson I don't want help.
3. Don't give my children any more money than their allowances.
4. Ask Dennis to drive the children to school on mornings of my class.
5. Tell Dad he can't criticize the kids anymore in my presence.
6. Take a full day for myself. Do things *I* enjoy, like shopping, reading in the park, seeing my friends, etc.
7. Tell Dorothy (friend) I am angry she is not pulling her share of the kids' carpool.
8. Tell Dennis how I feel when he criticizes me in front of other people.
9. Tell Dennis it is not acceptable for him to criticize me when I haven't done anything wrong or in front of other people.
10. When Dennis and I go shopping for the couch, state my preferences instead of just giving in to his.

---

3. Start Forming Your Own Preferences and Opinions in Many Aspects of Your Life: Movies, Foods, Leisure Time, Politics, Current Controversial Issues, Time Usage, etc. Learn About Yourself and Your Needs.
This involves a shift in your focus of attention. Instead of pouring your mental energy into figuring out what the other person wants and feels, start paying attention to what *you* want and feel. Think about what *you* prefer.

THERAPIST: *What movie did you two see the other night?*
CARLTON: Presumed Innocent.
THERAPIST: *Did you like it?*
CARLTON: *Uh, I don't know. It was okay. Erica liked it. I hadn't really thought about it.*
THERAPIST: *Well, try to think about it now.*
CARLTON: *Well, it was a little far-fetched.*
THERAPIST: *So much that you didn't like it?*
CARLTON: *No. I liked it. It kept me interested. It kept me guessing who the murderer was.*

Make yourself the source of your opinions, not the people around you.

4. Make a List of What You Do or Give to Others, and What They Do or Give to You. How Much of the Time Do You Listen to Others? How Much of the Time Do They Listen to You? Look at the give-get ratio in your relationships. Pick the most important ones: your lover, spouse, children, best friend, parents, or boss. Make a list for each one with two columns: "What I give the person" and "What the person gives me." Making these lists can help you see immediately how the relationship is off-balance.

MARY ELLEN: *I made a list about Dennis and me. (She gives me the list.)*
THERAPIST *(reads list): That's interesting. The list of what you give Dennis has thirty-two items—"Listen to his problems about work," "Buy his clothes," "Cook his food," "Take in his dry-cleaning," "Buy his gifts," "Wash his clothes," and so on. And the list of what Dennis gives you has one—"Financial security."*
MARY ELLEN: *Right. I know. No wonder I'm pissed off.*

Our eventual goal is for you to achieve a balance in your relationships. We do not want you to stop giving, but you need to stop giving so much, beyond what you would wish if you were more in control. And we want you to start getting the things you give—being cared for, listened to, supported, and respected.

5. Stop Behaving Passive-Aggressively. Push Yourself Systematically to Assert Yourself—Express What You Need or Want. Start with Easy Requests First. In order to change, you must be willing to experiment with new ways of behaving that are more assertive and expressive of your needs. You must be willing to make changes in the way you *relate* to people.

Changing the way you behave with someone changes the way you feel about them. For example, it is hard to remain intimidated after you have dealt with someone assertively. Most important, changing your behavior changes the way you think and feel about *yourself*. Positive behavior change creates self-confidence and self-esteem. It builds a sense of mastery.

The next step is for you to begin to behave in a more assertive fashion. We know this will not be easy for you. For this reason you should work gradually. Start by behaving assertively in situations that are relatively easy for you, and slowly work up to more difficult situations.

Take the list you constructed, of situations in which you subjugate yourself. Rate how difficult each item would be for you using the following scale:

SCALE OF DIFFICULTY

0 Very Easy
2 Mildly Difficult
4 Moderately Difficult
6 Very Difficult
8 Feels Almost Impossible

Here is how Mary Ellen rated the items on her list:

STEPS I COULD TAKE TO "UN-SUBJUGATE"	DIFFICULTY
1. Tell the paper boy to bring the paper to the door when it's raining.	2
2. Tell a salesperson I don't want help.	3
3. Don't give children any more money than their allowances.	5
4. Ask Dennis to drive the children to school on mornings of my class.	4
5. Tell Dad he can't criticize the kids anymore in my presence.	7
6. Take a full day for myself. Do things *I* enjoy, like shopping for wool, reading in the park, seeing my friends, etc.	4
7. Tell Dorothy I am angry she is not pulling her share of the kids' carpool.	5
8. Tell Dennis how I feel when he criticizes me in front of other people.	7
9. Tell Dennis it is not acceptable for him to criticize me when I haven't done anything wrong, or in front of others.	8
10. When Dennis and I go shopping for the couch, state my preferences instead of just giving in to his.	4

Work on each item from your list, starting with the easier ones and progressing to the more difficult ones. Here are some guidelines for you to follow.

Keep in mind that your goal is to complete the item. Do not let the pull of your Subjugation lifetrap lead you astray. For example, when Mary Ellen completed item #7 on her list, telling her friend Dorothy that she is angry about the carpool situation, she had to keep reminding herself that her goal was to express her anger, *not* to make Dorothy like her. Do not get distracted by what is always a subjugated person's hidden agenda: pleasing the other person.

Whatever the other person does, calmly keep restating your position. If the person attacks you, *do not get defensive.* Do not get lost in defending yourself. Stick to your point. For example, here is part of a role-play we did with Mary Ellen so she could practice confronting Dorothy about the carpool. We played the part of Dorothy.

MARY ELLEN: *Dorothy, there's something I've been meaning to talk to you about. I have been feeling angry about the whole carpool situation. For the past five Tuesdays, you've asked me to drive for you. It really is too hard for me to drive twice a week.*

THERAPIST *(playing Dorothy): I can't believe you're being so petty as to bring this up!*

MARY ELLEN: *Call me petty if you like, Dorothy, but it is really too hard for me to drive twice a week.*

Be direct. Do not make a speech. You have a much greater chance of being heard if what you say is short and to the point. Use the word "I" and speak in terms of your own feelings. (Interestingly, many subjugated people avoid the word "I" whenever they talk about their feelings. Instead of saying, *"I* felt angry when you cut me off," they say such things as *"People* feel angry when they are cut off that way.") Speaking in terms of your own feelings is an important component of assertiveness. This is, in part, a practical matter. No one can argue with your feelings. If you say, "I was right, you were wrong," a person can argue; but if you say, "I felt angry when you did that," no one can argue. No one can say, "No, you didn't feel angry." By expressing what you feel, you make a statement that how you feel *matters.*

Take at least a week to complete a hierarchy item. Do each item again and again, until you have mastered that level of difficulty. If the item can only be done once, substitute other items at the same level of difficulty from elsewhere in your life.

To help the exercises generalize into all the areas of your life, begin to behave assertively in a more spontaneous way, as relevant situations arise. Try to regard each situation that calls for assertive behavior as a cue for you to practice refining your assertiveness skills.

6. Practice Asking Other People to Take Care of You. Ask for Help. Discuss Your Problems. Try to Achieve a Balance Between What You Give and Get. Ask people to give you more. Talk about yourself. Many subjugated patients tell us that when they talk about themselves for "too long," they start to get anxious, and they switch back to the other person. When you feel anxious in this way, understand that it is *okay* to talk about yourself. It is *okay* to talk about your problems and ask for help. You will find that it brings you closer to people. And if there are people who simply do not want to listen, then it is time to reevaluate their importance in your life.

7. Pull Back from Relationships with People Who Are Too Self-Centered or Selfish to Take Your Needs Into Account. Avoid One-Sided Relationships. Change or Get Out of Relationships Where You Feel Trapped. When we first started as therapists, our tendency was to try to preserve every relationship in the patient's life. If the patient was married, our impulse was to try to preserve the marriage. If the patient was having a love affair, our impulse was to try to preserve the affair. But we no longer feel that relationships should be preserved at all costs. Some relationships are simply too damaging, and have too few prospects for change.

There will be some people in your life who will refuse to adjust to your attempt to balance the relationship. If you are married or if they are part of your family, you can give them every opportunity to change. But if, in the final analysis, they will not change, then you have to pull back from the relationship. You may even have to end it.

Carlton's marriage survived. As he became more assertive, Erica at first fought it tooth and nail. But at some level she also welcomed it. In her heart she was glad to have him become stronger. And at some level it was a relief for her to have limits set on her demandingness. She felt more secure, more contained.

However, Mary Ellen's marriage did not survive. Dennis could not accept her growth. He was too invested in being the one in control. Eventually Mary Ellen left him. She is working and putting herself through school. She is starting to date other men.

8. Practice Confronting People Instead of Accommodating So Much. Express Your Anger Appropriately, as Soon as You Feel It. Learn to Feel More

Comfortable When Someone Is Upset, Hurt, or Angry at You. You must learn to express your anger appropriately and constructively. Instead of continuing to let your anger control you, you must learn to *use* your anger to improve the relationships in your life.

There are guidelines for you to follow. The basic principle is: *Whatever the other person does, keep calmly restating your position.* Do not let the other person trick you into becoming defensive. Stick to your point.

Stay calm. Do not yell and scream. You are much more powerful when you are calm than when you are screaming. Screaming is a sign of psychological defeat. Try not to attack the person. Simply state what they have *done* that has upset you.

If you have a basically good relationship but want to say something negative or critical to a person, start by saying something positive. Try to instill an attitude in the person of openness to what you are about to say. People can only listen when they are in a receptive state. If you make people angry, they will become defensive and shut you off. Starting on a positive note enhances the receptivity of the listener.

For example, Carlton began one of his more difficult items ("Tell Erica not to reprimand me in front of other people") with the statement, "Erica, I know you love me." Say something that is positive and *true;* do not just make something up. Next, direct your criticism not at the person, but at the person's *behavior.* Carlton did not tell Erica, "You are an insensitive person." Rather he told her that there is something she does that he wishes she would stop: "You criticize me at times in front of other people." It is important to request specific behavior change. The person is more likely to comply when you have given a clear description of the specific behavior change you would like to see. Finally, end on a positive note. Carlton concluded his request by saying, "I really appreciate that you were able to stand here and listen to me."

Use good timing. Do not choose a time in which either of you is in a highly emotional state. Wait until the matter can be discussed in a calm atmosphere. In addition, be assertive not only in your words, but in your body language and tone of voice. Look the person directly in the eyes. If it will help you, practice assertiveness exercises in front of the mirror before you try them out in the world.

9. Do Not Rationalize Your Tendency to Please Others So Much. Stop Telling Yourself That It Doesn't Really Matter. It is time for you to express your preferences in relationships with other people. Try to do this at every opportunity. Begin with seemingly trivial matters and progress to more important ones.

CARLTON: *This may sound strange, but I really believe that the moment I started to change in therapy was one night when Erica asked me what I wanted for dinner, steak or hamburger. I started to tell her that I didn't really care, and I stopped. And I* picked *steak.*

Weigh the positives and negatives to decide which you prefer. Make a choice and communicate that choice.

10. Review Past Relationships and Clarify Your Pattern of Choosing Controlling or Needy Partners. List the Danger Signals for You to Avoid. If Possible, Avoid Selfish or Irresponsible Partners Who Generate Very High Chemistry for You. Make a list of the most important relationships in your life. What are the common patterns? What are the danger signals for you to avoid? Are you drawn to domineering partners? Do you melt into the lives of your partners so that you have no separate sense of self? Are you drawn to people who bully you with threats, or guilt-trip you? Or are you drawn to helpless, dependent people who need you to take care of them?

The patterns you identify are the ones for you to avoid. We know this will be hard for you because you tend to be most attracted to exactly these types of partners. The chemistry is high, but you cannot sustain these relationships. The cost to you is too great. In the long run, you become angry and unhappy. It is better to choose relationships in which you have equality, even if the chemistry is slightly lower.

11. When You Find a Partner Who Cares About Your Needs, Asks Your Opinions and Values Them, and Who Is Strong Enough to Do 50 Percent of the Work, Give the Relationship a Chance. If you find yourself in a good relationship with a partner who believes in equality, give the relationship a chance to work. Do this even though it feels strange to you. Subjugated people frequently give up too soon on good relationships, claiming they just are not interested, the relationship does not feel right, something is missing, or there is not enough chemistry. As long as you feel *some* chemistry—even a moderate amount—give the relationship a chance. As you become more accustomed to your new role, the chemistry might increase.

12. Be More Aggressive at Work. Take Credit for What You Do. Do Not Let Other People Take Advantage of You. Ask for Any Promotions or Raises You Might Be Entitled To. Delegate Responsibilities to Other People. Apply all your assertiveness techniques at work. Correct situations where you subjugate yourself. Are you indirect with your boss and then passive-aggressive later? Do you sacrifice your interests to those of your subordinates? Do you let coworkers and adversaries walk all over you? *Correct* these situations. It may be scary at first, but you will find that it feels good to be assertive, and this will motivate you to continue. Do not become overly aggressive, but get your fair share.

13. (To the Rebel:) Try to Resist Doing the Opposite of What Others Tell You to Do. Try to Figure Out What You Want, and Do It Even If It Is Consistent with What Authority Figures Tell You. For those of you who are rebels, liberate yourself from outside influence—from those you rebel against. Look to yourself for your opinions and direction. You do not know yourself any better than other subjugated people, and you are not any freer. As long as your decisions are dictated by other people, you are as oppressed—and as angry. Give yourself the freedom to *agree* with authority figures.

Follow all the other steps of change. You, too, need to learn to become more assertive, rather than overly aggressive. Try to even out the give-get ratio in your life, so you are giving as much as you are getting.

14. Make Flashcards. Use Them to Keep You on Track. When you find that you are having trouble, use flashcards. A flashcard can remind you of your right to be assertive. Here is an example of a flashcard written by Carlton. The subject was refusing unreasonable requests.

A SELF-SACRIFICE FLASHCARD

I have the right to say "no" when people ask me to do unreasonable things. If I say "yes," I will only get angry at the other person and at myself. I can live with the guilt of saying "no." Even if I cause the other person a little pain, it will only be temporary. People will respect me if I say "no" to them. And I will respect myself.

And here is one written by Mary Ellen, about her relationship with Dennis.

A SUBMISSION FLASHCARD

What I want is important. I deserve to be treated with respect. I don't have to let Dennis treat me badly. I deserve better than that. I can stand up for myself. I can calmly demand that he treat me with respect or the discussion is over. If he can't grow enough to give me my equal rights in this relationship, then I can leave the relationship and find one that better suits my needs.

Carry the flashcard with you. When your lifetrap is triggered, and it is time for you to be assertive, take out the card and read it. Flashcards are valuable in making the slow transition from intellectual understanding to emotional acceptance.

SOME FINAL WORDS

As you work to change, it is important to give some recognition to each bit of progress. Give yourself credit where it is due. Change is much harder when you forget to reward yourself for the steps along the way. Try to keep looking back at how far you have come, rather than looking forward to how far you have to go. When you make any change, no matter how slight, take a moment to feel good about it. As you take a step out of your subjugation, give yourself the acknowledgment you deserve.

Remember that your Subjugation lifetrap has the strength of a lifetime of memories and of a multitude of repetitions and confirmations that it is right. Subjugation *feels* right to you. Your lifetrap is central to your entire self-image and view of the world. Naturally, it is going to fight very hard for survival. You find comfort and reassurance in holding onto your lifetrap, regardless of its negative consequences for your life. You should not become discouraged because change is slow.

It is tempting to berate yourself for your subjugation. Mary Ellen says, "I am such a wimp. It makes me hate myself." But this attitude can only hinder your efforts to change. Try to respect the reasons your lifetrap developed in the first place. In your childhood, it was essential for your emotional survival. But what was once a help to you is now hurting you, and it is time to give it up. It is time for you to begin the slow journey out of self-denial and self-defeat, and to reclaim your life for yourself.

15

"It's Never Quite Good Enough"
The Unrelenting Standards Lifetrap

PAMELA: FORTY YEARS OLD. SHE IS STRESSED BY THE NEED
TO BE PERFECT IN BOTH HER PRIVATE AND PROFESSIONAL
LIVES.

Pamela is the so-called superwoman. She does it all. She is a doctor and is director of the anesthesiology department at an Ivy League university. She not only excels in the practice of administering anesthesia, one of the most difficult areas in medicine, but she also heads a large-scale research program. She has won grants from federal and private organizations, publishes in top journals, and travels all over the world to present at professional meetings. She earns over two hundred thousand dollars a year.

At the same time she is a perfect wife and mother. Her husband, Craig, is an executive in a large corporation, and practically every week she either attends or throws some business-related social function. Through it all, she insists on being there for her children, and makes sure to schedule time each day to spend with them. She also schedules time each day to exercise and is an excellent tennis player. Her house is immaculate, and the grounds around it are gardened perfectly. Pamela tells me that she regrets that she cannot do all of the gardening herself.

THERAPIST: *So you're a person in life who tries to do it all.*

PAMELA: *That's right, and I guess I do do it all. The only problem is that I'm doing so many different things that I'm a mess. It's go, go, go all the time.*

THERAPIST: *It sounds like it's too much for you.*

PAMELA: *I'll say it's too much. I'm not enjoying life. You would think, with all I have, I would enjoy it a little. But I don't. In fact, I've been feeling really depressed. Overwhelmed and depressed. That's why I've come to therapy. It's getting so that I don't want to get out of bed.*

THERAPIST: *Have you actually stopped doing things?*

PAMELA: *Of course not. I still do it all. I still get out of bed. Nothing has changed. But maybe it's that I just turned forty. I want something more out of life. I want some time for* myself.

KEITH: FORTY-TWO YEARS OLD. HIS RELENTLESS QUEST FOR SUCCESS IS DESTROYING HIM PHYSICALLY.

Keith is also successful at what he does. He is a television newscaster for a major New York station. He is good-looking and exudes a faint air of superiority. He is careful to tell me in an offhand way about all his achievements. He is famous, knows famous people, is powerful at the station, is rich, and dates beautiful models and actresses. But through it all, Keith is still dissatisfied. He wants more. He is *driven*.

THERAPIST: *Why have you come to therapy?*

KEITH: *I'll be honest with you. I don't want to be here. The only reason I've come is that my doctors tell me that my irritable bowel and headaches are caused by stress. I have to learn to relax.*

THERAPIST: *So you want to get rid of the irritable bowel and headaches, but leave everything else the same?*

KEITH: *Yeah. I'm not about to stop pushing to get ahead.*

THE UNRELENTING STANDARDS QUESTIONNAIRE

Fill out this questionnaire to measure the strength of your Unrelenting Standards lifetrap. Use the scale on the following page.

1 Completely untrue of me
2 Mostly untrue of me
3 Slightly more true than untrue of me
4 Moderately true of me
5 Mostly true of me
6 Describes me perfectly

If you have any 5's or 6's on this questionnaire, this lifetrap may still apply to you, even if your score is in the low range.

SCORE	DESCRIPTION
	1. I cannot accept second best. I have to be the best at most of what I do.
	2. Nothing I do is quite good enough.
	3. I strive to keep everything in perfect order.
	4. I must look my best at all times.
	5. I have so much to accomplish that I have no time to relax.
	6. My personal relationships suffer because I push myself so hard.
	7. My health suffers because I put myself under so much pressure.
	8. I deserve strong criticism when I make a mistake.
	9. I am very competitive.
	10. Wealth and status are very important to me.
	YOUR TOTAL UNRELENTING STANDARDS SCORE (Add your scores together for questions 1–10)

INTERPRETING YOUR UNRELENTING STANDARDS SCORE

10–19 Very low. This lifetrap probably does *not* apply to you.
20–29 Fairly low. This lifetrap may only apply *occasionally*.
30–39 Moderate. This lifetrap is an *issue* in your life.
40–49 High. This is definitely an *important* lifetrap for you.
50–60 Very high. This is definitely one of your *core* lifetraps.

THE EXPERIENCE OF UNRELENTING STANDARDS

The primary feeling is *pressure*. You can never relax and enjoy life. You are always pushing, pushing, pushing, to get ahead. You fight to be the best at whatever you do, whether it is school, work, sports, hobbies, dating, or sex. You have to have the best house, the best car, the best job, make the most money, and look the most handsome or beautiful. You have to be perfectly creative and perfectly organized.

The name of the lifetrap is from the point of view of the outside observer. It was we, not Pamela and Keith, who felt their standards were unrelenting. To Pamela and Keith, it was just a normal level of trying to achieve. People who have the Unrelenting Standards lifetrap are usually successful at whatever they do, but this success is from the point of view of other people. *Other* people think that you have achieved a lot, but you take your achievements for granted. They are only what you have expected of yourself.

Physical stress symptoms, such as the irritable bowel and headaches experienced by Keith, are common. You might have high blood pressure, ulcers, colitis, insomnia, fatigue, panic attacks, heart arrhythmias, obesity, back pain, skin problems, arthritis, asthma, or any number of other physical problems.

KEITH: *It is as though my body is telling me I can't do this, I can't push this hard.*
THERAPIST: *Something has to give.*

For you, life is only *doing*. Life is having to work or achieve all the time. You are always straining at the edge of your limits. There is never a chance to take a break, to stop and enjoy things. Everything, including activities that could be enjoyable, such as games or swimming, becomes an ordeal. Pamela and Craig discussed this in one of our marital sessions.

PAMELA: *I can't really relax when I play tennis. It's like I'm watching my game and worrying about perfecting every shot. And I get really pissed off when I can't get it right.*
THERAPIST: *So even your play is work.*
CRAIG: *It's true. I really don't like playing with her for that reason. She takes the game so seriously, and gets so tense. Each game is a life-and-death matter. And she gets upset when she loses. She's really not a good sport.*

Unrelenting Standards can create the full gamut of negative emotions. You feel constantly frustrated and irritated with yourself for not meeting your standards. You may feel chronically angry, and certainly you feel high levels of anxiety. You obsess about the next thing you have to do right. A major focus of your anxiety is *time:* You have so much to do and so little time. You are always aware of time and feel a constant sense of time *pressure.* And you can feel depressed at the grimness of your life and at the emptiness of what you have achieved.

You might ask *why* you continue to push yourself this way. As exhausted as you are, instead of slowing down, you accelerate, taking on more and more responsibility. It is as though you believe that one of the things you do is finally going to bring you satisfaction. You do not realize that the way you approach everything makes genuine pleasure impossible. Inevitably, whatever you try to accomplish takes on that same cast, that same heavy feeling of pressure.

KEITH: *I keep thinking that if I could get to where I want to be, I could be satisfied.*
THERAPIST: *But no matter what you get, whether it's a new job, a new girlfriend, a new car, or a new trip, you always apply those same relentless standards. It's really those standards that have to change.*

You believe in the possibility of success—that if you keep striving you can actually achieve that wonderful state of perfection. Although you probably do not consider yourself truly successful, you feel that you are improving, getting closer to your goal. This sense of progress keeps you going. You imagine an end to the road, when you can finally relax and enjoy life. You fantasize about some future time when you will be released.

THERAPIST: *What is it that keeps you going at this frantic pace? Why
    don't you just stop?*
PAMELA: *I think about that a lot myself. I think it's that I always see the
    light at the end of the tunnel, when I can relax and have what I want.
    I feel like I'm getting there.*

But that state of peace that you hope to find at the end of your striving
never comes. Even if it did, you would just find something else, some other
relentless standard to meet. This is how your lifetrap reinforces itself. At
your core, you are not comfortable unless you are striving. It may not make
you happy, but it is familiar. It is the devil you know.

There are at least three common variants of the Unrelenting Standards lifetrap. You may be more than one type—you may be all three,
in fact.

THREE TYPES OF UNRELENTING STANDARDS

1. Compulsivity
2. Achievement Orientation
3. Status Orientation

• COMPULSIVITY •

The *compulsive* is the person who keeps everything in perfect order. You
are the type who attends to every detail no matter how slight, who fears
making any mistake no matter how minor. You feel frustrated and upset
when things are not just right.

KEITH: *My date with Sharon was a disaster. When we got to the theater,
    we were off center by at least six seats. I was so irritated, I could barely
    pay attention to the play.*
THERAPIST: *That's a shame. I know making time to see this play meant
    a lot to you. Too bad you couldn't enjoy it.*

When Keith goes somewhere, no detail escapes him. The seat has to be
perfect, the food has to be flawless, and the room temperature has to be
exactly right. Of course, something is wrong every time, and he just cannot
settle down and enjoy himself.

Keith gets angry at his surroundings for disappointing him. But not
all compulsive people get angry at their surroundings. Some get angry at

themselves. It may be that you blame yourself more than your surroundings. Pamela is this way. Like Keith, she is the compulsive type, but most of her anger is directed at herself.

THERAPIST: *How did your dinner party go?*
PAMELA: *It went okay, except the rice was a trifle overcooked. I was really mad at myself about that rice.*

When Pamela thinks about her dinner party, her mind fastens on the one detail that did not go quite right. She reproaches herself for not getting this detail right.

Obsessive *self*-control is common. In fact, the whole issue of control is central to this type. When you feel *out* of control in other aspects of your life (because of Vulnerability or Subjugation, for example), compulsivity can be a way to cope so you feel *in* control.

• ACHIEVEMENT ORIENTATION •

This is the so-called workaholic. You are the person who works sixteen-hour days, seven days a week. You place an excessive value on a high level of achievement at the expense of your other needs. You have to be the best.

PAMELA: *When I was in college I remember I once couldn't sleep all night because I was worrying that I was going to get a "B" in my calculus course. I was thinking I wouldn't get to be valedictorian with that "B." I was just so mad at myself for blowing that course.*

It is important to distinguish Unrelenting Standards from the Failure lifetrap. Failure is the sense that you have failed relative to your peers, that you are below average. Unrelenting Standards is the sense that you are at least average, but that you are constantly striving to meet very high, perfectionistic standards. The person with the Failure lifetrap will attempt a task and then think, "I can't do anything right, I messed it up." The person with Unrelenting Standards will attempt that task and think, "I did okay, but I could do better."

PAMELA: *It's not that I think I'm going to fail. I know I'll do a good job. My fear is not of failing, but of being merely* mediocre, *of not standing out from the crowd.*

The Unrelenting Standards lifetrap can sometimes lead to a sense of failure. If your unrelenting standards are so high that you cannot come close to meeting them, then you may begin to feel incompetent, a failure.

It may be that you fall so far short of your goals that you feel you have not achieved anything at all.

Many workaholics exist in a state of chronic irritability or hostility. This is the Type-A personality. Type-A's get angry at anyone who outdoes them or who blocks their ambitions. Or, if the blocks are internal, they get angry at themselves. They are not pushing hard enough, or doing well enough at something. They feel a constant sense of internal irritation.

You may have a less severe form of Achievement Orientation. Perhaps the balance between work and play is slightly off in your life. You cannot really relax, but at least your life is not totally consumed with work. And you may be a workaholic about things other than your job. It may be decorating your house, shopping for clothes or sales, or hobbies and sports. It could be anything—any form of activity that you turn into work and that enslaves you.

• Status Orientation •

Status orientation is an excessive emphasis on gaining recognition, status, wealth, beauty—a false self. It is often a form of Counterattack, to compensate for core feelings of Defectiveness or Social Exclusion.

If you have an excessive Status Orientation, you never feel good enough, no matter what you do. You tend to be self-punitive, or to feel *ashamed,* when you fail to meet your high expectations. You are caught in an endless struggle to amass more and more power, money, or prestige, yet it is never enough to make you feel good about yourself.

THERAPIST: *It's funny, but even though you managed to get invited to such an exclusive party, and you brought, as you said, "the most beautiful woman there," it still sounds like you were unhappy the whole time.*

KEITH: *I was upset about where they sat us at dinner. It made it obvious that we weren't really part of the inner circle.*

Keith is never *satisfied.* It is never demonstrated to his heart's content that he is worthwhile. He feels driven to ever higher levels of success. But no matter what he gains, deep inside he still feels ashamed of who he is.

The status-orientation can be a way of making up for feelings of Emotional Deprivation as well. You may try to fill your emotional emptiness with power, fame, success, money—substituting status for genuine emotional connection. Yet the status is never enough. One patient like this, Nancy, married a rich, unloving man and spent most of her time buying *things*. She had the best of everything. She would sit alone in her big house, surrounded by all her things, and wonder what was missing.

There are four common origins:

THE ORIGINS OF UNRELENTING STANDARDS

1. Your parents' love for you was *conditional* on your meeting high standards.
2. One or both parents were *models* of high, unbalanced standards.
3. Your Unrelenting Standards developed as a way to *compensate* for feelings of defectiveness, social exclusion, deprivation, or failure.
4. One or both parents used *shame* or *criticism* when you failed to meet high expectations.

Growing up in an atmosphere of conditional love is the first common origin. Your parents may have only given you affection, approval, or attention when you were successful or perfect. This is what happened to Pamela.

PAMELA: *It was as though I didn't exist for them except when I won some award or got the highest grade. I remember when they told me I was valedictorian, my first thought was rushing home to tell my parents, that they would be happy with me. Most of the time they just didn't seem to care.*

With conditional love, your childhood is spent running a race to win your parents' love. The race is endless, with few points of reinforcement along the way. One time we asked Pamela to give us an image of her childhood:

PAMELA: *I'm running and running toward my house, but the house keeps receding, and the faster I run, the further away the house becomes.*

Alternately, you may have had loving parents who gave you *lavish* love and approval when you met their high expectations. The important thing is that meeting some standard of school achievement, beauty, status, popularity, or sports became the most effective way for you to win your parents' love, respect, or perhaps even adulation. Your parents may have placed you on a pedestal because of your success.

Your parents may have been *models* of unrelenting standards. They themselves were perfectionistic, orderly, status oriented, or high achieving.

You learned their attitudes and behavior. Often this origin is striking because no one in the family knows that the standards are so high. They feel normal to everybody.

PAMELA: *Until I started therapy, I never really thought of my standards as unrealistic. I never used to think of my parents as perfectionistic. I always thought of them as just normal average people with normal average standards.*

It wasn't until I started looking at it more closely that I realized my mother had to have the house perfect. There was never a trace of mess. If I walked in and left a piece of paper on the table, within five minutes my mother would be asking me to put it away where it belongs.

And my father was completely perfectionistic about his work. He owned his own business, and whatever it was, even hanging up a sign, he had to do it himself and do it perfectly. He was always working.

No one ever said to Pamela, "You must do very well." She learned it purely through modeling, by observing her parents. If you have parents who themselves have high standards, they have, either subtly or directly, communicated those high standards to you.

High parental expectations are particularly common in affluent suburbs where many professionals live. The more professional the parent is, the more likely it is that the child is going to be subjected to these pressures. The whole culture supports high expectations of achievement. However, we have also had many patients with Unrelenting Standards from working-class families. You can have parents with Unrelenting Standards who are mechanics, cashiers, painters, or musicians—they come from all rungs of the social ladder.

We have some patients whose Unrelenting Standards resulted from trying to rise above their childhood environments. You may have felt inferior relative to your peers, or felt that your parents were inferior, and tried to compensate through high achievement or status. This was true of Keith. Keith grew up in a working-class neighborhood and was ashamed of it. He went to a school that was mostly working-class, but Keith envied the rich students from the wealthy part of town.

KEITH: *I felt like where I came from wasn't good enough. I wanted to get to where the rich kids were. I wanted the things they had. I decided early on I was going to get the things the rich kids had.*

Keith planned his whole life around advancing his social class. His Unrelenting Standards were a reaction to shame regarding his family's Social Exclusion.

Unrelenting Standards can also tie in to other lifetraps. For example, you may have the Emotional Deprivation lifetrap. As a child, you found that praise for your accomplishments could make up *somewhat* for too little love. Success can be a strategy for making a connection to others. Unfortunately, it is usually a pale substitute for real nurturance and understanding.

A parent may have spurred you on. Keith's mother felt that she belonged in a higher class and had married beneath her. She fulfilled her desire for status vicariously through Keith. Consequently Keith could never relax. She was always in the background. He once gave us this image of his mother:

KEITH: *I'm in bed trying to sleep, and I hear her voice going on and on. She's saying, "You better get going, there are things you should be doing. Have you finished your homework, don't you need to practice your tennis, don't you have friends to call?"*

Although people with Unrelenting Standards are usually remarkably successful as adults, their childhood memories rarely focus on feelings of success. In fact, they are much more likely to remember feeling defective, excluded, or lonely. Regardless of how hard they tried, they rarely got the respect, admiration, attention, or love they wanted.

PAMELA: *I have so many memories of coming home from school with a top grade and not even getting any attention for it. It had to be something* extraordinary *for me to get attention.*

In Pamela's family, doing very well was treated as just average. Praise was rare. When we ask these patients if they are perfectionistic, they say "no." When we ask if their parents were perfectionistic they say "no" as well. By their standards, they are far from perfection.

Parents can either fail to give praise when a child does well or actually withdraw love when the child falls short of their expectations.

KEITH: *In my freshman year of college, I didn't get asked to pledge the top fraternity. My mother wouldn't talk to me for a week.*

Another patient told us that her mother would suddenly stop hugging and kissing her whenever she got less than an "A" in school.

You may have vivid memories of failures. We had one patient whose father used to mock him when he played sports with his brothers and lost. The whole emphasis in the family was on competition, on having to be the best. He and his brothers would fight to see who was the toughest. Though he became an excellent athlete, all he remembers is disappointment and pressure. There can be memories of striving very hard, yet failing to meet that impossibly high standard.

If your parents used shame or criticism when you fell short of their expectations, you almost certainly have a Defectiveness lifetrap as well.

UNRELENTING STANDARDS LIFETRAPS

1. Your health is suffering because of daily stresses, such as over-work—not *only* because of unavoidable life events.
2. The balance between work and pleasure feels lopsided. Life feels like constant pressure and work without *fun*.
3. Your whole life seems to revolve around success, status, and material things. You seem to have lost touch with your basic self and no longer know what really makes you happy.
4. Too much of your energy goes into keeping your life in order. You spend too much time keeping lists, organizing your life, planning, cleaning, and repairing, and not enough time being creative or letting go.
5. Your relationships with other people are suffering because so much time goes into meeting your own standards—working, being successful, etc.
6. You make other people feel inadequate or nervous around you because they worry about not being able to meet your high expectations of them.
7. You rarely stop and enjoy successes. You rarely savor a sense of accomplishment. Rather, you simply go on to the next task waiting for you.
8. You feel overwhelmed because you are trying to accomplish so much; there never seems to be enough time to complete what you have started.
9. Your standards are so high that you view many activities as obligations or ordeals to get through, instead of enjoying the process itself.
10. You procrastinate a lot. Because your standards make many tasks feel overwhelming, you avoid them.
11. You feel irritated or frustrated a lot because things and people around you do not meet your high standards.

The basic problem with Unrelenting Standards is that you lose touch with your *natural* self. You are so focused on order, achievement, or status that you do not attend to your basic physical, emotional, and social needs.

PAMELA: *Sometimes I feel like a machine, like I'm not really alive. Like I'm running on automatic.*

Things like love, family, friendship, creativity, and fun—the things that make life worth living—take a back seat to your obsessive quest for perfection.

CRAIG: *We went up to our summer house, and the kids and I changed into our bathing suits and went swimming in the lake. We were laughing and splashing and having a great time. Meanwhile Pamela was in the house cleaning, unpacking all our bags, and doing I don't know what. We kept yelling to her to come out and swim. She kept saying, "Just a minute, just a minute," and she never came out.*

Your Unrelenting Standards are costing you a great deal. You are foregoing many opportunities for happiness and fulfillment in your life.

Your reward is a measure of success. In whatever arena you have chosen to perfect yourself, you are probably one of the best. If we go to the top of any organization, the chances are good of finding someone with Unrelenting Standards. Who else would put in the time and energy necessary to reach the top? Who else would be willing to sacrifice so many other parts of their life? If you read interviews with famous people, you constantly hear about their perfectionism, their dedication, their attention to detail, how they drive themselves and other people.

However, you do not stop to *enjoy* your success. When one thing is accomplished, you simply shift focus to the next thing, rendering the thing you just accomplished meaningless. And sometimes your success *is* meaningless. This is when you are perfectionistic about trivial things. Does it really matter in the larger scheme that your kitchen drawers are perfectly organized or that your children's rooms are perfectly neat? Does it matter that your date is the best-looking person in the room, or that you are the best-dressed? Does it matter that you got a 99 instead of a 100?

Your intimate relationships almost certainly suffer. You may want the perfect partner and be unable to settle for less. The one woman Keith considers perfect for him is so beautiful, talented, and successful that dozens of other men pursue her as well; she has no interest in Keith.

Once you are in a relationship, you can be extremely critical and demanding. You expect other people (especially those closest to you, like your spouse or children) to live up to your standards. And without realizing it, you probably devalue them for not meeting the standards you set. Of course, because these standards do not seem high to you, you feel that your expectations are normal and justified.

You may be attracted to perfectionistic partners who have their own Unrelenting Standards, or you may be attracted to partners who are the opposite, relaxed and easygoing. You might choose someone who offsets your pressured life—who brings to your life all the things you have lost. This kind of relationship can become your one avenue of relief and enjoyment.

You probably have little time left to spend with the people you love. If you are single, you neglect your friends and lovers; if you are married, you neglect your family. You just do not have the time. You are too busy working, or putting the house in order, or advancing your status. You keep thinking that the time will come when you can relax and find a partner or spend time with your spouse and children. Meanwhile life slips by, and your emotional life is empty.

When you do spend time with the people you love, you are apt to do so in that same pressured, relentless way. Pamela schedules time each day to spend with her children, but she does not enjoy it, and neither do her children.

CRAIG: *Pamela is always on the kids' backs about something. I think she puts too much pressure on them. Look at our daughter, Kate. She has headaches and stomachaches. She's only in third grade, and already she's worried about how she's doing at school.*

Unrelenting Standards are passed down through generations in this way. Your parents give them to you, and you give them to your children. Even your time with your children is spent pushing. You do not stop to appreciate them. This deprives you of pleasure and contributes to their unhappiness.

It is not unusual for someone with this lifetrap to take on a large project, then become paralyzed and unable to get started. The procrastinator is often someone with Unrelenting Standards. The level at which you expect to perform is so high that it is overwhelming. The more invested you are in a project, the more likely it is that you will put it off. At some point, you may even collapse and stop functioning. You just cannot stand the thought of having to meet those expectations again.

Because of your Unrelenting Standards, you rarely feel *content*. The dogged pursuit of your standards destroys your chances for positive feelings like love, peace, happiness, pride, or relaxation. Instead you feel irritation, frustration, disappointment, and, of course, pressure. It is time for you to wake up to what your standards are costing you. Is it really worth it?

Here are the steps to changing your lifetrap:

CHANGING UNRELENTING STANDARDS

1. List the areas in which your standards may be unbalanced or unrelenting.
2. List the *advantages* of trying to meet these standards on a daily basis.
3. List the *disadvantages* of pushing so hard in these areas.
4. Try to conjure an image of what your life would be like *without* these pressures.
5. Understand the origins of your lifetrap.
6. Consider what the effects would be if you lowered your standards about 25 percent.
7. Try to *quantify* the time you devote to maintaining your standards.
8. Try to determine what reasonable standards are by getting a consensus or objective opinion from people who seem more balanced.
9. Gradually try to change your schedule or alter your behavior in order to get your *deeper* needs met.

---

1. List the Areas in Which Your Standards May Be Unbalanced or Unrelenting. Depending on whether you are Compulsive, Achievement Oriented, or Status Oriented, your list might include keeping things in order, cleanliness, work, money, creature comforts, beauty, athletic performance, popularity, status, or fame. It could be any area of your life where you feel a sense of constant pressure.

2. List the Advantages of Trying to Meet These Standards on a Daily Basis. The advantages will almost certainly have to do with your level of success. They are the benefits that accrue from *having* order, achievement, status. These benefits can be impressive. Our culture provides a great deal of reinforcement for people with Unrelenting Standards. Here is Keith's list:

ADVANTAGES OF MY UNRELENTING STANDARDS

1. I can buy what I want.
2. I feel special.
3. People are jealous of me and want what I have.
4. I can have almost any woman I want.
5. I move in desirable social circles.

On the surface, Keith seems to have a lot. However, what he has does not make him happy. He does not enjoy any of it. He is perpetually discontent. Keith is always looking toward the next purchase, the next woman, the next step up the social ladder. Nothing he has satisfies him.

Here is Pamela's list of advantages.

ADVANTAGES OF MY UNRELENTING STANDARDS

1. I make a lot of money.
2. I am almost at the top of my field.
3. I have won awards and prizes.
4. My house looks almost perfect most of the time.
5. My house runs in an orderly way.
6. My performance level as an anesthesiologist is high.

Once again, the advantages are powerful. Pamela has achieved a great deal and deserves to be proud. But still, the fact remains that she is not happy. Instead, she feels a constant pressure to keep performing.

This is probably true of you as well. You may seem to benefit a great deal from your high standards, but in truth you are unhappy. What good is having a spotless and perfect house when you are running yourself ragged to keep it that way and resenting everyone who gets in your way? What good is a top-level job when it leaves no time in your life for pleasure and love? What good are your creature comforts when you are too exhausted to enjoy them?

3. List the Disadvantages of Pushing So Hard in These Areas. The disadvantages are all the negative consequences, all the things you sacrifice along the way. They may include your health, happiness, desire to relax, and mood. As you make your list, consider the quality of your emotional life—how your Unrelenting Standards affect your relationships with family, loved ones, and friends.

This is Pamela's list of disadvantages:

DISADVANTAGES OF MY UNRELENTING STANDARDS

1. I am physically exhausted.
2. I don't have any fun.
3. My marriage is suffering.
4. I put too much pressure on my children. I don't enjoy being with my children. They seem afraid of me.
5. I've let a lot of close friendships go.
6. I don't have any time for myself.

Keith's list of disadvantages had two items.

DISADVANTAGES OF MY UNRELENTING STANDARDS

1. My health is suffering.
2. I'm not happy.

Now you have to weigh the advantages and disadvantages, and decide what makes the most sense. Do the advantages make it all worthwhile? Or do the disadvantages clearly outweigh the advantages?

4. Try to Conjure an Image of What Your Life Would Be without These Pressures. Sometime when you are under pressure, when you feel that familiar drive, stop and imagine what it could mean to your life to let some of that pressure go. Sit back and close your eyes, and let an image come. What else might you be doing that is really more important in life? When Keith did this exercise, he realized that being seen with the perfect woman (Sheila) was not as gratifying as the fun he could have been having with Beth:

KEITH: *I was at a dinner party with Sheila the other night, and I kept thinking of Beth. I knew it made more sense to be there with Sheila, she's better looking than Beth, she's richer. It's better to be seen with Sheila. But I kept wishing I was there with Beth anyway. It would have been more fun.*

This exercise can help you understand that the disadvantages of your life are directly linked to your Unrelenting Standards. If you lowered your standards, you could eliminate many of these disadvantages.

5. Understand the Origins of Your Lifetrap. How did your Unrelenting Standards originate? Did you have a parent who gave you conditional love? Were your parents models of Unrelenting Standards? As we have noted, this lifetrap might well be tied to others in your childhood. Your Unrelenting Standards might be part of another lifetrap which is closer to the core, such as Defectiveness, Social Exclusion, or Emotional Deprivation.

6. Consider What the Effects Would Be If You Lowered Your Standards about 25 Percent. First, we have to attack the all-or-nothing thinking that goes along with Unrelenting Standards. You believe that something is either perfect or a failure. You cannot imagine just doing something well. On a scale from 0 to 100, if your performance is not 100, or maybe 98 or 99, then it might as well be 0, the way it feels to you. You have to learn that it is possible to do something 80 percent or 70 percent and still do a very good job. You can still take pride in your work. Between perfection and failure there is a whole gray area.

PAMELA: *I was making lasagna for a dinner party the other night. Craig's parents were coming over. Well, I used a store-bought sauce. It was really hard for me to do that. I kept feeling guilty all night, like whenever someone complimented me on the lasagna, I felt guilty, like I didn't really deserve it.*

I really worked with myself about it. I kept telling myself that the dinner party was beautiful, that it didn't matter in the whole picture that I had used a store-bought sauce.

If you could settle for this lower level instead of insisting on perfection, you would still get a lot of the same rewards in terms of career advancement, financial success, praise, or status without having to pay such a heavy price. You would have to make *some* sacrifice in terms of these rewards, but the sacrifice would be greatly outweighed by the advantages of less stress, a healthier body, more time to relax, a happier mood, and better relationships.

7. Try to Quantify the Time You Devote to Maintaining Your Standards. One technique you can use is time management. Make a time chart, in which you allot time for each project that you have to do during the day. You are not allowed to spend any more time than is allotted for the project and must tolerate whatever level of success you have achieved when the time period is over.

Pamela used this technique to write a journal article. She allotted six hours to write the paper.

PAMELA: *And at the end of the six hours, that was it. The paper had to stay as it was, with no more perfecting of it. It was hard for me. There was so much I still wanted to do. But what stopped me was remembering my children. It was more important that I spend time with them.*

When you are deciding how much time to allocate for each project, be sure to consider how *important* the goal is to your overall happiness; then, allocate the most time to the areas of your life that are most important. People with Unrelenting Standards often lose their sense of perspective; all tasks become equally important. You may devote as much time to making a plane reservation as you do to writing an important report. You may apportion your time based on how long it takes you to finish a task perfectly, regardless of how much impact the task has on your quality of life.

Pamela had estimated it would take twenty hours to do her paper perfectly. But her family is more important to her than her paper, so she decided to allot more time to her family and less to the paper.

Through this process, we hope you will learn that perfection is not worth *any* price. You can stop *before* the point of perfection, and your life can go on much as before, only better. Allot a reasonable amount of time to complete each task; then accept whatever level of achievement you have attained at the end of that time period. Otherwise, the time you take to do things constantly expands, and your life spins rapidly out of control.

8. Try to Determine What Reasonable Standards Are by Getting a Consensus or Objective Opinion from People Who Seem More Balanced. This is one function we serve for our patients with Unrelenting Standards. We can offer a more objective opinion about reasonable standards, or help the patient think through how to get more objective opinions. It is important that you do this as well, because unbalanced standards do not *feel* unbalanced to you. You cannot trust yourself in this matter. Ask other people what they feel is reasonable. If there are people in your life who seem to lead balanced lives, who seem to have high standards but still manage to enjoy life, ask them how much time they spend working, relaxing, with family, with friends, exercising, vacationing, and sleeping. Try to map out the structure of a more balanced life.

9. Gradually Try to Change Your Schedule or Alter Your Behavior in Order to Get Your Deeper Needs Met. Gradually change your life until it matches this more balanced structure. This is what Pamela and Keith both tried to do. Pamela made excellent use of time management techniques. She restricted the time she spent working at the hospital and turned over responsibility for some of her research projects to an assistant professor in her department. She learned how to *delegate.* She began spending more time with her husband and children. She started hiking and spending more time outdoors—although, as you might imagine, she had to resist becoming perfectionistic about this.

PAMELA: *Once I started to let go a little in my career, I immediately saw that my life was better. I just became a much happier person. Everyone is happier. And that's what keeps me going. That's what helps me keep letting go.*

Pamela carries this flashcard around to remind her: "I can lower my standards without having to feel like a failure. I can do things moderately well, feel good about them, and not have to keep trying to perfect them."

For Keith, changing meant something different. It meant shifting his perspective entirely about what was really important to him. Meeting Beth was one of the primary catalysts. Keith surprised himself and actually fell in love with Beth.

KEITH: *Spending time with Beth feels like the lifting of a weight. I just find myself wanting to spend a quiet evening with Beth, just cooking dinner or going to a movie. That whole social scene, I just don't care as much about it anymore.*

Both Pamela and Keith illustrate the trade-off. Let go of your need for perfect order, achievement, or status in exchange for a higher quality of life and more fulfilling emotional relationships with the people you love.

16

"I Can Have Whatever I Want"
The Entitlement Lifetrap

Before we had even met Mel, we found ourselves growing irritated with him. In our first phone contact, he asked if we had an opening on Thursday evenings. We told him that we only worked Monday and Wednesday evenings. "So there's no chance I can come in on a Thursday?" he asked. We told him again that we did not work on Thursday evenings. We made an appointment for the following Monday. Twice more before we met that Monday, he called. "Isn't there any way I could come in on a Thursday?" he wanted to know. "It would really be much better for me."

Mel was twenty minutes late for our first appointment. When he walked into our office, the first thing he did was comment on how inconvenient it was for him to come on a Monday. "I have to come all the way across town," he said. He sat down on the couch and noted that it was uncomfortable. "Can I move it a bit?" he asked.

We asked him why he had come to therapy.

MEL: *It's my wife Katie. She's threatening to leave me unless I go into therapy. I don't want her to go.*
THERAPIST: *Why is she threatening to leave?*
MEL: *She found out I was having an affair again.*

314

THERAPIST: *So it's happened before?*
MEL: *Yeah. It's the second time she's found out.*
THERAPIST: *Is it your second affair?*
MEL: *Nah (laughs). It's a little quirk of mine. I just can't be satisfied with one woman.*

As time went on, we found that there were other reasons Katie was threatening to leave Mel. Katie talked about it in one of our marital sessions.

KATIE: *I just can't take it anymore. He just always has to have everything his way, and I'm sick of it. He's like a spoiled child. Everything has to be his way.*

Mel seemed baffled by Katie's behavior. "She makes such a big deal about everything!" he complained.

NINA: THIRTY YEARS OLD. SHE CANNOT HOLD DOWN A JOB.

Nina also was late for our first appointment. "I'm sorry," she said, "lateness is a problem for me."

THERAPIST: *Well, why don't we start with you telling me why you've come to therapy.*
NINA: *Well, my husband Raymond wants me to get a job. We're having money problems.*
THERAPIST: *Do you want to get a job?*
NINA: *No. Really, I think it's very unfair after all these years for him to start making me work. It really bothers me.*
THERAPIST: *But it sounds like you're looking for a job nevertheless.*
NINA: *Yeah. I've been looking. I mean, I have no choice. We're really having money problems. The problem is I'm having trouble finding a job. And to tell the truth, when I did work, I really had trouble holding on to a job.*
THERAPIST: *What was the problem?*
NINA: *I guess it's that I find working boring. I really can't be bothered to do everything they want.*

Nina strikes us as childish. It seems her true purpose in coming is to get us to ally with her against her husband and convince him she should not have to work.

THERAPIST: *Do you think your husband might be willing to come to therapy with you?*

NINA: *Yeah. That would be great. I wish you would talk to him and get him to see reason. I'm really not cut out for work.*

THERAPIST: *Well, if you want him to know that, you'll have to tell him yourself.*

When it becomes apparent we will not intervene in the way that she wants, Nina becomes petulant. "Why are you doing this to me?" she asks.

THE ENTITLEMENT QUESTIONNAIRE

Use this questionnaire to measure the strength of your Entitlement lifetrap. Answer the items based on the following scale:

SCORING KEY

1 Completely untrue of me
2 Mostly untrue of me
3 Slightly more true than untrue of me
4 Moderately true of me
5 Mostly true of me
6 Describes me perfectly

If you have any 5's or 6's on this questionnaire, this lifetrap may still apply to you, even if your score is in the low range.

SCORE	DESCRIPTION
	1. I have trouble accepting "no" for an answer.
	2. I get angry when I cannot get what I want.
	3. I am special and should not have to accept normal constraints.
	4. I put my needs first.
	5. I have a lot of difficulty getting myself to stop drinking, smoking, overeating, or other problem behaviors.
	6. I cannot discipline myself to complete boring or routine tasks.

	7. I act on impulses and emotions that get me into trouble later.
	8. If I cannot reach a goal, I become easily frustrated and give up.
	9. I insist that people do things my way.
	10. I have trouble giving up immediate gratification to reach a long-range goal.
	YOUR TOTAL ENTITLEMENT SCORE (Add your scores together for questions 1–10)

INTERPRETING YOUR ENTITLEMENT SCORE

10–19 Very low. This lifetrap probably does *not* apply to you.
20–29 Fairly low. This lifetrap may only apply *occasionally.*
30–39 Moderate. This lifetrap is an *issue* in your life.
40–49 High. This is definitely an *important* lifetrap for you.
50–60 Very high. This is definitely one of your *core* lifetraps.

THE EXPERIENCE OF ENTITLEMENT

There are three types of Entitlement, each with its own characteristic experience. The types overlap—you can be more than one.

THREE TYPES OF ENTITLEMENT

1. Spoiled Entitlement
2. Dependent Entitlement
3. Impulsivity

• SPOILED ENTITLEMENT •

You see yourself as special. You are demanding and controlling, and want everything your way. When other people balk, you get angry.

KATIE: *We've been fighting because I want to take this course, and he doesn't want me to.*

MEL: *She won't be there when I get home from work.*
KATIE: *I'll be home within a half-hour of when you get home.*
MEL: *But you won't be able to make my dinner.*
KATIE: *Mel, it's only one night a week. We can order our dinner or go out.*
MEL: *You don't understand. I work hard. It's a matter of my comforts. (Yells) And my comforts are important to me!*

You have little empathy or concern for the feelings of others. This leads you to be inconsiderate and perhaps even abusive.

You are indifferent to normal social expectations and conventions. You consider yourself above the law. You believe that although *other* people should be punished when they violate social norms, you should *not* be punished. You do not expect to have to pay the normal consequences for your actions.

MEL: *Sorry I'm late. I was waiting for this bastard to pull out of the tow-away zone so I could park there.*
THERAPIST: *You parked in a tow-away zone?*
MEL: *Yeah. But it's okay. I borrowed my brother-in-law's car. He has "MD" license plates. Even if I got a ticket, I could talk my way out of it.*

You take what you want without guilt because you feel entitled. You expect that you will somehow manage to escape the negative consequences other people would incur for acting similarly. You will get away with it or manipulate the situation so you do not have to pay the consequences.

• DEPENDENT ENTITLEMENT •

If you are the dependent type, you feel entitled to depend on other people. You place yourself in the weak, incompetent, needy role, and expect other people to be strong and take care of you.

You feel entitled much in the same way as a child feels toward a parent. It is your *right*. People *owe* it to you.

NINA: *Raymond is really mad at me 'cause he found out I was stealing from the food money to buy clothes.*
THERAPIST: *Why were you doing that?*
NINA: *Well, he cut my clothing allowance. It really bothers me. What am I supposed to do? Just keep wearing the same old crappy clothes?*
THERAPIST: *I know. He cut your clothes allowance because you two are having such money problems.*
NINA: *Well, he's supposed to be taking care of things better! It's not supposed to come to this!*

Like Nina, you may expect to be supported financially. You let other people assume responsibility for your everyday affairs and for much of your decision-making.

You are more likely to be passively than actively aggressive. When someone fails to take care of you, you feel like a victim. You are angry, but you probably restrain yourself. You express your resentment in other ways—through pouting, passive-aggressive behaviors, hypochondriacal complaints, whining, and occasionally a childlike temper tantrum.

You do not necessarily feel that you are special. In fact, you may try very hard to please and be accommodating. Yet you feel entitled to be dependent. Your entitlement comes from the fact that you feel weak and vulnerable. You need help, and people *must* give it to you.

• IMPULSIVITY •

This is a lifelong pattern of difficulty controlling your behavior and feelings. You have problems with impulse control. You act on your desires and feelings without regard for the consequences.

You have trouble tolerating frustration enough to complete long-term tasks, especially boring or routine ones. You have a general lack of organization and structure. You are undisciplined.

NINA: *Well, I didn't get the travel agency job.*
THERAPIST: *Oh. So you finally went down there. What happened?*
NINA: *Actually I couldn't get through the application. They wanted me to fill out all these long forms I didn't understand, and to do all this paperwork. I couldn't find anyone who would really help me go through it step by step. I thought that if this was what the application process was like, I definitely wouldn't like the job. It's just not the kind of place I want to work in.*

Like Nina, you may have a tendency to procrastinate. When you finally do the task, you do it half-heartedly or passive-aggressively. You just cannot get yourself to focus and persevere. Even when you *want* to stick to something it is hard for you. You have a problem with short-term versus long-term gratification.

Your difficulty postponing short-term gratification may also take the form of addictions such as overeating, smoking, drinking, drugs, or compulsive sex. However, problems with addictions do not necessarily indicate that you have this lifetrap. Addictions are only one of several indicators. For you to have the Entitlement lifetrap, the addictions must be part of a more general pattern of problems with self-control and self-discipline.

You may have trouble controlling your emotions, particularly anger. Although you may have some depression, anger is your predominant emotion. You are not able to express your anger in a mature way. Rather, you are like an enraged child. You get impatient, irritable, angry.

KATIE: *The way he yells, it's so embarrassing. He doesn't care where we are or who's listening. All of a sudden he'll start screaming. We can be in public, at a friend's house, anyplace.*
MEL: *That's right. When I'm angry, I want people to know it.*
KATIE: *And I'll tell you, it works. I give him whatever he wants just to shut him up. Everybody does.*

You are self-indulgent about expressing your anger. You feel you should be free to vent any emotion. You do not consider the impact on other people.

Your problems with anger and impulse control put you at risk. At the extreme, your problem controlling your impulses could lead to criminal behavior. More typically, they occur as explosiveness, temper tantrums, or inappropriate behavior.

NINA: *I got this great new dress for the party Friday.*
THERAPIST: *How did you swing that? I thought Raymond wasn't giving you any more money for clothes.*
NINA: *Well, if you swear not to tell him, actually I stole it. It was really easy. I just sneaked it into the dressing room and slipped it into my bag.*
THERAPIST: *How are you going to explain it to Raymond?*
NINA: *Oh, he won't notice. It's really his fault anyway, because he won't give me the money.*

Raymond *did* find out about the dress. He was so angry that he told Nina he wanted a trial separation. This was the last thing Nina wanted. She had acted impulsively, without considering the consequences. Between the *impulse* and the *action,* she had to learn to place *thought.*

Unlike many of the other lifetraps—which cause you to suppress your needs—the Entitlement lifetrap involves the *excessive* expression of your needs. You lack a normal degree of restraint. Whereas other people inhibit and discipline themselves appropriately, you do not.

Most patients with Entitlement do not feel any real distress about their pattern. This sets Entitlement apart from all the other lifetraps in this book. We have never had a patient come to us saying that he or she was in pain as a result of feeling entitled or special.

However, many of our patients have *partners* with serious Entitlement issues. This is how an entitled person shows up most often in therapy—as the partner of one of our patients. (We often ask the partners of our patients to come to some sessions as well.) To put it bluntly, rather than seeking therapy yourself, more often you are the person who drives others to seek therapy.

Your life becomes painful only when you are no longer able to avoid the serious negative consequences that result from your Entitlement—for example, when you actually lose your job because you cannot complete the work properly, or when your spouse threatens to leave you. Only then will you acknowledge that other people are not happy with your behavior and that your entitlement is a problem. You finally realize that the lifetrap has a cost—that it can really damage your life.

ORIGINS OF ENTITLEMENT

Entitlement can develop in three quite different ways. The first involves weak parental limits:

ORIGIN 1: WEAK LIMITS

Weak limits is the most obvious origin for Entitlement. These parents fail to exercise sufficient discipline and control over their children. Such parents spoil or indulge their children in a variety of ways.

(A) Spoiled Entitlement:
　　Children are given whatever they want, whenever they want it. This may include material desires or having their own way. The *child* controls the *parents*.

(B) Impulsivity:
　　Children are not taught *frustration tolerance.* They are not forced to take responsibility and complete assigned tasks. This may include chores around the house or schoolwork. The parent allows the child to get away with irresponsibility by not following through with aversive consequences.

　　They are also not taught *impulse control.* The parents allow children to act out impulses, such as anger, without imposing sufficient negative consequences. One or both parents may themselves have difficulty controlling emotions and impulses.

When we discuss *limits,* we mean reasonable rules and consequences. Both Mel and Nina had weak parental limits as children. In a sense, they were brought up by their parents to be entitled. Both were raised in permissive, laissez-faire environments where they were spoiled and indulged. They never learned appropriate limits.

Parents serve as models for self-control and self-discipline. Parents who are out of control produce children who are out of control.

MEL: *Yeah, I guess my father used to storm around the house in the same way. He was always losing his temper and yelling at us. I'm a lot like him.*

KATIE: *And what about your mother? His mother is a total pushover who just takes whatever his father dishes out.*

MEL: *Yeah. I guess neither one was a paragon of good behavior.*

It was acceptable in Mel's household for his father to behave like a child. When adults cannot control themselves, they are unlikely to control their children. It is through parental self-control that we learn to control ourselves. We do to ourselves what was done to us. When we have parents who provide clear, consistent, and appropriate limits, then we learn to apply these limits to ourselves.

Patients brought up with weak limits usually do not learn the notion of *reciprocity* as a child. Your parents did not teach you that, in order to get something, you have to give something back. Rather, the message they gave you was that they would take care of you, and you did not have to do anything in return.

Mel and Nina had an interesting commonality: Mel was the only boy and Nina the only girl in their families.

NINA: *I was the baby and I was the only girl. My mother really wanted a girl. She went through three boys to get me. I got everything I wanted as a child. I was just like a little princess. And everyone took care of me, my parents and my brothers.*

It is possible that certain children—only children, the youngest child in the family, the only child of that sex—are more apt to develop the lifetrap. This is because they may be more likely to be indulged.

ORIGIN 2: DEPENDENT OVERINDULGENCE

The origin of Dependent Entitlement is parents who overindulge their children in ways that make the children dependent on them. The parents take on everyday responsibilities, decisions, and difficult tasks for the child. The environment is so safe and protected and so little is expected of the child that the child comes to *demand* this level of care.

The difference between the Dependence lifetrap and "Dependent Entitlement" is one of degree. The more dependent you are allowed to be—the more you are overprotected and given everything—the more you will tend toward Dependent Entitlement. If you belong to this type, you should read the chapter on Dependence as well.

ORIGIN 3: ENTITLEMENT AS COUNTERATTACK FOR OTHER LIFETRAPS

For the majority of our patients, Entitlement is a form of Counterattack, or overcompensation, for other core lifetraps—usually Defectiveness, Emotional Deprivation, or Social Exclusion. For the origin of these Entitlement cases, see the chapter relevant to the underlying core lifetrap.

If you developed Entitlement as a means for coping with early Emotional Deprivation, then you were probably cheated or deprived as a child in some significant way. Perhaps your parents were cold and non-nurturing, so you were emotionally deprived. You Counterattacked by becoming entitled. Or perhaps you were materially deprived. The families around you had money, but you were relatively poor. You wanted things that you could not get. Now, as an adult, you make *sure* that you get everything.

Your Entitlement may have been an adaptive, healthy means of coping when you were young. Entitlement may have offered you a way out of the loneliness, the lack of loving, caring, and attention that you experienced as a child. Or it offered you a way out of the material deprivation. The problem is that you went too far. As an adult, you were so afraid of being deprived or cheated again that you became demanding, narcissistic, and controlling. You began to alienate the people closest to you. In trying to make sure that your needs got met, you began to push away the very people who could most meet them.

It is an interesting question why some children who are deprived develop Entitlement as a coping style. How do they come upon this strategy? We believe a number of factors come into play. First, there is the child's temperament. Some children are more aggressive. Their disposition pushes them to respond in an active way, rather than Surrender to feelings of deprivation.

Another factor is whether the family allows the child to Counterattack. An emotionally depriving parent might allow a child to be demanding in other ways. A third factor is whether the child is gifted in some way— whether the child is particularly bright, beautiful, or talented. A child can compensate by getting attention for such a gift. In that one area, at least, the child gets *some* needs met.

Anger is another factor that can drive a person to develop Entitlement as a coping mechanism for deprivation. Extreme anger can be a strong motivating force for people to overcome the conditions of their childhood. It gives them the will to set right something they see as unfair.

Although Entitlement is most often a reaction against feelings of emotional deprivation, it can also be a response to other lifetraps. Certainly someone who feels defective or socially undesirable may compensate by feeling special. If your underlying feeling is, "I'm inferior," you can counterattack by saying, "No, I'm special, I'm better than everyone else."

Problems with frustration tolerance and impulse control may also be forms of Counterattack for feeling subjugated (although this is not usually the origin of impulsivity). In these cases, the child was inordinately disciplined and controlled and later acts out by rebelling against discipline and emotional control.

DANGER SIGNALS IN PARTNERS

These are signs that your choice of partner is lifetrap-driven. That is, you have chosen someone who reinforces your sense of entitlement.

SPOILED ENTITLEMENT

You are attracted to partners who:

1. Sacrifice their own needs for yours.
2. Allow you to control them.
3. Are afraid to express their own needs and feelings.
4. Are willing to tolerate abuse, criticism, etc.
5. Allow you to take advantage of them.
6. Do not have a strong sense of self, and allow themselves to live through you.
7. Are dependent on you, and accept domination as the price of being dependent.

DEPENDENT ENTITLEMENT

You are drawn to strong partners who are competent and willing to take care of you (see the chapter on Dependence).

IMPULSIVITY

You may be drawn to partners who are organized, disciplined, compulsive, etc., and who thus offset your own tendency toward chaos and disorganization.

In sum, you are drawn to partners who support, rather than challenge, your sense of Entitlement. Both Mel and Nina had been in many relationships that bore this out. Before getting married, Mel had been involved with other warm, giving women whom he had bullied and treated badly, and Nina had been involved with other strong men.

Probably, if you look at your life, this will be true of you too. *Most* of your relationships will follow the pattern. They allow you to reenact the Entitlement of your childhood.

Of course, we also say that people who accept a relationship with you are acting out lifetraps of their own. It takes two to do the dance.

The tables that follow list the most common life patterns into which people with each type of Entitlement fall:

SPOILED ENTITLEMENT LIFETRAPS

1. You do not care about the needs of the people around you. You get your needs met at their expense. You hurt them.
2. You may abuse, humiliate, or demean the people around you.
3. You have difficulty empathizing with the feelings of those around you. They feel you do not understand or care about their feelings.
4. You may *take* more from society than you *give*. This results in an *inequity* and is unfair to other people.
5. At work, you may be fired, demoted, etc., for failing to consider the needs and feelings of others, or for failing to follow rules.
6. Your partner, family, friends, or children may leave you, resent you, or cut off contact with you because you treat them abusively, unfairly, or selfishly.
7. You may get into legal or criminal trouble if you cheat or break laws, such as tax evasion or business fraud.
8. You never have a chance to experience the joy of *giving* to other people unselfishly—or of having a truly equal, reciprocal relationship.
9. If your Entitlement is a form of Counterattack, you never allow yourself to face and solve your underlying lifetraps. Your *real* needs are never addressed. You may continue to feel emotionally deprived, defective, or socially undesirable.

DEPENDENT ENTITLEMENT LIFETRAPS

1. You never learn to take care of yourself, because you insist that others take care of you.
2. You unfairly impinge on the rights of people close to you to use their own time for themselves. Your demands become a drain on the people around you.

3. People you depend on may eventually become fed up or angry with your dependence and demands, and will leave you, fire you, or refuse to continue helping you.
4. The people you depend on may die or leave, and you will be unable to take care of yourself.

IMPULSIVITY LIFETRAPS

1. You never complete tasks necessary to make progress in your career. You are a chronic underachiever, and eventually feel inadequate as a result of your failures.
2. The people around you may eventually get fed up with your irresponsibility and cut off their relationships with you.
3. Your life is in chaos. You cannot discipline yourself sufficiently well to have direction and organization. You are therefore *stuck*.
4. You may have difficulty with addictions, such as drugs, alcohol, or overeating.
5. In almost every area of your life, your lack of discipline prevents you from achieving your goals.
6. You may not have enough money to get what you want in life.
7. You may have gotten into trouble with authorities at school, with police, or at work because you cannot control your impulses.
8. You may have alienated your friends, spouse, children, or bosses, through your anger and explosiveness.

It is important for you to consider these lifetraps carefully because your motivation to change may be low.

The issue of motivation to change is a big one with the Entitlement lifetrap. Unlike the other lifetraps, your entitlement does not *feel* painful. Rather, it seems to feel *good*. It is the people around you who are in pain.

THERAPIST: *Mel, you're going to have to let Katie pursue a career. What you're doing isn't fair.*
MEL: *Why should I? Why should I do the things you say I should? I like things the way they are. I like Katie centered on* me.

It is easy to see Mel's point of view. Indeed, why *should* he change? On the surface, his lifetrap only seems to benefit him. Similarly, why *should* Nina bother learning to do things for herself when she can get other people to do them for her?

When we work with Entitled patients, we are always looking for the *leverage*. Why should they change? How is the lifetrap hurting them in their personal and work lives?

Consider carefully what the lifetrap is costing you.

CHANGING ENTITLEMENT

As we were writing this chapter, we kept commenting upon a certain sense of futility. We recognize that few people with the Entitlement lifetrap will ever read this chapter. People with this lifetrap rarely want to change. They usually do not read self-help books. They resist going to therapy. Instead, they blame others for their problems and fight to stay the same.

If you are an exception—a person with an Entitlement lifetrap who is reading this chapter—it is probably because your lifetrap is proving so costly to you that you cannot ignore the issue anymore. Your spouse has asked for a divorce, your lover is about to abandon you, or you are about to lose your job. Something has happened to throw you into crisis.

We realize that many of the patterns associated with Entitlement that we discussed earlier in this chapter do not really matter to you. You probably do not care, for example, that your Entitlement is unfair to other people. You do not care that you are bringing other people pain. You are self-centered. You care only about yourself. This is a great drawback in terms of building motivation.

We have divided this change section into two parts. The first part is directed toward those of you who have the lifetrap and want to change.

However, we believe that the majority of people reading this chapter are victims of entitled people. That is, you are not entitled yourself. You are reading this to try to *understand* an entitled person—your lover, spouse, or parent.

We have included a section for you too.

HELPING YOURSELF OVERCOME ENTITLEMENT PROBLEMS

These are the steps to changing your lifetrap.

HELPING YOURSELF OVERCOME ENTITLEMENT PROBLEMS

1. List the advantages and disadvantages of *not* accepting limits. This is crucial to motivate yourself to change.
2. Confront the excuses you use to avoid accepting limits.
3. List the various ways that your Limits problem manifests itself in everyday life. Fill out the Limits Chart.
4. Make flashcards to help you fight your Entitlement and self-discipline problems in each situation.
5. Ask for feedback as you try to change.
6. Try to empathize with the people around you.
7. If your lifetrap is a form of Counterattack, try to understand the core lifetraps underlying it. Follow the relevant change techniques.
8. If you have self-discipline problems, make a hierarchy of tasks, graded in terms of boredom or frustration level. Gradually work your way up the hierarchy.
9. If you have difficulty controlling your emotions, develop a "time-out" technique.
10. If you have Dependent Entitlement, make a hierarchy of tasks, graded in terms of difficulty. Gradually start doing the things you allow other people to do for you. Start proving to yourself that you are competent.

1. List the Advantages and Disadvantages of Not Accepting Limits. This Is Crucial to Motivate Yourself to Change. In terms of the disadvantages, be sure to list: the harm you are causing others; the possibility that friends and family will withdraw from you; the possibility of being fired or not being promoted; the possibility of legal action against you; etc. If you have impulsivity problems, be sure to consider the likelihood that you will never reach your life goals if you fail to tolerate frustration better. *Be sure to include any negative consequences you have already experienced.*

Here is the list Mel composed:

Advantages and Disadvantages of My Entitlement

Advantages

1. I get things my own way and I like that.
2. I take what I want—money, women, my comforts.
3. By getting angry, I can usually get people to do what I want.
4. I can control most people and I like that.
5. I feel special.
6. I *am* special and shouldn't have to follow the rules.

Disadvantages

1. Katie is threatening to leave me.
2. People get angry at me a lot or avoid me.
3. People are afraid of me at work; they don't like me.
4. I don't have many close friends. A lot of people get mad at me after a while and stop associating with me.

You might note that, predictably, Mel did not include any items in the "Disadvantages" list about the pain he causes others or the injustice of his Entitlement. This would be the fruit of future work in therapy.

Get images of these bad events occurring, to make the consequences feel more real. Imagine your loved one abandoning you, your job lost. For example, one of Nina's items on her "Disadvantages" list was, "Raymond might leave me and I won't know how to take care of myself."

THERAPIST: *Close your eyes and get an image of what that would be like.*
NINA: *(Pause.) I see myself on the phone, calling my mother, calling my friends, trying to get them to do things for me. It's humiliating. I feel like I'm begging. It makes me angry, angry at Raymond. But no matter how angry I am, I can't get him back.*

Try to comprehend the cost of your Entitlement *before* the negative consequences occur. Between the impulse and the action, insert *thought*.

2. Confront the Excuses You Use to Avoid Accepting Limits. Make a list of
your excuses. For each excuse, write down why it is only a rationalization,
and not really valid. Start to counter the thoughts that maintain your
Entitlement.

Here are some excuses Mel collected in the course of our therapy:

EXCUSES FOR ENTITLEMENT

People should accept me for who I am.
I'm not hurting anyone.
Everyone's making a big deal out of nothing.
I'm special and deserve it.
I'll never get caught.
I look after myself, and other people can take care of themselves.
It's healthy to get all my anger out.
If I'm clever enough at manipulating, I'll be able to get my own way.

Nina's excuses focused more on her lack of self-discipline:

EXCUSES FOR IMPULSIVITY

If it's boring, why do it?
I can always catch up later.
I'll work on it tomorrow.
I can get by with my natural talent.
Someone could do this for me better.
Raymond will never really leave me.
Life is more fun when I do what I want.
I can't help it, it's just the way I am.

Your excuses help you deny the reality of the situation. If you continue the
way you are, you are going to pay some penalty for your Entitlement and
Impulsivity. The fact that you are reading this shows that *something* has
gone wrong already. Do not let your excuses cloud the negative consequences of your lifetrap.

3. List the Various Ways That Your Limits Problem Manifests Itself in Everyday Life. Fill Out the Limits Chart. We want you to develop a *very specific* list of the ways your lifetrap is manifested in your life. Ask friends and family members to help. They will be *more* than happy for an opportunity to point them out to you.

Consider various areas of life: At home—with your spouse—with your children—at work—in the car—at restaurants or hotels—with friends. For each area, fill out a Limits chart. This will give you an opportunity to compare your expectations to the norm.

The basic principle behind the norm is reciprocity, or reciprocal interchange. This is best expressed in the Golden Rule: "Do unto others as you would have them do unto you."

Here is a sample Limits chart, filled out by Mel for the situation, "Selecting a movie with Katie."

LIFE AREA	MY ENTITLEMENT	NORMAL EXPECTATIONS	NEGATIVE CON-SEQUENCES OF MY WAY
Selecting a movie with Katie.	Bully Katie into seeing my choice.	Reciprocity—Find a compromise movie we both like.	Katie won't go with me as often; she'll be mad at me all night.

We expect this step to take a long time. This is because we want you to fill out the chart for every area in your life where your Entitlement is an issue. The areas can be subtle; they may not be immediately apparent. For example, when Mel went to a restaurant, the room had to be the right temperature, the table had to be in the right spot, etc. His Entitlement had seeped into every aspect of his life.

If you are in therapy, your therapist can help you make this assessment. As we have stated, family and friends can help. It is important to ask others, because you will be unaware yourself of the many ways you act entitled.

4. Make Flashcards to Help You Fight Your Entitlement and Impulsivity Problems in Each Situation. Now we want you to struggle against your lifetrap. Whenever you come across a situation you have listed on your Limits chart, behave according to the norm rather than in an entitled, impulsive, or undisciplined way.

Flashcards can help. Make a flashcard for each situation. Use it before the situation to prepare yourself, and during the situation (if possible) to remind yourself.

As you write the flashcard, remember the following points:

WRITING AN ENTITLEMENT FLASHCARD

1. Tune into the needs of the people around you. Try to understand how they are feeling. *Empathize.*
2. Aim toward reciprocity, fairness, and equity as principles to guide your actions with others.
3. Ask yourself if your immediate need is important enough to risk the negative consequences (e.g., alienating friends, losing your job).
4. Learn to tolerate frustration as a means to achieving your long-range goals. As the saying goes, "No pain, no gain."

Here is an example of a flashcard Mel wrote, for the situation "Feeling attracted to another woman."

AN ENTITLEMENT FLASHCARD

I know that right now I am attracted to this woman, and I'm starting to plan how to go to bed with her. But doing this will make Katie very angry and very hurt. I don't want Katie sleeping around, so I shouldn't either. Having sex with this woman is not as important as my marriage to Katie. If I keep sleeping around, I'll lose her for sure. I love Katie and want to be with her for the rest of my life.

Mel had come to the verge of losing Katie. The possibility was very real and using the flashcard helped keep it real. Mel's love for Katie was the leverage that moved him to change.

Keep a checklist for each situation of how often you behave according to the norm versus how often you behave according to the lifetrap. The checklist can serve as an objective record of your progress.

5. Ask for Feedback as You Try to Change. It is important for you to get the people you trust involved in your efforts to change. Ask friends, colleagues, and loved ones how you are doing. Have they observed any change? What areas do they still feel need improvement?

Entitlement is so much a part of your existence that it is hard for you to see it. Other people can see it more easily. Getting feedback will help sharpen your vision of yourself.

It will also help you gradually understand normal expectations for behavior. What do people typically do for other people? What does it mean to be fair, to have equality in relationships? What are the conventions that people normally follow? Keep exploring these issues. Make explicit to yourself what most people understand already—the implicit rules of society.

6. Try to Empathize with the People Around You. Your lack of empathy is important in reinforcing your Entitlement lifetrap.

KATIE: *It's like Mel has no understanding of how it hurts me. He thinks he can have affairs and it's no big deal. No matter how much I cry, it doesn't seem to make a difference.*
THERAPIST: *Your pain does not stop him.*
MEL: *I just don't understand why it's such a big deal. Why do you make such a big deal about it?*

Mel had a real ignorance of other people's feelings. This is true of most people with Spoiled Entitlement. Being self-centered is such a lifelong pattern that they are largely unaware of how they are affecting others. A whole aspect of human relatedness is missing for them.

Other people's reactions are important cues in social situations. They help us decide how to act. Mel interacted without these cues. He was operating in a vacuum. He could not recognize when he was stepping beyond reasonable bounds. He just assumed that if it felt good to him, it was all right.

In couples therapy we do mirroring exercises to help people learn to empathize. Mirroring is a form of active listening. It has two parts. First, you reflect back what you heard the other person say. Next, you say how the person seems to feel.

KATIE: *I'm starting to get really mad about the way he orders me around the house. If we're watching television and he wants something to eat, he tells me to go and get it. And, if I tell him to wait until the commercial, he gets snippy.*

THERAPIST *(to Mel): Can you mirror that and then respond?*
MEL: *You're saying that I order you around the house too much, that I make you get me something to eat when we're watching television. And how do you feel? You're mad.*

Start paying attention to other people. Practice listening to their complaints and problems. Try to understand how *they* feel when you do not take their needs into account. Work on empathizing without getting defensive.

7. If Your Lifetrap Is a Form of Counterattack, Try to Understand the Core Lifetraps Underlying It. Follow the Relevant Change Techniques. If your Entitlement is a way of coping with another lifetrap—like Emotional Deprivation, Defectiveness, or Social Exclusion—follow the change techniques we recommend in the relevant chapters of this book. Unless you deal with the underlying lifetrap, it is going to be very hard for you to change.

One of the primary aspects of changing for you is getting in touch with your *vulnerability.* Your Entitlement is a drastic attempt to Counterattack so that you will not have to experience the pain of your vulnerability. Unless you experience that underlying feeling of deprivation, defectiveness, or social exclusion, you will not be able to change.

Your Entitlement is all-or-nothing. Either you get everything you want or you are deprived; either you are perfect or you are defective; either you are adored or you are rejected. You need to learn that there is a middle ground, that you can get your needs met in a normal way.

Find more appropriate ways of getting your core needs met—ways that respect the rights and needs of others. You do not have to be so demanding, controlling, and entitled to get what you want. Give up your Counterattacks. Start placing emphasis on intimate relationships, on trying to get your needs met through closeness with other people. Learn to ask for what you want without demanding it. Try being more honest with yourself. Be more open about who you are. Learn to say who you are, without trying to cover up, conceal, or impress.

We know this will be hard for you. You are afraid that you will be left vulnerable, helpless, and exposed, with no way of getting your needs met or feeling accepted by other people. But you will find that this does not have to be the case. In fact, your life can become much more rewarding. Following the change techniques presented in the chapters on your underlying lifetraps will help you stay in control of the process.

8. If You Have Self-Discipline Problems, Make a Hierarchy of Tasks Graded in Terms of Boredom or Frustration Level. Gradually Work Your Way Up the Hierarchy. This is a way for you to learn self-discipline. We want you to set tasks for yourself and force yourself to do them.

We know it is going to be difficult for you. Sometimes it will be boring, other times it will be frustrating. But think of yourself as in training. You are building your frustration tolerance. To keep yourself going, remind yourself of the long-term benefits.

Make a list of tasks to do, ranging from mildly difficult to extremely difficult. Use the following scale to rate the difficulty of the items on your list. Rate how difficult the item would be for *you*. For example, filling out a job application may not be difficult for most people, but it is *very* difficult for Nina.

SCALE OF DIFFICULTY

0 Very Easy
2 Mildly Difficult
4 Moderately Difficult
6 Very Difficult
8 Feels Almost Impossible

For example, here is the hierarchy Nina made.

TASKS THAT REQUIRE SELF-DISCIPLINE	DIFFICULTY RATING
Do the dishes.	2
Do the grocery shopping once a week.	3
Exercise twice a week.	4
Go through the want ads each day.	5
Draw up a household budget.	5
Make phone calls to set up job interviews.	6
Go to a job interview.	7
Fill out a job application.	7
Spend all the household money on the household, and not any on me, for the week.	8
Go through a job training program.	8

Try to complete at least one hierarchy item per week. You may choose to make some items part of your routine. After you have completed all the items, make it a general practice to sit down each week and set goals. Maintain your gains. Do not slip back into your old, undisciplined ways.

9. If You Have Difficulty Controlling Your Emotions, Develop a Time-Out Technique. Time-out techniques are particularly helpful for controlling anger. When you are about to act out in anger, they help you stop yourself and get out of the situation *before* you vent your feelings. Once you have regained control, you can make a rational decision about whether to express your anger.

What we want you to do is learn to use your rising anger as a *cue* to institute the control strategy. Use the following scale to rate your anger.

ANGER SCALE

0 Not at all Angry
2 Mildly Angry
4 Moderately Angry
6 Very Angry
8 Extremely Angry

Whenever your anger is 4 or higher on the 0–8 scale, use the time-out procedure. We want you to excuse yourself and leave the situation. (You can tell the other person something like, "I'm sorry, but I need to be alone to think for a moment. Let's finish this discussion in a few minutes.") If leaving the situation is impossible, start counting to yourself instead. Count to yourself until your anger goes below 4 on the scale.

Once your anger is manageable, spend some time pondering how you want to respond in the situation. You may find that you decide to express your anger to the person. But do it appropriately, assertively. Be calm and controlled in your presentation. Do not attack the person. State what the person has *done* that upsets you.

On the other hand, you may decide, upon reflection, *not* to express the anger. After all—how many times have you exploded in anger and then regretted it later?

10. If You Have Dependent Entitlement, Make a Hierarchy of Tasks Graded in Terms of Difficulty. Gradually Start Doing the Things You Allow Other People to Do for You. Start Proving to Yourself That You Are Competent. We want you to build your competence. That is, we want you to address the underlying Dependence lifetrap.

Make a list of the advantages and disadvantages of manipulating the people around you to take care of you. How does it affect your sense of self? How does it affect the lives of the people around you?

It was easy for Nina to list the advantages. She got things done for her, other people did them better, and she got what she wanted. It was harder for her to face the disadvantages.

NINA: *I feel behind everybody. I still can't do things people half my age can do. I mean, teenagers manage to get jobs and learn things.*

There is a tremendous loss of self-respect as a consequence of this lifetrap. You just cannot make progress in line with your peers. Your dependence is a drain on others and damaging to yourself.

Enlist the help of people close to you to gradually stop doing everything for you. It is important to get those reinforcing your lifetrap involved and to assume gradual responsibility for your own life.

Work out a hierarchy of tasks, and slowly move up the hierarchy. Do the easier tasks first, and work your way up to the most difficult ones. Build a sense of mastery and competence.

You have two lifetraps, Dependence and Entitlement. You need to address both. Follow the change techniques outlined in the Dependence chapter as well.

Here are some guidelines for helping *other* people overcome Entitlement.

HELPING SOMEONE YOU KNOW OVERCOME LIMITS PROBLEMS

1. Identify your sources of leverage. What do you have that he/she values? Your respect? Money? A job? Love?
2. How far you are willing to go to get change? Would you be willing to leave your partner? Fire an employee?
3. Approach the entitled person and express your complaints in a non-attacking way. Ask if he/she is aware of how you feel. Is he/she willing to work on changing?
4. If he/she is willing, go through the other steps in this chapter together.
5. If he/she is unreceptive, tell him/her the consequences if he/she will not try to change. Try to set up a hierarchy of negative consequences. Begin to implement them one at a time, until

the entitled person is willing to work with you. Try to empathize with how hard it is for him/her to change, but remain
firm.

6. Remember that it is often *impossible* to get someone with this
lifetrap to change. If you do not have enough leverage, you
will probably be unsuccessful. Be prepared to accept the price
of carrying through on your decision to push for change.
Make a list of advantages and disadvantages of pushing for
change by risking conflict and possibly ending your relationship. Make an informed choice.

Both Mel and Nina are among the unusual people with the Entitlement
lifetrap who are able to change. What made them different? Their partners
were certainly one factor. Both had partners who were willing to leave
them, and both had partners whom they loved. Love is leverage.

Stop waiting for your entitled partner to change. *You* have to change.
You have to learn to manage your partner. Learning to manage an entitled
partner is a skill which you can probably master. Basically, the skill is
setting limits. Entitled people are narcissistic. They lack empathy, they are
blaming, they feel entitled to more than they give. *They will never set their
own limits*. You have to set limits for them.

When Katie first started treatment, she believed that if only Mel could
see how much his affairs hurt her, he would stop. She kept showing him
her pain.

KATIE: *I couldn't understand it. I would never hurt him like that. I wouldn't
be able to stand it, seeing him hurt like that. I mean, there were times
I was almost suicidal. I just couldn't understand how he could see he
was hurting me and keep right on having affairs.*

Katie had to learn that her hurt was *never* going to stop Mel. You have to
learn this too. Demonstrations of hurt are almost always useless with an
entitled person.

What you have to do instead is to set limits. Use whatever leverage
you have. When Katie told Mel that she would leave the marriage unless
he entered therapy, she was using leverage to set limits. Of course, Katie's
job was not done. It was just beginning. Throughout therapy, Mel tried to
avoid changing any way he could. He kept trying to blame Katie, to get her
to be the one to give in.

Katie had to assert herself constantly. She had to learn to say, "Your behavior is unacceptable," and mean it. She had to set limits in every aspect of their life—from telling him, "If you have another affair I will leave you," to "If you leave your dirty clothes on the floor instead of putting them in the hamper, I won't wash them." Katie had to stop letting Mel manipulate her with guilt. She had to stop asking him for permission to live her *own* life. When she wanted to go out with friends or take a night class, she had to go ahead and do it, regardless of what Mel said.

This is not to say that Katie became mean to Mel. Rather, she learned to address him in a calm, controlled manner. In fact, Katie became much nicer. This was because what she was giving and getting began to even out in the relationship, so she felt less angry.

Deep inside, Mel wanted limits from Katie. They made him feel safer and more secure. And he began to respect Katie, which he wanted as well.

SOME FINAL WORDS

Studies have shown that the more distress patients display when they come for therapy, the more likely they are to change. For your sake, we hope you are in some distress. We hope you find some reason to overcome your Entitlement. Until you do, you will never fulfill your potential for love and work.

17

A Philosophy of Change

SEVEN BASIC ASSUMPTIONS

The process of change is a difficult one. We watch patients every day struggling to overcome deeply ingrained patterns. We also go through this same process of growth ourselves, and we observe how frustrating it can be to our friends and family members.

We know that self-help books, including this one, probably make change seem easier than it actually is. We wish there were some way to fully prepare you for the ups and downs of growing. We want you to expect change to be an erratic process. Patients always tell us that it's "one step forward and two steps back." There are many obstacles you can expect to encounter in trying to change. Chapter 5 describes many of them and offers solutions.

We have a philosophy underlying our approach to change that includes several basic assumptions. We have no way to prove these beliefs, except to say that we have found change easier when we assume these beliefs to be true. First, we believe that *we all have a part of ourselves that wants to be happy and fulfilled.* Sometimes this process is called *self-actualization.* We assume that this healthy self has somehow been buried under years of neglect, subjugation, abuse, criticism, and other destructive forces. The process of change involves reawakening this healthy side and giving it hope.

Second, we assume that *there are several basic "needs" or desires that will lead most of us to be happier if they are satisfied:* the need to relate and feel connected to other people; the need for independence, for autonomy; the need to feel desirable, competent, successful, attractive, worthwhile—to be "good" people among our peers; the need to express what we want and feel to others, to assert ourselves; the need for pleasure, fun, creativity—to pursue interests, hobbies, and activities that gratify us; and the need to help others, to show concern and love. We will discuss these needs in more detail later in this chapter.

A third core assumption in the lifetraps approach is that *people* can *change in very basic ways.* Some people are skeptical about this process. They believe that our basic personality is determined by the end of childhood, or even earlier by our genetic makeup, and that major personality change in adulthood is impossible or unlikely. We firmly reject this idea. We see people change every day in very fundamental ways. However, we acknowledge that changing core patterns is extremely difficult. Our inherited temperament, along with our early family and peer experiences, create very powerful forces that act against change. However, while our childhood histories create strong obstacles to change, they do not make change impossible. The more destructive these early forces, the harder we will have to work to change lifetraps, and the more support we will need from others.

A fourth assumption is that we all have strong tendencies to resist core change. This belief has important implications. It implies that *it is highly unlikely that we will change basic lifetraps without making a conscious decision to do so.* Most of us operate on automatic pilot, repeating habits of thinking, feeling, relating, and doing what we have practiced over our lifetime. These patterns are comfortable and familiar, and we are very unlikely to change them unless we make a concerted, deliberate, and sustained effort to do so; if we wait for fundamental change to happen on its own, it almost certainly will not. We are doomed to repeat the mistakes of the past and legacy of our parents and grandparents unless we make intentional and prolonged efforts to alter them.

A fifth assumption is that most of us have strong inclinations to avoid pain. This is good and bad. The good news is that most of us gravitate toward experiences that bring us pleasure and gratification. The bad news is that *we avoid facing situations and feelings that cause us pain, even when confronting them might lead to growth.* This desire to avoid pain is one of the most difficult roadblocks to change. In order to modify core lifetraps, we must be willing to face painful memories that stir up emotions like sadness, anger, anxiety, guilt, shame, and embarrassment. We must be willing to face situations we have avoided much of our lives because we fear they will result in failure, rejection, or humiliation. Unless we face these painful memories and threatening situations, we are doomed to repeat patterns that hurt us. Most of us shy away from painful feelings; many patients leave therapy rather than face these emotions. People become addicted to alcohol and drugs to avoid these feelings. We must commit ourselves to facing pain in order to change.

Sixth, *we do not believe that any one technique or approach to change will be successful for all people.* We believe that the most effective change approaches will be those that integrate and pull together a variety of different strategies. In the lifetrap approach, we draw on cognitive, behavioral, experiential, inner-child, psychoanalytic, and interpersonal techniques to help you change. Because we are combining several powerful change agents, we believe that more people will be helped with this therapy than by other therapies that only utilize one or two of these interventions. We strongly urge you to seek out approaches and therapists that combine several models, instead of just one or two. Although we do not expect to help everybody with our lifetrap approach, we hope to be more successful than single-technique treatments.

CREATING A PERSONAL VISION

Our final assumption about change involves the need to create a personal vision. Change is not just the absence of lifetraps. We must each discover who we want to be and what we want from life. We feel that it is vital to have this direction before going too far along the change process. We want you to look beyond the elimination of your individual lifetraps to an image of what will lead you finally to feel fulfilled, happy, and self-actualized.

Many of us go through life with only a fuzzy sense of where we are going. This explains why many of us reach middle-age or retirement feeling disappointed and disillusioned. We have never had a broad set of overriding goals to guide us. It would be like playing football without knowing where the goal posts are, or getting on a plane without knowing its destination. It is crucial for each of us to have such a blueprint. *The eleven lifetraps are obstacles to reaching our goals; they do not tell us what each of us uniquely needs to be happy.* Once you develop a set of life goals, you can begin to plan specific steps to get there. We urge you to approach change in a strategic way, not haphazardly.

To create a personal vision, you must discover your *natural inclinations,* which include those interests, relationships, and activities that inherently lead us to feel fulfilled. We believe that each person has an innate set of personal preferences. Perhaps the most vital task we can undertake in our lives is to discover what these inborn desires are. Our best clues to recognizing natural inclinations are our emotions and our bodily sensations. When we engage in activities or relationships that fulfill our natural inclinations, we feel good. Our body is content and we experience pleasure or joy.

Unfortunately, many of us are trained as children to disregard our natural inclinations and to do what is expected of us: We are forced to be tough when by nature we are sensitive; we are forced to pursue medicine, when our natural preference is for outdoor activities; we are forced to be conventional when by nature we are unconventional; we are forced to act in routine ways when by nature we prefer stimulation.

We could go on and on with examples of how parents and teachers, with the best intentions, encourage us to disregard our basic natures. Naturally, we cannot selfishly pursue only what we want to be happy. We must find a balance between the needs of society and our own personal fulfillment. We are not advocating a narcissistic philosophy of living. However, many of us have been overtrained, oversocialized. We have been pushed too far in the direction of doing what others expect.

Many of us must reverse this process in order to change. We must discover who we are. We must find out what makes us happy, without relying solely on what makes the people around us happy. Although we cannot, of course, develop this vision for you, we can guide you through the questions you have to ask yourself. We have already discussed the core needs that can lead us to happiness. (This was the second assumption in our philosophy.) Now we will go through them in greater detail with you.

The first area of change involves *relationships.* What is your vision of the relationships that you want in your life? Clarify the ways you want to connect to other people. Consider intimate relationships. What kind of intimate relationship do you want? What is most important to you— passion and romance, a companion, a family? What are your goals in finding a partner? How important is emotional closeness to you compared to sexual excitement?

Relationships are almost always a trade-off. Making intelligent trade-offs is a problem for many of us, because we are out of touch with our natural inclinations. Very few of us ever find a partner who provides us with everything we need, so we have to make choices. What is most important to you in choosing a partner? What are the less important qualities that would be nice, but which you would do without if you had to? For example, you might find yourself with someone you love and feel close to, but feel less passion for. We do not believe in a concept of the ideal relationship that *should* be right for everyone; you must decide what feels best to you.

What kind of social relationships do you want? What kind of friends? How involved do you want to be in a social "scene"? How committed do you want to be to groups in the community? Do you want to participate in a church or synagogue? Do you want to be involved in the running of schools or in local government? Do you want to participate in support groups? How much do you want to socialize with people at work? These are decisions you will have to make, using your natural inclinations as guides.

The Emotional Deprivation, Mistrust and Abuse, Abandonment, and Social Exclusion lifetraps are the biggest blocks to developing the kind of relationships you want in your life. Conquering these lifetraps will allow you to connect to people on a deeper and more satisfying level. Your relationship vision will guide you in fighting these lifetraps.

The second core area of change is *autonomy*. What is the optimal level of independence for you? Naturally, you want to operate in the world with a sense of independence and competence, with a strong sense of self. But what relative balance of autonomy and connection will make you happiest? For some people, spending most of their time in solitary pursuits is very fulfilling. Other people are happier spending a greater portion of their time socializing and relating than being alone.

Autonomy gives you the freedom to seek out healthy relationships, and to avoid or leave unhealthy ones. You are free to stay in a relationship because you *want* to stay, not because you *need* to. Many people with Dependence or Vulnerability lifetraps feel trapped in destructive relationships. They are afraid to leave and face the world on their own. These two lifetraps are the greatest blocks to developing a healthy level of autonomy.

Autonomy is a vital component in the pursuit of your natural inclinations. It involves developing a sense of identity. You are free to be who you uniquely are. Whether you prefer to be a musician, an artist, a writer, an athlete, a mechanic, a performer, a homemaker, a traveler, a nature lover, a caretaker, or a leader, you will feel free to pursue it. You are not too afraid to venture out into the world. You will not lose yourself in relationships, living your partner's life instead of your own.

The third component of change is *self-esteem*. Like autonomy, self-esteem provides a *context of freedom*. Instead of being blocked, you are free. The Defectiveness and Failure lifetraps are blocks to attaining self-esteem. Feelings of inferiority and shame weigh you down, causing you to avoid or mishandle opportunities. Your shame is like a heavy black cloud that surrounds you and leaves you unable to move—unable to connect, to express yourself, to get your needs met, to excel.

You want to choose a life that enhances your self-esteem. How can you strive to feel good about yourself, to accept yourself without being overly self-punitive or insecure? What are your strengths and how can you develop them? What are the weaknesses that you can correct?

The fourth area of change is *self-assertion and self-expression*. This involves asking to have your own needs met and expressing your feelings. Asserting yourself enables you to follow your natural inclinations and get pleasure out of life. In what ways can you express who you are?

Subjugation and Unrelenting Standards are blocks to self-assertion. With Subjugation, you give up your own inherent needs and pleasures in order to help others or avoid retaliation. With Unrelenting Standards, you give up your needs and pleasures in order to gain approval and recognition, and to avoid shame. Achievement and perfection become your goals in life, at the expense of happiness and gratification.

Passion, creativity, playfulness, and fun can help make life worth living. It is important to be able to let go sometimes, to include excitement and pleasure in your life. If you neglect self-assertion and self-expression, life feels heavy and you can begin to feel desperate. Your needs and those of the people around you are out of balance. *Change involves allowing yourself to fulfill your own basic needs and inclinations, without unnecessarily hurting those around you.*

The fifth area of growth, no less important than the other four, is *concern for others*. One of the most gratifying aspects of life is learning to give to other people and to empathize with them. Entitlement may keep you from showing concern for the people around you. It feels good to make a *contribution*. Social involvement, charity, having children and giving to children, helping your friends—these involve a connection to something greater than yourself and your individual life. How can you contribute to the world at large?

Spirituality and religious belief can be important components of feeling part of the world at large. Most religious and spiritual approaches share an emphasis on expanding beyond the narrow concerns of self and family, to the universe as a whole. Many forms of religious experience provide this added dimension and fulfillment.

Consider the areas we have mapped out as you develop your vision of life. The goals of life are probably universal: love, self-expression, pleasure, freedom, spirituality, giving to others—this is what most of us want. However, these goals often collide. For example, passion may conflict with stability, autonomy with intimacy, self-expression with concern for others. You will have to set priorities and choose the balance that feels right for you. We urge you to incorporate elements of these broader goals in your own unique way, in accord with your own unique needs and priorities.

EMPATHIC SELF-CONFRONTATION

We have developed a term to describe what we consider to be a healthy attitude toward change: *empathic self-confrontation.* Show compassion for yourself, while continually pushing yourself to change. Many people either criticize themselves too harshly when they do not feel they have changed enough, or they are too lenient and make excuses to let themselves off the hook.

The process of change is very difficult, as we have stated repeatedly. Above all, be compassionate with yourself. You are struggling to do your best. Be understanding of your limitations and flaws. Remember that lifetraps are hard to change. It is vital that you remember how you became the way you are. *Remember the origins of your lifetraps, and try to empathize with yourself when you were a child.*

However, it is also important to take responsibility for changing. Many self-help groups have been criticized for encouraging members to feel like victims of their parents without teaching them to take responsibility for changing. We think this is a serious risk. It is vital that you keep confronting yourself. Be persistent. Do not keep putting off change, waiting for a more convenient time. The best time to begin changing is now. No matter how damaged you were as a child, this does not excuse you from taking responsibility for change. *Childhood pain explains why change is so difficult and takes so long; it does not explain why someone allows destructive patterns to continue without working hard to alter them.*

Be honest with yourself. Place a high value on facing reality. So many people delude themselves, holding on to illusions of what they would like themselves to be or what they would like other people to be. They are unwilling to face the reality of what they are like—of their coldness, their sadness, their anger, their anxieties. Look at the reality of your situation. Self-delusion will only lead you to continue acting in self-defeating ways, and keep you from having genuine relationships.

Confront yourself to change at the speed and level you can handle. We cannot face everything all at once, so we usually have to confront lifetraps in gradual increments. Have faith that you can reach the place you want to go. Faith will help you ride out failure and disappointments in between your successes. Be patient. If you persist, you will eventually achieve your vision.

Unfortunately, some changes cannot be accomplished in small steps. They require a leap of faith, a high level of risk. Sometimes we must make major changes in order to grow; these include leaving a relationship, switching careers, or moving to another city. As we become more aware of our natural inclinations and overcome our lifetraps, we may have to make major breaks with the past. You may have to surrender the security of childhood patterns in order to grow into the adult you want to be.

ENLISTING THE HELP OF OTHERS

It is hard to change alone. Change is easier when you have support. Reach out for help to the people who love you. Let friends and supportive family members get involved. Tell them what you are trying to do and enlist their assistance.

Sometimes friends or supportive family members can serve as mentors or role models for reaching your personal goals. They can provide advice, guidance, and inspiration. Knowing someone well who has already met some of your goals can make the process more *real* to you, and can give you faith that change is possible.

Friends and supportive family members are often more objective than you are. They can help you to analyze the evidence, and push you to confront the tasks you are avoiding. It is going to be difficult for you to change without the help of *some* person who can see you clearly and realistically, because you will have trouble seeing your own distortions.

Unfortunately, turning to family and friends may not be an option for you. You may not have close family and friends, or they may be too disturbed themselves to be of much help to you. Often family members reinforce your lifetraps, rather than help you change. If this is the case, consider seeking professional help.

There are other times to consider seeing a professional. When your symptoms are so severe that they interfere with your functioning; when you have been stuck for a long time and do not know how to change; when change feels hopeless—these are times to consider getting professional help. Consider it when you are going through a life crisis, such as the break-up of a long-term relationship or the loss of a job; at these times, you need support and may be more receptive to change. Consider help if you had a traumatic childhood that included emotional, physical, or sexual abuse. Finally, if you are hurting other people because of your problems, then professional help is clearly indicated.

If your symptoms are very serious, psychiatric medication might help you. For example, you might be seriously depressed: you feel worthless, your eating and sleeping are disturbed, you feel slowed down, you cannot concentrate, you have lost interest in things that used to give you pleasure, or you are actually doing less. You may even be considering suicide. If you have symptoms of depression, especially if you feel suicidal, seek professional help immediately.

You may have serious symptoms of anxiety, such as panic attacks, multiple phobias, obsessive-compulsive symptoms, or intense generalized anxiety. You may be so fearful of social situations that you avoid them, wreaking havoc on your social and work lives. If these symptoms of anxiety characterize you, getting professional help is advisable.

You may be addicted to alcohol or drugs. You may have "post traumatic stress disorder," in which something from your past is haunting you. You may have flashbacks or nightmares, or you may feel numb and detached. Or you may have a serious eating disorder, such as bulimia or anorexia. Your desire to lose weight is so intense that you binge on foods and then somehow purge them, or you eat less and less, becoming dangerously thin. By all means, seek out a professional if you suffer from these serious disorders.

SELECTING A THERAPIST

Once you have decided to seek professional help, you have to grapple with the question of what type of therapist to see. There is no single answer that is right for everybody. Rather, selecting a therapist is another example of following your natural inclinations.

It is important to select a therapist with adequate credentials. In general, we believe it is better to see a professional therapist than a nonprofessional. After all, you are entrusting your well-being to another person. You want someone well trained and bound by a code of ethical standards. Although we are psychologists ourselves, we also recommend social workers, psychiatrists, and psychiatric nurses, *if they have had experience with your kind of problem.* All of these professions require at least a university degree and a state license. By selecting one of these professions, you are more likely to find a therapist with adequate knowledge, clinical training, connection to professional associations with high standards and codes of ethics, and accountability to the public. The more serious your symptoms, the more crucial it is that you select one of these professionals.

There are also many different schools of therapy. As we stated earlier in this chapter, we believe that it is usually a mistake to select a therapist committed to only one approach or model. We feel that the best therapists can blend a variety of techniques and strategies, depending on the needs of the patient. That is why we have a preference for integrative therapists.

It is extremely important that you find a therapist with whom you "mesh" emotionally. You want someone who is warm and accepting of you, who makes you feel safe. You want someone who is empathic and understands you. You want someone who seems genuine, whom you can trust. And you want someone who can handle you—who sets clear limits and confronts you when you get off track. Be skeptical of a therapist who always agrees with you and makes you feel good, who seems cold or distant, who is too critical of you, or who seems to have ulterior motives for working with you.

Avoid inappropriate "chemistry" in therapy that might be generated by your lifetraps. For example, if you have a Defectiveness lifetrap, you might feel a lot of attraction to a critical, "superior" therapist, even though this is destructive to you. You would do better with a therapist who seems to like and respect you. If your problem is disconnection, a therapist who is cold and remote is not the one for you. You need someone who will push you to relate. You do not want a therapist who generates chemistry, but someone who will provide a healing environment for your particular problem.

In some respects you want a therapist who can be the parent you never had. We call this "limited reparenting" in therapy. One aspect of therapy involves providing a *partial antidote* to problems in your childhood. If you did not get enough nurturing, your therapist nurtures you. If you were overly criticized, your therapist supports and validates you. If you had a parent who was too intrusive, your therapist respects your boundaries. If you were abused, the therapist contains and protects you.

Naturally, you cannot expect a therapist to substitute completely for the parenting you lacked. This is unrealistic. There is only so much reparenting you can receive in one or two therapy hours a week. In fact, we urge you to be wary of therapists who encourage you to be too dependent on them, or who promise a level of support that is unprofessional and goes beyond the limits of psychotherapy.

Your therapist can also be a role model in a domain where you are having difficulty. For example, your therapist can be assertive where you are timid, or demonstrative where you are closed. Your therapist can model effective ways of resolving problems.

We also encourage you to join reputable self-help groups. Twelve-step programs such as AA (Alcoholics Anonymous), ACOA (Adult Children of Alcoholics), AL-ANON (relatives of alcoholics), CODA (Codependents Anonymous), NA (Narcotics Anonymous), and OA (Overeaters Anonymous), are well established and nationally recognized. These groups have programs designed to help you change in specific ways.

Beware of "cult" groups. These are groups that have charismatic leaders, require you to recruit new members (proselytizing), and generally cost large sums of money to join or complete. Cult groups foster dependency and subjugation. Members are made to feel special, that they have a secret that no one else does. In reality, cult members are encouraged to remain children rather than come to grips with the demands of adulthood. They are encouraged to follow the rules of the leader, instead of discovering their own natural inclinations. If you are considering joining a group and are not sure whether it is reputable, you can consult with one of the mental health professionals mentioned above or call their respective professional associations.

If you would like a referral to a therapist in your area trained in the lifetrap approach, feel free to contact us. Furthermore, if you would like to share your experience using our approach (positive or negative), we welcome your feedback. Tell us your personal story. Although we cannot provide direct psychological assistance by mail, we would genuinely like to hear from you as you go through the process of change. You can write or call us at:

Jeffrey Young, Ph.D.
Cognitive Therapy Center of New York
3 East 80th Street, Penthouse
New York, New York 10021
(Phone: 212-472-1706)

Janet Klosko, Ph.D.
Cognitive Therapy Center of Long Island
11 Middleneck Road
Great Neck, New York 11021
(Phone: 516-466-8485)

We would like to conclude with a quotation from T. S. Eliot's *Little Gidding*:

> We shall not cease from exploration
> And the end of all our exploring
> Will be to arrive where we started
> And know the place for the first time.

REFERENCES

BECK, AARON T. (1988). *Love Is Never Enough*. New York: Harper & Row.

BECK, AARON T. (1976). *Cognitive Therapy and the Emotional Disorders*. New York: International Universities Press. Paperbound edition published by New American Library, New York, 1979.

BOWLBY, JOHN (1973). *Separation: Anxiety and Anger*. (Vol. II of *Attachment and Loss*). New York: Basic Books.

BRADSHAW, JOHN (1988). *Healing the Shame That Binds You*. Deerfield Beach, Fla: Health Communications, Inc.

BURNS, DAVID D. (1980). *Feeling Good*. New York: William Morrow & Company, Inc.

FREUD, SIGMUND (1920). *Beyond the Pleasure Principle: The Standard Edition of the Complete Psychological Works of Sigmund Freud*. (Volume XVIII: 1955). New York: Basic Books, Inc.

HENDRIX, HARVILLE (1988). *Getting the Love You Want*. New York: Henry Holt & Company.

PERLS, FREDERICK S., HEFFERLINE, R. F., and GOODMAN, P. (1969). In W. S. Sahakian, *Psychotherapy and Counseling*. New York: Rand McNally.

WINNICOTT, D. W. (1986). *Home Is Where We Start From*. Reading, Mass.: Addison-Wesley Publishing Company, Inc.

YOUNG, JEFFREY E. (1990). *Cognitive Therapy for Personality Disorders: A Schema-Focused Approach*. Sarasota, Fla: Professional Resource Exchange, Inc.

INDEX

AA (Alcoholics Anonymous), 38, 149, 351
Abandonment lifetrap, 6–8, 58–82
  absence of one stable maternal figure and,
    69–70
  based on dependence, 64–65
  based on instability or loss, 64, 65
  basic safety and, 26–27
  case histories, 58–60
  changing, 76–81
    avoid clinging, jealousy, and overreaction
      to separations, 82
    avoid the wrong partners, 79–80
    pitfalls of abandonment, 79
    monitoring your feelings, 78–79
    review past romantic relationships and
      clarify patterns, 79
    trust a committed partner, 80–81
    understanding your childhood
      abandonment, 77–78
  cycle of abandonment, 63–65
  divorce and, 70
  feeling of, 62–63
  fighting parents and, 70
  intimate relationships and, see Intimate
    relationships, Abandonment lifetrap
    and
  loss of parent and, 68–69
  new family member, withdrawal of
    attention to, 70
  origins of, 66–71

  overprotective parent and, 70–71
  overview, 16–17
  as preverbal trap, 62
  questionnaire, 60–62
  temperament and, 67–68, 77
  triggers of, 62–63
  unstable mother and, 69–70
Abusive person:
  Mistrust and Abuse lifetrap and. *See*
    Mistrust and Abuse lifetrap
  Subjugation by, 271
Acceptance of lifetrap on rational level, 54
Accomplishments, listing your, 252
Achievement orientation, 300–01
ACOA (Adult Children of Alcoholics), 351
Adolescence, Social Exclusion lifetrap in, 138
Adult Children of Alcoholics (ACOA), 351
Agoraphobia, 162
AL-ANON, 351
Alcohol, 319
  abuse and, 89
  Defectiveness lifetrap and, 222
  as Escape, 53, 213, 226
  Subjugation lifetrap and, 271
Alcoholics Anonymous (AA), 38, 149, 351
Alcoholism, 38, 134
  parent with, 25, 136, 271, 273–74
  self-help groups, 351
Anger:
  in abandonment cycle, 63

Anger *(cont.)*
  emotional deprivation lifetrap and, 120
  Entitlement lifetrap and, 320, 324, 337–38
  Subjugation lifetrap and, 263, 264, 265,
    266–68, 277, 280–81
    learning to handle anger appropriately,
      289–90
  unexpressed, 32
  venting, during imagery, 101–02
Anorexia nervosa, 269
Anxiety, 11
  in abandonment cycle, 63
  Dependence and, 162–63
  separation and, 66
  in social situations, 129, 131–33
  Vulnerability and, 187
Anxious attachment, 67
Assertiveness, 236
  Subjugation lifetrap and, 280, 286–88, 292
Assumption about change. *See* Philosophy of
    change, assumptions
Ativan, 4–5
Autonomy, 28–29, 345

Basic Safety, 26–27
Bass, Ellen, 100
Beck, Dr. Aaron, xiv, 10–11
Behavior change, 252–53
Behavior therapy, xiv
Believing lifetrap is true, 53–54
Biological predisposition to lifetraps. *See*
    Temperament
Blame:
  placing blame on others, 33, 39–40
  stop blaming partner for emotional
    deprivation, 127
  stop blaming yourself for abuse, 102
Boarding school, 69
Bowlby, John, 66

Career. *See* Work
Catastrophic thinking, 191
Changing lifetraps:
  dislike for change, 160
  obstacles and their solutions, 52–57
    accepting lifetrap on rational level, 54
    Counterattacking instead of
      acknowledging and taking
      responsibility, 52–53
    emotional validity of lifetrap, 55–56
    Escaping from experiencing lifetrap, 53
    lack of systematic, disciplined approach,
      56
    plan is missing an important element,
      56–57
    problem is too entrenched to correct on
      your own, 57

starting with a lifetrap or task that was
    too difficult, 54–55
  philosophy of change. *See* Philosophy of
    change
  steps in:
    build a case against your lifetrap, 45–47
    examine lifetrap patterns in careful
      detail, 49
    feeling your lifetrap, 44–45
    forgiving your parents, 51–52
    keep trying, 51
    label and identify your lifetraps, 43–44
    pattern-breaking, 49–51
    understand the childhood origins, 44–45
    write letters to the person who helped
      cause your lifetrap, 48–49
  See also specific lifetraps
Childhood:
  autonomy in, 28–29
  basic safety in, 26–27
  connection to others in, 27–28
  destructive early environment, 25
  lifetraps originating in. *See specific lifetraps*
  needs to thrive in, 26–33
  realistic limits in, 32–33
  self-esteem in, 29–30
  self-expression in, 30–32
  understanding origins of lifetrap in, 44–45
Cleaning, compulsive, 38
Clinging in a relationship, 72, 81
Co-dependency, 274
Cognitive therapy:
  development of, 10
  premise of, 10
Cognitive Therapy and Emotional Disorders
    (Beck), xiv
Competition between parent and child, 244,
    245–46
Compulsivity, 299–300
Concern for others, 346
Conditional love of parent, 302
Confronting oneself, 51
  continually, 3
  empathy in, 347–48
Confronting the person who makes you feel
    like a failure, 251
Confronting your abuser, 103–05
Control. *See* Subjugation lifetrap
Conversation, initiating, 152–53
Coping styles, 35–41
  Counterattack, 39–41
  Escape, 38–39
  Surrender, 36–38
Counterattack:
  as coping style, 39–41
  Defectiveness lifetrap and, 39–41, 210, 211,
    225–26

to Dependence, 163–64
Entitlement as Counterattack for other
    lifetraps, 323–25, 334–35
instead of acknowledging and taking
    responsibility, 52–53
of Mistrust and Abuse lifetrap, 93
of Social Deprivation lifetrap, 144–45
Subjugation lifetrap and, 268–69
Counterdependence, 163–64, 173–74, 182–83
Courage to Heal (Bass and David), 100
Criticism:
    from parent or sibling, 30, 37
        Defectiveness lifetrap and, 213–14, 215,
            216, 231–33, 237–38
        Failure lifetrap and, 243–44
        Social Exclusion lifetrap and, 137
        Subjugation lifetrap and, 271–72
        Unrelenting Standards lifetrap and,
            304–05
    from partner, Defectiveness lifetrap and,
        221
    sensitivity to, 221–22
Cult groups, 140, 351

Danger, exaggerated fear of, 188–89, 193,
    194–95, 196–97
Davis, Laura, 100
Day-care centers, 69
Defectiveness lifetrap, 207–38
    career and, 222–23
    case histories, 207–08
    changing, 223–38
        accept love from people close to you,
            235–36
        evaluate seriousness of current defects,
            229–30
        if you're the critical partner, stop putting
            down your partner and others, 237–38
        list partners who have attracted you
            most and least, 227
        list signs of negative coping style, 225
        list your defects and assets as child and
            teenager, and your current defects and
            assets, 227–29
        monitor your feelings of defectiveness
            and shame, 226–27
        start a program to correct changeable
            flaws, 230–31
        stop allowing people to treat you badly,
            236–37
        try to be more genuine in close
            relationships, 234–35
        try to stop behaviors designed to Escape
            or Counterattack, 225–26
        understanding your childhood
            defectiveness and shame, 223–25
        write a flashcard, 233–34

write a letter to your critical parent(s),
    231–33
coping styles, 36–41
    Counterattack, 39–41, 210, 211–12,
        225–26
    Escape, 38–39, 210, 213, 225–26
    Surrender, 36–38
critical parent and, 213–14, 215, 216,
    231–33
criticism and, 213–14, 215, 216, 218,
    231–33, 237
experience of defectiveness, 210–11
flashcard, 233–34
humiliation and, 216
intimate relationships and. See Intimate
    relationships, Defectiveness lifetrap
    and
narcissism and, 211–12, 215
origins of, 213–17
overview, 21
protective shell, 216–17
public speaking and, 223
questionnaire, 208–10
real defect, not based on, 217
self-esteem and, 29–30
self-hatred, 211, 212
shame and, 210, 211, 212, 214, 223, 226–27
siblings, comparison to, 216
Social Exclusion lifetrap and, 132, 136
Dependence, Abandonment lifetrap based on,
    64
Dependence lifetrap, 155–83
    anger and, 161–62
    anxiety and, 162–63
    autonomy and, 28–29
    case histories, 155–57
    change, dislike for, 160
    changing, 174–83
        avoid strong, overprotective partners,
            180
        counterdependence, acknowledging,
            182–83
        don't complain when your partner/boss
            refuses to help enough, 181–82
        upon failure, don't give until mastering
            the task, 178–79
        give a healthy relationship a chance to
            work, 180–81
        give yourself credit when you succeed,
            179–80
        list challenges, changes, or phobias
            you've avoided, 176–77
        list everyday situations in which you
            depend on others, 176
        list lifetraps to avoid, 179–80
        review past relationships and clarify
            patterns of dependence, 179–80

Dependence lifetrap *(cont.)*
  systematically force yourself to tackle
    everyday tasks without help, starting
    with easy tasks first, 177–79
  take on new challenges at work,
    gradually, 182
  understanding your childhood
    dependence, 175–76
  Counterattackers, 163–64
  counterdependence, 163–64, 173–74, 182–83
  dependent entitlement, 161–62
  depression and, 163
  Escape to reinforce, 161
  experience of dependence, 159–61
  imagery to understand, 175–76
  inadequacy, feelings of, 159
  incompetence, sense of, 159, 160
  indecisiveness, 159–60
  independence, 164–65
  intimate relationships and. *See* Intimate
    relationships, Dependence lifetrap and
  origins of, 164–65
    overprotective parents, 164, 165–69
    underprotective parents, 164, 169–71
  overcompensating, 163
  overprotective parents and. *See*
    Overprotective parents, Dependence
    lifetrap and
  questionnaire, 157–58
  subordinating role, taking a, 161
  Surrendering to, 160, 172–74
  underprotective parents and, 164, 169–71
  at work, 172–73
Dependent entitlement, 161–62, 318–19, 323,
    325, 326–27, 337–38
Depression, 11
  in abandonment cycle, 63–64
  Dependence and, 163
  Failure lifetrap and, 243
Despair, separation and, 66–67
Detachment, separation and, 67
Different, feeling, 130, 133, 134–35
  overcompensation for, 145
Disappointment in other people, 114
Disciplined approach to changing lifetrap,
    56
Disproving your lifetrap, 45–47
Dissociation:
  Mistrust and Abuse lifetrap and, 86–87,
    92
  multiple personalities, 93
Divorce, abandonment lifetrap and, 70
Drug abuse, 319
  abusive situation and, 89, 95
  Defectiveness lifetrap and, 222
  as Escape, 38, 52, 53, 213, 226
  Subjugation resulting from parent's, 271

Emotional Deprivation lifetrap, 2–3, 109–28
  case histories, 109–11
  changing, 121–28
    avoid cold partners, 124–25
    give healthy relationship a chance,
      125–27
    list pitfalls to avoid now, 125
    monitor your feelings of deprivation
      now, 123–24
    outlook for change, 127–28
    review past relationships and clarify
      patterns, 124–25
    stop blaming your partner and
      demanding your needs be met, 127
    understanding your childhood
      deprivation, 121–23
  chronic disappointment in other people,
    114
  connection to others and, 27–28
  coping styles, 120
  demandingness in relationships, 120–21
  empathy deprivation, 122
  experience of deprivation, 113–14
  father's protective role, 116–17
  imagery to understand, 123, 124
  intimate relationships and. *See* Intimate
    relationships, emotional deprivation
    lifetrap and
  maternal nurturance, insufficient, 114–17
  nurturance and, 113, 114–17, 122, 123–24
  origins of, 114–17
  overview, 20
  protection, deprivation of, 122
  questionnaire, 111–12
Empathic self-confrontation, 347–48
Empathy, 264
  deprivation, 122
  Entitlement lifetrap and, 318, 334
Enmeshment, 169
Entitlement lifetrap, 314–40
  anger and, 320, 324, 337
  case histories, 314–16
  changing, 328–29
    ask for feedback as you try to change,
      333–34
    confront the excuses you use to avoid
      accepting limits, 331
    develop time-out technique, 337
    fill out limits chart, 332
    if lifetrap is form of Counterattack, try to
      understand core lifetrap, 335
    list advantages and disadvantages of not
      accepting limits, 330
    list various ways your limits problem
      manifests itself in everyday life, 332
    make and work up hierarchy of tasks,
      336, 337–38

make flashcards, 333, 338–39
    try to empathize with others, 334
as Counterattack for other lifestyles, 323–25
dependent entitlement, 161–62, 318–19, 323,
    325, 326–27, 337–38
empathy and, 318, 333–34
experience of entitlement, 316–21
flashcards, 333, 338–39
impulsivity and, 319–22, 325, 329
intimate relationships and. *See* Intimate
    relationships, Entitlement lifetrap and
origins of, 321–24
overindulgence of parents, 323
overview, 21–22
patterns of, 326–27, 328–29
questionnaire, 316–17
realistic limits and, 32–33
setting limits on partner with, 339
spoiled entitlement, 317–18, 321, 325, 326
weak parental limits, 321–23
Environment:
    destructive early, 25
    heredity and, 24–25
Envy, 221
Escape:
    as coping style, 38–39
    Defectiveness lifetrap and, 38–39, 210, 212,
        225–26
    Dependence reinforced by, 161
    Failure lifetrap and, 242–43, 245, 247, 253
    instead of experiencing lifetrap, 53
    Social Exclusion lifetrap and, 141
        hierarchy of groups, 151–52
Experiential therapies, 10

Failure lifetrap, 239–57
    case histories, 239–40
    changing, 248–56
        assess whether your feeling of failure is
            accurate or distorted, 248–49
        become aware of your abilities, 251–53
        flashcards, 255–56
        get in touch with inner child, 248–49
        help inner child understand you were
            treated unfairly, 250–51
        involve loved ones, 256
        plan to change your patterns, 254–55
        try to understand pattern in your
            failures, 253–54
    competitive parent, 244, 245–46
    critical parent and, 244
    depression and, 243
    Escape to reinforce, 242–43, 245, 247, 253
    experience of failure, 242–43
    flashcards, 255–56
    impostor syndrome, 240
    inferior feelings as child and, 244

intimate relationships and, 247–48
    origins of, 244–46
    overview, 21
    parents who didn't care if you were
        successful, 244–45
    patterns of failure, 246–48
    questionnaire, 240–41
    self-discipline, failure to learn, 244, 245
    self-esteem and, 29–30
    as self-fulfilling prophesy, 246
    self-sabotage, 243, 246
    siblings, comparison to, 244
    very successful parent and, 244
Family:
    destructive early environments and, 25
    enlisting help from, 348
    lifetraps and adaptation to, 24
    Social Deprivation lifetrap and, 134,
        136–37, 139
    Unrelenting Standards and feeling ashamed
        of, 303–04
    see also Childhood
Fathers, lifetraps related to behavior of. *See*
    specific lifetraps
Feeling your lifetrap, 44–45
Fighting parents, Abandonment lifetrap,
    70
Financial ruin, exaggerated fear of, 189–90,
    194
Flashcards:
    Abandonment, 46, 82
    Defectiveness, 233–34
    Failure, 255–56
    Social Exclusion, 150
    Subjugation, 292–93
    Vulnerability, 202–03
Forgiving, 51–52
Freud, Sigmund, 5, 95
Friendships, Abandonment lifetrap and, 76
Frustration tolerance, 322, 324

Gays, Social Exclusion lifetrap and, 135
Gestalt therapy, 9
Gifted children, 135
Grief in abandonment cycle, 63–64
Groups, joining, 140
Guilt:
    over sexual abuse, 90–91
    Subjugation out of, 263–66, 272, 273–74,
        275–76

Heredity:
    environment and, 24–25
    temperament and. *See* Temperament
Hierarchy:
    of groups escaped in Social Deprivation
        lifetrap, 150–52

Hierarchy *(cont.)*
    of situations in which you subjugate
        yourself, 286–88
    of tasks for person with Entitlement
        lifetrap, 337–38, 339
Humiliation, 135, 142, 216
Hypervigilance, Mistrust and Abuse lifetrap
    and, 87
Hypochondriacs, 187–88, 192, 194, 319

Identifying your lifetraps, 43–44
Illness type of Vulnerability lifetrap, 187–88,
    192, 194
Imagery:
    to change Failure lifetrap, 249, 250–51
    to change Subjugation lifetrap, 283–84
    in overcoming Social Deprivation lifestyle,
        148
    in overcoming Vulnerability, 203–05
    to remember abuse, 100
    to understand childhood dependence,
        175–76
    to understand Emotional Deprivation,
        123–24
    venting anger during, 101–02
Immediate gratification, 32
Impostor syndrome, 240
Impulse control, 322, 324
Impulsivity, 319–22, 325, 329
Inadequacy, feelings of, 159
Incompetence, sense of, 159, 160
Indecisiveness, 159–60
Independence, 164–65
    steps toward, 164
    See also Dependence lifetrap
Independent functioning, 28–29
Inferiority, feelings of, 131, 135, 244
Inner-child:
    talking to your, 44–45, 203–04, 249–51
    therapy, 10
Instability, Abandonment lifetrap based on,
    64, 65
Intimate relationships, 27, 28
    Abandonment lifetrap and, 71–72
        avoiding clinging, jealousy, and
            overreaction to separations, 82
        danger signals in early stages of dating,
            72–73
        partners to avoid, 79–80
        trusting a committed partner, 80–82
        undermining good relationships, 73–76
    Defectiveness lifetrap and:
        accept love from people close to you,
            235–36
        chemistry, 222
        critical partner, 218
        danger signals while dating, 217
        devaluing of partner, 220

        envy, 221
        jealousy, 221
        masochistic relationships, 218
        patterns of behavior, 218–23
        putting-down partner, 219, 220
        sensitivity to criticism, 221–22
        stop allowing people to treat you badly,
            236–37
    Dependence lifetrap and, 171, 173
        danger signals in early stages of dating,
            171–72
        give a healthy relationship a chance to
            work, 180–81
        high chemistry partners, avoiding, 180
        strong, overprotective partners, avoiding,
            180–81
    Emotional Deprivation lifetrap and, 116–17,
        118–19
        danger signals in early stages of dating,
            118
        giving healthy relationships a chance,
            125–27
        partners to avoid, 125
        sabotaging the relationship, 119
        stop blaming your partner and
            demanding your needs to be met, 127
    Entitlement lifetrap and, 325–26
        danger signals in choice of partner,
            325–26
        setting limits, 339–40
    Failure lifetrap and, 247–48
    Mistrust and Abuse lifetrap and, 94–99
        changing choice of partners, 106–07
        danger signals in partners, 94–95
        lifetraps in relationships, 96
        of sexually abused, 99
        personal vision of, 344–45
    Social Exclusion lifetrap and, 138–40
    Subjugation lifetrap and:
        avoiding one-sided relationships or one
            where you feel trapped, 289
        avoid selfish or irresponsible partners,
            291
        choice of partners, 275–77
        danger signals in potential partners,
            274–75
        give healthy relationship a chance, 291
        review past relationships and identify
            patterns, 291
    Vulnerability lifetrap and, 193–94

Jealousy, 72, 81, 221

Klosko, Janet, 351

Labeling your lifetraps, 43–44
Letters, writing, 48–49
    confronting abuser by, 103, 104

to critical parent, 231–33
to person who makes you feel like a
    failure, 251
Lifetraps:
    as adaptations to family life, 24
    changing. See Changing lifetraps
    coping styles, 35–41
        Counterattack, 39–41
        Escape, 38–39
        Surrender, 36–38
    defined, 1–2
    development of, 24–34
    feelings triggered by, 2
    questionnaire, 15–17
    recognition of, 23
    sample score sheet, 16–17
    scores, interpretation of, 18
    summary, 18–22
    See also individual lifetraps
Lifetrap therapy as outgrowth of cognitive
    therapy, 10
Loneliness, 2, 28
    Social Exclusion lifetrap and, 130, 131,
        133
Losing control, fear of, 190–91, 202
Loss:
    Abandonment lifetrap based on, 64, 65–66
    of parent, 68–69

Manageable tasks, only attempting, 54–55
Masochistic relationships, 218
Materialism, 120
Meditation, 204
Memories:
    of abuse, 87
        imagery, 100–02
        unclear, 87–88
    of social exclusion, 142–43
Mental illness, 134, 271
Mistrust and Abuse lifetrap, 11–13, 83–108
    abused as abuser, 93–94, 107
    basic safety and, 26–27
    case histories, 83–85
    changing, 99–107
        become involved with partner who
            respects your rights, 106–07
        confronting your abuser, 103–05
        cutting off contact with abuser(s), 103
        do not abuse people close to you, 107
        imagery to remember abuse, 100–02
        stop blaming yourself, 102
        stop tolerating abuse in current
            relationship, 105
        therapist, seeing a, 100
        try trusting people who deserve it,
            105–06
        venting anger, 101–02
    Counterattacks, 93

dissociation and, 87, 92
drug and alcohol abuse and, 89, 95
experience of abuse, 86–88
hypervigilance, 87
inability to trust, 87
intimate relationships and. See Intimate
    relationships, Mistrust and Abuse
    lifetrap and
lack of protection, feeling, 90, 91
learned by example, 94
memories of abuse, 9
    imagery, 100–02
    unclear, 87–88
origins of, 88–94
overview, 18
physical abuse. See Physical abuse
questionnaire, 85–86
self-help groups, 100
sexual abuse. See Sexual abuse
verbal abuse. See Verbal abuse
volatile moods and, 86
Modeling, learning through, 192
Money, exaggerated fear of not having,
    189–90, 194
Mothers, lifetraps related to behavior of. See
    specific lifetraps
Moving frequently in childhood, 134–35
Multiple personalities, 93

NA (Narcotics Anonymous), 351
Nannies, being raised by succession of, 68
Narcissism, 3, 115, 120, 324, 339
    Defectiveness lifetrap and, 212, 215
Narcotics Anonymous (NA), 351
Natural inclinations, 344
Nurturance, 113–14
    Emotional Deprivation lifetrap and, 113–14,
        116, 122, 123–24

OA (Overeaters Anonymous), 351
Obsessive-compulsive behavior, Vulnerability
    lifetrap and, 196–97
Obstacles to change. See Changing lifetraps,
    obstacles and their solutions
Overcompensating:
    Dependency lifetrap and, 163
    Social Deprivation lifetrap and, 153–54
Overeaters Anonymous (OA), 351
Overeating, 319
    as Escape, 38, 53, 213
Overindulgence of parents, 33, 323
Overprotective parent, 4, 28–29
    Abandonment lifetrap and, 70–72
    Dependence lifetrap and, 164, 165–69
        enmeshment, 169
        intrusiveness, 166
        undermining of child's efforts, 167

Panic attacks, 162, 190–91, 192, 194, 196, 202
Parents, lifetraps related to behavior of. *See specific lifetraps*
Passive-aggression, 267, 280–81, 286, 319
Passivity, 137
   Subjugation lifetrap and, 261–62, 263, 275
Patterns:
   in Abandonment lifetrap, 79
   breaking, 49
   in Dependency lifetrap, 179
   in Emotional Deprivation lifetrap, 124–25
   in Entitlement lifetrap, 326–27, 328–29
   in Failure lifetrap, 246–48, 253–54
   in Subjugation lifetrap, 291
   in Unrelenting Standards lifetrap, 305–08
   in Vulnerability lifetrap, 194–97
Perfectionism, 32, 306
Permissive parents, 33
Personality, 137
Personal vision, creating a, 343–47
Philosophy of change, 341–52
   assumptions:
      need to create a personal vision, 343–47
      no one technique will be successful for all people, 343
      people can change in very basic ways, 342
      self-actualization, 341–42
      there are basic needs that will lead us to be happier if they are satisfied, 342
      we have strong inclinations to avoid pain, 342–43
      we have strong tendencies to resist core change, 342
   empathic self-confrontation, 347–48
   enlisting help of others, 348–49
   selecting a therapist, 349–51
Physical abuse, 91–92
Physical characteristics, Social Deprivation lifetrap and, 134, 135, 136, 139
Possessiveness, 72
Poverty, exaggerated fear of, 189–90
Pressure from Unrelenting Standards lifetrap, 297, 298, 310–11
Protection, deprivation of, 122
Psychosomatic illnesses, Vulnerability lifetrap and, 195, 196
Public speaking, 223

Questionnaires:
   Abandonment, 60–62
   Defectiveness, 208–10
   Dependence, 157–59
   Emotional Deprivation, 111–12
   Entitlement, 316–17
   Failure, 240–41
   lifetrap, 14–17

Mistrust and Abuse, 85–86
   Social Exclusion, 130–31
   Subjugation, 259–61
   Unrelenting Standards, 295–97
   Vulnerability, 186–87

Realistic limits, 32–33
Rebels, 268–69
   resist doing opposite of what others tell you, 292
   at work, 281–82
Reciprocity, 33, 322
Rejection by peers, 30
Relaxation techniques, 204
Religious beliefs, 346
Repetition compulsion, 5, 95
Rogerian therapy, xiv

Sabotaging the relationship, 119
Sadism, 93, 94
Safety, exaggerated concern for, 188–89, 193, 194–95, 196–97
Schema, 6
Secrecy:
   sexual abuse and, 90–91
   Social Deprivation lifetrap and, 153
Self, undeveloped sense of, 29
Self-assertion, 346
Self-confrontation, 51
   continually, 3
   empathic, 347–48
Self-control:
   excessive, 269, 300
   inadequate, 322
Self-discipline problems, 33, 244, 245
Self-effacement, 31
Self-esteem, 346
   Subjugation lifetrap and, 262
Self-expression, 30–32, 346
   symptoms of problems with, 31–32
Self-hatred, 210, 211
Self-help groups, 100, 351
Self-sabotage, 243, 246
Self-sacrifice, 263, 264–65, 272, 273–74, 275–76
Separation, 66
   controlling overreactions to, 81
   phases of, 66–67
Separation (Bowlby), 66
Setting limits on partner with Entitlement lifetrap, 339–40
Sex, compulsive, 319
Sexual abuse, 89–91
   adult intimate relationships and, 99
   dissociation, 92
   extent of, 89–90
   feeling of not being protected, 90, 91

guilt over, 90
secrecy of, 91
shame and, 91
Shame, 30
  Defectiveness lifetrap and, 210, 212, 214,
    223, 226–27
  over sexual abuse, 91
  Unrelenting Standards and, 301, 302,
    303–04
Siblings, comparison to, 216, 244
Sickness, fear of, 187–88, 192, 194
Smoking, 319
Social connections, 27
Social Exclusion lifetrap, 129–54
  adolescence, developed in, 138
  anxiety in social situations, 129, 132–33
  case histories, 129–30
  changing, 141–54
    be yourself in groups, 153
    initiate conversation in groups, 152–53
    list everyday social situations in which
      you feel uncomfortable, 143–44
    list qualities in yourself that make you
      feel alienated, vulnerable, or inferior,
      145–47
    list social situations you avoid, 144
    list ways you overcompensate, 145
    make flashcard for each flaw, 150
    make hierarchy of groups you've been
      escaping, 151–52
    reevaluate importance of flaws you
      cannot change, 149–50
    stop trying so hard to overcompensate,
      153–54
    understanding childhood social
      exclusion, 142–43
    write down steps to overcome real flaw,
      148–49
  connection to others and, 27–28
  Defectiveness lifetrap and, 132, 136
  Escape as means of coping with, 141
  experience of social exclusion, 131–34
  feeling different, 130, 133, 134–36, 138
  overcompensation for, 145
  flashcards, 150
  groups, joining, 140
  imagery in overcoming, 148
  inferiority, feelings of, 131, 134, 135, 138
  loneliness, 130, 131, 133
  maintaining, ways of, 138–40
    career and, 138, 141
    in social relationships, 139–40
  origins of, 134–38
  overcompensating, 153–54
  overview, 20
  partner, choice of, 140
  passivity and, 137

psychosomatic symptoms related to, 134
questionnaire, 130–31
secrecy and, 153
stress and, 134
Unrelenting Standards lifetrap and, 136
Spirituality, 346
Spoiled entitlement, 318–19, 322, 326, 327
Spontaneity, lack of, 32
Status:
  Failure lifetrap and, 242
  overemphasizing, 225–26
  Unrelenting Standards lifetrap and, 301
Steps in changing lifetrap. *See* Lifetraps,
  steps in changing
Stress:
  Social Exclusion lifetrap and, 134
  Unrelenting Standards lifetrap and, 297
Subjugation lifetrap, 8–10, 258–93
  alcoholic parent, 271, 273–74
  anger and, 263, 264, 265, 266–68, 277
    learning to handle anger appropriately,
      289–90
  assertiveness and, 280, 286–88, 291–92
  case histories, 26–57, 272–74
  changing, 282–83
    assert yourself, 285
    avoid one-sided relationships, 289
    avoid relationships where you feel
      trapped, 289
    avoid selfish or irresponsible patterns,
      291
    do not rationalize your tendency to
      please others so much, 290–91
    feeling the subjugated child inside of
      you, 283–84
    flashcards, 292–93
    give healthy relationship a chance, 291
    learn to confront people, 289
    learn to handle anger appropriately,
      289–90
    list everyday situations in which you
      subjugate or sacrifice your own needs,
      284–85
    look at get-give ratio in your
      relationships, 286
    practice asking others to care for or help
      you, 289
    rebel, advice for the, 292
    review past relationships and clarify
      patterns, 291
    start forming your own preferences and
      opinions, 285
    stop passive-aggressive behavior, 286
    understanding your childhood
      subjugation, 283–84
    at work, 291–92
  co-dependency, 274

Subjugation lifetrap *(cont.)*
  Counterattacking, 268–69
  criticism and, 271–72
  description of patterns of, 276–77
  experience of subjugation, 261–69
  feeling trapped, 261, 262
  flashcards, 292–93
  imagery to change, 283–84
  intimate relationships and. *See* Intimate
      relationships, Subjugation lifetrap and
  origins of, 270–74
  out of fear (submissiveness), 263–64,
      265–66, 275
  out of guilt (self-sacrifice), 263, 264–65, 272,
      273–74, 275–76, 280–81
  overview, 21
  passive-aggression, 267–68, 270–71, 280–81,
      286
  passivity, 261–62, 263, 275
  questionnaire, 259–61
  rebels, 268–69
    advice for, 292–93
    work and, 281–83
  self-control, excessive, 269
  self-esteem and, 262
  self-expression and, 30–32
  self-sacrifice, 263, 264–65, 272, 273–74,
      275–76, 280–81
  submissiveness, 263–64, 265–66, 275
  work and, 277–82
    becoming more assertive, 291–92
    the rebel, 281–83
Submissiveness, 263–64, 265–66, 275
Subordination, self-, 161
Success:
  Failure lifetrap. *See* Failure lifetrap
  overemphasizing, 225–26
Superiority, attitude of, 39–41, 215
Surrender:
  as coping style, 36–38
  Defectiveness lifetrap and, 36–38, 210
  to dependence, 160, 173–74
  in Emotional Deprivation lifetrap, 120

Talents, listing your, 252
Teasing, 135, 142
Temperament, 24, 35, 65
  Abandonment lifetrap and, 66–67, 76
  reaction to abuse and, 24–25
Temper tantrums, 319, 320
Therapy:
  for the abused, 99–100
  selecting a therapist, 349–51
  times to consider, 348–49
  when to seek, 57
Time management, 312–13
Time-out technique, 337

Trust:
  in intimate relationship, 80–81
  Mistrust and Abuse lifetrap and, 87
  trying to trust people who deserve it,
      105–06
Type-A personality, 301

Underprotective parent, Dependence lifetrap
    and, 164, 169–71
Understanding the childhood origins of your
    lifetrap, 44–45
  Abandonment lifetrap, 77–78
  Defectiveness lifetrap, 223–25
  Dependence lifetrap, 175–76
  Emotional Deprivation lifetrap, 121–23
  Social Exclusion lifetrap, 142–43
  Vulnerability lifetrap, 197
Unrelenting Standards lifetrap, 294–313
  achievement orientation, 300–01
  case histories, 294–95
  changing, 308–13
    consider effects if you lowered your
        standards 25 percent, 311
    gradually try to change your schedule or
        behavior to meet your deeper needs,
        313
    list advantages of trying to meet
        standards, 308–9
    list areas in which your standards may
        be unbalanced or unrelenting, 308
    list disadvantages of pushing so hard,
        309–10
    try to determine what reasonable
        standards are, 312–13
    try to imagine life without these
        pressures, 310–11
    try to quantify the time devoted to
        maintaining your standards, 312
    understand origins of your lifetrap, 311
  as compensation for feelings of inferiority,
      303–04
  compulsivity, 299–300
  conditional love of parent and, 302
  criticism from parents when falling short of
      their expectations, 304–05
  experience of, 297–301
  origins of, 302–05
  parent as model of, 302–03
  patterns of, 305–08
  perfectionism, 306–07
  physical stress symptoms, 297
  pressure, feeling of, 297, 298, 310–11
  questionnaire, 295–97
  shame and, 301, 302, 303–05
  status orientation, 301–02
Unstable mother, Abandonment lifetrap and,
    69–70

Unstable partners, Abandonment lifetrap and attraction to, 79–80

Verbal abuse, 91–92, 93–94
Vision, creating a personal, 343–47
Volatile moods, Mistrust and Abuse lifetrap and, 86
Vulnerability, getting in touch with your, 336
Vulnerability lifetrap, 4, 184–206
    anxiety and, 186, 195
    autonomy and, 28–29
    case histories, 184–86
    changing, 197–206
        begin to tackle each of your fears in imagery, 205
        develop hierarchy of feared situations, 198
        enlist loved ones' support in helping you face your fears, 197–98
        examine probability of feared events occurring, 201–02
        list specific fears, 197–98
        practice relaxation techniques, 204
        reward yourself for each step you take, 206
        tackle each fear in real life, 205
        talk to your inner child, 203–04
        understanding the origins of the lifetrap, 197
        write flashcard for each fear, 202–03
    danger, 188–89, 192–93, 194–95, 196–97
    danger signals in relationships, 193–94
    experience of vulnerability, 187–91

flashcards, 202–03
health and illness, 187–88, 192, 194
imagery in overcoming, 203–05
losing control, 190–91, 202
obsessive-compulsive behavior and, 196–97
origins of, 191–93
overview, 19
panic attacks and, 190–91, 192, 194, 196, 202
patterns of, 194–97
poverty, 189–90, 194
psychoanalytic illnesses and, 195, 196
questionnaire, 186–87
relaxation techniques, 204
types of vulnerability, 187–91

Winnicott, D. W., 26
Work:
    Defectiveness lifetrap and, 222–23
    Dependence lifetrap and, 173
        don't complain when your boss refuses to help enough, 181–82
        take on new challenges gradually, 182
    Failure lifetrap and. *See* Failure lifetrap
    Social Exclusion lifetrap and, 138, 141
    Subjugation lifetrap and, 277–83
        becoming more assertive, 291–92
        the rebel, 281–83
Workaholics:
    Escaping by becoming, 38–39, 53, 213
    Unrelenting Standards lifetrap, 200–01

Young, Jeffrey, 351

ABOUT THE AUTHORS

JEFFREY E. YOUNG, PH.D., is Founder and Director of the Cognitive Therapy Centers of New York and Fairfield County. He completed his bachelor's degree at Yale University. After receiving his doctorate from the University of Pennsylvania, he remained there to complete a post-doctoral fellowship with Aaron Beck, founder of cognitive therapy, at the Center for Cognitive Therapy. He then went on to serve as the Center's Director of Research and Training. Using well-known procedures and materials he has developed over the past ten years, he has trained over a thousand cognitive therapists at workshops throughout the United States and Europe. Dr. Young has numerous publications on cognitive therapy, and is co-author of a major psychotherapy outcome study evaluating the effectiveness of cognitive therapy. Dr. Young is on the faculty in the Department of Psychiatry at Columbia University.

JANET S. KLOSKO, PH.D., is a training therapist at the Cognitive Therapy Center of New York, and co-director of the Cognitive Therapy Center of Long Island, in Great Neck. She also has a residence in the Albany, New York, area, where she has a private practice. She received her Ph.D. in clinical psychology from the State University of New York at Albany, and interned at Brown University. She has done extensive work researching treatments for anxiety disorders. She won the Albany Award for Excellence in Research, and the Dissertation Award from the American Psychological Association Section on Clinical Psychology as a Science. She has written numerous publications on treating anxiety. Since completing her graduate training, Dr. Klosko has worked with Dr. Young doing schema-focused therapy with individual patients and couples, and supervising and training other therapists. In addition, she has a master's degree from McGill University, and a B.A. from Union College.